Neoliberalism and neo-jihadism

Manchester University Press

Neoliberalism and neo-jihadism

Propaganda and finance in
Al Qaeda and Islamic State

IMOGEN RICHARDS

Manchester University Press

Published by Manchester University Press
Oxford Road, Manchester M13 9PL

www.manchesteruniversitypress.co.uk

British Library Cataloguing-in-Publication Data
A catalogue record for this book is available from the British Library

ISBN 978 1 5261 4320 4 hardback
ISBN 978 1 5261 7190 0 paperback

First published 2020
Paperback published 2023

The publisher has no responsibility for the persistence or accuracy of URLs for any external or third-party internet websites referred to in this book, and does not guarantee that any content on such websites is, or will remain, accurate or appropriate.

Typeset by
Sunrise Setting Ltd

Contents

Acknowledgements

I am indebted to the many colleagues, friends, and family who supported me physically and emotionally in preparing this book. First and foremost, special thanks go to Richard Jackson and David Whyte for providing invaluable feedback and advice during the writing process. Richard's advice on potential curative measures for what he termed the 'epistemological crisis' of contemporary counterterrorism was in the first instance vital to framing the book's investigation. The following consideration of how neo-jihadism and US counterterrorism can be conceptualised through a lens of 'power' and 'resistance' derived from Richard's contributions to peace and conflict research, and the Critical Terrorism Studies field, of which he is a founder. From legal studies and criminology, David's guidance on information sequencing, streamlining, and overall coherence was also instrumental to my revisions of this work at early stages. Moreover, David's advice on theoretical debates about political violence within and beyond academia, and the importance of frank author positioning in relation to those debates, informed a central pillar of the book's argumentation.

Criminology departments at Monash and Deakin Universities then provided the resources and opportunities that enabled my pursuit of this research and ultimately made the book possible. Academic and professional staff provided me with opinions and insights from their many combined years of research experience, including through shared sub- and 'anti'- disciplinary expertise. At Monash, Jude McCulloch provided steadfast support in supervising the research for this book from 2015–2018. Her insights about criminology, political economy, and counterterrorism, significantly shaped my early understanding of issues the book explores. Thanks also must go to Jarrett Blaustein for providing invaluable feedback and for sharing his perspective of where this work might sit in the broader scholarly field. Jarrett's knowledge of global governance and theories of power across diverse intellectual traditions was also greatly influential in my initial planning of the investigation.

At Deakin University, staff within and beyond the department of criminology were of immense help in their willingness to share perspectives on contentious political matters examined in this book. I reflected at various stages of writing on how to discuss with critical and ethical merit matters concerning counter/terrorism. Considerations included in particular my own 'Global North' perspectives on developing-nation situations, within a broader context of the criminalisation, suffering, and structural disadvantage experienced by those affected with political violence in various forms. Reece Walters was in particular helpful in bringing such issues into focus and offering encouragement for my approach.

Also at Deakin, I extend my appreciation to Mark Wood and Chad Whelan for providing constructive comments on the intersectional nature of political economy, security, and culture with regard to the representation of these subjects in the following chapters. Support and encouragement from Mary Iliadis, Matthew Sharpe, Emma Ryan, Danielle Tyson, Bree Carlton, Andrew Groves, Ian Warren, and many others at Deakin also made the process of preparing for publication much more manageable and enjoyable than would otherwise have been possible. Further appreciation must be extended to Robert Byron, Lucy Burns, Jen Mellor, and the editors and staff at Manchester University Press for their positivity, dedication, and professionalism. I am especially thankful to Tim Hyde and the team at Sunrise Setting for their invaluable feedback, advice, and support throughout the production process.

Of my friends, in particular I thank Arwen Johns for reading drafts, listening to all manner of cogitation, and providing perceptive and constructive insights that made all the difference. Luke Todd, Shane Tas, Max Thurnwald, Craig Willis, Abbey Kendall, and Paris Dean also shared much appreciated enthusiasm about the project and provided me with support in a number of ways – in particular listening to more than a few repetitive reflections and staying positive when my own endurance was waning. Without their enthusiasm and assistance, the process of organising my thoughts for writing, and translating these into practice, would have been significantly more daunting.

Finally, I am very grateful to my family for discussing ideas, sharing opinions, and being unwavering in their support. Hayley, Erica, Ryan, Simon, and Deb, you have all borne a lot of reflection and some rumination on my part without complaint. Thanks for your encouragement during these years and for having faith that this exploration would make a meaningful contribution to my life and to the broader social field.

Abbreviations

7/7	Al Qaeda attack on the London Underground on 7 July 2005
9/11	Al Qaeda attack on the US on 11 September 2001
ACLU	American Civil Liberties Union
AQ	Al Qaeda
AQAP	Al Qaeda in the Arabian Peninsula
AQI	Al Qaeda in Iraq
AQIS	Al Qaeda in the Islamic Subcontinent
BIF	Benevolence International Foundation
CAT	Center for the Analysis of Terrorism
CIA	Central Intelligence Agency
CNN	Cable News Network
CPA	Coalition Provisional Authority
CTS	Critical Terrorism Studies
DFI	Development Fund for Iraq
FAO	Food and Agriculture Organization of the United Nations
FATF	Financial Action Task Force
FBI	Federal Bureau of Investigation
GCC	Gulf Cooperation Council
GDP	Gross Domestic Product
GFC	Global Financial Crisis (2008)
GI	Generation Identity
GWOT	Global War on Terrorism
IBC	international business corporation
ICSR	International Centre for the Study of Radicalisation and Political Violence
IFI	international financial institution
IGC	Iraqi Governing Council
IMF	International Monetary Fund
IRRF	Iraq Relief and Reconstruction Fund
IS	Islamic State

ISI	Inter-Services Intelligence
ISIL	Islamic State of Iraq and the Levant
ISKP	Islamic State Khorasan Province
LDC	less developed country
MAK	Maktab al-Khidamat
NATO	North Atlantic Treaty Organization
NCB	National Commercial Bank
OECD	Organisation for Economic Co-operation and Development
OFAC	Office of Foreign Assets Control
PDPA	People's Democratic Party of Afghanistan
PNAC	Project for a New American Century
SAP	structural adjustment programme
UNESCO	United Nations Educational, Scientific and Cultural Organization
UNOCAL	Union Oil Company of California
USAID	United States Agency for International Development
WTO	World Trade Organization

Introduction

The contemporary type of political violence sometimes referred to as 'neo-jihadism' developed in a dialectical, political-economic relationship with its US-directed military and counterterrorist opposition. While the neo-jihadist organisations, Al Qaeda (AQ) and Islamic State (IS), have since their inception propagandised on the basis of widespread anti-capitalist sentiments, at the same time they exploit and contribute to the mechanisms of neoliberal and late modern capitalist finance they condemn. The nature of the dialectic between AQ, IS, and their US opposition is to this end multifaceted, entailing elements of causation, reflexivity, and mirroring. Where few investigations have to this point looked beyond linear cause and effect to explore AQ and IS, I adopt a holistic approach based on a criminological interpretation of dialectics to analyse the individuals and entities in question. The analysis features a grounded focus on these organisations' material and idealistic interests, represented in high-profile examples of their propaganda and finance, through discourse and documentary evidence.

Recognising that other factors beyond political economy, the West, and the US inevitably come into play in the rise to prevalence of groups such as AQ and IS, this book begins from the premise that dialectical engagements between neo-jihadism and neoliberalism are significant and worthy of further critical reflection insofar as they denote the political-economic reciprocity and interdependence of opposing, politically violent actors. I argue in the following chapters that while dispossession, marginalisation, and violence perpetrated by Western actors against majority-Muslim populations have often been cited by those who claim religious precedent and justification for their behaviour in the years following the AQ attacks on the New York World Trade Center and Washington Pentagon on 11 September 2001 (9/11), AQ and IS have selectively drawn from the tenets of Islam to justify acts of violence prosecuted through distinctly late modern capitalist methods.

In this light, AQ and IS are understood as neo-jihadist, constituting 'a late twentieth and early twenty-first century form of ideological expression, subculture, and militancy that combines novel understandings and interpretations of Islamic theology and jurisprudence, with other *non-Islamic* forms of social organization and interaction' (Lentini 2008, 26; my emphasis). Differing from jihadism, which describes the 'peripheral current of extremist thought whose adherents demand the use of violence in order to oust non-Islamic influence' (Brachman 2008, 4), neo-jihadist organisations are transnational in their orientation, often asserting religious and/or historical justification for their violent, expansionist aims. In conceptualising neo-jihadism, Pete Lentini (2008, 2013) emphasised such entities' reliance upon modern technology and selective interpolation of religion, despite their often anti-modern political positioning. In *Neoliberalism and neo-jihadism* I similarly explore characteristics of AQ and IS that are 'diverse' and 'syncretic' (IISA 2014); I differ from Lentini, though, in describing these organisations as neo-jihadist, primarily in light of their engagements with the neoliberal dimensions of late modern capitalism.

Where AQ and IS are referred to in this book as 'Islamist', this refers to their role within radically and sometimes violently enacted political movements that aspire to 'the re-instauration of the Islamic might in the world' (Mozaffari 2007, 17). All Sunni and Shia examples of Islamism mentioned in the following chapters are construed as seeking the (at least) domestic instantiation of Islamic governance, a form of political organisation sometimes defined as the Islamic law of sharia. Islamism, then, denotes a politicisation of the Islamic religion and not a form of Islamic worship, while the type of militant quasi-Islamism exercised by AQ and IS, understood as neo-jihadism, entails the use 'bombings, inflammatory language, terrorist activity, and so forth' (Wintrobe 2002, 25).

Recognising that neo-jihadist violence has been examined extensively, this book looks beyond the physical violence of AQ and IS to better apprehend their less well understood political-economic aspects. Drawing on cases of AQ and IS propaganda and finance, the following chapters investigate how and in what ways these organisations profess to oppose neoliberalism while at the same time relying upon its philosophical and practical exigencies to conduct their day-to-day operations.

The characteristics of neo-jihadism explored in the following chapters might thus, from a strategic standpoint, be said to demonstrate only a superficial contradiction between the 'terrorists' and 'counterterrorists' in question, and to shed light on the seeming 'hypocrisy' of AQ and IS's anti-capitalist and anti-modern positioning. On a deeper, structural level, on the other hand, philosophical and practical reciprocity between the opposing structures and agents of neoliberalism and neo-jihadism, extending to US counterterrorism, might be anticipated. Resistance movements throughout modern history, including in Mao Zedong's China, Iraq under the Hussein administration, and the 1917 Russian Revolution, have often ended up resembling the various authoritarian, autocratic, and corrupt state institutions they first overthrew (Bloom 2016). Non-state movements with feminist, post-colonial, labour and ecological agendas have also variously been co-opted, diluted, and repurposed such that they ultimately served to re-enshrine forms of power they originally mobilised against (Tarrow 2002). As Jeff Ferrell noted (2019), resistance by its very nature has the potential to become subsumed within existing orders, while its exponents can sometimes lack progressive or reformist ideations. As cultural criminologists have observed (Hayward and Schuilenburg 2014), resistance-to-power has also sometimes been symptomatic rather than fundamental, distracting from the broader, structural issues at play.

From an epistemological perspective, wherein 'terrorism' constitutes a form of resistance, albeit one often characterised by the abuse of power, I investigate how AQ and IS exist in a dialectical relationship with the dominant political-economic paradigm of neoliberalism. The investigation begins from the premise that 'power and resistance' discourses from the Enlightenment period to international colonialism, anarchism, communism, and the birth of late modern capitalism have defined the limits of possibility for opposition to oppressive political, social, and economic conditions (Bloom 2016). Drawing on propaganda produced by AQ and IS, these discourses and the political activity they justify are investigated here for the extent to which they perpetuate structural inequities in power distribution experienced by and constituted through the subjectivities of resistance-movement participants.

With its focus on neoliberalism and neo-jihadism, this work builds upon Bloom's contention that the emergence of late modern capitalism was materially and ideologically foundational for contemporary political movements, marked as it was by 'the construction of an economy premised on a discursive grammar of power and resistance (innovation, competition and the struggle for profit)' (2016, 88). Reflecting Bloom's philosophy, AQ and IS exploit anti-capitalist ideological discourses in their propaganda, while materially they rely upon the philosophical and practical affordances of neoliberalism for their continued existence.

The interplay between ideology and materiality in AQ and IS's neo-jihadist engagements with neoliberalism is investigated in the following chapters through a lens of Bourdieusian theory. Pierre Bourdieu's (1984, 1986, 1998b) concepts of habitus and field, neoliberalism, and the interrelationship between social, cultural, symbolic, and economic forms of capital, are specifically applied to explain the generative power of ideology and the material conditions that reinforce ideology's practice. In the analysis, Hegelian idealism, in which identity and beliefs are determinants of real-world events, is integrated with a Marxist dialectical materialist emphasis on the power of physical situations to reproduce metaphysical social systems (Hegel 1901, 1969; Marx 1992). Through its 'structuralist constructionist' approach, the analysis interpolates Bourdieu's perspective that reality is determined by the practices of individuals and institutions, but it is also compelled by the outcomes of previous actions, which exist as structural constraints (Bourdieu 1977, 1984; Swartz 1997, 2008). In Bourdieu's work, and in the subjects of this book, these constraints are correlated with relational inequalities in the distribution of capital, which are also self-perpetuating.

Far from endorsing the violence of organisations such as AQ and IS, understanding neo-jihadism in dialectical relation to the dominant political-economic environments it operates in provides an avenue through which to address a prevailing 'epistemological crisis' in contemporary counterterrorism (Jackson 2015). As Critical Terrorism Studies (CTS) scholars have long highlighted, this crisis has been characterised by a mythologising of terrorism (Zulaika 2009) and embrace of 'expert ignorance' since 9/11 (Zulaika 2012; Stampnitzsky 2013; Lindahl 2017). In light of this situation, comparative investigations such as *Neoliberalism and neo-jihadism* provide a necessary alternative to reductive Othering interpretations of neo-jihadism, which are often predicated on racism, including Islamophobia, and a lack of information (Poynting 2015; Zempi and Awan 2016). Though reductive demonological rhetoric is often used to describe neo-jihadism in Western policy statements and news media (Richards 2017; Jackson 2018), this book shows that neo-jihadism in fact represents a complex transnational criminological phenomenon worthy of critical and transparent investigation.

AQ and IS are therefore referred to in this book as 'terrorist', but this term is used while recognising its intense historical and ongoing political disputation. As has been well noted, the matter of subjectivity central to any political resistance is highlighted by the cliché 'one man's terrorist is another man's freedom fighter' (Seymour 1975, 62). Scott Poynting and David Whyte illustrate, for example, that state-based violence may to an extent be labelled 'terrorist' insofar as it seeks to inspire terror in civilian populations, promote political agendas, and disrupt productive economic capabilities (2012; see also Stohl 1984; George 1991). As David Wright-Neville explains, on the other hand, labelling state violence 'terrorism' is inherently problematic given the difficulty of determining its unlawful characteristics, which derives, in part, from protections for politically motivated violence attributed to states by sovereignty clauses in the 1648 Treaty of Westphalia (Wright-Neville 2010, x; see also Whyte 2014).

In the following chapters, AQ and IS are categorised as 'terrorist' for specific comparative reasons: to demonstrate behavioural reflexivity between terrorist and counterterrorist organisations and to highlight their targeting and exploitation of disempowered civilians. 'Terrorism' in the following discussions therefore denotes the behaviour of politically violent, non-state organisations that use acts of aggression to enact political change by instilling fear in civilian populations, while 'counterterrorism' refers to state-based measures used to inhibit the efforts of terrorist organisations (Mythen and Walklate 2016; Lindahl 2017).

Challenges to reductive and polarising explanations of the contemporary and high-profile form of terrorism known as (neo-)jihadism that are influential to this book have emerged from CTS and from the cross-disciplinary traditions of critical criminology. These include the research of Gabe Mythen and Sandra Walklate, who in various studies have synthesised theories of political economy and risk-based securitisation to explore how the relative deprivation and suffering experienced by counterterrorism targets generates the disaffection, anger, and lack of understanding that, in turn, fuels political violence (2006, 2008; Mythen et al. 2009, 2013). Also instrumental is Jock Young's argument that a late modern 'vertigo', characterised by globalisation, instability, (in)security, and exclusion, has the potential to contribute to an intensification and escalation of international crime (2003, 2007). The investigative approach of this book is, furthermore, grounded in political-economic perspectives on the US 'war on terror' presented by David Whyte (2007, 2010, 2015) and Ronald Kramer and Raymond Michalowski (2005, 2011; see also Chambliss et al. 2013). The exploration of neo-jihadist finance in particular draws on Whyte's account of US-directed neoliberal incursions in the Middle East that deprived civilian populations of access to basic goods and services and created political-economic environments in which terrorism thrives.

Although a degree of policy research has emphasised the individual actions of terrorist and counterterrorist organisations to reveal strategic contradictions in their behaviour, these investigations often ignore the 'subjugated knowledges' that render terroristic ideologies convincing (Jackson 2012). While my investigation is interested in the extent to which paradox or contradiction between the anti-capitalist propaganda of neo-jihadist organisations and their quasi-capitalist financial practices might occur, *Neoliberalism and neo-jihadism* initially reflects on the various reasons why this contradiction might be investigated.

From a strategic, counterterrorist perspective, such an investigation has the potential to destabilise the narratives of neo-jihadist organisations by revealing their non-religious and paradoxical modes of operating. As demonstrated in earlier strategic counterterrorism approaches, however, including civilisational-theoretical strategies adopted in the aftermath of 9/11 (Huntington 1993, 1996; Hellmich 2011), and the US government's unsuccessful Center for Strategic Counterterrorism Communications (CSCC) campaign to contest IS and AQ's social media propaganda, revealing the 'hypocrisy' of neo-jihadist organisations is often unsuccessful at reducing their support base (Richards 2016a, 2016b). This is because these approaches often reaffirm reductive Othering interpretations of such organisations, which neglect the root causes of political violence, encouraging both discrimination and the entrenchment of political divisions. At other times, they disregard the narrative of entities including AQ and IS that engaging in *taqiyya* (the denial of religious belief in the face of persecution) is acceptable in what they depict as 'war-time' situations (Hoffman 2013). By exploiting the weapons of their enemies, AQ and IS in fact practise a long-established method of warfare first popularised in the fifth century BC by Sun Tzu (Griffith 1963). Moreover, in the contemporary political-economic context, these tactics have been used extensively in the anti-capitalist activism of, for instance, left-wing agitprop groups (Brown 2013).

If this book's aim was to identify ideological discordance within the movement of neo-jihadism that might be used to strategically undermine the ideology of AQ and IS, it might illuminate how exploitative and criminogenic characteristics of neoliberalism perpetuate, sustain, and constitute the various aspects of neo-jihadism. My primary purpose in writing this book, however, is not to explore in rigorous detail the many deleterious impacts of neoliberal economic systems. Rather, it is to shed a critical criminological light on the political-economic dialectics that underwrite neo-jihadism as a contemporary, high-profile, and persistent form of political violence.

The evolution of neo-jihadism

To understand the political economy of AQ and IS, it is necessary to reflect initially on their various institutional characteristics. Although there has been relative consensus regarding the changing structure of AQ since 2001, there has not been a corresponding consensus regarding the constitution of 'Al Qaeda' per se. As Christina Hellmich explains in *Al-Qaeda: From global network to local franchise* (2011), from the events of 9/11, with regard to the post-Cold War activities of AQ actors, until her time of writing in 2011, there has been a lack of ontological certainty about what AQ actually *is* and how it is best described. Where some accounts have described AQ as an organisation, others posit AQ as a network (Hoffman 2004), a loose-knit collective of disparate, 'leaderless' actors (Sageman 2011), or best conceptualised as an ideology (Burke 2004) that variously incorporates characteristics of a transnational corporation (Basile 2004). While this uncertainty remains in 2020, the desire to attain a rigid ontological certainty regarding AQ has in fact impeded open and inductive terrorism research (Hellmich 2011, 1–22). Evidence suggests that, to an extent, 'Al Qaeda' incorporates numerous characteristics of these phenomena, and that to engage in an empirically grounded exploration of AQ, it may be necessary to dismiss reductive tropes about its definition.

While leading scholars and pundits have over the years more or less agreed that AQ may be generally classified as a terrorist organisation (Hoffman 2013), definitions of IS to this point have been more varied. Some argue that in its early manifestation, IS was best understood as a religiously motivated terrorist group whose regional dominance had international security ramifications (Stern and Berger 2015). Others assert that IS's paramilitary operations, state-building practices, and declaration of a Middle Eastern Caliphate warrant its more apt description as a non-terrorist, quasi-state entity (Cronin 2015). Still another school of thought has framed IS as a mobilisation of regional and international Salafi jihadism better understood as an ideological movement (Armstrong 2014). For many, IS and AQ's institutional arrangements suggest that both may be effectively likened to modern post-industrial corporations (Gray 2003; Daragahi and Solomon 2014). In this work, I differentiate IS and AQ as exclusive examples of modern neo-jihadist organisations. AQ, like IS, is described most often as an organisation, in part because it has a discernible membership, governance, and structure, and otherwise for the purposes of comparison with its US-directed counterterrorist opposition.

The US invasions of Afghanistan in 2001 and Iraq in 2003 gave rise to the late, decentralised form of AQ, in the aftermath of 9/11, within a context in which international communities were concerned with a perceived proliferation of 'Islam-associated' violence (Zempi and Awan 2016). This concern was exacerbated by attacks committed by AQ under decentralised governance: the organisation's bombings of a Sari nightclub in Bali in 2002, a Madrid commuter train system in 2004, and the London Underground in 2005, and in shootings at the Parisian satirical magazine *Charlie Hebdo* in 2015, though contention surrounds the perpetrators (Hoffman and Reinares 2014; Cook 2015).

In 2013, two years into the Syrian civil war, where the AQ precursors of IS were present, the organisation known as 'ISIS', 'ISIL', 'Daesh', or 'IS' emerged as a notorious neo-jihadist organisation alongside AQ, and it too was widely recognised and feared for attacking international targets. Continuing in the tradition of AQ, these included a series of bombings and firearm attacks on restaurants and a concert theatre in Paris in 2015, and on an airport and metro in Brussels in 2015 (Gerges 2017), the bombing of an Ariana Grande concert in Manchester in 2017, claimed influence over the bombing of churches and hotels across Sri Lanka in 2019 (Wood 2019), as well as a series of IS-inspired and IS-affiliated firearm, knife, and vehicular attacks in Australia, Germany, Tunisia, the US, and elsewhere.

In addition to its recent success at executing and inspiring attacks, IS's distinction from other organisations, and its neo-jihadist, transnational dimension, became apparent in April 2013, at which time Abu Bakr al-Baghdadi, the leader of the Iraqi branch of AQ, renamed that branch the 'Islamic State of Iraq and al-Sham', sometimes translated as 'Islamic State in Iraq and Greater Syria' (ISIS), or 'Islamic State of Iraq and the Levant' (ISIL) (Laub and Masters 2014). Baghdadi also declared that with this rebranding, ISIS, or 'IS', would assume autonomous control over Iraqi and Syrian AQ forces. However, the restructure was rejected by both AQ Central leadership and Abu Mohammed al-Jawlani, who commanded AQ forces (under Baghdadi's leadership) in Syria. Though early members of IS had for several years, therefore, been engaged in conflict with Iraq's Nouri al-Maliki administration and various Iraqi militias, from 2013 the organisation also fought the Syrian Bashar al-Assad regime and oppositional Sunni rebels, including AQ's Syrian branch, Jabhat Fateh al-Sham (previously Jabhat al-Nusra) (Lister 2015).

When IS's proposed merger with Jabhat al-Nusra was rejected by the leadership of AQ Central in 2013, the organisation became officially independent. While it had previously fomented violence between jihadist forces, from this time IS members executed Middle Eastern civilians en masse, forced dissidents into sexual and economic slavery, and put foreign prisoners to death (Lister 2014). Then in June 2014, IS announced the establishment of a 680km Syrian and Iraqi quasi-nation state under violent quasi-Islamist governance and administration, hereafter referred to in the organisation's words as the 'Caliphate' (Lister 2014, 1). Although some see IS as a direct product of the Syrian civil war, in reality its organisational roots extend as far back as 2006. To understand IS, it is necessary to realise how the organisation and its leadership evolved from the AQ-affiliated Islamic State of Iraq.

Islamic State of Iraq was formed in 2006 from the merger of Al Qaeda's Iraqi branch (AQI) and two local insurgent factions, the Mujahideen

Shura Council and Jund al-Sahhaba (Dhiman 2015, 4). From 2004 to 2006, AQI had engaged in frequent, vicious attacks throughout Iraq, targeting civilian centres while inciting and perpetuating sectarian violence. With the tacit approval of AQ Central, its primary aim was the establishment of a Sunni-led Iraqi Caliphate (Lister 2014). In June 2006, the Jordanian leader of AQI, Fadeel al-Nazal al-Khalayleh, aka Abu Musab al-Zarqawi, was executed by a US drone strike. An Egyptian man named Abu Ayyub al-Masri briefly assumed AQI leadership; however, when the Islamic State of Iraq alliance was created that same year, the elusive figure of Hamid Dawoud al-Zawi, aka Abu Omar al-Baghdadi (who, it was speculated, had back-filled the role of a fictional ISI figurehead), apparently became its leader (Kilcullen 2016). When al-Zawi was also reportedly killed by a US strike in April 2010, the Iraqi-born Ibrahim Awad Ibrahim Ali al-Badri al-Samarrai, aka Abu Bakr al-Baghdadi, became his successor. Abu Bakr al-Baghdadi spearheaded Islamic State of Iraq's passage from Iraq into Syria against the instructions of the then AQ Central leader, Ayman al-Zawahiri (Gerges 2017), and remained the leader, or 'emir', of IS until his execution by US forces on 26 October 2019.

Although Baghdadi held the position of emir, or 'Caliph', meaning that within IS he was considered a biological descendent of the Prophet Muhammad, influential parties also view Zarqawi as a kind of deified founding father. Due in part to this ideological heritage, IS has sought to sustain its historical reputation for breakaway politics and brutal violence, differing from AQ Central in its advocacy of sectarian slaughter and the endorsement of a transnational Caliphate (Hashim 2014). Though AQ envisioned that a collective Caliphate would be achieved at some point in the undefined long-term future, its leaders foregrounded organisational diplomacy between AQ parties as of utmost importance. Despite these differences, IS has been tangibly influenced by operational advice provided to Zarqawi by the AQ leaders Osama Bin Laden and Ayman al-Zawahiri (Holbrook 2015, 94). Moreover, similarities and differences between the organisations derive from their cultural and leadership histories, which, as Neoliberalism and neo-jihadism demonstrates, are reflected in a number of their ideological and material practices. Contiguity between their histories also means that IS arguably cannot be understood without reference to AQ after 9/11.

Neoliberalism

To explore the political-economic dimensions of neo-jihadism I apply a neo-Marxist interpretation of neoliberalism for two primary reasons. First, it is relevant to the historical dimension of the analysis, which pertains to the formation of AQ at the close the Cold War, a conflict in which the primary political disagreement pertained to capitalism. Second, Marxism as a historical discourse constitutes capitalism's most famous ideological antagonist, as set out in Karl Marx's detailed multi-volume critique of capital (1992). It is also frequently associated with the command-economy variation of communism of the totalitarian regimes of the Union of Soviet Socialist Republics (USSR, also referred to as the Soviets) and its allies during the Cold War. These regimes referred to themselves as communist and claimed to be inspired by Karl Marx.

As such, *neo*-Marxist perspectives are useful in highlighting dominant critiques of the late modern version of capitalism known as neoliberalism, and are most directly relevant to neo-jihadist propaganda and finance. Drawing on a critical criminological interpretation of neoliberalism with neo-Marxist strains, the following analysis is overtly critical in nature, purposefully investigating the deleterious outcomes of neoliberalism and the anti-capitalist basis on which organisations such as AQ and IS campaign. In doing so, it establishes a frame of inquiry through which dialectical tensions between neo-jihadist organisations' anti-capitalist posturing and their quasi-capitalist practices are investigated.

Neoliberalism as an analytic concept in this book is explained in Chapters 1 and 2 as entailing cross-national privatisation, deregulation, and financialisation. The analysis broadly follows David Harvey's description of neoliberalism as:

A theory of political economic practices that proposes that human well-being can best be advanced by liberating individual entrepreneurial freedoms and skills within an institutional framework characterized by strong private property rights, free markets, and free trade. The role of the state is to create and preserve an institutional framework appropriate to such practices. (2005, 2)

Neoliberalism is deliberately unhyphenated to avoid confusion between its economic principles and the democratic principles of classical liberalism, two ideologies that, given neoliberalism's lack of deontology, are variously in conflict (Jessop 1982; Thorsen and Lie 2006). While, like jihadism and neo-jihadism, liberalism and neoliberalism share the same conceptual genesis, as Chapters 1 and 2 explain, optimistic 'classical liberal' protections of freedom and civil rights are often undermined by neoliberalism's 'demand for total liberty for the talented and their enterprises' (Thorsen and Lie 2006, 16). Through analysis of neo-jihadist propaganda and finance, this book reflects on the fact that neoliberal policies are themselves often referred to as 'violent' (Giroux 2004; Springer 2015), while the politically violent domain of neo-jihadism can be said to epitomise criminogenic risks associated with neoliberalism's often undesirable policy outcomes.

Outline of the book

This introduction has set out the rationale for and approach of the book, clarified several important characteristics of the phenomena of neo-jihadism and neoliberalism, and explained the evolutionary attributes of neo-jihadism that inform the following chapters. Building on this background, Chapter 1 provides a history of neoliberalism, extending from the US and UK administrations of Margaret Thatcher and Ronald Reagan, beginning in 1979 and 1980 respectively. Here, I elaborate on neo-Marxist geo-economic theory, presented by David Harvey, Bob Jessop, and Jamie Peck, in preparation for its application to AQ and IS's geo-economic interests. Theories of neoliberalism, capital, and dialectics in Bourdieusian theory are also outlined, as is Bourdieu's influence on the research design. The final part of Chapter 1 explains the data collection and methods of analysis used in the chapters as well as the key sources used and some research limitations.

Further detail of neoliberal philosophies and policies, as they relate to both neo-jihadism and the Global War on Terrorism (GWOT), are then set out in Chapter 2. Drawing on Hall (2011; Hall et al. 2015) and Ali (2003), I discuss the positivist philosophical premises of neoliberalism, along with its fundamentalist and neo-colonial philosophical attributes. Extending these philosophies to a consideration of neoliberal policies, the second half of this chapter comprises an account of high-profile neoliberal case studies, from the 2008 Global Financial Crisis (GFC) through deregulated labour conditions in less developed countries to US military industries. Extending Thomas Piketty's 2014 *Capital in the twenty-first century*, I also examine how the monetarist precepts of neoliberal reasoning and its 'meritocratic extremism' have contributed to exacerbating wealth inequality within the US and internationally.

Interpolating insights about neoliberalism from Chapters 1 and 2, Chapter 3 commences an account of AQ propaganda. My discussion and analysis here are influenced by interpretations of neo-jihadism articulated in the work of activist-scholars Iain Boal, T. J. Clark, Joseph Matthews, and Michael Watts, as well as by insights from investigative journalism. The analysis in this chapter also features Islamist ideologues that influenced AQ at its 1988 inception, before reflecting on how the organisation's political-economic propaganda engaged with dominant anti-capitalist and anti-US perpsectives prior to and following 9/11, and

after the 2008 GFC. This discussion addresses the discourse of prominent figures who influenced AQ and who variously spoke on behalf of
the organisation, including Osama Bin Laden, Abdullah Azzam, Ayman
al-Zawahiri, and Adam Gadahn. Drawing on Bourdieusian theory, I explore
how AQ leaders appeal to social, cultural, and symbolic capital through
their propaganda, while their collective expression of an anti-capitalist
'habitus' corresponds to a changing 'field' of anti-capitalism that developed over time.

The investigation of neo-jihadist propaganda continues in Chapter 4
with a reflection on ideologues that were uniquely influential to IS, and
a consideration of how, following its announcement of a Caliphate in
2014, the organisation appealed to anti-US and anti-capitalist sentiments in its multiplatform propaganda. As with Chapter 3, I begin with
an account of historical and contemporary ideologues influential to IS,
drawing on insights from Will McCants and Robert Manne, before
proceeding with a critical analysis of IS speeches and audiovisual propaganda produced and disseminated by leading figures and entities affiliated with the organisation. These figures include the former IS 'emir'
Abu Bakr al-Baghdadi, Abu Muhammad al-Adnani, and the production
entities Al Hayat and Al Furqan. My critique of these documents is again
informed by Bourdieu's theory, including his emphasis on the dialectical
interdependence of materiality and idealism, discussed here with reference to what might be interpreted as the 'historical materialism' focus of
certain IS media. Reflecting on IS's geo-economic orientation, I interpret
this feature of IS media as related to the organisation's strategic interests,
including its need to retain and exploit territory in governing the Caliphate during its peak, from 2014 to 2017. Further to the focus on neo-
jihadist propaganda, then, Chapters 3 and 4 consider the extent to which
AQ and IS's respective geo-economic orientations are reflected in their
political-economic propaganda, in relation to AQ's decentralisation and
in IS's case in terms of the Caliphate. In comparing and contrasting these
organisations, my discussion examines various ways in which AQ and
IS, as differentiated examples of neo-jihadism, portray themselves as
anti-capitalist actors.

The second major aspect of the investigation, in Chapters 5 and 6,
investigates fundraising and financial governance on the part of AQ and
IS over select years: from the 1990s to 2014 for AQ and from 2014 until
2017 for IS. I discuss the extent to which the philosophies and policies
of neoliberalism set out in Chapters 1 and 2 can reveal how AQ and IS's
financial practices reflect and resemble the behaviours of US military and
counterterrorist actors in the extent of their neoliberal dimensions.
Insights from research institutions such as the Center for the Analysis of

Terrorism and the International Center for the Study of Radicalisation are particularly influential here.

Before the analysis of AQ finance in Chapter 5, I outline the US-directed intervention in Afghanistan during the Afghan–Soviet War (1979–89) and discuss precepts of Islamic finance that conflict with the political and economic policies of neoliberalism. Insights from declassified Western government intelligence material, testimony from figures within governments and intelligence organisations, and reliable information from think tanks are also applied to the documentary discussion of AQ finance. After a description of US-led political-economic interventions prior to the announcement of the establishment of AQ in 1988, the analysis explores the relative significance of wealthy donors and charities in the Middle Eastern region, alternative remittance systems, and the broader commercial activities of AQ actors on behalf of the organisation. I conclude by providing a brief account of the discordance between Islamic finance decrees and neoliberal economic managerial mechanisms. With reference to Bourdieu's theory, this part of the investigation considers how AQ's financial behaviour can be explained as representing the organisation's collective expression of habitus within a field and doxa of normalised neoliberal political-economic relations.

Extending the focus on neo-jihadist finance, Chapter 6 accounts for US interventions in Iraq from the 1990s to 2003 and discusses key fundraising and financial management practices on the part of IS from 2014 to 2017. Drawing on think-tank research, declassified intelligence reports, and administrative materials produced by IS actors, this analysis reflects on the relative importance to the organisation's historical fundraising of financial institutions, oil and gas, other natural resources, and the administration of the Caliphate's financial governance. These practices are again analysed for their neoliberal features, with reference to Bourdieusian and neo-Marxist ideas.

I do not attempt in Chapters 5 and 6 to examine all examples of neo-jihadist finance. Rather, the investigation emphasises and interrogates those financial characteristics of neo-jihadism most relevant to the dialectics of AQ, IS, and neoliberalism, and the US military and counterterrorism. Using a neo-Marxist lens to compare the financial behaviours of AQ and IS, I again consider the extent to which these behaviours exist in a recursive and representative relationship with the organisations' respective geo-economic orientations. The divergent geo-economic and territorial interests of AQ and IS are therefore a primary point of focus in these chapters, as is the extent to which they can be said to characterise differentiated organisational models of neo-jihadism.

The conclusion of the book reflects on the significance of research presented in light of political-economic developments regarding neo-jihadism from 2017 to 2020, and within the global economic system. It incorporates comparative consideration of other political philosophies and movements, from anarchism and left-wing activism to the GWOT and a twenty-first-century rise in far-right politics and (neo-)fascism. Furthermore, I elaborate a brief consideration of evolutionary developments within the phenomenon of neo-jihadism, including several forecasts of the political activities of AQ and IS.

Drawing on theoretical and strategic inferences about the variegated nature of neo-jihadism, and the empirical insights of the research presented in this book, I ultimately suggest a reframing of the extant strategic emphasis on surface-level contradictions or paradoxical relationships between the political-economic propaganda and financial practices of AQ and IS. In other words, I advocate attention to underlying structural connections between these groups and the Western neoliberal organisational entities and societal systems they externally oppose. With insights from social theory and critical commentary, including the perspectives of Jeff Ferrell and Peter Bloom, this investigation reflects on how the cases and events examined reveal the overarching influence of the paradigm of neoliberalism on the continued development of neo-jihadism.

I

Neoliberalism, Bourdieu, and neo-Marxism

In *Neoliberalism and neo-jihadism*, AQ and IS's propaganda and finance are analysed through a lens of Bourdieusian theory and with reference to a neo-Marxist interpretation of neoliberalism. Ideological and philosophical tenets of Marxist-Leninism are relevant to the historical dimension of this book's investigation, including the evolution of neo-jihadism since the formation of AQ in 1988, at the close of the Cold War (Burke 2004). Marxist theory has long been the dominant epistemological critique of capitalism, and neo-Marxist ideas are a foundational antagonist of neoliberal capitalism. They are to this end reflected in popular anti-capitalist commentary, including neo-jihadist organisations' political-economic campaigns.

Extending Bourdieusian and neo-Marxist theory from a criminological perspective, the approach to the investigation of AQ and IS's propaganda and finance outlined here is overtly critical in nature, purposefully investigating the deleterious outcomes of neoliberalism and the anti-capitalist bases on which these organisations campaign. In doing so, this chapter establishes a frame of inquiry through which dialectical engagements between neo-jihadist organisations' anti-capitalist posturing and their quasi-capitalist practices are investigated. After a descriptive section on neoliberalism's origins, I outline neo-Marxist principles on the geo-economics of neoliberalism, and the relevant aspects of Bourdieusian theory. Drawing on Bourdieu's ideas, I then describe the research design as well as the discourse and documentary methods used in the analysis.

Neoliberalism in history

Proponents of neoliberal policies often trace their ideological roots to the principles of classical economic liberalism laid out in Adam Smith's *The wealth of nations* (1776). As David Harvey has highlighted (2005), though, Smith's text predated the vital economic restructuring that occurred during the Industrial Revolution, and, as such, a more material history of neoliberalism might be constructed with reference to the financial catastrophe of the 1930s. Following the Great Depression, 'neoliberalism' denoted a series of re-regulatory reforms implemented in developed Western countries to curb the apparent crisis tendencies of unrestrained capitalism. In the 1940s, these reforms were guided by the protectionist welfare principles recommended in John Maynard Keynes' *The general theory of employment, interest, and money* (1936). After several decades of Keynesian influence, a global order characterised by relatively unrestricted markets with allowances for state capital controls came to be described as 'embedded liberalism' (Ruggie 1982). While for some, contemporary neoliberalism represents an extension and intensification of nineteenth-century early modern capitalism and twentieth-century embedded liberalism (Rowthorn 1980), as Harvey (2005) and others highlight, certain distinct political-economic traditions that might be defined as 'neoliberal' emerged in the Thatcher and Reagan administrations.

The post-1980s incarnation of 'neoliberalism' to which this book refers entailed drastic reductions in Keynesian welfarism, widespread international trade, privatised services, and deregulated capital controls, along with a cohort of other context-specific methods. Following the international proliferation of neoliberal economic policies in the 1980s, their harmful socio-political and socio-economic effects included degradation of the environment (Gonzalez 2004), community and household marginalisation (Brenner et al. 2010), a lack of ready public access to basic services, and exacerbation of wealth disparity in domestic and international settings (Navarro 2007). Neoliberalism's advocacy of competition and autonomy was revealed through ethnographic research to produce an erosion of social cohesion, civic functionality, and awareness of the 'common good' (Brenner and Theodore 2005). In a high-profile twenty-first-century example of their social and economic effects, the profit-driven policies of neoliberal financialisation were deemed by scholars and economists to be the primary impetus behind the 2008 GFC (Mirowski 2013).

The Thatcher and Reagan governments are often cited as the context in which neoliberalism emerged. Thatcherism is generally understood to entail significant reductions in public expenditure combined with tax benefits for large commercial entities, whereas Reaganomics is typically explained via the logic of supply-side, or trickle-down, economics (George 1999). Under monetarist economic policy management during these years, the UK saw interest rates rise to 17 per cent, while the US witnessed a decrease in tax rates to 20 per cent, from 78 per cent, for the country's wealthiest citizens (Reitan 2003, 29; Dorian 2010, 166). Although the tactics and diplomacy of the administrations differed in several respects, both operated according to a belief that rapid fiscal growth would trickle down from major industries and benefit their respective countries. Both administrations also committed to neoliberal programmes under the influence of the Viennese economist Friedrich Hayek (1937) and the Chicago School economist Milton Friedman (1962).

Following the widespread international adoption and acceptance of neoliberal policies in decades since the 1980s, critics have deconstructed its 'ostensibly rational response to the "crisis of Atlantic Fordism"' (Jessop 2002, 4; Brenner et al. 2008). These deconstructions contradict the conservative notion that undesirable economic conditions in developed Western countries during the 1970s, such as stagflation, were the result of taxes imposed on the wealthy, strict regulation, and the suppression of free markets (Stiglitz 2011). In one example, Paul Krugman (1987) (an economic advisor to Martin Feldstein during the Reagan administration) blamed the conditions prior to US neoliberalism on expenditure during the Vietnam War and the country's resulting balance-of-payments deficit. Later, he suggested that unhinging the dollar from the gold standard, rather than crippling regulation, caused US share worth to plummet internationally (Krugman 2009). In relation to the UK, cultural theorist Stuart Hall put forward a similar argument, that structural adjustment programmes (SAPs) led by the UK 'provided the catalyst' Margaret Thatcher needed to debilitate trade power, create nationwide stagflation, and introduce 'get on your bike' neoliberal policies (2011, 707). Collectively, these accounts demonstrate how economic emergencies during the 1970s, and the apparent recovery of the US and UK economies, appeared to vindicate Milton Friedman's (1962, xvi) statement that 'only a crisis – actual or perceived – produces real change'.

Beyond the US and UK, a pattern of crisis-producing neoliberalism materialised in a number of ways. While the broad-based impacts of neoliberal policies in domestic and international settings are explained in more detail in Chapter 2, further to Klein's (2007) explication of 'disaster capitalism', Iain Boal and his co-authors offered a compelling explanation for the role that neoliberal policies play in wartime situations. The Retort activists who authored *Afflicted powers* (Boal et al. 2005) argue that oil exists within the broader landscape of neoliberal economic restructuring that occurred in Iraq and elsewhere in the nascent days of the GWOT, a US empire of capital accumulation they describe as 'military neoliberalism'. For Boal et al. (2005, 45) this characterises a 'deadly alchemy of permanent war, capitalist accumulation, and the new enclosures – all now conducted under conditions of spectacle'. Here, 'political Islam' assumes the form of a distinctly modern resistance movement, outfitted with a revolutionary vanguard, despite Bin

Laden's significant inheritance from his family's construction business and AQ followers' ostensible interest in financial markets. Far from a single determinative commodity that yields political-economic effects only in the extent of its 'facticity', for Boal and his co-authors oil represents:

> Neoliberalism mutating from an epoch of 'agreements' and austerity pro-grammes to one of outright war; the plural and unstable relations among specific forms of capital, always under the banner of some apparently dom-inant mass commodity; and those periodic waves of capitalist restructuring we call *primitive accumulation*. (Boal et al. 2005, 52; my emphasis)

Drawing on ideas such as those set out by Boal et al., the analysis in this book does not attempt to establish historical cause and effect, nor does it assume that neoliberalism is mono-faceted. For the sake of exploring the noteworthy political-economic connections, a number of debates must inevitably be omitted. There is, for example, little space given to account-ing for Aiwa Ong's (2006) resistance to institution-centric explanations of 'big N' neoliberalism, or Maurizio Lazzarato's (2009) elaboration of de-politicised financialisation. It is also impractical to differentiate between paleoliberal economics and neoliberal structuralism, or to explain the advent of German ordoliberalism, regardless of their ongoing social and political influence.

This book also rejects the notion that neoliberalism has experienced a linear developmental trajectory since the late 1980s. Neoliberalism is, in short, understood in Jamie Peck's (2010, 7, 9; see also Connell and Dados 2014) terms as a 'messy hybrid' of ideological principles, expressed through 'philosophy, politics, and practice'. To demarcate 'actually exist-ing neoliberalism' (Brenner and Theodore 2002), it explicitly investigates AQ and IS's political-economic behaviour, as represented through their propaganda and finance, with discourse and documentary evidence.

The geo-economics of neoliberalism

To illuminate similarities and differences between the political economy of AQ and IS, and variegated neo-jihadist engagement with the para-digm of neoliberalism, the analysis of propaganda and finance also reflects on these organisations' geo-economic orientations. Drawing on Harvey (1995, 2003, 2005), it compares AQ and IS's global interests with their internal, centrifugal concerns, including their differentiated interactions with territorial and economic priorities characteristic of nation states or international financial institutions (IFIs). In the first instance, I emphasise Harvey's explanation that the interests of states and IFIs converge correlative to neoliberalism's divergent agendas, as they are bound both by spatial and temporal fixes, and by territorial and capitalist logics of power. Where fixes are economic managerial measures designed to rectify the inherent 'crisis tendencies' of capitalism (Marx 1992), territorial and capitalist logics refer to the key actors, main logic, core features, role of space and territory, secondary logic, interdependencies, mode of steering, crisis reactions, and imperialist tendencies of political-economic entities (Harvey 2001, 2003; Jessop 2006). To conceptualise the relative importance of territory and economy for AQ and IS, the following chapters also draw on Bob Jessop's (2006) theoretical revision of ideas set out by Harvey (2001, 2003).

In the first instance, Harvey suggested that capitalism always takes political precedence over territoriality in neoliberal societies, which is explained as the implementation of 'spatio-temporal fixes', or 'solutions to capitalist crises through temporal deferment and geographical expansion' (Harvey 2003, 65, cited in Jessop 2006, 152). One example of a spatio-temporal fix in the US-led GWOT, which Harvey (2003) terms 'accumulation by dispossession', is 'the transfer [of] assets and channel [of] wealth and income either from the mass of the population towards the upper classes or from vulnerable to richer countries' (Harvey 2007, 34).

Diverging from Harvey, Jessop then offers a new interpretation of how, in conditions of neoliberal governance, capitalism and territoriality become mutually interdependent. Jessop (2006) argues that territoriality and capitalism interrelate, but that territoriality itself should not necessarily be interpreted as subsumed within the overarching precepts of economic capitalism. First, he asserts that the 'fictitious' price-setting of non-commodities such as land, labour, and money is needed for the effective functioning of capitalism, as is diplomacy that will regularise political governance and alleviate 'strategic dilemmas inherent in the capital relation' (Jessop 2006, 162). Second, Jessop suggests that capital accumulation demands a 'regional structural coherence', whereby state and non-state 'alliances emerge to defend regional values and coherence and to promote them ... through the provision of new economic and extra-economic conditions favourable to further accumulation' (2006, 153, 260). I raise Jessop's ideas for the purpose of considering how neo-jihadist organisations are economically interdependent with certain local US-allied nation states and their representatives, 'diplomacy' through neo-jihadist propaganda operating to normalise and extend a neoliberal status quo within the region.

Lastly, in combination with insights from Harvey and Jessop, Jamie Peck's (2010) concept of neoliberal 'layering' is incorporated to explain how the evolution of neo-jihadism is built off the back of a history of US neo-colonial incursions in the Middle East and elsewhere. Neoliberalism is here understood as an amorphous hybrid of philosophies, policies, and practices, which chronologically constitute a series of 'prosaic forward failures' (Peck 2010, 25). Following Peck (2010, xi, 7–8), neoliberalism is neither capable of autonomously reproducing itself, nor of existing without ongoing political antagonism. The investigation also considers that Peck's theory derives from John Clarke's (2008) reflexive multiplication and doubling theory, in which a process of 'part–whole doubling' occurs and individual cases of neoliberalisation are both influenced by and constitutive of a transnational neoliberal 'whole'. Extending this primarily temporal understanding of economic development, Peck (2008, 2010) argued that the process involves a 'redoubling', or 'doubling back', whereby a series of re-regulatory and deregulatory tendencies accumulate within specific geographies to create layers of successive neoliberalisation. In this book, these layers of neoliberal policies, evoked in neo-jihadist propaganda and practice, are contextualised with reference to neoliberalism's overarching political and philosophical dimensions. These dimensions are then interpreted as part of a broader transnational neoliberal paradigm, which has permeated neo-jihadist modes of organisation.

Although this theory of neoliberal 'redoubling' is useful for framing the political-economic approach of this book, as Jessop (2011) remarked in relation to *Constructions of neoliberal reason* (Peck 2010), Peck's overwhelming concern with macroeconomic policy renders his investigation both abstract and inattentive to neoliberalism's extra-economic social and political effects. While Harvey has paid attention to the multifarious effects of neoliberalism (2001, 2005), this book applies neo-Marxist theory to phenomena that exist beyond the market, in general. For this reason, Peck's, Harvey's, and Jessop's ideas are integrated under a framework of Bourdieusian theory, which accounts for the discursive, ideational, and non-economic environments in which neoliberalism's philosophical and political effects are generated.

Bourdieu's theory: Dialectics, habitus and field, doxa and capital

My approach to dialectics in this book derives from Bourdieu's (1977) 'structuralist constructivism' emphasis on the objective structures that determine actor experience, and the reciprocal effect that subjective agency has on real-world situations. Sometimes termed 'habitus' and 'field', this understanding of the relationship between subjective and objective circumstance represents a confluence of structuralism (Durkheim et al. 1963; Levi-Strauss 1963; Althusser and Matheron 2003), ethnomethodology

(Schutz 1967; Garfinkel 1972; Berger and Luckmann 1991), and earlier dialectical thinking. Central to Bourdieu's theory and the subject of this book's investigation is how dialectical interactions between subjective agency and objective circumstances lead to the performance of what he calls 'practices' (Bourdieu 1977). For Bourdieu, these practices are dialectical such that they become mutually reinforcing.

In contrast to Hegel's dialectic theory (1901, 1969), in which practices and outcomes are considered to interact, destroy, and replace one another in a series of moments, Bourdieu posited that relative positions between agents are mutually constitutive, such that oppositional forces and their practices are always in part constituted by each other (Fogle 2011, 74). Through practices, these forces mutate and merge in ways that forge new paradigmatic situations (Bourdieu 1984). This represents a non-linear approach to social phenomena, applied here to elucidate how neo-jihadism interacts with its US-led military and counterterrorist opposition and with the broader neoliberal environments in which it operates.

To understand the contingent role of institutions and actors in the dialectical comparisons, several theoretical concepts presented by Bourdieu are relevant. Initially, the analysis incorporates Bourdieu's (1985a, 1993) explanation that interactions between individual actor agency and environmental circumstance can be understood via the concepts of habitus and field. Habitus, for Bourdieu, is 'a system of lasting transposable dispositions which, integrating past experiences, functions at every moment as a matrix of perceptions, appreciations, and action and makes possible the achievement of infinitely diversified tasks' (Bourdieu 1977, 78). It consists of the psychological structures internal to a person, produced by their upbringing, education, and subjective interpretation of life experiences, in addition to their corresponding conceptualisation of explicit external conditions. Although a collective habitus based on shared experiences may develop (Bourdieu 1984), no two persons' habitus is exactly the same.

The field against and within which the habitus is negotiated can then be defined as a 'system of deviations on different levels and nothing, either in the institutions or in the agents, the acts or discourses they produce, has meaning except relationally, by virtue of the interplay of oppositions and distinctions' (Bourdieu 1982, 185). According to Bourdieu (1986), it constitutes the arena in which agents compete for social (status, belonging), cultural (education, class), economic (money), and symbolic (meaning) capital. These forms of capital are also inextricable with the means by which the habitus is formed, once more rendering reactions and events, and subjectivity and objectivity, endlessly relational (Bourdieu 1990).

Synthesising Bourdieu's theory of practice with a neo-Marxist interpretation of neoliberalism, my political-economic analysis of AQ and IS propaganda considers their appeal to different forms of capital, while the discussion of these organisations' finances reflects on their relative engagement in economic capital exchange. Cultural capital is understood in Bourdieusian terms as (1986, 47) the 'unequal scholastic achievement' of people 'originating from the different social classes by relating academic success ... to the distribution of cultural capital between the classes and class fractions'. It represents investment in *embodied*, *objectified*, and *institutionalised* states – for example, with social conditioning, the attainment of cultural goods, and the acquisition of formalised education. Social capital, on the other hand, 'is the aggregate of the actual or potential resources which are linked to possession of a durable network of more or less institutionalized relationships of mutual acquaintance and recognition – or in other words, to membership in a group' (Bourdieu 1986, 51). Symbolic capital, as an overarching form intersectional with cultural and social capital, is 'capital – in whatever form – insofar as it is represented, i.e., apprehended symbolically, in a relationship of knowledge or, more precisely, of *misrecognition* and *recognition*, presupposes the intervention of the habitus, as a socially constituted cognitive capacity' (Bourdieu 1986, 56; my emphasis).

To investigate IS's state-like acquisition and display of capital, the investigation also incorporates the Bourdieusian notion that state-building entails the 'culmination of a process of concentration of different types of capital: capital of physical force or instruments of coercion (army, police), economic capital, cultural capital or (better) informational capital, and symbolic capital' (1998a, 41). Herein, the state becomes the holder of a type of 'metacapital' (1998a, 41), which helps to reinforce its perceived legitimacy in governing populations and territory. While this can constitute an institutional strength, it can also create a weakness, wherein different holders and forms of capital become increasingly interdependent. In the financial investigation of IS specifically, the organisation's acquisition and retention of territory is demonstrated as correlative with its fundraising and political influence, both through its propagandised citation of the Caliphate and through its management of finance through territorial means.

While multiple forms of capital are therefore necessary for the exercise of political power, Bourdieu (1984) emphasises that the perpetuation of capital relations is guided primarily by economic capital as 'mercantile exchange', which exists in concert with, and is convertible to, other non-economic types of capital: its social, cultural, and symbolic forms. Like the aforementioned critical neo-Marxist theorists and commentators,

Bourdieu argues that an emphasis on neo-classical economic calculation in conditions of neoliberalism often falsely portrays economic capital as separate and distinct from broader social and political situations (Bourdieu 1986). Agents that maintain control over capital do so by presenting the 'rules' that govern capital distribution as objective and 'disinterested' in social and political conditions (Bourdieu 1998a, 1998b). Through this process, the 'science' of neo-classical economics becomes incontestable, while social concerns such as declines in educational and living standards, and public health crises, are sublimated beneath economic concerns such as productivity. These processes provide for what Bourdieu deems to be a 'utopia of exploitation', in which the masses are perpetually disenfranchised and wealth endlessly consolidates (Bourdieu 1998b). For Bourdieu, and some neo-Marxists, this process of semantic separation is artificial and contrived. In reality, economic capital is regularly converted through physical and ideological methods into cultural, social, and symbolic capital, and vice versa.

Bourdieu's interpretation of neoliberalism underwrites his (earlier historical) interpretation of dialectics and corresponds to the broader neo-Marxist perspective of this book. According to Bourdieu, owing to its convertible nature, economic capital in conditions of neoliberalism facilitates concentrations of power among political and social actors who dictate 'that maximum growth, and therefore productivity and competitiveness, are the ultimate and sole goal of human actions; or that economic forces cannot be resisted' (Bourdieu 1998b, 31). The inevitability of 'neoliberalism' as a dominant paradigm that promotes productivity over social progress and equality is then enshrined as a 'doxa' (Bourdieu 1998b). Deriving from the semantic traditions of 'heterodox', this entails 'an adherence to relations of order which, because they structure inseparably both the real world and the thought world, are accepted as self-evident' (Bourdieu 1977, 471).

With an emphasis on the economy, Philip Cerny's (2008) notion of 'embedded neoliberalism' can further explicate the doxa to which Bourdieu refers. It is understood to entail the entrenchment of 'pro-market rules, institutions and policies' and survival-of-the-fittest mentalities, such that they become recognised as 'common sense' (Cerny 2008, 10). As Bourdieu directly explains, neoliberalism as a doxa is ultimately reinforced through the mobilisation of academic, political, and popular discourses that are replete with references to 'flexibility' and 'deregulation', and which collectively 'imply that the neo-liberal message is a universalist message of liberation' (Bourdieu 1998b, 31).

The practical installation of a Darwinian, survival-of-the-fittest worldview in conditions of neoliberalism would not have succeeded, according to Bourdieu, foreshadowing neo-Marxist human geographers (for example, Peck 2010), without the existence of a 'destabilised habitus' (Bourdieu 1998b, 98), facilitated by conditions of insecure employment, growing wealth disparity, and the various mechanisms of socio-cultural subjugation that neoliberal capitalism entails. Extending the work of 'disaster capitalism' theorists (Klein 2007; Dupuy 2010, 2011; Perez and Cannella 2011) and research on neoliberal developmentalism (Ong 2006; Peck 2010), neoliberalism is accordingly explored in the following chapters to the extent of its influence in the domains of politically violent organisations, which themselves germinate in 'post-disaster' situations.

Finally, the historical aspect of this investigation extends to the evolution of neo-jihadism, and is explained with reference to the Bourdieusian concept of 'inherited history'. To explain the importance of inherited history for interpreting the chronology of political events and situations, Bourdieu quotes from Emile Durkheim (2013). In *The logic of practice*, he states:

> In each of us, to differing degrees is contained the person we were yesterday ... our past *personae* predominate, since the present is necessarily insignificant compared with the long period of the past ... It is just that we do not directly feel the influence of these past selves precisely because they are so deeply rooted in us. They constitute the unconscious part of ourselves. (Bourdieu 1990, 56; emphasis in original)

This notion of inherited history was further elaborated in Bourdieu's *Acts of resistance* (1998b). In a similar manner to Boal et al.'s (2005) conceptualisation of 'military neoliberalism', Bourdieu used a dialectical frame to explain that security and economics can become inextricable within a field of neoliberal relations pertinent to the emergence of political violence and the actions of powerful nation states. In his explanation, 'the reason, which cannot be separated from the abuses of power which are armed or justified by reason (economic, scientific or any other)', imposed by the US through international institutions and foreign policy on and against 'Arab', 'South American', or 'African peoples', creates conditions that can, in turn, become generative of international terrorism (Bourdieu 1998b, 20). For Bourdieu, 'terrorist violence, through the irrationalism of the despair which is almost always at its root, refers back to the inert violence of the powers which invoke reason' (Bourdieu 1998b, 20). In a dialectical sense, the habitus of politically violent entities as 'irrational' exists as a 'product of our rationalism, imperialist, invasive and conquering' (Bourdieu 1998b, 20).

Bourdieu's perception of the impact of historical neoliberal and neo-colonial domination may be considered in relation to his distinction between the individual and collective habitus. Although all individuals have different 'habituses' (Swartz 2002, 636), for Bourdieu (1984) the collective affinities yielded by similar structural experiences (typically in distributions of capital) propagate group-specific habitus characteristics. Far from the Durkheimian notion of collective consciousness, or a 'system of collective beliefs and practices that have special authority' (Lukes 1969, 14), habitus for Bourdieu is in a constant process of renegotiation based upon a subject's practical engagement in real-world events (see also Swartz 2008). From a historical materialist perspective, Bourdieu's inherited history and his notion of a collective habitus explain how political-economic dialectics are created by distributions of capital effected by powerful political-economic agents. In this book, through a Bourdieusian lens, the powerful agents in question are US-directed military, counterterrorist, and neoliberal economic entities. Their interventions in the Middle East and elsewhere, extending from the Afghan–Soviet War to the twenty-first century, are here critically analysed for the extent to which they dialectically influenced the development of AQ and IS.

While I do not attempt a theoretical revisioning of Bourdieu or seek to draw from his ideas in wide-ranging theoretical detail, the analysis does extend his understanding of capital and dialectics to explore the multifaceted nature of neo-jihadism, with reference to the cases of AQ and IS. Chapters 3 and 4 are interested in exploring how, via their expression of habitus, these organisations seek to acquire and display cultural, social, and symbolic capital through their political-economic propaganda; and Chapters 5 and 6 consider how they manage economic capital in political-economic settings where neoliberal methods of fundraising and financial management are normalised, expected, and tolerated. From an overarching perspective, neoliberalism is explored as both a doxa and field, while, consistent with a core supposition of this book, capital acquired via their discourse and financial behaviour is seen to create a situation in which AQ and IS dialectically perpetuate dominant neoliberal paradigms that, within and beyond the GWOT, are accepted as 'self evident' (Bourdieu 1998a).

Research design

Dialectical relationships between neoliberalism and neo-jihadism are explored in this book through comparative analysis, with Bourdieusian and neo-Marxist ideas, and through qualitative discourse and documentary analysis methods. Primary documents include personal, private, and public communications produced by AQ, IS and individuals affiliated with these organisations. They also include reports produced by the US government, multilateral organisations such as the UN, and by international public and private think tanks. Documents for analysis were selected on the basis that they reflect the criteria John Scott (2014, 1) identifies as critical to documentary research: 'authenticity', 'credibility', 'representativeness', and 'meaning'. Following a long-standing social-science ambition, they are used 'less to test what is already known, but to develop new empirically grounded theories' (Flick 2009, 15), in this case to map out a theoretical and empirically informed approach to investigating neoliberalism and neo-jihadism.

The documents were gathered by either 'proximate' or 'mediate' access (Scott 2014) – that is, directly or through a third party, as determined by their availability and by the need for translation. Proximate materials consist of publicly available intelligence and financial reports, administrative materials, policy documents, internal communications, press releases, written propaganda, and audiovisual propaganda produced and distributed by AQ and IS. These are all either original English-language materials or materials that have been translated to English by AQ and IS. Mediated materials include primarily Arabic-language documents translated by a second party and accessed through an open-source data-collection method. Examples include transcripts of neo-jihadist propaganda and eyewitness accounts of events and situations by investigative journalists and researchers, the sources of which are discussed in more detail below.

The number of primary documents in the analysis is extensive (thirty-seven documents produced with or by AQ or IS, and 300 documents from other sources), and the historical and practical scope of the project necessitated that decisions be made regarding data selection. The epistemological basis for data inclusion reflects an approach to social-science research derived from Bourdieusian philosophy. Methodological reflexivity was important, as was the role of the researcher in creating content and meaning through subjective interpretation (Bourdieu 1990; Bourdieu and Wacquant 1992). While the analysis acknowledges critiques of Bourdieu's research theory that challenge the veracity of his argument to achieve an epistemologically rigorous researcher objectivity (Maton 2003), I also reflect on a counter-argument, that illustrative scientific social observation can only be revealed through ongoing self-reflection (Bourdieu 1990; Loadenthal 2019). Research for this book commenced from the premise that interactions between neo-jihadism and neoliberalism would demonstrate the contradiction between the former's anti-capitalist proselytising and its quasi-capitalist practices, but this was revised to incorporate greater consideration of the underlying structural connections that give rise to such dialectics, through a lens of power and resistance, for the purpose of revealing the mutually constitutive nature of the entities in question.

For the analysis in Chapters 3 and 4, neo-jihadist propaganda documents were obtained using a Boolean technique to search Google, Yahoo!, and Bing for various combinations of the keywords 'Islamic State', 'Al Qaeda', 'speech', 'video', 'English-language', 'English translation', from 1979 to 2014 for AQ and from 2014 to 2017 for IS. The credibility of the search results was assessed by the research method of triangulation (Rothbauer 2008) and with consideration of the political and economic context of their publication. The content of AQ and IS media, including text, audiovisual imagery, and sound, was captured using the qualitative-research program NVivo. Results were coded for the key theme of 'anti-capitalism' and the subthemes 'anti-US', 'anti-neo-colonial', 'anti-globalisation', and 'anti-neoliberal'. The results were then recoded using an axial approach for the cross-sectional criteria of 'cultural and social capital', 'symbolism and symbolic capital', 'anti-capitalist doxa', 'habitus', and 'field'. A third classificatory dimension was used to inform the analysis. This entailed identifying geo-economic references in the propaganda documents to 'idealism', 'historical materialism', and 'land'.

Documents for the analysis of AQ and IS finance in Chapters 5 and 6 were obtained through a similar Boolean search technique using the same search engines and on the news-media databases Factiva and Informit. Keyword searches were conducted using the terms 'Al Qaeda', 'Islamic State', 'economics', 'political economy', 'finance', and 'financial practices'. The results were again assessed for their reliability through a consideration of publication context and triangulation. Search results relating to AQ were grouped into the subthemes of 'Maktab al-Khidamat', 'donors and charities', 'alternative remittance systems', and 'commercial activities'. Results pertaining to IS were grouped under 'US interventions in Iraq', 'financial institutions', 'oil and gas', 'natural resources', and 'IS administration of finance'. The data for AQ and IS were cross-coded for 'financialisation', 'monetarism', 'public–private partnerships', and 'accumulation by dispossession', and the Bourdieusian concepts of 'economic capital' and 'neoliberalism as doxa'. They were then given a third interpretive layer, related to AQ and IS's respective geo-economic orientation. Documentary evidence of geo-economic interests was classified as either 'non-territorial quasi-corporation' or 'territorial quasi-nation state'.

Propaganda examples in Chapters 3 and 4 were analysed using a critical discourse method concerned with addressing 'opaque as well as transparent relationships of dominance, discrimination, power and control as manifested in language' (Wodak and Meyer 2009, 10). This entailed attention to the textual, contextual, and interpretive levels of discourse in the examined speeches, media, and texts (Ruiz 2009, 10). It also included consideration of relevant political events that preceded the publication of the documents, and it interpreted how mutually reinforcing discourses between neo-jihadist organisations and neoliberal entities function as mechanisms of political persuasion. The documentary method applied to examine AQ and IS's propaganda and financial practices in Chapters 3 to 6 emphasised the content or findings of the materials, and the 'frame of orientation', consisting of experience, politics, and practices (Bohnsack 2010). It considered pertinent features of the artefacts examined, including their content, format, publishing, authorship, and anticipated audience reception. In comparing the findings of the analysis chapters, and establishing evidence of dialectical relationships, the discussion reflected on how a Bourdieusian political-economic framework could be used to illuminate evidence of dialectical engagements such as 'causation', 'reflexivity', and 'mirroring'.

Mediated sources

One practical limitation of this project related to data selection is its use of translated and transliterated material. This is because the content of the material is compromised by the subjective positioning of the translator and by a lack of semantic equivalence between English and other languages. For this reason, and because targeting of 'the West' in certain neo-jihadist propaganda is relevant to the research questions, the analysis in Chapters 3 and 4 examines mainly English-language propaganda produced by AQ and IS. Where Arabic-language materials are used, the discussion draws from translations that were either conducted by the neo-jihadist organisations themselves or by credible others, such as think-tank researchers and academics. With respect to the materials translated by AQ and IS, the analysis considers material directed at an English-language audience. With respect to artefacts mediated (translated and transliterated) by others, here referred to as 'interpreters', it considers material directed primarily at Arabic-language audiences.

The extensive reliance on English-language and translated materials in this book poses a potential limitation related to equivalence and access; it is also a possible drawback for the research focus on neoliberalism. Propaganda produced in or translated into English by neo-jihadist-affiliated entities is likely to be oriented to a Western readership or audience and therefore to include anti-Western, anti-colonial, and anti-capitalist critiques likely to resonate with this audience. With this in mind, I do not propose that the political-economic patterns and trends examined pertain to the broad spectrum of neo-jihadist organisations' propagandised behaviour, or that political economy per se is necessarily an overwhelming focus of these organisations' broader politics. Rather, as mentioned in the Introduction, this book adopts a political-economic analytic lens for the purpose of exploring exclusively how neo-jihadist entities engage with neoliberalism, to the extent that these engagements demonstrate noteworthy reciprocity and interdependence. In short, the analysis is bound in its scope, and it may not be possible to extrapolate its meaning beyond the limits of enquiry outlined.

Other issues for consideration regarding language mediation include the credentials of the interpreter, their positioning both within and outside of the translation and transliteration processes, and the manner in which they have logistically handled a potential lack of conceptual and linguistic equivalence (Squires 2009). To address these issues in relation to non-English-language material, this book posits a (structuralist) constructivist understanding of the interpreter's identity and motivation during the translation or transliteration processes (Temple 2002). Once more in contrast to positivist accounts that interpret translations as technically absolute and accurate, this method allows for an acknowledgement of the determinative influence of the context in which the material was originally mediated (Temple and Young 2004). With respect to translated and transliterated material, the analysis primarily reflects on its political and academic context. This constructivist approach to mediated material is appropriate given the research interest in the political environments in which interactions between neo-jihadist and counter-terrorist entities take place. It reflects Bourdieu's (1990) emphasis on self-reflexivity and his understanding of the impact that research fields have on the habituses that define individual researchers' subjectivity.

Extensive translations of AQ and IS's written and audiovisual propaganda were performed and distributed by the organisations themselves, and translations of various internal and external communications were also performed by researchers of (neo-)jihadism. These researchers have worked in the fields of investigative journalism and academia, for private and public think tanks, and they have collaborated with commercial and government entities.

The book draws from primary material and on insight from books and news media chronicling the emergence of AQ and IS written by Michael Weiss, Hassan Hassan, and Abdel Bari Atwan. Weiss is a columnist for the US-based news-media outlets the Daily Beast, *Foreign Policy*, and Cable News Network (CNN). Hassan, who performed the translations, is a journalist for multiple outlets in both Western and Middle Eastern locations. He has testified before the US Senate and Homeland Security and been a national security advisor to US governments. Atwan is the editor-in-chief of a London-based, Arab-world newspaper, *Rai al-Youm*, and he interviewed policymakers and counterterrorism targets following 9/11, the 2003 US invasion of Iraq, and the emergence of IS. He often expresses critical interest in how Western governments' foreign policy may be generative of political violence.

Demonstrating the importance of investigative journalism for this book, the analysis also draws extensively on the work of award-winning *Guardian* correspondent Jason Burke. Since the 1990s, Burke has written high-profile accounts of AQ, IS, and of militant Islamism more broadly. During his investigations, he lived in Pakistan and Somalia and travelled to multiple conflict zones in Gaza, Kurdistan, Thailand, Algeria and elsewhere. He has conducted interviews with residents of these regions and members of designated terrorist organisations. Combining insights from these interviews and a number of texts produced by the entities in question, he synthesised critical accounts of Western foreign policy, published in books and editorials.

Arabist and non-Arabist researchers from public and private think tanks whose translations and findings are also used extensively include Charles Lister (2014, 2015), Stefan Heißner, Managing Partner of EY Fraud Investigation & Dispute Services (of Ernst & Young Global Limited), and his co-authors at the International Centre for the Study of Radicalisation and Political Violence (ICSR), an independent, 'non-partisan' research organisation hosted at the Department of War Studies at King's College, London (Winter and Saltman 2014; Heißner et al. 2017), Will McCants (2015), and Laurence Bindner and Gabriel Poirot, who have worked with Jean-Charles Brisard and Damien Martinez at the Center for the Analysis of Terrorism (Brisard and Martinez 2014; Bindner and Poirot 2016). In contrast to investigative journalists, these researchers, representing their institutions, have generally adopted a strategic counterterrorist approach to analysing organisations including AQ and IS. Charles Lister, for example, is a Senior Fellow at the Middle East Institute in Washington and previously worked as a Visiting Fellow at the Brookings Institution's Doha Center in Qatar. He has been the head of counterterrorism research teams, and he engaged in three years of intensive correspondence with insurgent groups in Syria.

A number of other Arabic speakers whose work informs the analysis in this book are affiliated with the ICSR. In addition to Heißner and colleagues (Heißner et al. 2017), these include Aymenn Jawad al-Tamimi, a doctoral candidate at Swansea University, author at The Washington

Institute for Near East Policy, and graduate of Oxford University. Tamimi's research is unique in its field, given his ability to identify, access, translate, and interpret internal IS documents. Chapter 6's discussion of IS finance draws on these documents, available via his website, Twitter, and subscription services.

Other senior research fellows at the King's College Centre whose work the book draws on include Charlie Winter, who is well known for his critique of neo-jihadist organisations' online activity, and Aaron Zelin, also an alumni of the Centre, and the editor of Jihadology.net, which provides translations of and access to primary neo-jihadist documents, such as the IS speeches and audiovisual material examined in Chapter 4. Zelin is now a fellow at The Washington Institute and a visiting fellow at Brandeis University.

From private think tanks, the book draws most extensively on the translations and perspectives of Will McCants from the Brookings Institution and of researchers at the Center for the Analysis of Terrorism (CAT). McCants is a director of the research initiative, US Relations with the Islamic World, and Senior Fellow in Foreign Policy, based at Brookings, and he has a long history of Islamic linguistics and theological studies, teaching at US universities including Johns Hopkins. The Brookings Institution is based in Washington, DC and is differentially referred to as a 'conservative' and 'liberal' research affiliate of institutions that influence US foreign policy. The Center for the Analysis of Terrorism (CAT) is a comparable European counterpart, and its website byline is 'a research center aiming at becoming a European leading think tank on the analysis of terrorism. The CAT is recognized as an institution of public interest' (CAT 2017). The founders of the institute, Jean-Charles Brisard and Damien Martinez, have both worked in federal law enforcement related to counterterrorism, 9/11 in particular. Martinez also maintained affiliations with commercial entities including Credit Suisse and Thomson Reuters Risk, and he is the founding Chief Executive Officer of the insurance service firm Facepoint.

The translations of statements by Bin Laden and other leading jihadist figures examined in Chapter 3 were published by researchers for other think tanks and government-affiliated institutions. These are the Combatting Terrorism Center, which undertook the translations, and the Investigative Project on Terrorism, which published an unclassified CIA memorandum about and featuring the fatwa in question. The Combatting Terrorism Center is an academic institution at the US Military Academy in West Point, New York; the Investigative Project on Terrorism focuses exclusively on 'radical Islamic groups' (2018) and is directed by Steven Emerson, a US journalist accused of expressing Islamophobic opinions (Clifton 2011). While these research entities, like CAT and Brookings, are constitutive of and contribute to the military industries critically addressed in this book, they are deemed to be appropriate sources for pursuing the book's comparative research interests. This is because they provide comprehensive accounts of neo-jihadist organisations' propaganda and finance, and because they do not (and are the least likely to) exhibit a critical political bias of establishing evidence of reflexivity, mirroring, or causation between the US, Western commercial entities, and neo-jihadist organisations.

As news media is inherently politicised, subjective, and consumer-driven, this must be accounted for when using journalistic data. There are, on the other hand, merits to these sources that potentially outweigh limitations. The first of these is that journalism, the fourth estate, is an invaluable informational resource. Second, news-media perspectives serve as a historical artefact of neoliberalism's evolutionary development. For example, writers for *New Left Review* during the 1980s pioneered political confrontation of neoliberal interventionism during the nascent phases of the Reagan doctrine (Halliday 1978; Habermas 1990). The inclusion of these sources arguably counterbalances what might otherwise be an over-reliance on official organisational narratives, in particular the strategic anti-terrorism incentives that might influence certain sources' language mediation. As demonstrated by their professional affiliations, other sources have worked for commercial and government-sponsored research initiatives. They represent the wide spectrum of political thought that is a major focus of this book. The institutional and organisational origins of the translations are therefore important for the framing of the analysis. To the extent to which material resulting from research conducted for strategic counterterrorism purposes can be said to illuminate dialectical relationships between neo-jihadism and neoliberalism, it is also useful in clarifying reflexivity in terrorist and counterterrorist behaviour. Reflecting on these sources provides insight into the knowledge available to counterterrorist actors and reveals knowledge accessible to English-language supporters of AQ and IS.

As with any investigative and exploratory project, this book does not profess to, nor can it, examine every situational variable and scenario relevant to its study, in this case ideology and finance. The argument instead follows that although neoliberal intersections may not be dominant across all neo-jihadism-related political continuums, their occurrence is strategically significant, given that neo-jihadist organisations profess in many ways to be anti-capitalist, and given the impacts of neo-jihadist violence in neoliberal environments.

Within the book's limits, then, I seek to provide an exacting account of key political-economic intersections between neo-jihadism and neoliberalism, extending to neoliberal aspects of US-led military and counterterrorist activity. Through reference to documents and discourses, I assess ideological and material affinities between the relevant organisations and entities, and lay the groundwork for an empirically supported theory of neo-jihadism in its political-economic dimensions. In preparation for the investigation of AQ and IS's propaganda and finance, the following chapter outlines neoliberal philosophies and policies that have yielded significant international effects, including in the politically violent domain of neo-jihadism.

2

Neoliberalism in action

Dialectical engagements between neoliberalism and neo-jihadism correspond to a history of Western economic development and to neoliberal philosophies and policies that have yielded undesirable social, political, and economic outcomes. In this chapter, I outline a number of philosophies and policies that are subject to widespread criticism and that have been variously intersectional with the GWOT and neo-jihadism.

Superficial contradictions in the political economy of neo-jihadist organisations' propaganda and practice are apparent, and neoliberalism also evinces a number of internal and external contradictions. Two of those relevant to neoliberalism's early and late modern foundations are the principle that neoliberal policies derive from and uphold the classical liberal ideals of protections for freedom and human rights; and the belief that neoliberalism derives empirically and ideologically from the secular, rational, and scientific ideals of the Enlightenment. These principles are explored in the first part of this chapter, together with an account of neoliberalism's fundamentalist and neo-colonial aspects. Several deleterious policy outcomes of neoliberalism are then analysed, with a consideration of those that remain prevalent and subject to sustained critique.

Neoliberal philosophies

Modernity

While 'modernity' is often associated with various points in Western history, in the following investigation it refers to the major societal changes that took place in western Europe during the Enlightenment (seventeenth to eighteenth centuries). Neoliberalism, as a late modern form of capitalism (existing from around 1980 to the present day), persists via the common belief that as an economic model it provides a means for underprivileged workers to improve their quality of life. This has proven a popular fallacy, inconsistent with the reality of much neoliberal economic enterprise.

A core philosophical contradiction of neoliberalism is that it pro-motes the values of individualism and competition, despite the fact that the means by which people can compete to improve their socio-economic situations are often limited. Resembling the individualising ideals of early modern capitalism, the individualist ideology of neolib-eralism is reinforced by restrictions on collectivised political and indus-trial action, and governments' de-funding and erosion of public spaces where people can freely associate (Brenner and Theodore 2002). These factors produce social environments where people internalise blame for their socio-economic situation, and victim-blame in cases of violence and exploitation (Stringer 2014). Like the 'autonomous' subjects of the Enlightenment, the subjects of neoliberalism assume responsibility for their circumstances in the manner of 'rational', 'moral' actors. Consis-tent with the historical effects of capitalism, when neoliberal subjects experience ongoing deprivation they become spiritually and physically isolated (Braedley and Luxton 2010).

The neoliberal values of secularism, liberalism, and science may be understood as internally contradictory in light of the paradigm's early and late modern roots in the epistemological traditions of positivism. Despite neoliberalism's 'Enlightenment' affiliations, and its derivation from both the Vienna Circle (Ayer 1966), and Austrian and Chicago School economic theory (Becchio and Leghissa 2016; see also Hayek 1937 and Friedman 1962), as a philosophical and political-economic school of thought it is ideologically grounded in the positivist, scientific religion expounded by August de Comte (1789–1857), inspired by the theories of Henri de Saint-Simon (1760–1825).

As Gray highlights (2003), insofar as neoliberalism derived from early and late forms of positivism, it also inherited their predisposition towards scientific-spiritual fanaticism. The spiritual roots of Comte's positivist theory, for example, were his 'religion of humanity', replete with a lit-urgy, priesthood, calendar, ritualistic meetings, and fasting (Comte 1858; Wright 1986). In contemporary societies, the modern 'cult of neoliberal-ism' (Peck 2010) is predicated on neo-classical economic theory (Smith 1776; Rodrik 2000; 2011; Hall 2011, 709) and characterised by a dom-inant belief that a philosophical pursuit of liberty should equate to a dogmatic observance of the 'science' behind economic freedom (Jessop 1982; Gray 2003; Crouch 2011). Echoing Bourdieu's theories about a culturally pervasive doxa of neoliberalism, enshrined through the trans-ferability of different forms of capital (1986, 1998a, 1998b), productiv-ity, rather than feasibility or social benefit, has become the 'quantifiable' measure of economic success, despite the often deleterious social out-comes of neoliberal programmes (Hall et al. 2015).

Fundamentalism

The 'cult' of neoliberalism typically denotes its proponents' dogmatic dedication to deregulation, privatisation, and other 'market fundamentalist' policy approaches (Harvey 2001), but neoliberalism may also be considered fundamentalist in terms of its extension to contemporary Western politics. This was particularly evident in the neoliberal–neoconservative nexus that characterised the George W. Bush administration after 9/11 (Ali 2003; Jackson 2005; Pyszczynski et al. 2008; Kurtulus 2012; Vlahos 2012). Contrary to neoliberal proponents' claims of modernity and progress, fundamentalist religiosity during this period served as a political rationale for US public and private entities to pursue neoliberal economic agendas in military activity and counterterrorism. This was particularly so in the direct aftermath of the attacks, where overtly religious and fundamentalist rhetoric fomented support within the US for its activity in the Middle East during the nascent phases of the GWOT.

After 9/11, for example, neo-jihadist violence on the part of AQ was discussed in terms of Good, Evil, and the Devil (Jackson 2005, 2006, 2011). US foreign policy was explained in political discourse and news media using Manichean tropes about the 'inexplicable' nature of the 'Evil terrorists' versus the 'Enlightened' rationality of US citizens, as 'God's chosen people' (Vlahos 2012; Richards 2017). Following the attacks, Bush openly speculated: 'what if God has been holding his peace, waiting for the right man and the right nation and the right moment to act for Him and cleanse history of Evil?' (Beatty 2003), while a 2002 CNN poll found that up to a quarter of Americans believed that the events of 9/11 were prophesied in the Bible (Scherer 2004). Demonstrating the correlation of such pseudo-civilisational narratives and the government's economic pursuits, shortly after the US invasion of Iraq, Bush stated: 'by expanding trade, we spread hope and opportunity to the corners of the world, and we strike a blow to the terrorists. Our agenda for freer trade is part of our agenda for a freer world' (Juhasz 2006). His advisor and future president of the World Bank Robert Zoellick pledged to 'counter terror with trade' (Juhasz 2006).

The philosophical roots of the neo-conservative–neoliberal nexus under George W. Bush were first apparent in a 1992 memorandum written during George Bush Senior's time in office by George W. Bush's future Deputy Secretary of Defense Paul Wolfowitz and Wolfowitz's assistant Lewis 'Scooter' Libby. The memorandum, titled 'Defense Planning Guidance of 1992', in many ways recalled both the militaristic policies of the Reagan administration and the moralistic political views expressed by the founders of neo-conservatism, Irving Kristol and Robert Kagan (Kristol 1972, 1978; Kristol and Kagan 1996). Advocating increased US military presence in the Gulf region, the document stipulated that the US's primary concerns were 'access to raw materials, primarily Persian Gulf oil, proliferation of weapons of mass destruction and ballistic missiles, and threats to U.S. citizens from terrorism' (Tyler 1992).

Resembling the tone and message of the 1992 document, a 1997 think-tank report written by members of the neo-conservative Project for a New American Century (PNAC) was a further policy directive for pursuing US political and economic hegemony. The authors were academics, advisors, and commercial magnates, including the future Bush administration Secretary of Defense Donald Rumsfeld, US publishing executive Steve Forbes, and future vice president under Bush, then CEO of US oil conglomerate Halliburton, Dick Cheney. The report outlines a plan to export US-style democracy and liberal trading conditions through military activity, concluding with this statement:

> Such a Reaganite policy of military strength and moral clarity may not be fashionable today. But it is necessary if the United States is to build on the successes of this past century and to ensure our security and our greatness in the next. (Abrams et al. 1997)

The social and cultural conditions in the US that promoted public support for its governments' neoliberal and neo-conservative agendas before and after 9/11 are highlighted in Andrew Strombeck's (2006) analysis of the *Left behind* (LaHaye and Jenkins 2011) book series. As Strombeck explains, the series, which is sold at Walmart outlets across the US, tells the story of an American evangelical apocalypse, synthesising a hybrid religious and economic cultural logic predicated on neoliberal privatisation and consumer-driven citizenship. As Laurie Goodstein (2003) earlier demonstrated, speeches by US religious leaders have also been illustrative of conflated religious, economic, and military policy agendas. When advocating US military offensives against insurgent activity in the Middle East, for example, the Christian evangelist 'CEO' Franklin Graham characterised Islam as 'a very evil and wicked religion', while Jerry Vines, a former pastor of the country's third largest Southern Baptist church, labelled the Prophet Muhammad a 'demon-possessed pedophile' (Goodstein 2003). Harking back to political-economic tensions of former years, Richard Cizik, the Vice-President for Governmental Affairs of the National Association of Evangelicals, which comprises 45,000 congregations, compared the religion of Islam with societal fears of communism during the Cold War, declaring that 'Muslims have become the modern-day equivalent of the Evil Empire' (Goodstein 2003).

The role that political actors play in perpetuating neoliberal and religious fundamentalist exceptionalism in the US, particularly with regard to the GWOT, has been explored at length by Tariq Ali (2003), and Noam Chomsky and David Barsamian (2010; see also Kirkpatrick 2006). Drawing on autobiographical evidence and first-hand testimony, Ali argued in *The clash of fundamentalisms: Crusades, jihads and modernity* (2003) that, in light of events such as the Spanish Reconquista, Islam's conservative tenets had historically assumed dominance over its progressive ones, but that in comparison with the religiosity of other states, 'American imperialism' is 'the mother of all fundamentalisms' (2003, 307). Chomsky and Barsamian (2010) highlighted that 'Christian-Zionist' US members of Congress have for some time convinced their constituents of the necessity of providing military support to Israel by promoting a narrative in which, when the apocalypse occurs, all Jewish people will be automatically converted to Christianity, and everyone else will be 'smote' from the earth. Indicating the persistence of religious fundamentalism in contemporary GWOT debates, a 2012 *Life-Way* research poll revealed that 32 per cent of US respondents believed 'the battles in Syria are all part of the prophecies of the Book of Revelation' (Hafiz 2013). Indeed, fundamentalist, religious, and moralising attitudes continue to serve as justification for the pursuit of political-economic agendas in US military and counterterrorism campaigns at the time of this book's writing.

Neo-colonialism

Beyond its extension to counterterrorist and military activity, another philosophical characteristic of US-directed neoliberalism that has been criticised for yielding undesirable outcomes is its tendency to neo-colonialism. While Harvey's (2001) previously discussed theory of 'accumulation by dispossession', described by Jessop (2006, 151) as a state of affairs in which 'resources are expropriated once and for all from a "commons" that has been built up over many years', helps to explain broad patterns of neo-colonial activity, William Clark's (2005) concept of 'petrodollar warfare' illuminates the specific case of US control over Middle Eastern energy.

In Clark's explanation, power over the world's energy extraction and distribution regions both directly and through proxies has allowed the US to stipulate that all primary international oil trade must be conducted in US Federal Reserve dollars. In turn, US control over international oil distribution has ensured that nation states are required to hold reserves of US currency, thus maintaining the authority of the US dollar and allowing the country to run trillion-dollar budget deficits. Clark identifies a cyclical dimension to this situation, given that significant US budgetary expenditure is dedicated to military efforts, which, in turn, operate independently, through the North Atlantic Treaty Organization (NATO) and various international partnerships, to guard geographical areas where major oil extraction and (initial) distribution takes place. As Chapters 3 and 4 of this book will show, Clark and Harvey's ideas are relevant in conceptualising the political impacts of the GWOT, particularly the extent to which AQ and IS explicitly use terminology such as 'petrodollar' and 'dispossession' in their propaganda.

Another neo-colonial tenet of US neoliberal activity often highlighted in political-economic commentary is the international economic influence of US and US-affiliated multinational corporations. The neoliberal dimensions of international commerce manifest in relaxed global trading conditions, 'flexible' capital accumulation (Harvey 1989), a homogenisation of diverse societies and cultures (Sheppard and Leitner 2010), and the reliance of vulnerable populations upon the patronage of powerful nation states such as the US, inflaming geopolitical tensions (Duggan 2012). The consumption of products distributed by Western multinationals has undermined domestic industries, contributed to a trend in cultural commodification sometimes described as 'McDonaldization' (Ritzer 1992; Barber 1995), and variously, as in the case of neo-jihadism and other violent social movements, resulted in civil unrest and parochialism (Crothers 2012; Pieterse 2015).

In regions of the world disadvantaged by economic disparity created by US-led neoliberal enterprise, the values of commodification, individualism, and competition, and the products they are attached to, can carry negative connotations. They have in particular been criticised by international spectators and the residents of non-Western nations as indicative of a Western cultural elitism. At the same time, industrial conditions in countries where US, UK, or European-owned goods are produced have been described as 'neo-colonial', given the common and persistent occurrence of low wages, unsafe work spaces, and lack of 'flow-down' profits to local workers from corporate elites.

Historically, and until the emergence of early modern capitalism in western Europe, governments and nation states had been the main perpetrators of neo-colonial exploitation. Now private industries, often supported by US-directed institutions such as the International Monetary Fund (IMF) and World Trade Organization (WTO), and the neoliberal programmes of host states control and colonise domestic economies, imposing various social and economic harms on local populations (Welch 2008). AQ and IS's political and practical response to such philosophical environments of neoliberalism are explored in the chapters that follow; outlined below are specific cases and characteristics of US neoliberal policies and the broader programmes to which they belong.

Neoliberal policies

As explained in Chapter 1, the Western tradition of neoliberalism used as an analytical comparison in this book derives ideologically from the radical free-market tendencies of Friedman's Chicago School liberalism and the social conservatism of Hayek's Austrian school of theory (Harvey 2005), broadly advocating deregulation, privatisation, monetarism, and open international borders to allow for increasingly globalised flows of people, goods, and services. It also derives from a dual-pronged approach to domestic and international economics, founded upon theories of income distribution and aggregate employment determination. As explained by Thomas Palley (2005, 20), these are the theories that labour and capital resources 'get paid what they are worth' through automatic re-stabilisation of the supply and demand process, given that 'free markets will not let valuable factors of production – including labor – go to waste'. Neoliberal economic policy guidance is supported by the socio-political reinforcement of individual enterprise, the advocacy of public–private partnerships, and a broad-based reduction in centralised power exercised by conventional sovereign states.

With the overarching aim of ensuring expanded capital mobility, neoliberal policies promote the growth of financial(ised) industries and transfers of responsibility for public services to private entities, via the curbing of restraints on corporations posed by labour unions, taxes, and other barriers to trade (Cerny 2008; Mirowski 2013). Contrary to the neoliberal philosophies of individualism, innovation, capital growth, and freedom from government intervention, 'actually existing neoliberalism' (Brenner and Theodore 2002) in reality intensifies inequality, insecurity, scarcity, and the absence of legitimate competition. As neatly summarised by Piketty (2014, 1), 'modern economic growth and the diffusion of knowledge have made it possible to avoid the Marxist apocalypse but have not modified the deep structures of capital and inequality'. Drawing on Piketty's (2014) analysis and a series of high-profile case studies, in the remainder of this chapter I explore neoliberal policies that have been subject to widespread critique internationally, including in the political-economic propaganda of neo-jihadist organisations.

The 2008 GFC

Perhaps the most often criticised aspect of neoliberalism has been its proponents' advocacy of privatisation, deregulation, and financialisation.

The 2008 GFC was an exemplary case of the application of these neoliberal approaches to policy; as Chapters 3 and 4 demonstrate, it was also extensively cited in post-2008 propaganda communicated by AQ spokespersons. For critics more broadly, the policies that led to the 2008 GFC illustrate the deregulation of business investment and financial assets leading to undesirable outcomes (Montgomerie and Williams 2009). While catalysts for the crisis were cumulative and complex, the 'Levin–Coburn report', published 13 April 2013, foregrounded the failure of US-directed neoliberal market logic, mentioning 'high risk, complex financial products; undisclosed conflicts of interest; the failure of regulators, the credit rating agencies, and the market itself to reign in the excesses of Wall Street' (Levin and Coburn 2013, 1) to be major contributing factors to the crisis. Three other catalysts often identified were the bursting of the 2006 US housing bubble, the mass accumulation of financial assets in the US and internationally, with credit-default swaps and other financial derivatives encouraging sub-prime lending, and the fact that prior to the GFC, the labour model characterising US–China trading relations had seen a 'decade long period of unsustained tilting' (Mason 2012, 107). Added to this were deregulated international trading conditions that secured capital flows in favour of US corporations (Brunnermeier 2009).

After the GFC, critics observed an increase in rates of homelessness and unemployment in developed countries, with European citizens in particular subject to the harsh austerity of significant cuts to investment in public goods and services (Johnson 2009; Wight 2012). Due to less developed countries (LDCs) being economically reliant upon the US, many people residing in these countries were also significantly affected by the GFC, although their experience was less frequently reported in mainstream Western news media. In addition to the direct impacts of the GFC, these impacts resulted in part from the neoliberal Washington Consensus and WTO 1999 trade agreement that collectively enabled the US and EU to penetrate the borders of LDCs and force an internationalisation of their trade policies (Chomsky 1999, 67). It was also a result of SAPs provided by the IMF and WTO, which enabled foreign investors and creditors to interfere with domestic social and political institutions in LDCs. As Wendy Brown (2009, 38) put it, debt packages provided by neoliberal nations allowed the US and EU to 'yank the chains of every aspect of Third World existence'. Given international economic dependence during the GFC, in 2009 Cambodia's gross domestic product (GDP) growth reduced to zero, while Kenyan horticultural exports fell by 35 per cent, and in Zambia 30,000 mining jobs were eradicated (Velde 2010).

In the aftermath of the GFC, risky financial activity on the part of domestic and international financial institutions was still recognised as permissible, given nepotistic social networks and institutional linkages between public and private actors in the US. Lobbyists were seen to contribute billions of dollars in donations to political parties who promised to implement neoliberal finance and trade policies, ensuring sustained economic deregulation and transfers of public wealth and services to private hands (Panitch and Konings 2009). Despite the risks that led to the GFC, in 2010 the US Supreme Court rejected a motion from the Citizen's United Group to restrict private investment in US elections (Lubin 2012, 186). Moreover, as former World Bank Chief Economist Joseph Stiglitz (2011) famously observed, 85 per cent of members of the US Senate were part of a 1 per cent population margin controlling the majority of the country's wealth. In *America at the crossroads: Democracy, power and the neoconservative legacy* (2007), Francis Fukuyama, a former member of the PNAC and key contributor to the Reagan Doctrine, explained the nature of neoliberal financial arrangements between public and private actors in the US:

> The problem comes from politicians who want to use public money to maintain patronage networks that are critical to their political survival. Asking them to be fiscally responsible may be tantamount to asking them to commit political suicide, something they are understandably reluctant to do. (Fukuyama 2007, 124)

Although it may be reductive to assign responsibility for the GFC solely to the US's role in neoliberalism's 'ecological dominance' (Jessop 2000), political and economic decisions made in the US during this period constitute a vital example of neoliberal policies producing devastating outcomes. Extreme wealth inequality underlay many of the direct causative mechanisms that led to the crisis, and it resulted from neoliberal approaches to economic policy since the 1980s.

From 1977 to 2007, in fact, the richest 10 per cent of the US appropriated three quarters of its total economic growth, while the wealthiest 1 per cent absorbed nearly 60 per cent (Piketty 2014, 373). In these conditions, the wages and purchasing power of those on lower and middle incomes stagnated, while a severely deregulated financial sector embraced predatory lending, which, in turn, contributed significantly to the GFC. As Piketty (2014) has brought to light, historical correlations in distributions of wealth that precede such crises present significant cause for reflection. The share of US national income held by the top ten per cent peaked twice in the country's history, in 1928 and 2007; an economic crash ensued in both of the following years.

Wealth inequality

Further to the GFC, neoliberal economic policies reinforcing privatisation and deregulation have generally yielded deleterious outcomes to the
extent to which they contribute to wealth inequality on an international
scale. This too represented a prominent focus in neo-jihadist media,
including AQ and IS's emphasis on metaphorical 'enslavement' caused
by insufficient remuneration for labour in the West (AQIS 2014; Al
Hayat 2015a), and Bin Laden's (2007) analogy of late modern capitalism and the 'shackles' and 'attrition' of early modern feudalism.

The unequal conditions to which critics of the US and neoliberalism
more broadly refer were accounted for comprehensively in Piketty's
Capital in the twenty-first century (2014). One function of this work
was to address widespread justifications of neoliberalism predicated on
the belief that economic advantage is won by 'merit', and that restrictions on wealth aggregation will somehow hurt a society's lowest
socio-economic strata. To explain how neoliberal policies relegate those
less advantaged by birth or ability to exploitation by the 'capitalist class',
Piketty (2014) draws on the World Top Incomes Database, estate tax
returns, and national wealth indicators. He explains that if conditions at
his time of writing were to continue, the international rate of return
from capital would ultimately exceed the combined international rate of
growth of income from labour combined with output, as it did in the
nineteenth century; or, as Piketty denotes this equation, '$r > g$' (Piketty
2014, 33). These conditions include, specifically, a return to prominence
of private capital (or 'wealth') relative to national income, significant
global income earned from capital relative to labour, and, in the US case
in particular, extreme disparity in remuneration for labour both within
and between markets.

Piketty's investigation reveals that ratios of private capital to national
income increased significantly in the wealthy countries of the US,
Germany, the UK, Canada, Japan, France, Italy, and Australia from 1970
to 2010. In what he describes as the rise of 'patrimonial capitalism', private wealth at the start of the 1970s represented 'between two and three
and a half years of national income in all the rich countries, on all con-
tinents', while in 2010 it was 'between four and seven years of national
income' (Piketty 2014, 215). This occurred in part because of deregulated trading conditions and the growth of financial industries, but it
also occurred because of 'public dissaving', meaning in this case a
decrease in assets earned through taxation and the investment of public
capital. Direct transfers of assets from public to private hands by governments adopting neoliberal economic models since the 1980s also
contributed (Harvey 2003; Braedley and Luxton 2010). Moreover, much
of the extent and nature of this private wealth is unknown, given that,

by Gabriel Zuman's conservative estimate, drawing on Swiss bank data, at least 10 per cent of global GDP resides in tax havens (cited in Piketty 2014, 592).

While there is some irony to AQ and IS's condemnation of situations such as this, given their own exploitation of tax havens, elaborated in Chapter 6, spokespersons for the organisations more broadly cite the social injustices of extreme wealth disparity in pejorative references to 'elites' (see, for example, Naji 2006). Indicating the field of anti-(neoliberal) capitalism that neo-jihadist propaganda operates within, broader anti-globalisation and anti-capitalist resistance movements, such as the Occupy movement in the US, the Indignados in Spain, and the Arab Spring across North Africa and the Middle East, have also been prolific in their opposition to economic wealth disparity, citing its creation of harmful and unjust living conditions.

While the extent and nature of anti-capitalist activism in the neoliberal era is as diverse as it is complex, a well-known example within the US was the Occupy movement's appropriation of Stiglitz's (2011) finding that 1 per cent of the US population controlled 40 per cent of the country's economic capital and a quarter of its income, while the incomes of men with only high-school degrees declined 12 per cent in the year prior to the publication of Stiglitz's research, 2010. Amost a decade later, in 2018, the People's Policy Project revealed that since 1989, the richest 1 per cent in the US had increased their net worth by US$21 trillion, while in the same period the net worth of the poorest 50 per cent decreased by US$900 billion; in other words, the top 'one per cent' at this book's time of writing owns '[US$]30 trillion of assets, while the bottom half owns less than nothing' (Bruenig 2019). Indicating the international dimensions of this situation, an Oxfam paper in 2017 revealed that eight men owned the same amount of global wealth as half of the world's population: 3.6 billion people. This paper also indicated that between 1988 (the year of AQ's inception) and 2011, 'the incomes of the poorest 10 per cent increased by just [US]$65 per person, while the incomes of the richest grew by $11,800 – 182 times as much' (Oxfam 2017).

To explain in part how wealth disparity in the US and internationally reached such 'eye-popping' levels (Bruenig 2019), with reference to his own data set, Piketty (2014) outlined the emergence of what he terms 'supermanagers'. He shows that while wage disparity in the US in the 1950s was relatively low compared to western Europe, from the 1970s onwards the top 1 per cent of US wage earners were awarded an increasingly bigger percentage of total wages in the country, rising from 25 to 35 per cent during the forty-year period, much faster than the (stagnating) growth rate of the average US wage (Piketty 2014, 377). In 2013, these supermanagers constituted 60 to 70 per cent of the top 0.1 per cent of income earners, receiving more than US$1.5 million per year for work at both financial and non-financial firms (Piketty 2014, 380). Moreover, the neo-colonial dimensions of this situation are apparent in the fact that the supermanager is a definitively Anglo-Saxon phenomenon (Piketty 2014). Demonstrating this, 'the transfer of income to "the 1 per cent"' between 1980 and 2010 'involves only two to three [percentage] points of national income in continental Europe and Japan compared with 10 to 15 points in the United States – 5 to 7 times greater' (Piketty 2014, 404). Piketty also reveals that this trend is replicated in the English-first-language countries of the UK, Canada, and Australia, albeit to a lesser degree of severity than in the US.

Also contributing to a growth of economic inequality in the US was a very substantial increase in income from existing wealth, or capital, which contributed to around 'one third of the increase in income inequality' during the 1970 to 2010 period (Piketty 2014, 377). Moreover, while inequality of income from labour and capital remain pronounced in the US, inegalitarian ownership of capital is pronounced everywhere. Inequality of capital ownership in the most egalitarian societies in history, such as Scandinavian countries in the 1970s and 1980s, in fact exceeded wage inequalities in the US in the early 2010s (Piketty 2013, 322). The upper 10 per cent in Europe in 2010 owned approximately 60 per cent of total wealth, while in the US they owned 70 per cent of national wealth. The poorest 50 per cent of the population in Europe and in the US, meanwhile, owned 5 per cent of total wealth available, the same as they did in 1910 (Piketty 2014, 327) – a historical comparison often signposted by neoliberalism's critics (Hudson 2012; Mirowski 2013). Again indicating the international dimensions of this situation, in 1987 billionaires owned just 0.4 per cent of global private capital, whereas in 2013 they owned 1.5 per cent (Piketty 2014, 547), representing a tripling of the wealth in the hands of billionaires during this period.

The undesirable social, political, and physical outcomes of such extreme wealth inequality were explored in Richard Wilkinson and Kate Pickett's *The spirit level: Why equality is better for everyone* (2009). Drawing on data about income levels for labour in twenty-three countries and all US states, derived primarily from the UN, the WTO, and the World Health Organization (WHO), Wilkinson and Pickett show that extreme inequality within rather than between countries, when basic standards of living are met, has detrimental effects on rates of mental health and drug use, life expectancy, educational performance, teenage pregnancy, criminal justice, social mobility, community life, and social relations. Drawing, too, on criminological research and UNICEF data

(Currie 1998; Gilligan 2001), they show, for example, that more unequal societies experience higher rates of homicide, increased incidence of disruptive and violent behaviour among children, and greater percentages of people expressing beliefs that 'they would do better than average in a fist fight' (Wilkinson and Pickett 2009, 141).

Such research shows that modern social and economic transformations have not been due to a reduction in global wealth inequality so much as the rise of a patrimonial, propertied 'middle class'. Despite some increases in socio-economic mobility, economic inequality in neoliberal environments is likely to intensify while supported by policies that reinforce reduced taxes on corporations and high incomes, the privatisation of state-run goods and services, deregulated trade, and increased financialisation. This situation remains unlikely to change, short of the introduction of radical corrective measures such as a progressive international taxation on capital (Piketty 2014), especially as investors' success in labour markets tends to lead to capital ownership, while economic capital, including existing investments, typically yields greater returns for longer periods of time than do increases in labour income and productive output combined:

> The entrepreneur inevitably tends to become a rentier, more and more dominant over those who own nothing but their labor. Once constituted, capital reproduces itself faster than output increases. The past devours the future. (Piketty 2014, 746)

Inequality created through inherited initial wealth and the fact that rates of return on capital often exceed the growth of income and output from labour destabilise the neoliberal argument that exorbitant rewards are required to encourage successful entrepreneurialism. Though arguments in support of entrepreneurialism are often used as justification for the extension and continuation of neoliberal economic policies, as Piketty (2014, 562) explains:

> No matter how justified inequalities of wealth may be initially fortunes can grow and perpetuate themselves beyond all reasonable limits and beyond any possible rational justification in terms of social utility.

In this light, neoliberal assertions of the need to protect entrepreneurialism and innovation might be interpreted (significantly, given the point of comparison here) as 'meritocratic extremism' (Piketty 2014). As in France in the nineteenth century, when a small number of civil servants received enormous salaries relative to the average worker, those in receipt of super-salaries in modern times are often supported by a capitalist societal belief that they should have access to the same mass capital investment opportunities as rentiers, who live on their investments alone. Rather than their 'nobility', those in higher wage brackets now tend to justify this privilege by citing personal attributes of 'rigor, patience, work, effort, and so on' (Piketty 2014, 529). While compelling for some, this logic exists in a dialectical relationship with the logic of AQ and IS's violent extremism. It also runs contrary to the popular beliefs of many followers of other violent and non-violent resistance movements, reflecting a wider rise in prevalence of those disenfranchised by neoliberal capitalism and thus with anti-(neoliberal) capitalist grievances.

Monetarism and trickle-down economics

For supporters of neoliberalism, policies such as those above are justified beyond claims of merit by the often less decipherable pseudo-scientific contentions of neo-classical economic modelling. Notably, these include the neo-classical theory of monetarism, which underpins public faith in trickle-down economics (Steger and Roy 2010). As a policy approach, monetarism was originally theorised by Milton Friedman (1983), and it has often been associated with neoliberalism (Harvey 2005; Brenner et al. 2010; Steger and Roy 2010). Although not all aspects of Friedman's relatively purist monetarist perspective have been directly reflected in the policies of US governments or IFIs, key aspects of his theory inform contemporary neoliberal economic reasoning.

In the first instance, advocates of monetarism argue that the chief determinant of economic behaviour within the business cycle is the supply of money that enters the system. They maintain that as the supply of money expands, so too will the economy, increasing GDP and ensuring stable market growth. Though Friedman (1983) recognised that excessive supplies of money were inherently inflationary and on this basis advocated replacing the Federal Reserve banking system with a computer, he also argued, consistent with US policy, that a centralised monetary authority should maintain stable pricing within markets by adjusting interest rates in accordance with changing supply and demand (Jahan and Papageorgiou 2014). While neo-jihadist actors in the 2000s condemned the 'enormity of [US] capital control' (Bin Laden 2009), for Friedman and those who follow his logic, 'the surest road to a healthy economic recovery is to increase the rate of monetary growth' (Friedman 1998, 1).

In its de-linking from other policy considerations, such as social benefit, monetarism reflects a major component of neo-classical economics, particularly as it has informed various Western governments' embrace of neoliberal policies. Consistent with the broader pseudo-scientific characteristics of neoliberalism that Bourdieu recognised (1998a, 1998b), Friedman and other supporters of monetarism advocate managing labour and commodity demand through the money supply, rather than through discretionary fiscal policies.

Neoliberal governments' adoption of monetarist strategies and their embrace of supply-side economics have created economic environments financially beneficial for multinational corporations but not typically for working populations. 'Supply-side' in this context refers to the idea that more money in a financial system will overall have a beneficial effect, given that corporate profits will 'flow down', and the wages of workers at every level will eventually rise (Canto et al. 2014). In accordance with this philosophy, central monetary authorities' manipulation of the money supply and interest rates in neoliberal countries has been accompanied by the implementation of reduced tax rates for businesses (Martinez and Garcia 1998, 2; Peck 2010, 98). Since the initial introduction of neoliberal policies by the UK Thatcher and US Reagan Governments between 1979 and 1981, which followed the post-1973 'neoliberal experiment' in Chile under the US-backed Augusto Pinochet government (Drake and Frank 2004), Friedman's trickle-down monetarist economic logic has justified the broad liberalisation of the US economy and led to the formation of the current US banking system.

Though it is not feasible within the limits of this book to explore in detail how US banking operates, it is useful to elaborate briefly on the country's fractional-reserve system, given that its wide-ranging impacts feature in neo-jihadist and other prominent anti-US commentary (Wall and Bollier 2015). In short, the system is based on debt that exists in the US economy, such that the US Federal Reserve controls the amount of money created in commercial banks by issuing credit, manipulating interest rates, and stipulating cash-reserve requirements. For every loan that is issued by a commercial bank, the Federal Reserve on average requires commercial banks to hold 10 per cent of the loan in cash reserves, allowing 90 per cent of the loan to be based solely on new money created through credit (Mankiw 2014; US Federal Reserve 2017). This process increases the amount of money in the system overall and can lead to inflation or hyperinflation, with the overall effect that the value of US currency decreases.

As discussed above, the trickle-down-economics thesis is destabilised by the reality that in the US, wages growth in deregulated conditions of labour have not kept pace with the rate of inflation (Ip 2017). Underemployed and low-income workers domestically are increasingly unable to afford rent, healthcare, and the minimum cost of living, particularly when these pressures are combined with ongoing debt repayments augmented by increased interest rates (Caplan and Ricciardelli 2016). Moreover, given that the US Federal Reserve dollar constitutes the 'gold standard', global deregulatory trade policies benefit US-led industries, and fractional-reserve banking has been adopted internationally, the negative effects of this system in the US on low-income workers have been replicated internationally (O'Brien and Williams 2016).

Crisis-lending, resources, and military industries

Combined with high financial returns on capital relative to labour, and poor remuneration for labour, monetarist approaches to economic management, a key component of neoliberalism, are widely recognised for exacerbating social and economic harm on an international scale. These impacts were highlighted by researchers at the IMF in 2016. Although Jonathan Ostry, the IMF Deputy Director, asserted that a report of which he was the lead author was not intended as an attack on 'the entire neo-liberal agenda or the Washington Consensus' (Ostry et al. 2016), its authors critically reflect on the impacts of austerity measures in developed countries, and programmes that created unpayable debt for LDCs. The first part of the report targets 'crisis lending' practices on the part of the US, IMF, and WTO that require exposed countries to privatise national industries and open their markets to international competition. It highlights that, contrary to its intended consequences, 'financial openness' often appreciably increases inequality and generates significant risks of a financial crash occurring:

> Although growth benefits are uncertain, costs in terms of increased economic volatility and crisis frequency seem more evident. Since 1980, there have been about 150 episodes of surges in capital inflows in more than 50 emerging market economies ... about 20 percent of the time, these episodes end in a financial crisis, and many of these crises are associated with large output declines. (Ostry et al. 2016, 39; see also Ghosh et al. 2016).

The second part of the report criticises austerity measures for the extent to which they reflexively 'generate substantial welfare costs due to supply-side channels' and reduce consumer demand, negatively impacting economic growth and employment (Ostry et al. 2016, 40). Citing Ball et al.'s (2013) findings, the authors assert that consolidating debt via increased wages or reductions in public spending, rather than through long-term growth, has on average had long-term adverse effects on employment and increased income inequality in the seventeen Organisation for

Economic Co-operation and Development (OECD) countries surveyed in Ball et al.'s study by 1.5 per cent within five years, using the Gini coefficient measure. The report argues in sum that the economic costs and risks associated with economic inequality are undesirable, and inequality itself is contributed to significantly by states' adoption of neoliberal economic policies. The perceived benefits of perpetual growth motivating these policies are meanwhile revealed as difficult to determine. To the extent that ongoing economic growth remains desirable, the authors also highlight that greater inequality in the medium to long term holds negative prospects for sustained economic growth. Echoing the earlier concerns of critical neo-materialists (Clarkwest 2008), Ostry et al. (2016) also emphasise that neoliberal policies designed to reduce risk and offset the potential for crisis may in fact be generative of financial risks. Although the impacts of neoliberal policies highlighted by the IMF researchers are typically not referred to directly by organisations such as AQ and IS, importantly, as Chapters 3 and 4 show, they provide the ideological backdrop on which their anti-capitalist discourses are articulated.

Cases of crisis-lending to LDCs, such as in joint-run World Bank, IMF, and US Agency for International Development (USAID) projects in Haiti during the 1980s and in 2010, demonstrate some of the undesirable effects referenced in the IMF report. These effects in fact extended Haiti's long legacy of debt servitude, since its independence, including payment of reparations for a century from 1804, albeit since the 1980s in neoliberal forms (Hallward 2007). In the 1980s, creditors imposed policies that required the offshore privatisation of Haiti's local infrastructure; redevelopment projects, which were granted to US companies; and the promotion of deregulated trading conditions, which led to the inundation of local markets with US agriculture, undermining local industries. Also under creditors' direction, domestic policies were introduced that curbed expenditure on health, education, and subsidies for local services (Easterly 2006). Following the Port au Prince earthquake in 2010, billions of dollars of international aid flowed into Haiti from all over the world. Until this book's time of writing, however, the majority of this money has remained either in the hands of foreign redevelopment contractors or has been seized by neoliberal brokerage partnerships between local governments and the wealthiest 5 per cent of the country's population (Dupuy 2010).

In non-crisis conditions, the neoliberal pursuit of corporate deregulation and intensified foreign private investment in LDCs by US- and UK-led multinationals led to the implementation of labour conditions that disadvantaged local populations (War on Want 2017). While these impacts are not often cited by politically violent actors, including neo-jihadists, they show how economic expropriation is experienced by the disadvantaged LDC populations to which spokespersons for AQ and IS, imprecisely though explicitly, refer (Bin Laden 2007; Naji 2006, 101; Al Hayat 2015a).

The harmful impacts of labour conditions in deregulated industries are illustrated by the fires in Pakistan and Bangladesh between 2010 and 2012 that resulted from poor building standards and led to the death of 500 workers, paid as little as 18 US cents per hour (Nova 2012). As Action Labor Rights highlighted in 2016 in their interviews with 1,200 employees at thirty-nine Korean-owned clothing factory sites in Myanmar, almost 30 per cent of the factories did not abide by the sixteen-hours-per-week maximum-overtime rule, and interview participants reported being unable to live on full time wages (ALR 2016). In addition, two 2018 reports published by Global Labour Justice revealed more than 540 allegations of sexual and physical abuse endured by workers at Gap and H&M clothing factories (Hitchings-Hales 2018). Such deleterious working conditions result from multinational employers taking advantage of the home-country standard with regard to low wages and industrial conditions in LDCs, and host governments' failures to enforce a 'universal standard' of internationally recognised labour rights (Hijzen and Swaim 2010).

Despite the harmful impacts of some economic activity sanctioned by multinational corporate employers, it is necessary to recognise the importance of investment by multinational companies in LDCs in the neoliberal economy, given that knowledge and technology transfer represent the most sustainable path to long-term economic development, and pay and other working conditions provided by multinational employers tend to be more favourable than local alternatives (Buckley and Clegg 2016). On the other hand, exploitative industrial manufacturing in LDCs leads to the production of goods sold for very high prices in developed countries, intensifying the rate of accumulation by dispossession from one country to another, and to a multinational elite. This is also the case with neoliberal trading policies that create environments favourable to foreign ownership of natural resources within LDCs. US and European multinationals have, through foreign investment, historically extracted oil, water, wood, and essential minerals from African, Middle Eastern, and Central Asian countries. As revealed at the Proceedings of the American National Academy of Sciences in 2008, 'about 40 percent of all of the raw materials consumed around the world were used to manufacture exported goods – some 70 billion tons of raw material', and the amount of raw materials used to produce goods imported by Western countries vastly exceeded the amount of resources consumed locally (Rinat 2013).

A further contentious characteristic of US- and US-led neoliberal economic policies corresponds to the previously discussed conflation of religious and market fundamentalism in US foreign policy after 9/11, particularly the armaments and funding provided by the US to regions dominated by populations of certain faiths (Sharp 2010; Griswold 2015). In 2016, for example, the US pledged to deliver a US$38 billion military funding package to Israel over the next decade (Green 2016); annually it provides more total aid to Israel than any other state (Chughtai 2018). Indicating the interdependent economic and market logic underpinning such commitments, the US has also provided support in the form of intelligence, armaments, and (until 2019) aerial refuelling to the Saudi coalition responsible for the post-2015 humanitarian crisis in Yemen (Laub 2018).

Privatisation, deregulated trading conditions, and US foreign policy have also broadly contributed to the expansion of a contemporary political-economic circumstance often termed the US 'military–industrial complex' (Singer 2007). As will be discussed in Chapter 4, US expenditure in the GWOT and burgeoning private military industries were mentioned repeatedly in IS audiovisual media from 2014 to 2017. Referring to the massive growth of US private military and security industries since the 1970s, neoliberal-military connections in this 'complex' pertain to revolving-door associations between federal agencies, lobbyists, and companies that have trillion-dollar investments in the privatisation of war (Percy 2013; Stanger 2014; McFate 2017). For many, developments in the GWOT and the US reliance's upon private military firms call to mind former US President Dwight Eisenhower's warning:

> In the councils of government, we must guard against the acquisition of unwarranted influence, whether sought or unsought, by the military–industrial complex. The potential for the disastrous rise of misplaced power exists and will persist. We must never let the weight of this combination endanger our liberties or democratic processes. (quoted in Schmidt et al. 2006, 107)

In contemporary political-economic settings, these war economies include formerly public military services outsourced to armed combat companies, such as the former Blackwater (renamed Xe Services and then, in 2009, Academi) and others with major stakes in resource provision, including ammunitions, food, and services (Smart 2016). Jonathan Turley, a professor at George Washington University who testified about these matters before the US Congress on several occasions, highlighted that 'in the first 10 days of the Libyan War alone, the administration spent roughly [US]$550 million' (Turley 2014). As a 2016 report for the Brown University Watson Institute's Cost of War Project also revealed, since 2001, the US spent US$4.79 trillion in the GWOT on the combined costs of domestic security, and conflicts in Afghanistan, Pakistan, Syria, and Iraq (Crawford 2016, 1).

Though the examples discussed in this chapter are only several of many ways in which neoliberal economic decision-making can yield harmful effects on large populations, they are those most readily exploited in neo-jihadist propaganda and, differentially, in the resistance discourses of progressive anti-(neoliberal) capitalist entities (Eschle 2004; Escobar 2004). The widespread impacts of neoliberalism are, in fact, what differentiate it as an economic model from other, earlier forms of capitalism. In particular, neoliberals' reliance upon state and international entities to bolster the power and outward autonomy of private industries has been a prominent object of critique. The advocacy of deregulated commercial practices, outsourcing to private entities, and protections of financialisation and monetarism in neoliberal policy decisions are also widely condemned for eroding possibilities for equitable participation in domestic and international markets, and fostering mass aggregations of wealth among the world's most powerful businesses and individuals (Giroux 2004; Hall et al. 2015).

The philosophies and policies discussed in this chapter also demonstrate that although neoliberal policy guidance can produce undesirable social outcomes, which can, in turn, prompt amendments to policy, this has not led to neoliberalism's failure and eradication. In reality, neoliberal policies are often introduced in response to crisis situations that occur either independently or as a product of neoliberalism's own making. Neoliberal policies can thus be understood as a series of layers upon which successive neoliberalisations, both within and beyond neo-jihadist environments, are predicated. In line with Peck (2010, 7), neoliberalism here constitutes a 'messy hybrid' of philosophies, policies, and practices that survives 'by virtue of the very unattainability of its idealized destination'.

While neoliberalism has been justified by the idealistic notion that entrepreneurial freedoms, trickle-down economics, and access to unrestricted competition will provide a means by which disadvantaged people can improve their quality of life, in reality neoliberalism operates as a series of 'prosaic forward failures' (Peck 2010, 23), increasing extreme wealth inequality and undesirable societal outcomes, proliferating even in previously non-economic domains.

Extending the critical insights about neoliberalism set out here, in the following chapters I explore how negative ramifications of neoliberal reforms, including the undermining of human and civil rights, are variously intersectional with neo-jihadism. Chapters 3 and 4 highlight how neoliberalism and anti-capitalist resistance discourse is exploited in AQ and IS's propaganda, and Chapters 5 and 6 explore how AQ and IS finance operates in and via neoliberal economic systems. These discussions consider that neoliberal globalisation has provided for the tangible, physical extension of neoliberalism beyond states and licit commercial industries to illicit arenas such as terrorism.

3

Al Qaeda's political-economic propaganda

AQ's targeting of the New York World Trade Center and Washington Pentagon on 9/11 marked a watershed moment in public and political understandings of the phenomenon of neo-jihadism. While Al Qaeda and the ideological movement with which it was associated were in many contexts perceived as a civilisational threat (Ali 2003; Dreyfuss 2006), the symbolic nature of 9/11 and its propagandised after-effects also drew attention to neo-jihadism's political-economic dimensions. Some explored how the relative meaning of image-based propaganda is integral to the identity and expression of terrorists groups, given that terrorism itself is founded in resistance to hegemonic power, and the power of terrorist groups is constituted by their ability to inspire 'terror' in populations, rather than to effect tangible political change (McNair 2009; Weimann 2011). Others emphasised that neo-jihadist organisations became reliant on the mediatised production and narrating of terrorist events and the effects on the viewer this produces, that production having been made possible by the technologised products of late modern capitalism (Laqueur 2000; Laqueur et al. 2002; Awan 2014).

Building on this research, and paying attention to evidence of dialectics between neo-jihadism and the US, this and the following chapter begin from the premise that US-directed neoliberalism has been a prominent feature of AQ and IS propaganda. Drawing on ideas set out in the previous chapters, the analysis reflects on how propaganda produced by AQ and IS evoke neoliberal agendas in US counterterrorist and military endeavours, and philosophies and policies more broadly associated with Western neoliberalism.

The investigation considers that while 'anti-capitalism' is an inherently amorphous descriptor of diverse political positions, and it has been used to characterise a broad swathe of political-economic situations, as Simon Tormey (2013) notes, following the GFC the term was most often used to describe broad-ranging opposition to neoliberal capitalism. Anti-globalisation and anti-US neo-colonial movements of the 1990s and 2000s, for instance, were not all necessarily opposed to the core and enduring tenets of capitalism as an economic model, although they were often relatively united in their rejection of neoliberal policies that encourage intensified flows of international finance in favour of US and US-affiliated individuals, governments, and corporations (Eschle 2004). The contemporary popularity of democratic socialism in 2018, for example, was represented in the support base of former UK Labour leader Jeremy Corbyn, US Congresswoman Alexandria Ocasio-Cortez, and former US presidential candidate Bernie Sanders (Day 2018). The following year, this popularity was also indicated in a Gallup poll that revealed 43 per cent of US respondents viewed socialism as a 'good thing' (Younis 2019). Ideological tenets of democratic socialism, or, more aptly, forms of 'social democracy', do not denote a cross-national desire to overthrow capitalist models of governance. Rather, they (perhaps somewhat paradoxically) incorporate differentiated political-economic desires to bring about financial policies and regulatory models of governance similar to those prevalent in Western countries during the post-World War II years of 'Atlantic Fordism' (Wittner 2018).

Socialism, then, refers to the overarching characteristics of a number of diverse political traditions. It refers to the democratic socialism of movements advocating the (re-)nationalisation of private industry, radical wealth redistribution via taxation and other fiscal policies, and a comprehensive promotion of 'socialistic measures to complement private economy activity' (Tormey 2013, 90), as well as to anarcho-socialism and the communist-socialist tenets of Marxist and Trotskyist ideologies prevalent during the Cold War era, which were predicated on a rejection of Western notions of economic liberalism and individualistic tenets of social liberalism (Schumpeter 2010). Anarcho-socialism (aka 'social anarchism') can refer to anarcho-collectivism, anarcho-communism, or anarcho-syndicalist traditions, variously combining the (non-authoritarian) socialist political-economic principles of collectivist, non-hierarchical, and decentralised organisation of workplaces and municipalities, with protections for social freedom and provisions of mutual aid (Bookchin 1996; Escobar 2005). Marxism, then, broadly represents the promotion of collective social emancipation via radically redistributive and centralised economic planning, initially (often) enacted via nation states, though eventually expanding to unite an international, stateless proletariat (Krassó and Mandel 1968).

In their historical, securitised, and Anglocentric usage, Marxism and socialism have often been associated with Cold War-period Soviet-aligned states opposed to liberalism, the West, and the US in particular (Sassoon 1997). The perspectives of critics during the Cold War in the Eastern bloc and elsewhere are, moreover, continuous with the perspectives of some contemporary 'anti-American' forces that oppose neoliberal capitalism today. Their diverse historical socialism or anti-capitalism, however, should not be interpreted as consistent or necessarily coherent with popular rejections of neoliberalism and contemporary advocacy of socialist values (Bronner 2019). Although further nuance might be added to explain contemporary and historical situations, the propagandised messaging of neo-jihadism, rather than shifting political-economic environments per se, are the focus of this chapter. For this reason, 'socialism' and 'anti-capitalism' are here taken to refer to political-economic positionalities critical of neoliberal philosophies and policies, including those outlined in Chapters 1 and 2. As mentioned above, socialism also denotes the promotion of public, communal goods, social collectivisation, and equality of opportunity and outcome, albeit in variously more or less egalitarian forms, depending on historical socio-political context (Cohen 2009). With reference to these ideas, I interpret political-economic characteristics of AQ propaganda in comparative relation to neo-Marxist and Bourdieusian traditions of enquiry outlined in previous chapters.

Through its focus on AQ's political-economic campaigns, this chapter contributes to critical investigations of AQ and to operational and organisational understandings of the phenomenon of neo-jihadism. The discussion explores how and in what ways AQ has engaged with the political-economic paradigm of neoliberalism through its propaganda from 1996 to 2014, paying attention to US-directed neoliberal politics and behaviours. Here Bourdieu's theory is applied to examine how AQ spokespersons appeal to social, cultural, and symbolic capital, and how the expression of habitus via their propaganda exists in a dialectical engagement with the political-economic field of neoliberalism in which it operates. Extending the outline of Bourdieusian concepts provided in Chapter 1, the habitus is taken to constitute the 'learned set of preferences or dispositions by which a person orients to the social world', entailing 'a system of durable, transposable, cognitive "schemata or structures of perception, conception and action"' (Bourdieu 2002, 27, cited in Edgerton and Roberts 2014, 195). The 'socialised subjectivity' of the habitus is also shaped and constrained by its socio-cultural field, which itself comprises 'formal and informal norms … organized around specific forms of capital or combinations of capitals' (Edgerton and Roberts 2014, 195).

By applying the concepts of habitus, field, and capital to a dialectical interpretation of neoliberalism and neo-jihadism, the investigation emphasises how AQ reflexively constructs its external political identity at least partly on the basis of its political-economic opponents. Beginning in the lead-up to the formation of AQ in 1988, at the close of the Cold War, I first consider nascent ideological influences on AQ, before investigating high-profile statements made by AQ spokespersons before and after 9/11, and following the 2008 GFC.

The different examples of propaganda in AQ's history are in this discussion interpreted as an expression of its evolving collective habitus, not to be confused with collective consciousness, which in the Durkheimian interpretation connotes 'a system of collective beliefs and practices that have special authority' (Lukes 1969, 14; Durkheim 2008). Habitus for Bourdieu is, rather, in a constant process of renegotiation, based upon a subject's practical engagement in real-world events (Swartz 2008). Individual and collective examples of AQ's expression of habitus accordingly reflect culturally prevalent anti-capitalist sentiments, which change over time, and the dominant global political-economic environments they respond to. Consistent with Bourdieu's (1984, 1986) understanding of capital conversion, where the mercantile exchange of economic capital exists in concert with, and is convertible to, non-economic types of capital, AQ's propagandised appeal to social, cultural, and symbolic capital correlates with wider distributions of economic capital in neoliberal economic environments, albeit to the extent of AQ's (and IS's) 'anti-capitalism', in a negative or inverse way.

To the extent to which AQ's appeal to diverse forms of capital does occur, this indicates that AQ and neo-jihadism more broadly is fundamentally conditioned in and through the political economy of neoliberalism. The widespread societal acceptance of this state of affairs for supporters of and commentators on neo-jihadism might hereby be said to reflect a doxa, where neoliberalism's 'utopia of exploitation' is indeed normalised, expected, and tolerated. In this situation, discourses of resistance on the part of AQ (and then IS) become vital to neo-jihadist identity formation.

Finally, through their propagandised 'capital accumulation', AQ and IS can be said to participate in an entrenchment of the socio-political competition foundational to neoliberal capitalism's materialistic ideology and its discursive political support base. What Bloom (2016, 88) terms the 'discursive grammar of power and resistance' here serves a pacifying function, delimiting the 'spectrum of acceptable opinion' (Chomsky 1998, 43, cited in Bloom 2016, 88), such that anti-capitalist commentary on the part of AQ and IS is limited, superficial, and antagonistic, serving ultimately to enable neoliberal conditions and environments to persist relatively unrestricted. In this situation, neo-jihadist spokespersons primarily bemoan a lack of access to the political-economic competition and access that proponents of neoliberalism often promise, failing to call into question the underlying (often contradictory) philosophical and logistical premises of neoliberal capitalism itself (Stringer 2014). In so doing, the examples of neo-jihadist propaganda outlined in this and the following chapter broadly re-enshrine modes of subjectivity founded upon individualism and difference, which themselves underpin the social and economic reproduction of capitalist political-economic systems.

Recognising that this supposition might be contentious, the application of theory and political-economic ideas in this chapter also provides direct insights into the significance of the different forms of capital for the propagandised dimension of neo-jihadism, including how practices, environments, and actors in the neo-jihadism–neoliberalism dialectic become self-perpetuating. These dialectical engagements extend beyond wider political-economic engagements to the shifting geo-economic orientation of AQ from its emergence in 1988.

Early ideological influences

To understand the political-economic rationality of AQ at its inception, it is necessary to reflect on how the organisation was situated ideologically within the late Cold War period. During this time, AQ demonstrated an awareness of the changing international political-economic field and the 'rules of the game' (Bourdieu 1986, cited in Iellatchitch et al. 2003) in which it operated. Its external political-economic orientation in the 1980s was characterised by a shift from its Mujahideen predecessor's 'anti-socialist' behaviour during the 1979–89 Afghan–Soviet conflict, including the Mujahideen's rejection of Soviet presence and influence in the country, to a post-war embrace of anti-capitalist and anti-US sentiments. As explained by Bourdieu's (1977) theory of mutable habituses within changing fields, this shift in ideology was apparent in AQ's rhetorical articulation of dominant political-economic perspectives that opposed and dialectically responded to the global exercise of power by the atheistic Soviets, and then the US 'imperialists' (Harvey 2003). Statements made by high-profile AQ spokespersons in this period in particular illuminate the organisation's differentiated decision-making, as 'variegated logics of social action' (Wacquant 2011, 82), and demonstrate that AQ's nascent habitus was predicated on a politics of emancipation (Bourdieu 2005). They also show that the organisation sought to garner support by appealing to a political-economic field of neoliberalism, characterised by an emergent doxa of popular anti-capitalism.

In the first instance, statements made by Osama Bin Laden in the late 1980s and early 1990s revealed that AQ members believed the

Mujahideen's expulsion of Soviet forces from Afghanistan in 1989 was divinely sanctioned. According to these statements, leaders of the early AQ believed that the Mujahideen were directly responsible for the dissolution of the Soviet Empire, and that it was only a matter of time before AQ was successful in driving the US from the Middle East and ending US political-economic hegemony. In an exclusive 1993 interview with Robert Fisk of the *Independent*, for example, Bin Laden declared 'we believe that God used our holy war in Afghanistan to destroy the Russian army and the Soviet Union' (Fisk 1993). In a 1994 interview with *Rai al-Youm* editor-in-chief, Abdel Bari Atwan, he stated: 'I took up arms against the Soviets in Afghanistan for 10 years, and we believe that our battle with the United States is easily compared with the battles in which we engaged in Afghanistan' (Foreign Broadcast Information Service 2004).

In light of AQ's historical anti-establishment and anti-imperial posturing, it is perhaps unsurprising that the radical proselytising of Islamist social critics, such as Sayyid Qut'b and Abdullah Azzam, as explained further below, was attractive to the organisation's leaders. What is more surprising, from a geopolitical perspective, is the resemblance such rhetoric bears to that of the twentieth-century 'revolutionary' movements aligned with pro-Soviet forces (Burke 2004; Blanchard 2007), given Bin Laden's animosity towards the Soviets and AQ's Mujahideen predecessors' support of anti-revolutionary, capitalist-funded, elitist feudalism (Halliday 1980). As Boal et al. (2005, 149–50) note, on the other hand: 'the creed of revolutionary Islam ... is utterly hybrid. Its tactics and strategies borrow heavily from the Marxist canon: vanguardism, anti-imperialism, revolutionary terror, and popular justice'. As they usefully explain, this may have been so because 'the Islamist intelligentsia was most often the product not of the religious schools but of universities with a curriculum (official or otherwise) centred on Marxism, Third Worldism, and the literature of national liberation struggle' (Boal et al. 2005, 150); and the prevalent anti-US-capitalism in Cold War environments may be another reason why the early pseudo-Leninist-Marxism of 'revolutionary Islam' was to be expected.

Though AQ's antecedents condemned Soviet-style Marxism and US-style Western liberalism, they drew on pseudo- and quasi-socialist ideals in their early political-economic campaigns. These ideals included aversion to democracy, liberalism, and commercial materialism, the advocacy of universal revolution through collective violent action, and faith in equality through submission, albeit in this instance to a religious higher power rather than to a nation or political group. Following the Muslim Brotherhood, Jihad Organization (Tanzim al-Jihad), Islamic

Liberation Group (Takfir ae'l Hijra), Denouncers of the Kafirs (Mukaf-aratiya), and God's Soldiers (Jund Allah) (Boal et al. 2005, 147), the early shift in the focus of AQ, from resisting Soviet influence to promoting Leninist revolutionary violence, reflected an emergent trend in the region (Sassoon 1997). This ideological orientation also fostered sympathy for AQ's cause within the broader political-economic field and ultimately facilitated its rise to eminence following its political and strategic break with the Mujahideen.

This break represented a significant shift in focus for AQ, given that, during the Cold War, the Mujahideen had in effect worked in support of Western-style capitalism, through its alliance with the US, and ideologically and physically opposed the communist-socialist policies of Nur Muhammad Taraki, the leader of the Khalq faction of the People's Democratic Party of Afghanistan (PDPA). Among these policies was a thirty-nine-point programme Taraki committed to in a speech on 9 May 1978, after a coup on 27–28 April led to the overthrow of Mohammad Daud Khan's government and the installation of the PDPA. Taraki promised to eradicate feudal property relations between landowners and peasants, radically distribute countryside resources, guarantee freedom of religion, award greater rights to national and religious minorities, and ensure universal access to primary education (Magnus and Naby 2002). The most contentious and significant policies put forward by Taraki related to land ownership, the cancellation of debts owed by peasants to landlords, a ceiling of 15 acres on individual landholdings, and sweeping redistributions of existing titles further to the proposed abolition of usury on which many peasants' working contracts were predicated (Halliday 1978; Rais 1992). Not only did Taraki put forward these policies, he followed up with action towards implementation. He also announced a minimum 51 per cent nationalisation of all major private enterprise and the implementation of foreign-trade controls, declaring that 'the goal of our revolution is a total break with our feudal past. We aim for the elimination of poverty, adversity and class exploitation, and the uplifting of the Afghan people' (Holmes and Dixon 2001, 19). Hafizullah Amin, who engineered the 1978 coup and served as PDPA Deputy Prime Minister until March 1979, when he became prime minister, and then as president from September 1979 until his execution in December that year, stated that the reforms constituted 'a revolution that heralds a socialist revolution' (Holmes and Dixon 2001, 19).

Although, as explained further in Chapter 5, usury, or *riba*, has historically been condemned in Islamic finance, Taraki's proposed governmental decree was heavily criticised by the fundamentalist support base of the Mujahideen, while critics of the Soviets and Soviet-style communism internationally condemned the PDPA's broad-ranging reforms, alleging that they would wreak havoc on Afghanistan's economy. Critics argued that although modifications to land ownership were intended to provide greater labour and income equality, alternative working arrangements for the country's lowest socio-economic strata would be scarce (Westad 1994). Following the introduction of Taraki's reforms, peasants were no longer beholden to landowners, and many experienced insecure employment, while agricultural productivity weakened. Socio-culturally, such redistribution, along with pro-socialist restructurings of education, religion, and gender, was perceived to destabilise long-held traditions of 'tribe', 'clan', and 'family' (Gibbs 2006). Clerics in tribal areas were, in fact, often wealthy landowners; for fundamentalist sects, redistribution was interpreted as an apostate rejection of wealth divisions prescribed by Allah (Gould and Fitzgerald 2011). In a likeness of neoliberalism's fundamentalist philosophical origins, the Mujahideen precursors of AQ were underwritten by US support for the religious-elite, and they collectively benefited from concentrated economic capital in the region.

Given its emergence from the relatively 'pro-capitalist' Mujahideen, AQ's expression of quasi- (and pseudo-) socialist sentiments following the war was an overt volte-face from the organisation's founding principles. Where the field here might be taken to represent 'a space of relations which is just as real as a geographical space, in which movements have to be paid for by labour, by effort and especially by time' (Bourdieu 1982, 100), AQ's positioning indicates its enactment of an early practical habitus, the type Bourdieu described as a 'strategy generating principle enabling agents to cope with unforeseen and ever-changing situations' (1977, 72). This evolutionary characteristic of AQ is significant to the phenomenon of neo-jihadism, given AQ's influence from international politics and its early transnational aspirations. AQ's integration of anti-capitalist and anti-US rhetoric demonstrates both its popular opposition to US political and economic hegemony after the Cold War and the historically contingent nature of its political displays.

What might therefore be termed an aggregated 'Islamist-socialist' rationality, outwardly embraced by AQ during its early development, was most evident in texts written by the well-known literary critic Sayyid Qut'b. While various Leninist tracts in Qut'b's opus were influential, such as *Islam: The religion of the future* and *In the shade of the Quran* (Roy 1996; Boal et al. 2005; Burke 2004), his 1964 text *Milestones* remains well known for prescribing a method of living under sharia law, in which an explicit interpretation of the Islamic religion would guide all aspects of society from 'administration and justice' to 'principle of art and science' (Qut'b 1981, 107). In Qut'b's vision, societies that are *Jahiliyyah* (signifying the 'Age of Ignorance' (Celso 2015)) are intolerable and should be attacked by a vanguard that will overthrow the governing political and economic classes. Qut'b proposed that the Islamist vanguard would adopt a twofold strategy of converting disbelievers to Islam and destroying 'the organizations and authorities of the Jahili system' through 'physical power and Jihad' (Qut'b 1981, 55). Although the movement would begin in the 'homeland', its ultimate objective would be to spread a sharia form of order and governance 'throughout the earth to the whole of mankind' (Qut'b 1981, 72).

For followers of Qut'b in the 1980s, leading up to the formation of AQ, his ideas likely held a contemporary relevance. They resonated with what was at the time an emergent societal backlash against the individualising, survival-of-the-fittest, 'get on your bike' ideological tenets of US and UK-directed neoliberalism, epitomised in the economic policies of the US and UK governments of Ronald Reagan and Margaret Thatcher (Harvey 2005). Anticipating critiques of capitalism prevalent in some political arenas at the end of the Cold War, *Milestones* advocated the establishment of a strong state, an eradication of private realms, the abolition of the 'selfish individual', and an end to the 'exploitation of man by man' (1981, 112).

Demonstrating this, a prominent scholar of Islamic theology and history, Shaikh Rabee bin Haadee al-Madkhalee (1995), recognised that Qut'b's advocacy for the confiscation and redistribution of wealth from privileged elites reflected the dominant socialist ideals during and after Qut'b's lifetime. Prior to his death in 1966, Qut'b incentivised oppositional Islamist political action in response to the establishment of Arab states and civic nationalism, resourced through petroleum revenue and strengthened by the political and economic effects of Soviet and US incursions into the Middle East. Western critics, including Jason Burke, the author of *Al Qaeda: The true story of radical Islam* (2004), referred to *Milestones* as an 'Islamicized communist manifesto' (2004, 54) for its energising and mobilising call to action, rather than its authentic incorporation of socialist values. Owing to its advocacy of offensive (rather than defensive) jihad, and its articulation of aspirations for a transnational Islamic State, *Milestones* has also been recognised as a primary influence on modern (neo-)jihadist organisations (Brachman 2008; Lister 2014). Its contribution to AQ was most apparent in the inclusion of Qut'b's rhetoric in texts and statements authored by the early AQ ideologue Abdullah Azzam (who was a personal friend of Qut'b), and by the organisation's current leader, Ayman al-Zawahiri.

Socialist ideologies in Qut'b's writing were initially influential for Azzam's vision for AQ, expressed in *Defence of the Muslim lands: The first obligation after faith* (1979) and *Join the caravan* (1987). An often cited example of Qut'bist ideological references is Azzam's mention in an *Al-Jihad* article of AQ as a 'vanguard' that 'constitutes the strong foundation (*al qaeda al-Sulbah*) for the expected society' (Al Qaeda 1988). Others include Azzam's repeated proclamation that all true Muslims were obligated to engage in a collective jihad against neo-colonial and imperialist intrusions in lands that had historically belonged to majority-Muslim populations. Following the style of expression characteristic of Qut'b, and of communist-socialist movements in the 1930s, such as the revolutionary international Bolsheviks and their differing, state-centric USSR-led Stalinist derivatives, Azzam described this strategy as a new 'mode of activism and a tactic' (Azzam 1979, 1987; Burke 2003).

The importance of Azzam's vision to AQ during the 1980s was further demonstrated by the 16–20,000 Mujahideen he recruited during the Afghan–Soviet War (Flannery 2015) and by an AQ training manual, the *Encyclopaedia of the Afghan jihad*, which allegedly mentions both Azzam and Bin Laden in its dedication (McGregor 2006). Bin Laden had been a pupil of Azzam's (and Sayyid Qut'b's younger brother Muhammad) at the King Abdul Aziz University in Jeddah in the 1970s, and, according to the testimony of sources present during the Afghan–Soviet War, he was originally persuaded by Azzam to join the jihad in Afghanistan after completing his education (Bergen 2006). Among Azzam's most infamous decrees pertaining to AQ and jihadism is his proclamation that 'those who believe that Islam can flourish [and] be victorious without Jihad, fighting, and blood are deluded and have no understanding of the nature of this religion' (cited in Scheuer 2002, 68). During the Afghan–Soviet conflict, Azzam started the Maktab al-Khidamat (MAK) financial services bureau with Bin Laden, which provided around US$1 million financial assistance to the Mujahideen. As discussed in Chapters 5 and 6, the social, economic, and physical networks established by the MAK remain foundational to the ongoing financial practices of AQ and IS.

While Azzam's contribution to the Afghan–Soviet conflict greatly influenced the establishment of AQ, at least equally important was Ayman al-Zawahiri, Bin Laden's deputy, who philosophically opposed and replaced Azzam following his assassination in 1989 and who, after Bin Laden's death in 2011, became the head of AQ Central. Zawahiri's influence was particularly vital to the organisation's shift in focus following the end of the Cold War. Where Azzam emphasised 'liberating' oppressed Muslims in Palestine, Bin Laden and Zawahiri believed that it was most important to challenge the 'far enemy' of the US, and regional, apostate governments that the organisation deemed US proxies (Blanchard 2007). AQ began to embody and define its mission according to internationally pervasive anti-US and anti-capitalist sentiments. Continuing from its prior resistance to Soviet occupation and influence, this orientation constituted a doxa in which violent opposition to powerful governments, and in particular the US as hegemon, became increasingly commonplace (Hollander 1992).

To a greater extent even than Azzam, Zawahiri drew on the 'calls to revolution' issued by Sayyid Qut'b. Not only did Qut'b's theories on the 'clash of civilisations' (1962, 2003) between Islam and disbelievers distinctly form the basis of Zawahiri's theological doctrine, there were other, deep links between the two, including Qut'b's legal representation by Zawahiri's uncle Mafouz Azzam for advocating violence and anti-government Islamism. Although Zawahiri never met Qut'b, he was regaled throughout his childhood with stories of Qut'b's sacrifice in the face of governmental oppression and the appalling conditions of Egyptian prisons. Zawahiri was fifteen in 1966, when Qut'b was executed, and the same year he started an underground movement that became the Egyptian Islamic Jihad, which subsequently challenged Gamel Abdel Nasser's secular government. During his time in Egypt, Zawahiri too spent time in prison, from which he emerged as an AQ leader, brutalised and militant (Wiktorowicz 2005). In his memoirs, Zawahiri wrote that following Qut'b's death, 'the apparent surface calm concealed an immediate interaction with Sayyid Qutb's ideas and the formation of the nucleus of the modern Islamic jihad movement in Egypt' (Bird 2010, 189). As Laurence Wright observed, this in fact merely re-enshrined a pledge Zawahiri had made at age fourteen to 'put Qut'b's vision into action' (Wright 2006, 37).

Beyond the immediate influence of Qut'b, Azzam, and Zawahiri on AQ, a broader, international field of pervasive anti-Western and anti-capitalist sentiments, extending to neo-jihadism, is apparent in literature written by Islamist theoreticians of the late twentieth century, who, further to the above-mentioned factors, influenced Qut'b himself. These theoreticians include Abul A'la Maududi, the Pakistani founder of Jamaat-e-Islami, the largest Islamist organisation in Asia, which is often deemed responsible for the establishment of an Islamic State in Pakistan (Halliday and Alavi 1988), and Ali Shari'ate, who was resident in France during the two years that Qut'b lived in the US (Tripp 2006). As one of the first to equate religious piety with absolute political obedience, Maududi imagined an Islamic State that resembled the totalitarianism of Cold War communist and (neo-)fascist regimes (Moten 2003). Moreover, despite the Shi'ite ideologue Shari'ate's divergence from the Sunni-Salafism of AQ, like Qut'b he contributed to an overarching ideological climate in popular Islamism that 'expressed revulsion at the world that European capitalism had brought into being' (Tripp 2006, 152). This animosity towards consumer capitalism was at the time reflective of wider anti-capitalist ideologies that were foundational to AQ.

A dominant Islamist perspective adopted by early AQ spokespersons in particular corresponded to anti-imperial, classless ideals of popular and oppositional pro- and quasi-socialist entities. Despite the Mujahideen's alliance with the capitalist US during the Afghan–Soviet War, AQ's early ideologies were rooted in a relatively collectivised, utilitarian opposition to US authority, signifying the organisation's dialectical engagement with a field of international political-economic developments. As Chapter 2 explored, this field was characterised by resistance to the actions of US-led neoliberal entities, beginning in the 1980s with widespread deregulation and privatisation in developed economies (Brenner and Theodore 2002) and the imposition of neoliberal programmes in LDCs, such as US 'shock therapy' in Chile and Nicaragua, and SAPs led by the US-directed IMF and WTO (Larner 2000). In line with Bourdieu's (1977) explanation of habitus as dispositions that are both relational and bound by opposition, AQ's early political-economic identity was bound by its post-Marxist opposition to US capitalist hegemony. Consistent with this trend, in the lead up to 9/11, AQ's external anti-capitalism continued to evolve in reflection of high-profile political opposition to the international effects of US-directed neoliberalism.

Before 9/11

While AQ continued to engage ideologically with 'activist' traditions in its early history, prior to 9/11 the focus of its propaganda shifted perceptibly from communist-socialist rhetoric apparent in the statements of Qut'b, Azzam, and Zawahiri during the Cold War to a reflection of anti-globalisation sentiments internationally prevalent in the 1990s. Statements by Bin Laden during this period can be said to reflect Bourdieu and Wacquant's (1992, 108) observation that, depending on their position in a given field, political agents have 'a propensity to orient themselves actively either towards the preservation of the distribution of capital or the subversion of this distribution'. In various cases on behalf of AQ, for example, Bin Laden expressed a desire to alter international distributions of economic capital and to acquire social capital in the form of political recognition. The social capital Bin Laden appealed to resembled a form characterised by Bourdieu as 'the sum of the resources, actual or virtual, that accrue to an individual or a group by virtue of possessing a durable network of more or less institutionalized relationships of mutual acquaintance and recognition' (1986, 51). This characteristic of AQ's political-economic strategy was primarily apparent in

Bin Laden's statements, within a field of international anti-globalisation activism, from 1988 to the early 2000s.

The wider field of anti-capitalism AQ responded to included the often non-violent mobilisation of anti-globalisation movements that staged protests during the 1980s and 1990s in response to neo-colonial labour and resource exploitation conducted by (primarily Western) IFIs and multinationals. A well-known example in 1988, the year of AQ's emergence, was a Berlin rally against the annual meeting of the IMF and World Bank. This was followed in 1989 by the French *ça suffit comme ça*, in which protestors opposed the G7 and advocated the cancellation of Third World debt incurred as a result of SAPs. There were then the 1994 Madrid riots, which drew attention to exploitation and ill-administered industrial practices implemented in LDCs by powerful multinationals (Lloyd 2001), the 'J18 protests' on 18 June 1999 in Oregon, Eugene, and London, and the N30 protests that restricted access to WTO meetings in Washington and Seattle (Eschle and Maiguashca 2005). In the early 2000s, anti-globalisation demonstrations continued and were accompanied by the establishment of civil entities such as the World Social Forum (2001) and European Social Forum (2002), which proposed alternatives to neoliberal economic planning (Escobar 2004).

Against an international background of anti-globalisation protests, official AQ public communiques during the 1990s were limited, despite the fact that AQ attacks at the time (including the 1992 Yemen Hotel bombings, the first (1993) attack on the World Trade Center, and the 1998 bombings of US embassies in Nairobi, Kenya and Dar es-Salaam, Tanzania) drew significant international attention (Wedgwood 1999). In the late 1990s, two written statements of significant import in defining AQ's anti-capitalist vision were Bin Laden's 1996 *Declaration of jihad against the Americans occupying the land of the two holiest sites* (Bin Laden 1996) and the 1998 fatwa *World Islamic front for jihad on the Jews and crusaders* (Bin Laden et al. 1998). Also influential were statements made by Bin Laden in televised interviews with *Independent* correspondent Robert Fisk in Sudan and Peter Arnett of CNN in Afghanistan in 1993 and 1997 respectively. Once again, excerpts from the transcripts of these interviews demonstrate the mutable nature of AQ's political-economic perspective, while detail in the written statements indicates Bin Laden's deviation from the broad-spectrum socialism apparent in the early writings of Azzam and Zawahiri. Several statements pertaining to US-directed neo-colonial and territorial endeavours also reflect the geopolitical interest of AQ prior to its post-9/11 decentralisation.

It is useful initially to examine the nature and substantive content of statements made by Bin Laden during his interviews with Fisk and

Arnett. In Fisk's 1993 interview, AQ's objective of undermining international US hegemony through violent means was not apparent, but Arnett's interview in 1997 is evidence of the intensity of Bin Laden's violent anti-Western and anti-capitalist perspective. When considered in relation to events during the 1990s, including anti-globalisation activism and AQ's late-1990s attacks, these statements demonstrate the changing 'psychosomatic' nature of AQ's habitus as a predisposition motivating future practices (Bourdieu 1984, cited in Rehbein 2011), in this case as rhetoric foreshadowing attacks. The embryonic nature of AQ spokespersons' habituses during this period is also discernible when comparing Bin Laden's statements from the early and late 1990s. In contrast to the violent anti-capitalist and anti-US rhetoric in AQ's 1996 and 1998 statements, at least one of Bin Laden's early interviews demonstrates his early implicit endorsement of late modern capitalism and high finance.

Within the scope of the cases examined here, Bin Laden's embrace of neoliberal market competition was apparent in Fisk's 1993 interview, where his innovation and business 'entrepreneurialism' is described. When asked about the possibility of establishing training camps for post-Cold War Mujahideen in Sudan to mount an armed resistance to US-sponsored governmental oppression, Bin Laden answered: 'if I had training camps in Sudan, I couldn't possibly do this job' (Fisk 1993). Fisk noted that Bin Laden was engaged in an 'ambitious job' of building 'a brand-new highway stretching all the way from Khartoum to Port Sudan' (Fisk 1993). Then, in response to a question regarding his opinion on the Bosnia-Herzegovina crisis occurring at the time, and his perspective on the potential role for Mujahideen there, Bin Laden asserted: 'the situation there does not provide the same opportunities as Afghanistan' (Fisk 1993). Fisk wrote that at the conclusion of the interview, Bin Laden refused to answer any further questions about political conflicts involving Muslim populations, including the Algerian War, although it was subsequently used as a justification for attacks by AQ (Lia 2010). Indeed, as the inaugural leader of AQ, Bin Laden's external politics during this period, at least in this interview, foreground personal ambition and economic interest over concerns with US activity, anti-capitalism, or AQ's future violence.

In comparison, Arnett's interview with Bin Laden in eastern Afghanistan in March 1997 focused primarily on US influence in the Middle East and North Africa, US energy trading, and AQ's related incentive to attack US military installations. Here Bin Laden articulated an AQ habitus predisposed toward violence, featuring a long-term strategy and obligation for global jihad (Arnett 2001), and he rationalised this predisposition by drawing a detailed political-economic critique of US-directed neo-colonialism and elaborating on comments made in the 1996

Declaration. He specifically referred to the US using Saudi Arabia as a 'proxy', and criticised the pressure it experienced from US commercial entities to increase oil production, dampen the price of oil, flood international markets, and reduce profits for Middle Eastern countries (Arnett 2001). The dialectical relationship in question is, then, multifaceted: further to the instrumental connection of US behaviour and neo-jihadist violence, a paradoxical circumstance, at least superficially, arises in relation to Bin Laden's own stake in high finance. As noted by *Forbes* in 2009, the Bin Laden family at that time had a net worth of US$7 billion, garnered through ownership of the largest construction firm in Saudi Arabia, while Bin Laden's personal will later stipulated that US$29 million should be dedicated to 'jihad' (Myre 2016).

Indeed, during the 1980s and 1990s, Bin Laden and his family benefited extensively from US-initiated oil-price setting in the region (Bergen 2006). From the mid-1990s, Bin Laden nevertheless justified AQ's plan for violence through reference to neo-colonial, territorial, and neoliberal aspects of US and US allies' economic behaviour. In the cases emphasised by Bin Laden, resources belonging to local Middle Eastern populations were either withheld or expropriated by foreign-controlled and directed institutions and companies, a circumstance that for critics like Harvey (2003, chapter 3) constituted 'accumulation by dispossession' in action. Similar accusations to those made in Bin Laden's interview with Arnett (2001) were made in the *Declaration* (Bin Laden 1996), including the statements that 'Muslims' blood became the cheapest and their wealth as loot in the hands of the enemies', creating 'injustice' for Muslim populations in both 'industry and agriculture' (Bin Laden 1996, 1, 2). This propaganda focus indicates AQ's early reliance on perceived shared experiences of dispossession by its audiences, in what might be described as a broader collective habitus of subjugation for Muslim people. Within a field of animosity and anger directed at Western neoliberal elites, the situation also reflected wider experiences of dispossession by people in LDCs at the time (ALR 2016; Ip 2017). Faisal Devji (2008) described Muslim people as the 'new [international] proletariat', who had assumed the role of 'spokespersons of humanity' by virtue of their status as economically and socially marginalised victims. And, as the *Declaration* (discussed below) suggests, this was underwritten by a stated belief that the shared subjugation of Muslim people was in particular a result of the structural inequalities of US-led capitalism.

Bin Laden's criticism of the US in the *Declaration* (Bin Laden 1996) is to some degree an educated critique of US-directed neoliberalism and its political dimensions. His statements also reflect broad-ranging characteristics of neoliberalism often cited by researchers of human geography

(Harvey 2001; Peck 2010), international relations, and sociology (Bourdieu 1998b). In doing so, such statements define the contextual landscape that characterised the symbolic triumph of capitalism over communism after the Cold War and are thus in some ways continuous with AQ's early quasi-socialism. This is indicated where Bin Laden signposts both the failings of the neoliberal Washington Consensus (Williamson 1993) and Anne-Marie Slaughter's (1997) critical perspective on US-directed international relations. He asserts explicitly: 'the most disgraceful case was in Somalia; where – after vigorous propaganda about the power of the USA and its post-Cold War leadership of the New World Order – you moved tens of thousands of international forces, including twenty-eight thousands [sic] American soldiers into Somalia' (Bin Laden 1996, 12). It is also evident when Bin Laden evokes a popular critical contention that the US 'exporting' liberal democracy typically produced economic benefits for the US and its allies and economic disadvantage for the target country (MacEwan 1999). Also highlighted in this statement is the US imposition of economic sanctions on Iraq following the Gulf War, during which time, Bin Laden highlights, 'more than 600,000 Iraqi children have died for lack of food and medicine' (1996, 15).

According to the *Declaration* (Bin Laden 1996), measures such as the Iraqi sanctions and international policies that fortify US economic hegemony in the Middle East produce 'injustice that had affected every section and group of the people: the civilians, military and security men, government officials and merchants, the young and the old people as well as school and university students. Hundreds of thousands of the unemployed graduates, who became the widest section of the society, were also affected' (Bin Laden 1996, 2). The perpetuation of this situation is then presented as linked to consumerism on the part of those in the 'Arabian Peninsula': 'the money you pay to buy American goods are transformed into bullets and used against our brothers ... by buying these goods we are strengthening their economy while our disposition [sic] and poverty increase' (Bin Laden 1996, 12). Through such statements, Bin Laden appealed also to a form of social capital by rhetorically signifying dispossession and collectivity, as well as his own personal concern for shared Muslim membership of a 'durable network' (Bourdieu 1984, 21) of extended mistreatment and abuse.

Useful in illuminating the practical characteristics of the *Declaration* (Bin Laden 1996), within the framework given here, is Lau's (2004, 276) observation that Bourdieu in fact borrowed the concept of habitus from Edmund Husserl (1973, 1989). Specifically, Lau and Husserl emphasise the function of habitus as a practical sense of what is coming, based on previous situations, rather than as a reflective interpretation of open-ended possibilities. Echoing such practical and reactive dimensions of AQ's Bourdieusian-style habitus in the *Declaration* (Bin Laden 1996), Bin Laden emphasises 'practices' and 'strategies' as a necessary response to his audience's experience of oppression. He advocates responding to US-directed neoliberalism by 'boycotting' US finance and denying 'these occupiers … the enormous revenues from their trade with our country' (1996, 10). A strategy for countering neoliberal trading practices, led by the US, is then discursively conflated with incentives to violent action, and reasoning that echoes often non-violent anti-globalisation movements' concern with neoliberal characteristics of institution-based international relations. He states, for example, that 'the USA and its allies' occupy traditionally Muslim lands and support locally oppressive regimes for economic ends 'under the cover of the iniquitous United Nations' (1996, 1). Emphasising AQ's transnational aspirations, Bin Laden identifies governments that have oppressed Muslim people and are thus legitimate targets of the organisation, such as those in Chechnya, Bosnia, the Philippines, Burma, Takijistan, and elsewhere (Bin Laden 1996). Through such selective interpolation of popular-resistance discourses, AQ and the neoliberal entities it opposes mutually relied upon the effects of capitalism's globalised exploitation to achieve power and legitimation.

Another characteristic of the *Declaration* (Bin Laden 1996) that renders it a formative example of trends in AQ propaganda, and indicates the organisation's overarching propaganda strategy, is Bin Laden's acquisition and display of cultural capital when demonstrating his knowledge and education about how US-directed neoliberal-neo-colonialism operates. While cultural capital can exist in embodied, objectified, and institutionalised states, collectively it denotes a measure of scholastic achievement and ability that corresponds both to the class one was born into and its related social mobility (Bourdieu 1986, 1998b). It is reproductive of educational strategies and the recirculation of knowledge, which, in turn, perpetuates distributive flows of the other forms of capital in social, symbolic, and economic domains. By expressing cultural capital through, for example, his comprehension of the global outcomes of US-directed competitiveness and global monetarism, Bin Laden insinuates that neo-jihadism as an ideology has a high principal worth, legitimised by academic intellect and political-economic education. This occurs in the *Declaration* where he explicitly and in detail refers to the compound effects of US-led international currency manipulation. Referring again to Saudi Arabia, Bin Laden asserts:

> Everybody talks about the deterioration of the economy, inflation, ever increasing debts and jails full of prisoners. Government employees with limited income talk about debts of ten [*sic*] thousands and hundreds of

thousands of Saudi Riyals. They complain that the value of the Riyal is greatly and continuously deteriorating among most of the main currencies. Great merchants and contractors speak about hundreds and thousands of million Riyals owed to them by the government. (1996, 3)

In its signification of cultural capital, through relatively informed references to inflation, debt, and deteriorating economies, this statement represents Bin Laden and AQ's most explicit early intellectual interaction with the monetarist precepts of neoliberalism. When considered alongside the examples provided in Chapter 2, it might be said to signpost the undesirable effects of inflation arising from US-initiated monetary policy (on an international scale), where money is generated by several countries' central banks based on credit, while stagnating wages struggle to keep pace with the rate of inflation, and the deregulation of US currency markets has international flow-effects for LDC populations and US trading partners (Mankiw 2014; US Federal Reserve 2017).

Attention to monetarism and financialisation in AQ propaganda might also, in terms of dialectics, be interpreted in comparison with AQ's own geopolitical decentralisation after 9/11. As US interventions in Afghanistan and actions in Pakistan debilitated AQ's leadership, increasingly from 2001 the organisation relied upon franchises, operative through decentralised governance, to conduct and manage operations. During this time, AQ spokespersons could be seen to target financialised, non-material flows of neoliberal economic activity, rather than economic neo-colonialism or the exploitation of land and territory, a shift in message that was potentially also ideologically resonant with its increasingly international (including the 'Global North') support base. Again demonstrating AQ's reflexive response to a changing anti-capitalist field, this shift in focus correlated with emergent anti-capitalist perspectives in Eastern and Western societies. As outlined in the discussions of neoliberalism in Chapters 1 and 2, economic trending towards financialisation, neoliberal governments' adoption of monetarist economic policies, and a widespread de-linking of assets from physical products had been subject to intensifying scrutiny since the commencement of this behaviour on Wall Street in the 1980s (Epstein 2005; Tremayne 2013).

Although Bourdieu's theory extends beyond economics, and he did not consider himself a Marxist (Bourdieu 1985b), as Michael Grenfell and Frederic Lebaron observe (2014), his social theory can expand empirical knowledge of historically bounded economic situations. While Bourdieu would likely have decried the violent behaviour of AQ, his treatises in the late 1980s and 1990s, which advocated a joining of the forces of educated, petit-bourgeois intellectuals and structurally disadvantaged populations, might thus be applied to explain Bin Laden's contemporaneous intellectualisation of political economy, and his collectivising rhetoric based on idealistic notions of economic liberation (Bourdieu 1998b; Swartz 2013). Bin Laden is in fact well known for his long-form and poetic prose and his relatively erudite articulation of regional Islamist forces' complex geo-economic situations (Bergen 2006; Hoffman 2008). If it were possible to quarantine its neo-jihadist petition for supporters to target civilians with violence, AQ propaganda during this period could be considered to epitomise the ethic of what Bourdieu (1998b) describes as the 'critical collective intellectual', mobilised in resistance to neoliberalism's 'utopia of exploitation'.

Despite a developing intellectualism, and a non-material political-economic focus in the *Declaration* (Bin Laden 1996), it is necessary to note that this by no means persisted through subsequent high-profile AQ propaganda. In the *World Islamic front for jihad on the Jews and crusaders* fatwa (Bin Laden et al. 1998), issued 23 February 1998 by Bin Laden, Zawahiri, and others in the jihadist leading circles, the focus on and critique of explicit US and US-influenced economic policies was less intricate, immediate, and intellectually nuanced than that in the *Declaration* (Bin Laden 1996). As with some aspects of the *Declaration*, though, the authors of the *World Islamic front* statement implore AQ supporters to adopt practical territory-based economic offensives in response to what they imply is a linear history of US-directed economic oppression. Citing a history of US-intervention in Iraq, Saudi Arabia, Egypt, and Sudan, for instance, the authors of the fatwa assert that 'the ruling to kill the Americans and their allies – civilians and military – is an individual duty for every Muslim who can do it in any country' (Bin Laden et al. 1998, 2).

In its incitement of practical action, the *World Islamic front* (Bin Laden et al. 1998) statement again affirms Lau's (2004) perspective that the Bourdieusian habitus serves *primarily* as a motivator of strategy. Extending Bin Laden's call for supporters to 'boycott' the US dollar and the authors' provocation of murder, it calls 'on every Muslim who believes in God [Allah] and wishes to be rewarded to comply with God's [Allah's] order to kill the Americans and plunder their money wherever and whenever they find it' (Bin Laden et al. 1998, 3). Indicating AQ's enduring neo-colonial emphasis during this period, this is contextualised within a broader imploring of supporters 'to liberate the al-Aqsa Mosque and the holy mosque [Mecca] from their grip, and in order for their armies to move out of all the lands of Islam, defeated and unable to threaten any Muslim' (Bin Laden et al. 1998, 2).

Although, as these statements indicate, the same expression of cultural capital (or educated reasoning) exhibited in the *Declaration* (Bin Laden

1996) is not apparent in *World Islamic front* (Bin Laden et al. 1998), its authors do invoke an anti-globalisation rejection of US economic imperialism and appeal to the notion of a ubiquitous, disenfranchised Muslim population. This is apparent in their repeated reference to a collective *ulema* of Muslim scholars, extended to incorporate 'leaders, youth, and soldiers', that has a duty to wage violence against the US (Bin Laden et al. 1998, 3). It is also apparent in their claim that the 'rulers' of the Arabian Peninsula had resisted yet were powerless to prevent US use of regional countries as a base for waging attacks against Iraq (Bin Laden et al. 1998, 2), presumably during the 1980s and 1990s. As addressed in the discussion of AQ finance in Chapter 5, AQ's petition to boycott the US dollar and resist US economic influence in the Middle East, is at first sight paradoxical, given the wealth of funding of AQ provided by individuals tied to US–Gulf states and individuals.

While *World Islamic front* (Bin Laden et al. 1998) does not therefore explicitly refer to the economic effects of neoliberalism on international financial markets, unlike the *Declaration* (Bin Laden 1996), it does emphasise structural geopolitical arrangements that sustain international US economic hegemony. Its statements about US influence also in some ways mirror the religious-fundamentalist characteristic of US neo-conservative policies in the Middle East, which, as previous chapters explained, were extensively highlighted by Jackson (2018), Chomsky (2003), and Ali (2003). Specifically, this is evident where US 'Christian-Zionism' is alleged to operate coterminously with US military support to Israel (Kaiser 2010) for the purpose of extending US satellite control over major energy and other trading in the Middle East. Demonstrating each of these ideological characteristics, the fatwa authors state:

> If the Americans' aims behind these wars are religious and economic, the aim is also to serve the Jews' petty State and divert attention from its occupation of Jerusalem and murder of Muslims there. The best proof of this is their eagerness to destroy Iraq, the strongest neighboring Arab state, and their endeavor to fragment all the states of the region such as Iraq, Saudi Arabia, Egypt, and Sudan into paper statelets and through their disunion and weakness to guarantee Israel's survival and the continuation of the brutal crusade occupation of the Peninsula. (Bin Laden et al. 1998, 2)

Though characteristic of AQ's broader anti-Semitic and violent political orientation, the above statement reveals the organisation's specific concern with Israeli settlements in Palestine, strategic-economic developments that from the 1990s were increasingly subject to widespread attention from the international political left (Mearsheimer and Walt 2007). Unlike the emphasis of left-wing commentators, however, the evidence of religious bigotry in the statement and the authors' reference to 'religious' and 'economic' motivations for US military activity might be read as characterising a causative dimension to the relationship of the external political-economic identity of AQ and fundamentalist-religious exceptionalism in US counterterrorism policy, signifying the mirroring of AQ and the fundamentalist and pseudo-religious philosophical characteristics of US neoliberalism. As Jeroen Gunning and Richard Jackson illustrate, though, contrary to civilisational 'religious terrorism' theses, AQ's propagandised rhetoric in fact reflects the rationale of an asymmetric conflict to a greater extent than it does 'cosmic war' (2011, 378). Indicating the economic dimensions of US political concerns, as Chapter 2 elaborated, a stark neo-conservative–neoliberal fundamentalism was evident in US foreign policy following 9/11 and the commencement of the GWOT by the Bush administration. Relatedly, the above statements demonstrate another characteristic of US economic behaviour exploited in AQ propaganda, in line with Jessop (2006) and Harvey's (2005) perspective. This is that the ongoing neoliberal period, from the 1980s until today, is characterised by an extension of economic effects beyond the market, and neoliberal supports that became operational in previously non-economic and extra-economic domains.

One key insight from the analysis on this point is that AQ propaganda articulated changing objectives over the years. In the *Declaration* (Bin Laden 1996) and the 1997 interview with Arnett, Bin Laden advised followers to target 'only military US installations' (Arnett 2001). Then in the *World Islamic front* (Bin Laden et al. 1998) statement, multiple AQ (and other jihadist) leaders call for their audience to 'plunder' US economic industries and 'kill the Americans and their allies – civilian and military' (1998, 2). The *World Islamic front* (Bin Laden et al. 1998) statement is therefore foundational for AQ's political violence, particularly given its contemporaneous publication with the 1998 attacks AQ perpetrated against US embassies in Nairobi, Kenya and Dar-es-Salaam, Tanzania (Hoffman 2003).

While the cases examined demonstrate AQ's engagement with a doxa of resistance to the early effects of neoliberal capitalism, its spokespersons' promotion of violence and economic counter-offensives evince its distinctive neo-jihadist ideological development within a broader political field of anti-capitalism. Also, by appealing to social and cultural forms of capital, AQ participated in a discursive political class struggle that over time sustained its US-led, neoliberal opposition (Hobsbawm 2010; Bloom 2016). In its practical dimensions, AQ propaganda shifted from engagement with the neo-colonial and neoliberal precepts of US neoliberal capitalism to a more permanent instantiation of habitus as a predisposition motivating strategies and actions; and after 9/11, anti-capitalist discourse in AQ propaganda transitioned from anti-globalisation and anti-neocolonial rhetoric to what might be understood as a more direct opposition to neoliberal policies.

After 9/11

The act of 9/11 is now widely recognised as demonstrating the importance of symbolism to AQ as part of its political-economic strategy (Harris 2002; Mitchell 2011). The World Trade Center was often seen as a symbolic Mecca of capitalism, an icon of US neoliberalism, while the other 9/11 targets – an unknown (potentially government) building and the Washington Pentagon (Nacos 2003) – symbolised the US government and military. AQ's combined actions, in a Bourdieusian assessment, might be interpreted as reflecting its implicit antagonism to public–private governmental partnerships, discussed in Chapter 2 as inherent to neoliberalism (Peck 2010). They also reveal the organisation's manifest desire to acquire symbolic capital through dialectical engagement with its political-economic opposition. Supporting this perspective, Baudrillard speculated that 9/11 demonstrated AQ to be a product of 'the machinery that secreted its own counterapparatus', creating 'the greatest symbolic impact' (2003, 9–11), while Klein (2002) argued that by attacking an 'effigy' of US-directed neoliberal capitalism, AQ fortified global antipathy towards the symbols, ideations, and outcomes of neoliberalism. Symbolic capital was in fact widely recognised as instrumental to AQ's international rise to prevalence. The investigation below shows how symbolism during this period joined in prominence with AQ's continued appeal to social and cultural capital and in so doing confirmed AQ as a neo-jihadist organisation with global aspirations.

Although in an interview Bin Laden originally denied responsibility for 9/11, statements made by AQ spokespersons following the attack outlined its proposed justification (Miles 2010). Recalling Bin Laden's display of cultural capital in the *Declaration* (1996), these statements provide insight into the organisation's emergent focus on the intangible and non-material dimensions of US finance. As the examples below demonstrate, AQ's critique of the neo-colonial philosophical characteristics of US policy was substituted by attention to specific neoliberal policies and strategies. After 9/11, AQ spokespersons also emphasised political-economic ideologies over historical and material situations in a manner that dialectically corresponded to AQ's own emergent de-territorialised, decentralised geo-economic orientation, described by Lawrence Husick of the Foreign Policy Research Institute (Charette 2007) and Jason Burke (2004) as comparable with venture capitalist franchising (see also Basile 2004; Hubbard 2014). As further explained by Peck's (2010) theory of neoliberal layering, AQ propaganda during this period primarily targeted international communities' acceptance of neoliberal political-economic systems and their tacit if not overt endorsement of its ongoing political-economic failures.

One example of the emergent symbolic focus on neoliberal policies in AQ propaganda in the immediate aftermath of 9/11 is Bin Laden's radio interview with Tayseer Alouni from the news broadcast service Al Jazeera. In the interview, Bin Laden stated that the attack had devastated not only US financial infrastructure but also its symbolic economic power as retribution for the instalment of a global political-economic system by which 'Americans take our money and give it to Israel to kill our children in Palestine' (Bin Laden and Alouni 2002). In a later *Letter to America* (2005), which originally appeared on the internet and was translated by AQ supporters in the UK, Bin Laden used emotive and metaphorical language to condemn the US and the West more broadly for its historical subjugation of Muslim people. To the presumed Western reader of the letter he states:

> You steal our wealth and oil at paltry prices because of your international influence and military threats. This theft is indeed the biggest theft ever witnessed by mankind in the history of the world. Your forces occupy our countries; you spread your military bases throughout them; you corrupt our lands, and you besiege our sanctities, to protect the security of the Jews and to ensure the continuity of your pillage of our treasures. You have starved the Muslims of Iraq, where children die every day. It is a wonder that more than 1.5 million Iraqi children have died as a result of your sanctions, and you did not show concern. Yet when 3000 of your people died, the entire world rises and has not yet sat down. (Bin Laden 2005, 163)

Further to its anti-Semitism, symbolism and emotional affect, this might be said to state AQ's practical incentive to enact a redistribution of global economic capital. While the reference to 'the biggest theft ever witnessed' signposts exacerbating wealth inequality and dispossession in neoliberal times (Piketty 2014; Oxfam 2017), the comment on 'theft' suggests that, in the eyes of AQ, behaviour in support of this economic process should be deterred, punished, and rectified through violence against its contributors and through a reallocation of wealth. It also, once more, appeals to a shared habitus of victimisation, of which Bin Laden, via self-inclusive prefixes, declares himself to be a part. Again, his personal financial dependence on US economic power in the Middle East (Hanieh 2016) renders the statement superficially hypocritical, while the detached yet empathic insinuation of his statement resonates with Bourdieu's (1984) notion of the 'collective intellectual'.

Indicating the emergent importance of discursive symbolism and educated reasoning for AQ, rhetorical techniques such as those in the above statement were atypical of earlier AQ propaganda. Given the widespread impact of these examples, and Bin Laden's own notoriety at the time, they furthermore signify AQ's new emphasis on idealism and the logic of thought, in contrast to its former focus on the material political and social impacts of territorially bound, US-led 'accumulation by dispossession' (Harvey 2001). This is also indicated in the letter where Bin Laden communicates an intersectional focus on the imperial philosophical dimensions of US neoliberalism, economic agendas pursued via partnerships between politicians and major corporations, and the overarching policy guidance that, as Chapter 2 explored, was reinforced by the influence of neo-conservative–neoliberal American exceptionalism. With reference to these ideas, Bin Laden writes:

> Your law is the law of the rich and wealthy people, who hold sway in their political parties, and fund their election campaigns with their gifts. Behind them stand the Jews, who control your policies, media and economy. That which you are singled out for in the history of mankind, is that you have used your force to destroy mankind more than any other nation in history; not to defend principles and values, but to hasten to secure your interests and profits. You who dropped a nuclear bomb on Japan, even though Japan was ready to negotiate an end to the war. How many acts of oppression, tyranny and injustice have you carried out, O callers to freedom? (Bin Laden 2005, 168)

The Bourdieusian, engaged nature of this pseudo-intellectual project is evident, given, for instance, the sardonic bent of statements such as 'o callers to freedom'. Likewise, the tone conveys Bin Laden's (and thus AQ's) aim of exploiting the contradictions of neoliberalism so often highlighted by critical academics (Peck 2008; Fuchs 2009; Whitehead and Crenshaw 2012). Of particular relevance is the inherent contradiction in neoliberalism's proponents' appeal to the select, idealistic classical liberal values of social and economic freedom, while neoliberal economic policies in reality intensify inequality and scarcity, restricting access to social and economic mobility (Braedley and Luxton 2010; Stringer 2014). Furthermore, Bin Laden's assertion in the letter that US 'principles and values' are sublimated by 'interests and profits' in US foreign policy (Bin Laden 2005, 168), though reductive in its assessment of neoliberal conditions, might reasonably be interpreted as citing US actors' incentives for waging a perpetual counterterrorism war. As Chapter 2 explored, these incentives include the economic agendas underlying US military activities (Singer 2007) and the revolving-door employment arrangements between corporations and governments, which sustain US wartime industries (Duncan and Coyne 2015).

Unlike the arguments of anti-globalisation activists and critical political-economists, Bin Laden's 2005 letter, like earlier cases of AQ propaganda, ideologically conflates religion and economics. This is reflexive of the fundamentalist religiosity that exists in the nexus between neoliberalism and neo-conservatism in the US, as revealed in Ali's (2003) and Gray's (2003) different accounts of AQ and the US's shared positivist Enlightenment origins. It is also consistent with Bourdieu's (1986) perspective that economic capital in neoliberal environments is interchangeable with its non-economic correlates. For example, Bin Laden conflates notions of anti-US-imperialism, popular in the early twentieth century, with a persecutory anti-Semitism, echoing the religious-fundamentalist rhetoric of US community and political leaders, who after 9/11 promoted US political and economic interventions in the Middle East while demonising Muslim communities. Such dialectics, as Breton et al. (2002) observed, can serve through their antagonistic tension to sustain politically violent actors at diverse or opposing ends of extremism spectrums. As will be explored in more detail in the Conclusion of this book, in a manner similar to often anti-Semitic neo-fascist groups profligately campaigning on the basis of the GWOT to racialise and demonise Muslims, neo-jihadist actors such as AQ erroneously blame Jewish populations for the effects of neoliberal globalisation (Richards 2019a, 2019b).

In years following 9/11, comparable though often less detailed critiques of the ideologies and policies that undergird US foreign policy were communicated by Bin Laden in texts and electronic media. During the mid-2000s, video recordings produced by AQ's As Sahab media department were prevalent internationally (Seib 2008). Although these videos were far less technologically sophisticated than media later produced by IS, the translations and graphics they featured were more advanced than videos produced by other jihadist organisations (Lia 2010). This was due in part to the input of a US AQ recruit, Adam Gadahn, who was responsible for editing and translating video content and who was the first man to be charged in the US with treason since

World War II. Significantly, Gadahn contributed both technological proficiency and an understanding of US domestic and international economics. In early 'As Sahab' media, the discursive expression of this knowledge was overlain with what is discernibly Bin Laden's own interpretation of the structural US political-economic system. Through their rhetorical complexity, these communications again evince Bin Laden's display of AQ's cultural capital, strengthened by the organisation's progressive, emotive concern for dispossessed Muslims, which, in turn, is articulated symbolically with thematic reference to US neoliberalism's ideological dimensions.

One video message in particular, released by the As Sahab AQ media department on 7 September 2007, demonstrates the increasingly intricate rhetoric used in AQ propaganda pertaining to connections between US foreign policy and neoliberal finance. In the video, Bin Laden discusses the economic implications of the US 'monopoly on the unjust right of veto' (2007), presumably referring to multilateral decisions about foreign conflicts made by the Permanent Members of the UN Security Council, or P5+1: China, France, Russia, the UK, and the US, plus Germany. To this end, certain statements in this message might be said to call to mind Harvey (2003) and Jessop's (2006) accusations of a 'new [US] imperialism', evidenced by its perpetration of the 2001 and 2003 wars in Afghanistan and Iraq. Again demonstrating the reflexive and dialectical religious-economic focus of AQ propaganda on fundamentalist US policy rhetoric, Bin Laden analogises Western finance both with generic interpretations of Western imperialism and with the eleventh-century Christian Crusades. He states:

> If you ponder it well, you would find that in the end it is a system harsher and fiercer than your systems in the Middle Ages. The capitalist system seeks to turn the entire world into a fiefdom of the major corporations under the label of 'globalization' in order to protect democracy ... as you liberated yourselves before from the slavery of monks, kings and feudalism, you should liberate yourselves from the deception, shackles and attrition of the capitalist system. (Bin Laden 2007)

Statements such as this one might furthermore be interpreted in relation to Bourdieu's (2000) notion of 'symbolic violence', as discussed in more detail further below. It is worth noting that the statement also significantly and implicitly signposts neoliberalism's contravention of the ideals of 'liberal democracy', including the modern, Enlightenment-inspired values of freedom and civil rights (Braedley and Luxton 2010). As noted in the Introduction, select classical liberal concerns with autonomy,

freedom, and access to competition, often also championed by proponents of liberal democracy, are recognised by critics as discordant with
neoliberal supports for major commerce (Brenner and Theodore 2002).
The contradictory nature of neoliberalism is, in fact, central to Bin Lad-
en's rationale in this video: that (neo)liberal democracy itself is condemned to fail. To make this argument, he uses a causation fallacy,
erroneously conflating broad democracy with war, destruction, and
political economy, stating: 'it has now become clear to you and the entire
world the impotence of the democratic system and how it plays with the
interests of the peoples and their blood by sacrificing soldiers and populations to achieve the interests of the major corporations' (Bin Laden
2007). Then, highlighting the undesirable socio-economic and political
impacts of 'democratic capitalism' (Bin Laden 2007), he implicitly promotes neo-jihadist iterations of theocracy as a preferable governance
model. Ultimately, this is expressed through the usage of negative reinforcement, when Bin Laden states:

> It is imperative that you free yourselves from all of that and search for an
> alternative, upright methodology in which it is not the business of any class
> of humanity to lay down its own laws to its own advantage at the expense
> of the other classes as is the case with you, since the essence of man-made
> positive laws is that they serve the interests of those with the capital and
> thus make the rich richer and the poor poorer. (2007)

AQ's external political-economic identity is therefore constructed in
oppositional relation to neoliberal capitalist (though 'democratic') political-economic alternatives. Moreover, this usage of competitive and oppositional rhetoric serves, in turn, to reinforce the competitive philosophical
premises of neoliberalism and, in the manner of 'resistance discourse'
described by Bloom, 'paradoxically stabilize [neo-jihadist] identity linked
to dominant power relations' (2016, 3). The dialectical interplay of neoliberalism with its political-economic opponents was described in Chapter 2 from a neo-Marxist perspective. As Peck summarised:

> Neoliberalism's burden – as a resilient, responsive and deeply reactionary
> credo – is that it can never remake the world in its own image. As a result,
> it is doomed to coexist with its unloved others, be these the residues of state
> socialism, developmental statism, authoritarianism, or social democracy.
> Like the idealized market to which it defers, neoliberalism is destined to
> remain a frustrated presence in an impure world, a condition with pro-
> found consequences for the righteousness and dogged momentum that
> have become long-run characteristics of the market revolution. (2010, 7)

Demonstrating its reinforcement of neoliberalism's 'reactionary credo', the rhetorical sophistication of AQ propaganda after 9/11, and its dialectical relationship with the evolving characteristics of US-affiliated neoliberalism, is also demonstrated in the video by Bin Laden's acknowledgement of economic interdependencies between AQ and the US. As Peck (2010) explained with reference to Clarke's (2008) 'part–whole doubling' theory, neoliberalism is in effect multilayered and cyclical, while its incorporation and adaptation in diverse political-economic situations, including through aid programmes, and the IFI enforcement of privatising and deregulatory policies internationally, leads to its proliferation in diverse socio-political domains. With reference to these conditions, Bin Laden states: 'many of America's policies have come under the influence of the Mujahideen ... even if our interests overlap with the interests of the major corporations and also with those of the neoconservatives' (2007). In doing so, he was also likely responding to a co-occurring political-economic field of the early 2000s characterised by the international attention paid to the energy and financial interests shared by Bin Laden's family and the George W. Bush administration (Huliaras 2006). The admission is therefore strategically significant, given that it reveals Bin Laden and AQ's awareness that a material-economic dialectic between the organisation and its US military–industrial opponents was both real and patent.

After the GFC

Although the interests AQ shared with US politicians extend beyond the finances of the Bin Laden family (Bowles 2003; Huliaras 2006), these were not openly acknowledged by Bin Laden's successor, Ayman al-Zawahiri. Moreover, although Bin Laden was not executed by US forces until 2011, his statements were much less frequent from 2001 to 2011, when he was in hiding (Bergen 2012). During this period, Zawahiri and other spokespersons, including Gadahn, issued global public statements on behalf of the organisation. The statements following the 2008 GFC evidence a third major shift in the focus of AQ propaganda. Following AQ's divergence from the quasi-socialist ideals of Azzam and Zawahiri to anti-globalisation and anti-neo-colonial discussions of economics and territory during the 1990s, AQ emphasised symbolism, ideology, and economic policies, with reference to the behaviour of neoliberal entities connected to the US following 9/11. After the GFC, AQ propaganda was characterised by resurgent quasi-socialist rhetoric similar to that popular at AQ's inception, combined with detailed commentary on neoliberalism's ideological and practical dimensions.

This last trend in AQ propaganda demonstrates a complexity that matched the organisation's late historical exploitation of the internet and digital media, an environment of 'cognitive capitalism' (Lucarelli and Fumagalli 2008), described by OECD researchers as a 'knowledge-based economy' (Foray and Lundvall 1996). Although it is infrequently cited in examinations of neo-jihadist organisations' digital activities, researchers including Gabriel Weimann (2014) and Anne Stenersen (2008) argued that terrorist networks at this time were becoming increasingly reliant upon a modern capitalist exchange value associated with online 'informationalism'. In relation to AQ propaganda, 'informationalism' may be understood with reference to its description in Manuel Castells' *The information age* (1996) trilogy. In *The rise of the network society*, volume one of the trilogy, Castells suggested the emergence of an international political-economic paradigm characterised by 'a new mode of development, informationalism, of which networking is the critical attribute' (1996, 162; see also Fuchs 2009). Within the context of such an environment, AQ's expression of habitus can be seen to entail a combined emphasis on social, cultural, and symbolic capital. Through the networked, discursive methods outlined in this chapter, its spokespersons appealed to a political-economic field that, with increasing intensity, via digital and informational means, reflexively targeted the networked financialised and monetary dimensions of US-directed neoliberalism.

Following 2008, then, AQ's globalised anti-capitalism was foregrounded to a greater extent than it had been in previous years (although, as we have seen, subjugation of Muslim people in LDCs on the part of neo-colonial entities was an early dominant AQ propaganda focus), in some respects ironically, given its usage of digital and commercial capitalist propagandising means. This emphasis was apparent in Bin Laden's continued and increasingly detailed intellectualisation of political-economic issues and Zawahiri's use of populist, intellectually accessible prose in AQ's audiovisual media. It also entailed AQ spokespersons' reference to popular conspiracies relating to the US government and commercial elites, and their allusions to symbolic violence on the part of the US. The latter might reasonably, for example, be seen in Bin Laden (2007) entreating his audience to recognise the 'enslavement' they experienced under the US-led 'capitalist system', insinuating that this system resembled feudalism in the Middle Ages, as will be elaborated with examples below. Moreover, the importance of symbolism in AQ statements during this period, epitomised through statements by Zawahiri, framed AQ's emergent figurative and populist attitude towards the US-led international financial system.

AQ's portrayal of its own political-economic position was often framed in relation to US government actions prior to and after the GFC. In the As Sahab video *Al Azhar – The lions' den* (Zawahiri 2008), for example, Zawahiri suggested that the fallout from 9/11 contributed to the GFC. While this suggestion is not supported by known facts, the significant shift in focus, subject matter, and tenor of AQ propaganda in these cases might have been compelling for its audiences. AQ propaganda during this time increasingly featured symbolism but also a developing consideration of the macroeconomic and microeconomic effects of US neoliberalism, rather than the previously relatively isolated macroeconomic conjecture. In the As Sahab video, Zawahiri discussed the harmful impacts of the GFC on individuals in the US, including their experience of debt-based economies and banking deregulation, asserting: 'the ones shouldering the burden are taxpayers, whose money was spent to rescue senior capitalists and to protect the fraudulent interest-based system from collapse' (Zawahiri 2008). Later in the video, Zawahiri states:

> There will be no reform in the Peninsula so long as Crusader forces continue to desecrate the Arabian Peninsula ... the political corruption which has thrown the country into a mire of submission to the West to ensure the survival of sons and grandsons in power ... has deprived the Ummah of any political participation and led to the financial corruption which has made everyone and everything above the ground and under it property of the ruling family which controls resources and markets. (2008)

Bourdieu explains symbolic violence as 'the coercion which is set up only through the consent that the dominated cannot fail to give to the dominator ... when their understanding of the situation and relation can only use instruments of knowledge that they have in common with the dominator' (Bourdieu 2000, 170). While the video indicates AQ's targeting of a mainstream, global audience through social and symbolic means, it also, in line with Bourdieu, incorporates a degree of populist expression and rhetoric. Demonstrating AQ's ongoing intellectual participation in public political-economic debates (Bourdieu 1984), rhetorically familiar statements are here used to connect with disparate, economically disenfranchised populations. Moreover, such statements hold dialectical significance in light of AQ benefiting from US-directed economic activity in the Middle East, as will be discussed in Chapter 5.

Although many communications on behalf of AQ following the GFC were delivered by Zawahiri, several less analysed documents imply an endorsement of Zawahiri's political-economic propaganda focus by Bin Laden. One example is an artefact from a declassified cache of documents authored by Bin Laden, which reflects his interest in condemning US financial elites, albeit, again, through long-form expressions of cultural capital as 'educated' political-economic reasoning. The letter, addressed by Bin Laden to the US public shortly before former US President Barack Obama's inauguration in 2009, combines the then AQ leader's characteristic emphasis on popular Islamist ideals with a complex and academic critique of political events related to US-led capitalism.

Referring to monetarist economic policy approaches to interest manipulation and credit creation on the part of the US Federal Reserve, Bin Laden asserts: 'your current president [Obama] warns you now about the enormity of capital control and it has a cycle whereby it devours humanity when it is devoid of the precepts of God's law' (Bin Laden 2009). Condemning the two-tiered Federal Reserve system that preserves the US dollar as the gold standard (Friedman 1962; Brenner and Theodore 2002), and the broader neoliberal state of affairs, he declares the organisation's affinity with a subjugated US population, as well as with Muslim people more broadly. Referring collectively to stagnating wages in the US, the power of banks and multinationals before the GFC, the US government's post-GFC bailout to banks of US$700 billion, and US companies' financial benefit from the 2003 Iraq invasion, he writes:

> The tyranny of the control of capital by large companies has harmed your economy, as it did ours … Tens of millions of you are below the poverty line, millions have lost their homes, and millions have lost their jobs to mark the highest average unemployment in 60 years. Your financial system in its totality was about to collapse within 48 hours had not the administration reverted to using taxpayer's money to rescue the vultures by using the assets of the victims. As for us, our Iraq was invaded in response to pressure from capitalists with greed for black gold. (Bin Laden 2009)

The letter also refers to widely condemned neoliberal public–private partnerships, including nepotistic industrial connections between the US government and private industry, and deregulated neoliberal lobbying sustained, for example, by the previously discussed 2010 US Supreme Court rejection of a motion from the Citizen's United Group to restrict private investment in US elections (Lubin 2012, 186):

> Any president who tries to move the train from the lobbyist's tracks to a track for the American people's interests will confront very strong opposition and pressures from the lobbyists. Your president described the decision by the court in favor of corporations to intervene in the political arena as a victory, but it is not [a victory] for the American people except for the big corporations. (2009)

Statements to this end made by AQ representatives since the GFC entailed a resurgent, quasi-socialist critique of US neoliberal policies and their international effects. This was particularly the case in contributions to networked global media by the US AQ recruit Adam Gadahn. In the glossy AQ magazines *Inspire* and *Resurgence,* Gadahn evoked myriad themes related to capitalism and contemporary US 'imperialism', including domestic and international policies enacted in the service of US and US-directed neoliberal industries. In the tenth issue of *Inspire,* for example, Gadahn used symbolic and euphemistic language, calling for the 'Government of the Crusader West' to:

> Prove that you are serious when you talk about turning over a new leaf and changing Western policy towards the Islamic world, by… calling off your proxies, agents, 'jackals' and 'economic hit men', [by] leaving the Muslims alone to rule themselves by themselves, free from the 'global governance' of your supranational organizations and institutions. (AQAP 2013, 37)

Later, in 'On targeting the heel of Western economies', an article in *Resurgence*, which is directed by Al Qaeda in the Indian Subcontinent (AQIS) rather than AQ Central, Gadahn designated commercial industries as legitimate and deserving targets of violence. As with the statements made in the *World Islamic front* (Bin Laden et al. 1998) fatwa, this articulation of an economic strategy demonstrates AQ's enduring attention and appeal to a collectivising habitus, grounded in an experience of oppression, as a political imperative to future action:

> Major Western companies and multinational corporations like Walmart, MacDonald's, Proctor and Gamble, Microsoft, Nestle and Unilever are symbols of the rampant Crusader globalization which is characterized by the exploitation of the weak and impoverished, and the destruction of local economies. It is our duty as Muslims and as Mujahideen to stop this at all costs. (AQIS 2014, 53)

Demonstrating AQ's intensifying historical emphasis on economic counter-strategies, Gadahn offered the following direction to readers:

> Muslims must avoid as much as possible banks and financial markets, because not only are they based on the so-called 'interest', which is nothing but usury, whose users, abusers and beneficiaries Allah has threatened with war (see al-Quran 2:275–281). Banks are also an integral part of the Western-run global economic system which has become a tool for enslaving the

Muslims and other oppressed people of the world ... Reinstating gold as a medium of exchange is also necessary for ridding ourselves of the usurious fractional reserve banking system that creates money from nothing, ties our markets and industries to the economies of the West, puts us at the mercy of the World Bank, International Monetary Fund and World Trade Organization, and makes us vulnerable to international sanctions, economic embargoes, and countless other forms of interference in our society, culture, government and religion. (AQIS 2014, 53)

Taking into account the changing nature of the political-economic field in which it was published, Gadahn's elucidation of a broad and specific economic strategy for AQ demonstrates a final noteworthy aspect of AQ's external, evolving political-economic ideology. This is the transformation from ideology to planning that would prefigure the organisation's attacks and its day-to-day financial practices. While Bin Laden's statements prior to and immediately after 9/11 advocated boycotting US finance, statements following the GFC indicated that AQ's direction for supporters to undermine the US economy, along with an intensification of explicitly anti-neoliberal capitalism, had become active and more practical in nature.

AQ's desire to challenge US control over the global oil trade and commerce was also communicated expressly in a September 2013 video in which Zawahiri implored followers to eschew the US 'petrodollar system' and 'bleed America economically' (Cowell 2013). In the video, Zawahiri explicitly argued that AQ supporters should 'abandon the dollar and replace it with a currency of other countries that are not taking part in the aggression against us' (Cowell 2013). Indicating the twofold nature of the approach, and AQ's budding attention to US military industries, Zawahiri also urged supporters to challenge the US 'by provoking it to continue in its massive expenditure on its security, for the weak point of America is its economy, which has already begun to stagger due to the military and security expenditure' (Cowell 2013).

As well as demonstrating the practical planning in AQ's anti-capitalist rhetoric, this statement is significant for what it reveals about the broader dialectical nature of AQ's political-economic identity in the extent to which it signifies ideological and material points of opposition and convergence between AQ and the US. Elaborating on this, Chapter 5 explores how the sources of donations to AQ are inextricable from major US-directed economic relations in the Middle Eastern region and how the organisation is deeply implicated in the neoliberal commercial exigencies of the international financial system. At the same time, as the examples in this chapter demonstrate, AQ externally opposed US economic actions globally while exploiting these actions for propagandising ends. Strategically and ideologically, AQ positioned itself in a dialectical relationship of opposition to and dependence on the neoliberal dimensions of the US's political and economic hegemony.

Attending to high-profile electronic and textual media directed primarily at Western (but also non-Western) audiences by AQ spokespersons and leaders, this chapter has revealed three primary shifts in AQ's propaganda from 1996 to 2014. In the 1990s, Bin Laden deviated from the quasi- and pseudo-socialist tenets of Azzam and Zawahiri's statements to an overarching anti-US and anti-neo-colonial posturing that reflected the rhetoric and discourse of co-occurring anti-globalisation movements. This new focus entailed a broad-based critique of the US–Israel alliance, which has been instrumental in facilitating US control over major energy in the Middle East (Chomsky 2003), and oppositional statements directed at the neoliberal exploits of US-directed multinational corporations, and IFIs. After 9/11, AQ engaged in a symbolic way with ideological and non-material, de-territorialised practices on the part of US and US-affiliated entities. Following the 2008 GFC, AQ spokespersons re-invoked the populist, quasi-socialist ideals prevalent in the immediate post-Cold War period. Throughout AQ's history, organisational spokespersons including Zawahiri, Gadahn, and Bin Laden have appealed to populist language and themes in combination with an educated critique of neoliberalism using relatively high-level rhetorical means.

AQ propaganda has furthermore focused distinctly on the aggregated domestic and international effects of US neoliberal policies. The increasing discursive sophistication of AQ's propagandising tactics, despite its often reductive reasoning, was demonstrated by its engagement with specific neoliberal policies, such as financialisation and monetarism. Over time, AQ expressed an ideological, de-territorialised perspective on US neoliberal philosophies and practices, which may have reflected its post-9/11 disaggregation. This perspective might also be interpreted as reflexive, given its twenty-first-century, neo-jihadist global orientation, demonstrated in AQ propaganda through the organisation's spokespersons' appeal to AQ's international support base. These examples might be said to exemplify Bourdieu's emphasis on neoliberalism's recursive effects. As he articulated in *Acts of resistance*:

> You cannot cheat with the law of the conservation of violence: all violence is paid for, and, for example, the structural violence exerted by the financial markets, in the form of layoffs, loss of security, etc., is matched sooner or later in the form of suicides, crime and delinquency, drug addiction, alcoholism, a whole host of minor and major everyday acts of violence. (Bourdieu 1998b, 40)

This chapter's Bourdieusian framework revealed how AQ's propaganda evolved within a changing field of neoliberalism and in relation to a doxa of popular anti-capitalism. It illuminated how various forms of capital were pertinent to different actors throughout AQ's evolution, and, in line with Bourdieu's understanding of socio-economic phenomena, how social, cultural, and symbolic capital in AQ discourse existed in a dialectical relationship with US-led economic capital distribution. A doxa of normalised and expected anti-capitalism became pronounced in line with widespread societal condemnation of neoliberal capitalism, in anti-globalisation protests and the fallout from the GFC. In line with Bourdieu's (2005) 'psychosomatic habitus', which serves as a motivator of future action, AQ's economic strategies targeting its political-economic opponents became more high-profile and more practical, though also more symbolic and less material, over time.

4

Islamic State's political-economic propaganda

Neo-jihadism's evolution beyond AQ saw the emergence of AQI, Islamic State of Iraq, and then IS. As with propaganda produced by AQ, propaganda produced by IS condemned US military and economic activity and sought to rationalise neo-jihadist violence and recruit audiences with anti-Western and anti-capitalist grievances. Also consistent with AQ, IS spokespersons' statements on the political economy of the US reflect the organisation's geo-economic ambition. Where AQ propaganda over time increasingly focused on the non-material, financialised, and ideological dimensions of US-directed neoliberalism, following IS's declaration of a Caliphate in 2014 its spokespersons persistently referred to the territorial characteristics of US military-economic behaviour, contextualised in relation to the organisation's own strategic interests. This chapter explores how IS propaganda engaged in a dialectical manner with the philosophies and policies of US-directed neoliberalism. Drawing on insights about neo-jihadism set out in the exploration of AQ media in Chapter 3, I investigate IS's engagement with neoliberalism from the lead-up to its announcement of a Caliphate in 2014 until 2017.

Although, since their emergence, AQ and IS have both incorporated ideological traditions of Islamism and jihadism, their respective propaganda focused on different material, ideological, and territorial aspects of US political-economic activity. In contrast with AQ propaganda, which emphasised the neo-colonial tenets of US economic activity embedded in the international financial system, IS propaganda from 2014 to 2017 referred explicitly to a geopolitical and material history of Western and US actions in the Middle East. This included events in Iraq that preceded IS's emergence, ranging from UN Security Council resolution (UNSCR) sanctions during the Iran–Iraq War (1980–1988), and the UN-directed Oil-for-Food Programme, to US-led economic reforms introduced in Iraq after the 2003 invasion, each of which is explored in more detail in Chapter 6. It also included a longer history of Western intervention now sometimes associated with the US, including the 1928

Red Line agreement, eleventh-century Christian Crusades (Richman 1991; Le Billon and El Khatib 2004; Fouskas and Gökay 2005), and twentieth-century US efforts at 'hegemonic stability' (Keohane 1980, 2005) and 'regime change' (Albrecht and Schlumberger 2004; Litwak 2007; Yetiv 2011).

Given its major subjects, IS propaganda might in some aspects be said to echo academic 'oil crusade' arguments, wherein US involvement in Middle Eastern conflicts after World War II was understood to be motivated by the country's incentive to control major energy resources in the region (Bidder and Nitzen 1996; Gendzier 2015). Other subjects of IS propaganda, however, offer a multivalent characterisation of US activity that accords more aptly with Boal et al.'s (2005) activist–scholar theory of US 'military neo-liberalism', albeit on the part of IS more cursorily than Boal et al.'s interpretation and with reductive political-economic critique. To elaborate, Boal and his co-authors (2005, 77) explain that US-directed activity (in the GWOT in particular) extends beyond 'blood for oil' to the protection and pursuit of intersectional political-economic enterprise, from revenue garnered through hydrocarbon trading and the sale of armaments to contracts for the reconstruction of critical infrastructure (see also Brauer 1999). Perhaps evoking Bourdieu's (1998a, 1998b) emphasis on the discursive and ideational effects of neoliberalism, Boal et al.'s (2005) research interpolates anti-war and anti-capitalist resistance discourses to emphasise how extra-economic dimensions of 'American empire' were constituted by 'neoliberalism', entailing 'geopolitics' and 'spectacle'.

Following Boal and his co-authors' attention to the intersectional impacts of political economy, military, and spectacle in the GWOT, in this chapter I explore how in its spectacular dimensions, media produced by IS extends neo-jihadism's engagement with the competitive ideologies and discursive practices characteristic of neoliberal capitalism (Bloom 2016), translated in the case of IS to contemporary conflicts that occurred in material and territorial settings. In doing so, the analysis also builds upon Henry Giroux's (2014) observation that after 9/11, with AQ and then IS, 'the visual theatre of terrorism mimics the politics of the "official" war on terrorism'. In certain respects, the analysis also echoes Giroux's argument, derived from Brian Massumi (1993), that IS media, like that of its Western capitalist counterparts, operates 'as a workstation in the mass production line of fear' (Giroux 2012). It rallies disenfranchised mass audiences to discursive resistance while fomenting support for a perpetual and profitable war on terrorism (see also Herman and Chomsky 2010).

IS propaganda incorporates brutal capitalistic spectacles of terrorism to a greater extent than that of AQ, spectacles which are facilitated via their coverage in international news and sophisticated technology media. In this manner, IS engages with what Bloom (2016, 95–97) described as the '(r)evolutionary capitalist history of modernisation', in which capitalist discourses and their mediatised representations become the dominant means by which resistance towards capitalism is articulated. Also differing from AQ, IS emphasises interdependencies between US economic and territorial interests (Jessop 2006), which, as discussed further in Chapter 6, dialectically reflect the organisation's own strategic and financial activity.

In light of its political-economic characteristics, IS propaganda in this chapter is taken to exemplify the Marxist historical materialist dimension of Bourdieu's habitus-and-field dialectic, whereas AQ propaganda, particularly after 9/11 and the 2008 GFC, was to a greater extent concerned with a quasi-Hegelian idealism. Where AQ propaganda reflexively alluded to the organisation's own decentralised and non-territorial agenda, within a changing international field of anti-(neoliberal) capitalist sentiments spokespersons for IS emphasised anti-capitalist ideologies relevant to its desired acquisition of territory and the US-led GWOT in the Middle East after 9/11.

Following the investigation of AQ propaganda in the previous chapter, social, cultural, and symbolic capital are here applied as an ideological trope to delineate IS spokespersons' efforts at mediatised persuasion. Consistent with the earlier analysis, in this chapter I argue that the acquisition and display of capital in IS propaganda demonstrate a dialectical relationship between the organisation's external habitus and the broader field of neoliberalism it operates within. On the other hand, while the discussion considers how IS propaganda appeals to a doxa of anti-capitalism among US-opposed groups in the region, this is demonstrated as being less explicit than is the case with AQ. Moreover, given the comparatively shorter time over which IS has been publishing and distributing propaganda at the time of this book's writing, the discussion emphasises how IS appeals coterminously to a differentiated doxa of anti-capitalist audiences and perspectives, rather than foregrounding how its propaganda reflects a doxa of anti-capitalism that evolved over time.

Early ideological influences

As discussed in Chapter 3, texts influential to the development of neo-jihadism included Sayyid Qutb's *Milestones* (1964), the writings of Sayyid Abul A'la Maududi (Moten 2003), and the quasi-socialist proselytising of Abdullah Azzam (1979, 1987). In the post-Cold War environment, the many expressions of opposition to capitalist governments by state and non-state actors' included the activist rhetoric espoused by Ayman al-Zawahiri (2008) and the anti-neo-colonial sentiments of Osama Bin Laden (Fisk 1993; Bin Laden 1996; Bin Laden et al. 1998). Early articulations of jihad were also rooted in the works of foundational scholars such as Taqī ad-Dīn Ahmad ibn Taymiyyah (aka Ibn Tamiyyah), the thirteenth-century ultra-conservative Sunni Muslim scholar whose rejection of classical Islamic traditions is often credited with influencing the advent of Wahhabism and Salafism, and Muhammad Ibn Abd al-Wahhab, the founder of modern day Wahhabism, who instructed Muhammad I ibn Saud ibn Muhammad ibn Muqrin Al-Maridi (aka Muhammad ibn Saud), the founder of the House of Saud, which rules the current, unified Saudi Arabia (Faksh 1997). Others who, in Robert Manne's (2016) description, sought to make Qut'b's vision 'operational' include the author of *The neglected duty* (Faraj 1986), the Egyptian engineer who led the Cairo branch of the Islamist group al-Jihad, Muhammad abd-al-Salam Faraj.

IS drew ideological and strategic inspiration both from these examples and from contemporary texts that appear to have been less influential on AQ or other militant quasi-Islamist groups (Jenkins 2015). Echoing statements made in 2008 by the then Interior Minister of Saudi Arabia (also a former Crown Prince and Deputy Prime Minister), Nayef bin Abdulaziz Al Saud, William McCants referred to one text in particular, *The management of savagery* (Naji 2006), originally published online, in 2004, as a 'blueprint' for the modus operandi of the future IS (McCants 2008; see also Manne 2016). McCants observed that *The management of savagery* was likely written immediately after 9/11, with sections added following the 2003 US invasion of Iraq. As Michael Weiss and Hassan Hassan, the investigative reporters and authors of *Islamic state: Inside the army of terror* (2016) note, a copy of this text was carried by IS foot soldiers and their commanders. Although the text bears the *nom de guerre* Abu Bakr Naji, his or her real name has not been verified. Moreover, though researchers at the Al Arabiya Institute for Studies (McCants 2015, 82) assert that Naji's real name is Muhammad Khalil Hasan al-Hakaymah and that he has contributed to online AQ publications, the methods outlined in *The management of savagery* in a number of respects typify the differences of political-economic philosophy and strategy between AQ and IS.

The following analysis of *The management of savagery* is based on McCants' (2006) translation, and it is considered in relation to IS's nascent political-economic strategies. These might be understood with reference to the Bourdieusian principle that ideology and material circumstance are mutually reinforcing, such that the habitus and field become reflexively situated. Detail in the text indicates, for example, that the political-economic ideology, or habitus, that precipitated sympathy for IS is firmly rooted in the field of material circumstances that followed 9/11, the 2001 war in Afghanistan, and the 2003 US invasion of Iraq. The text also indicates that the early ideology of those who would later form the membership of IS derives from Naji's (and Islamic State of Iraq leader Abu Musab al-Zarqawi's) explicitly stated territorial ambition.

Specifically, Naji argues that the habitus of the 'Mujahideen' (as he terms the neo-jihadists) should exploit opportunities presented by the field of political and economic devastation that the GWOT wrought on the Middle East. To do this, he instructs them to capitalise on conditions of chaotic governance in regions and countries they deem destined for Islamic governance, and to sow chaos in those not yet affected by disaster. According to Naji, in countries that have a relatively stable government the Mujahideen should implement 'vexation and exhaustion' campaigns (2006), and within those that are unstable they should begin the initial stages of implementing sharia leadership and governance administration. In practical terms, reflexively responding to US and UK entities' profit from 'disaster capitalism' (Klein 2007; Dupuy 2010) in Iraq during the post-2003 occupation, Naji directs the Mujahideen to profit from the destruction of Iraq's institutions and infrastructure, and the mass death of Iraqi civilians, via their acquisition of control over the country's resources and territory.

In several respects, Naji's directions for the Mujahideen foreshadow early high-profile actions on the part of IS (Ignatius 2014; Manne 2016). Further to his discussion of territory, these include Naji's justification of beheadings, reference to the original Caliph burning 'apostates' alive, and instructions for other local insurgent groups, such as what was then Jabhat al-Nusra in Syria, to 'choose between killing or joining us, or fleeing and abandoning their weapons' (Naji 2006, 104). While these statements are consistent with the overarching fundamentalism and Manicheanism of IS's neo-jihadism, Naji's instructions to polarise societies into camps of 'believers' and 'unbelievers' might be considered in dialectical relation to George W. Bush's statement after 9/11 that 'you are either with us, or you are with the terrorists' (2001b). Furthermore, deriving from and reinforcing contemporary Western stereotyped understandings of 'jihadist' terrorism, elsewhere he advocates 'liquidating' hostages in a 'terrifying manner', to fill 'the enemy's hearts with fear' (Naji 2006, 78). Extreme brutality is, in fact, promoted throughout *The management of savagery* (Naji 2006) in the service of the Mujahideen's political-economic ambition.

As with AQ, and resembling rhetoric in Western news media during the GWOT (Giroux 2014), at several points in *The management of savagery* (2006) Naji attempts to garner and display various forms of non-economic capital to render his ultimatums and incitements to war convincing. A tandem endorsement of both social and cultural capital is apparent, for instance, in an excerpt highlighting that audiovisual propaganda are vital for contemporary neo-jihadism by virtue of being a form of media accessible to the 'masses' as well as the intellectual 'elite' (Naji 2006, 110).

From a strategic perspective, Naji's request for his audience to appeal to the 'masses' and the 'elite' prefigured IS's later tactic, in 2014 and 2015, of disseminating propaganda in dozens of languages and various formats via more than 30 media departments (Zelin 2015). Furthermore, although social and cultural capital were important for AQ, and public media remains important for most politically violent groups, Naji's specific direction to appeal to a diversely educated audience foreshadowed a relatively unique characteristic of IS. Zawahiri, for instance, used populist rhetoric at AQ's foundation and following the GFC, while Bin Laden demonstrated his education in statements made over the course of several decades. Naji, on the other hand, advocated the articulation of both short-form 'populist' and long-form 'elitist' political-economic critique, for the purpose of appealing to a broad base of disenfranchised populations. As discussed further below, IS media did indeed appear to follow Naji's recommendation, in contrast to relatively unidirectional and mono-faceted statements on the part of AQ, though there were dissimilarities in the representations of some AQ authors, including Bin Laden and Zawahiri.

The practical significance of Naji's instructions is evidenced by their manifestation in IS's behaviour. Further to Naji's instruction for the Mujahideen to embrace mass media, chaos, and young international recruits (Fitzpatrick 2014), he endorsed brutal public executions. Naji referred to the original Caliph 'Baghdadi' burning two apostates alive (2006, 74), and IS burned to death Muath al-Kaseasbeh and two unidentified Turkish soldiers (Aboufadel 2017). Also reflecting Naji's repeated reference to beheadings, Zarqawi, the leader of the organisation that would later become IS, infamously filmed and broadcast on YouTube the beheading of the US contractor Nicholas Berg, an event which marked a transformation in neo-jihadist strategy from AQ to IS (Atwan 2013). Beyond his extremely brutal and public manner of executing prisoners, Zarqawi's strategy of murdering Sunnis and Shia and his incitement of chaos and violence among warring groups in Iraq after 2003 signifies the literal instantiation of Naji's 'vexation and exhaustion' operations, which, as discussed in the Introduction, would become the unique modus operandi of IS. The tactical directions for IS apparent in *The management of savagery* (2006) render the identification of links between Naji's text and later IS actions more compelling.

In a final instance of the text foreshadowing IS activity, Naji recommended that the Mujahideen target industries controlled by Western and international coalitions, explaining these attacks in 'rational' economic terms (2006, 109). In contrast to the de-territorial and relatively non-material financial strategy of AQ, including 'boycotting' US finance, Naji (2006, 98–99) directed the Mujahideen to target specific, geo-economic interests of the US and US-directed entities, at the same time employing 'a specialist in political-economic studies' to report via multi-platform media on US financial arrangements in the region and their implications for local citizens. While demonstrating the importance of propaganda for neo-jihadism in the years prior to IS, this strategy also indicates Naji's rejection of the widespread counterterrorist-military logic that Bourdieu describes. In Bourdieu's words:

> Great juridical multinationals which impose the traditions of American law on the whole planet, that of rational-action theories, etc. – is both the expression and the justification of a Western arrogance, which leads people to act as if they had the monopoly of reason and could set themselves up as world policemen, in other words as self-appointed holders of the monopoly of legitimate violence, capable of applying the force of arms in the service of universal justice. (1998b, 20)

In line with a Bourdieusian logic regarding the factors that contribute to political violence, Naji explains that neo-jihadism is to be sustained by 'our rationalism, imperialist, invasive and conquering' (Bourdieu 1998b, 20). Demonstrating similarities between IS and AQ in this respect, Naji's statements epitomise neo-jihadist actors' recognition of the power of the 'public intellectual' to bring about political and social change, leveraging the semblance of rationalism and intellectualism to influence public opinion (Bourdieu 1998a, 1998b).

The management of savagery

There are other similarities between the propaganda and planning of AQ and IS that signify continuity in the evolution of neo-jihadism. Sections of *The management of savagery* (Naji 2006) implore the Mujahideen to adopt economic strategies, later advocated by Zawahiri. In one case, as in Zawahiri's statements cited in the previous chapter, Naji implores his readers to 'drain' the economic power of the US and its allies, instructing them to target 'usurious' banks, so that other banks will have to be 'secured', weakening the international financial system (Naji 2006, 46). In another, he advises attacking petroleum and oil targets to prompt global superpowers to demand increased provision of security from overstretched US allies and bleed the resources of Mujahideen enemies (Naji 2006, 43).

Directions in *The management of savagery* (Naji 2006) followed by the organisation that would become IS are from an overarching perspective more material than the propagandised focus of AQ. Namely, they are more applied, practical, and territorially bound than Bin Laden or Zawahiri's statements on behalf of AQ. Moreover, as with Naji's advocacy of brutal executions, the material focus of his statements relating to Mujahideen plans for fundraising and attacks on the US, when considered in relation to IS's subsequent territorial and resource-related activity, are significant in revealing the distinct nature of IS's nascent political-economic orientation. Naji's recommendation to 'target banks', for example, entails the literal bombing of a building, unlike comparatively vague discussions about banks on the part of AQ spokespersons, with directions to AQ followers being far less detailed and practical than IS's plans for territorial, 'on the ground' attacks against US-backed commercial and military entities (Naji 2006, 97). Revealing the respective idealist and material emphases of these organisations, AQ propaganda following 9/11 symbolically cited the 'deception, shackles and attrition of the capitalist system' (Bin Laden 2007), while Naji directed the future IS to attack material assets, including physical institutions controlled by the US.

Following a post-Marxist ideological tradition, the shared habitus to which Naji appeals might here be understood as 'perceptions, aspirations, and practices that correspond to the structuring properties of earlier socialization' (Swartz 1997, 103), rather than, as with AQ, a psychosomatic driver of action bringing about change (Bourdieu 1984, cited in Rehbein 2011). Also indicating an important point of difference between AQ and IS's external political-economic identities, Naji's appeal is based on the goal of collectivised action against what he implies to be US neoliberal aggression, rather than, as with AQ, on a collectivised experience of subjugation. Naji's instructions, like the IS propaganda that followed them, are more practical and proactive than AQ's imprecise petitions for its supporters to 'target' and boycott US trade and currency.

This practicality is particularly evident in an extended passage in which Naji outlines a means by which the Mujahideen could seize control of Middle Eastern oil fields and disseminate propaganda about Western exploitation of local reserves for the purpose of fostering sympathy in potential supporters (2006, 98–103). As discussed below, statements made by the former IS leader Abu Bakr al-Baghdadi, and excerpts from the organisation's main English-language magazine, *Dabiq*, describe how IS did seize and control oil production in Iraqi fields, as well as in Syria, in accordance with Naji's directions. The strategic importance of these activities to IS finance, and the related dialectical engagements between its propaganda and practices, is discussed further in Chapter 6.

In line with the future activities of IS, Naji's practical instructions for his readers to seize and manage an oil rig include tactics for taking control of the facility and a propagandising method for garnering sympathy. While the tactics are explained step by step but are situationally unspecific, Naji's propaganda advice is extensive. Emphasising the role of political economy in the Mujahideen's politically violent ambition, he advises his readers to condemn the US neoliberal activity of commodity-price setting, a practice only alluded to in AQ propaganda by Bin Laden. As with certain statements made by Bin Laden, Naji's advice appears on the surface to be ideologically contradictory, given IS's later exploitation of economic managerial mechanisms available in neoliberal financial systems. As Benjamin Barber argued in his post-9/11 introduction to *Jihad vs McWorld*, however, 'what we face is not a war between civilizations but a war within civilization' (1995, xvi). Herein, 'jihad' and its opposing forces are connected in their 'global, networked and material future' (Barber 1995, xvi), extending in this context to IS's networked, financialised opposition to the exploitative and criminogenic dimensions of US-affiliated neoliberalism.

When considered in light of the philosophies of neoliberalism discussed in Chapter 2, Naji's directions relate to a primary discordance between classical liberal economic principles and neo-classical, neoliberal economic policies, and, in turn, indicate the extent to which neo-jihadist entities are sustained at a structural level by their (anti-)neoliberal positioning. One passage in Naji's text, for example, refers to the popular fallacy that late modern capitalist markets are 'liberal' and possess the ability to automatically stabilise, whereas, in reality, US financial entities use 'neoliberal' means to control capital by manipulating macroeconomic conditions of supply and demand (Thorsen and Lie 2006). As explained by Clark (2005), this occurs, in part, via economic processes whereby US-aligned governments and corporations maintain control over major oil extraction and distribution regions, and because the US Federal Reserve dollar remains the international gold standard. Engaging with these themes, Naji states:

> One of the media groups, which has a specialization in political-economic studies, undertakes a study in which the true price and value of petroleum

is established and (which explains) how, despite frantic searching, there is no substitute for it at the present time, but that it is the one commodity which is the most devalued in its prices compared with other commodities … This study should include a delimitation of a true or approximate price for barrels of oil in accordance with sound, economic criteria. It must also have an exposition of the political importance of petroleum and the extent of injustice and pillaging which the Umma has suffered for decades on account of its devalued price. Afterwards, the research must be submitted to a member of the committee who specializes in drafting statements of justification. This member will write a statement which should not include a justification which says that we are striking petroleum sectors because it is sold to infidels. That is an 'ijtihad' [independent reasoning] question and will expose us to media criticism which will turn our action away from its goal. (2006, 98)

Once more indicating the practical orientation of Naji's directions, and his reflexive, personal promotion of oil markets, he provides detail of what should be included in Mujahideen communiques to the media. Initially, and in a manner thematically similar to Bin Laden's *Declaration* (1996), Naji cites the devastating effects on Middle Eastern and North African economies of devalued international oil. He then implicitly condemns the neoliberal practices of tax avoidance and financial-sector deregulation, instructing the Mujahideen that funds garnered via the acquisition and distribution of oil should not go through 'a hole which goes straight to the banks of Switzerland' (Naji 2006, 100).

Foreshadowing the cessation of oil extraction that occurred at IS-held fields in Syria and Iraq, Naji continues in *The management of savagery* to urge and justify temporarily ceasing production if control over territory cannot be secured. He declares that this may be the only means to rectify unequal distributions of wealth in the region, stating: 'most of our income from petrol goes into bank accounts belonging to collaborationist rulers and their assistants and none of it is paid to the masses' (2006, 98). Demonstrating his appeal here to social capital as 'belonging' (Bourdieu 1986), and perhaps also the twenty-first-century resurgence of popular socialist values discussed in the previous chapter, Naji refers to himself as a member of the disenfranchised masses and cites the need to protect 'the welfare of the Umma' (2006, 98). This recalls Bin Laden's usage of self-inclusive prefixes to denote his own involvement in the economic situations he discusses. However, in contrast to AQ's comparatively one-dimensional propaganda, in Naji's text social and cultural capital – as belonging, quasi-socialist membership of a group, and educational awareness of complex political-economic situations – are mutually integrated.

Preceding IS's capture of the British Broadcasting Corporation (BBC) journalist John Cantlie (and, reflexively, the organisation's contemporary engagement in currency manipulation, discussed in Chapter 6), Naji's second step for the Mujahideen's oil seizure was to kidnap either a petroleum worker, an Arab Christian, or a Western journalist. He states that this person should be held hostage in protest at the 'injustice which afflicts the poor masses' to 'encourage the petroleum states in non-Islamic regions to raise the price of petrol' (Naji 2006, 101). From a historical perspective, this statement might be considered reminiscent of the Saudi government's activities as a trading partner of the US in 1975, during which time it orchestrated an oil crisis to protest US support for Israel (Venn 2016). It might also be interpreted as indicative of a broader trend in neo-jihadism, in light of Bin Laden's various expressions of support for the Saudi people and opposition to the Saudi government, the latter contingent upon the government's financial interdependencies and alliance with the US. Once more, Naji observes the importance of social capital for this activity, recommending that the findings of an 'economic study' of US-controlled trading environments within Islamic states, conducted by the 'political-economist', be communicated to 'as many people as possible among the economic, political, and media elites in the Islamic world and outside of the Islamic world' (2006, 101).

Although Naji's critique of capitalism and consumerism, targeting the neoliberal philosophies of anomie, normlessness, and individualism, resembles AQ rhetoric in its *Inspire* magazine, his vision for IS is more developed and multi-directional than political-economic commentary on the part of AQ. He outlines an anti-capitalist and anti-neoliberal philosophy condemning the worship of commodification and wealth, emphasising more detailed connections between material economic practices and consumer idealism than is apparent in AQ media. Furthermore, as will be demonstrated to be the case with the IS organisation's propaganda, Naji explains that the physical manifestation of consumer capitalist ideologies occurs in territory that falls outside of the proposed future Caliphate, as opposed to the alleged piety and nobility characteristic of those in the latter. Criticising the consumerism of contemporary societies, Naji writes: 'they strive to survive, but it is not just any survival … it is a survival which guarantees them an unruffled life of comfort and luxury' (2006, 88). Indicating a combined focus on consumerism and land, he then highlights the role of governments in Middle Eastern territories acting as proxies for the US, the hegemonic neoliberal nation state. For Naji, if such governments:

> Circled in the orbit of a new superpower or still flirted with the superpower that supported the previous regime, they mixed their social and economic

values with the values of the superpower in whose orbit they circled and imposed the mixture upon society, placing a sacred halo around these values, even if they were values that every rational mind refused. (2006, 14)

The political-economic aspect of this excerpt can be further illuminated with reference to Jessop's (2006) explanation of how capitalist and territorial interests are independent in some neoliberal nation states. According to Jessop, a 'regional structural coherence' (2006, 152) emerges in differentially governed territories within resource-intensive regions from the promotion of shared neoliberal values, under conditions of US economic influence (see also Haykel 2009). This might be said to characterise, for example, financial relationships between some Gulf region nation states and the US, constituted as they are by alliances that 'emerge to defend regional values and coherence and to promote them ... through the provision of new economic and extra-economic conditions favourable to further accumulation' (Jessop 2006, 153, 260). The financial and strategic implications for IS of this characteristic of contemporary inter-governmental relations is discussed in Chapter 6. Within the context of this investigation, it is relevant that there remains a fairly widespread critical emphasis in political-economic research on the role that capitalistic ambitions shared by state and state-like entities play in facilitating LDC civilians' experience of economic dispossession (see also Harvey 2001). In examples such as the above statement, Naji signposts this emphasis and, furthermore, exhibits a neo-Marxist association of territory, land, and trade with commercial capitalism.

When considered in relation to IS propaganda and finance, the above passage from Naji's text foreshadows IS's approach to Middle Eastern states such as Turkey, which they criticise for embracing the products of modernity and global capitalism. This is despite evidence suggesting that some prominent Turkish businesspersons trade with IS if they deem it financially worthwhile, as is explored in Chapter 6. Here the 'economic and extra-economic conditions favourable to further accumulation' (Jessop 2006, 260) are shared by IS as a local quasi-nation state with its regional state and non-state contemporaries. As can also be explained by Bourdieu's (1984) habitus and field theory, this situation signifies a merging of practices between opposing structures and entities, in this case of IS and its (outwardly strategically opposed) nation-state adversaries, within structural conditions of neoliberalism.

Given the quasi-capitalist characteristics of neo-jihadist finance discussed in the following chapters, including IS's exploitation of neoliberal political and economic partnerships in the region, Naji's criticism of commercial capitalist 'social and economic values' again illustrates evidence of a surface-level contradiction between neo-jihadist propaganda and practice, constituted by ideological antagonism and behavioural mirroring. This dialectic indicates that a broader mirroring between the entities in question could involve elements of causation and mimicry, where IS's propaganda and financial activity reflects and logistically responds to the historical behaviour of other political actors in the region. This contention is further supported by the fact that, despite IS benefiting from neoliberal economic relations in the region, as Chapters 5 and 6 will show, IS and AQ's political-economic development occurred in the aftermath of, and in some ways reproduced, a history of US-led military and economic intervention in the Middle East.

IS speeches

In Chapter 3, I argued that the key political events that influenced the evolution of AQ propaganda included the end of the Cold War, the emergence of anti-neo-colonial and anti-globalisation movements in the 1990s, the attacks of 9/11, and the 2008 GFC. By contrast, my discussion here begins from the premise that IS's political-economic propaganda corresponded to later events, including the post-9/11 US pre-emptive wars in the Middle East and IS's declaration of a transnational Caliphate in June 2014. Although IS spokespersons exploited anti-capitalist political-economic agendas on the part of their supporters, these statements were limited in comparison with the anti-capitalist rhetoric used by Bin Laden and Zawahiri, or the political-economic rhetoric featured in IS's later audiovisual media. Following IS's announcement of the Caliphate, its spokespersons campaigned extensively in opposition to US territorial and economic agendas, though a critique of 'capitalism' was not always readily apparent.

In speeches immediately following IS's 2014 declaration of a Caliphate in particular, IS spokespersons' references to capitalism were relatively understated in comparison with the overtly anti-capitalist views expressed by Bin Laden and Zawahiri following 9/11. Although the rhetorical characteristics of these speeches demonstrate the influence of Naji's text on IS and certain continuities with the political-economic positioning of AQ, IS spokespersons' discussions of US political economy were for the most part contextualised (relatively exclusively) with reference to land and the Caliphate, supported by excerpts from Islamic texts such as the Qur'an, Hadith, and Sunnah. Given that there were few internationally received public statements made by IS leaders, three key speeches made by the Caliph, Baghdadi, and three speeches by a leading spokesperson for the organisation, the late Abu Muhammad al-Adnani al-Shami (killed by US forces on 30 August 2016), are useful in explicating IS's early external political-economic positioning. Once more, signifying the organisation's dialectical determination, these speeches are characterised by an ideological engagement with materialism over idealism, and the leaders' preoccupation with IS's incentives for state-building, albeit in different ways to IS audiovisual media.

Although early speeches delivered by Baghdadi elaborate on the sanctity of the Caliphate in contrast with the apostasy of 'Evil' regimes, they refrain from specifying the source or practical detail of the organisation's external political-economic opinion. IS's first public speech, delivered on 4 July 2014, for instance, makes several obscure references to what might be interpreted as political-economic innovation, insinuating that innovation and late modern technology represent an abhorrent deviation from religious fundamentalism. These include: 'if you desire provision, fear Allah'; 'Strive to the cause of Allah with your wealth and lives'; and 'The worst affairs are newly invented matters. Every newly invented matter is a *bid'ah* [religious innovation], and every *bid'ah* is misguidance, and every misguidance is in the Hellfire' (Baghdadi 2014). Similarly, in a December 2015 speech delivered by Baghdadi following Russian and US-led coalition airstrikes in Syria, the only references to political-economic developments that might include capitalism pertain to the heresy of commodification and the desire to live a 'worldly life' (Baghdadi 2015).

Although explicit references to political economy in the July 2014 and December 2015 speeches are limited, certain Leninist excerpts of these speeches recall the tenets of Qut'b and Azzam's early writing, including Baghdadi's repeated reference to a Mujahideen 'vanguard'. These excerpts indicate continuity between IS and some outward ideological expressions of AQ. They also signify an attempt to evoke quasi-socialist sentiments popularised in Islamist rhetoric by Sayyid Qut'b and Abdullah Azzam (Burke 2004; Boal et al. 2005). Their socialist-collectivising aspect, however, is destabilised to an extent by Baghdadi's emphasis on his own attainment of cultural capital, demonstrated by persistent overt and covert insinuations that he rightfully possesses the privileged status to communicate 'Allah's will' to IS supporters. As researchers have noted, this is evident in Baghdadi's long-form prose, which is laden with more extensive and overt theological references than those evident in Bin Laden's widely disseminated propaganda (Armstrong 2014; McCants 2015). Baghdadi's ability and predisposition to incorporate such prose is often considered a reflection of his educational history, which included a bachelor's course in Islamic Studies at the University of Baghdad, and the attainment of a master's degree and doctorate in Quranic studies from the Saddam University for Islamic Studies (Lister 2014).

Researchers of IS have recognised that Baghdadi's long-form articulation of political grievances on behalf of the organisation do not only convey his academic background; for supporters of IS, they potentially add credence to his claim to theocratic leadership (Fromson and Simon 2015; Goodwin 2015; McCants 2015). This sets Baghdadi apart from other IS spokespersons and from the majority of IS supporters. Foot soldiers of IS, for example, typically do not have the requisite literacy to the read the Quran, let alone understand the complex doctrinal references throughout Baghdadi's addresses (Lister 2014; McCants 2015). As such, the inextricable nature of religious fundamentalism and political-economic critique in Baghdadi's statements will also perhaps not be evident to IS supporters. These supporters are unlikely to be able to recognise how conflated logic is also apparent in speeches made by IS's US opposition, including, for instance, George W. Bush's statements suggesting his own messianic role in the GWOT after 9/11 (Jackson 2018). Demonstrations of Baghdadi's display of education, his self-promotion, and his integration of political critique with religious fundamentalism include the following passage from a July 2014 speech:

> And your brothers the mujahideen, indeed did Allah, blessed and exalted, give them victories and conquests which came after many years of hardship and patience. And they were firm against the enemies of Allah, and He made them powerful in the land until the declaration of the Caliphate and choice of an imam. And this is a matter obligatory upon all Muslims. It is Waajib! (highest level of obligation). And it must be applied upon the earth entirely. Yet most of the people are ignorant. (Baghdadi 2014)

While the tenor of this statement denotes Baghdadi's elitism and educational background, differentiating him from other organisational leaders and members, from a Bourdieusian perspective his individual expression of habitus may be seen to exist in tension with the collective habitus of IS supporters (see Jawitz's (2009) interpretation of Bourdieu (1984)). This characteristic of IS propaganda is reminiscent of AQ propaganda in the 1990s, including Bin Laden's display of education. However, owing to the volume of short-form, simple, and intellectually accessible audio-visual propaganda IS disseminated following 2014, the contrast between Baghdadi's speeches and IS's other media is more apparent than the contrast between AQ's relatively mono-faceted long-form propagandised discourse in the 1990s and its other media. Recalling Naji's (2016) instruction, the diversity of IS propaganda formats and incorporation of diverse discourse renders its media appealing to a wide and disparate audience. From a teleological perspective, this correlates with neo-jihadism's increasingly globalised orientation and its proponents' practical and violent ambitions.

Further indicating the emergent diversity in IS media, while Baghdadi's November 2016 speech, 'This is what Allah and his messenger promised us' (Baghdadi and Al Hayat 2016), once more demonstrates his attainment of education as cultural capital, its content differs in political-economic focus from the July 2014 and December 2015 examples. In the 2016 speech, Baghdadi outlines a neo-colonial, territorial critique, which, like Bin Laden's 1996 *Declaration* and AQ and jihadist leaders' 1998 *World Islamic front* statement, alleges the collective, subjugated habitus of Muslim people. This critique is also less esoteric and quasi-theological in focus than prior statements made by Baghdadi on behalf of IS. He cites US military and economic endeavours as justification for IS's acts of violence. He also directs to IS supporters allegations that US-led coalitions will 'raid your lands under the pretext of waging war against the Islamic State', and regional 'rulers' have 'sold your issue and surrendered your affair and your land to your enemy' in 'the shade of the extensive corruption [that] the government of al-Salul [Saudi Arabia] engages in to secularize the land' (Baghdadi and Al Hayat 2016).

Again recalling Naji's political-economic treatise, these statements exemplify Jessop's (2006) idea that strategically powerful political-economic entities in the Middle East strive to create a 'regional coherence' favourable to capital accumulation. Baghdadi insinuates here, for instance, that regional governments act as proxies and allies of the US and in doing so promote 'non-Islamic' values and customs conducive to late modern capitalism.

Critiques of commodification, materialism, and internationalist values also feature in speeches delivered by leading IS spokesperson Abu Muhammad al-Adnani. In a September 2014 statement, 'Indeed your Lord is ever watchful', for example, Adnani (2014) refers to the heresies associated with desiring a 'worldly life' in association with the 'collapse of the [US] economy', although he does not elaborate on exactly what this might entail or elaborate a causal link between the two. Resembling AQ's early appeal to internationally widespread anti-neo-colonial and anti-globalisation sentiments, Adnani's remarks are then explained with reference to the widespread political and economic oppression of Muslim people. Like Bin Laden's neo-colonial critique in the *Declaration* (1996), for example, Adnani cites populations in 'Palestine', 'Burma', and parts of 'China' (2014), whom he alleges have been dispossessed of their wealth and freedom by US and US-allied political-economic actors. Adnani's speech herein exhibits a practical, historical materialist critique noticeably absent in Baghdadi's statements. This critique persists in

Adnani's later speeches, which emphasise practical plans for IS to undermine US finance through territorial means. In this dimension, they recall the strategic and operational guidelines for action provided by Naji.

Speeches made by Adnani in 2015 and 2016 in particular outline an ideological perspective on the part of IS regarding US military industries while explaining an organisational strategy for challenging US financial and military hegemony in the Middle East. In an October 2015 speech, 'Say to those who disbelieve you will be overcome' (Adnani and Al Hayat 2015), Adnani highlights the efforts of US forces to capture and defend the Iraqi Baiji oil refinery from IS before it was recaptured by IS militants in December 2014. Adnani's comments here are less complex and pedagogic than those of Baghdadi, perhaps indicating that social capital, via a politicised and populist emphasis on the ideal of collectivisation, is more relevant for an IS representative in his position than cultural capital. This tactic – individual organisational leaders communicate protracted and long-form explanations for neo-jihadist violence, and supporting spokespersons communicate with the 'masses' in straightforward, culturally resonant rhetoric – might be said to be similar to that used by AQ, although the latter's early deputy leader, Ayman al-Zawahiri, was not known for particularly charismatic media displays (Byman 2015).

Adnani's appeal to his audiences' assumed membership of a collective and resistant population, rather than a subjugated one, is nevertheless reinforced through his discussion of their shared experience of summary exploitation. Adnani implores his audience:

> Stand up against Al Salul (the House of Saud) and their committee of agents so that the Americans and their allies swiftly collapse, for it is from your lands that they set out and by your oil that they are financed, and by the fatawa of your devils that the Muslims are forsaken, handed over, driven out, and butchered. (Adnani and Al Hayat 2015)

The last speech Adnani delivered in May 2016, before his assassination in August, 'That they live by proof' (Adnani and Al Furqan 2016), features even simpler and more colloquial language than his previous speeches, explicitly denouncing US entities and their pursuit of neoliberal agendas in the Middle East. Adnani announces that '8 years of a destructive war … devastated America's economy', rhetorically asking his audience: 'why do they spend billions of their wealth against us?'; in answer to which he states: 'the whole world has not come together to wage war against us except because we command the worship of Allah, alone without partner, and we incite others to do so' (Adnani and Al Furqan 2016).

While Adnani's emphasis on US military industries and debt economies clearly indicates IS's opposition to the precepts of US-directed neoliberal financial systems, it also frames the dispute between IS and its opponents as a religious war, predicated on a fundamentalist ideology. Variously analogous to Bush (2001a, 2001b), Huntington (1993, 1996) and Qut'b's (1962) 'clash of civilizations' theses, Adnani's 2016 speech includes the passage: 'there are only two armies, two camps, two trenches. It is the war between kufr and iman. It is the war of wala and bara' (Adnani and Al Furqan 2016). This dualism is reaffirmed by a discursive framework of territoriality, including Adnani and Baghdadi's various invocations of tension between '*Dar al-Islam*' and '*Dar al-Harb*' (meaning, in this usage, the 'House of God' and the 'House of War') (Armstrong 2014; Jabareen 2015). Combined with Adnani's mention of 'camps' and 'trenches', these allusions to land (through houses or abodes) and religious morality are an extended Manichean and spatial analogy that, again in line with Jessop (2006), signifies reflexivity between IS and the US. In this regard, both IS and US policymakers who promoted interventions can be said to exhibit interdependent geographical and economic logics in their state(-like) reasoning, and both remain concerned with a neoliberal political-economic incentive.

In the six years from the announcement of the Caliphate in 2014 to the time of this book's publication in 2020, statements made by Baghdadi and (at an early stage) Adnani demonstrated a series of propaganda strategies for IS, including divergent emphases on cultural and social capital, expressed through intensifying focus on US military and counterterrorism endeavours. These speeches also accused the US of political or economic aggression, contextualised with reference to US geo-economic behaviour and IS's incentives to occupy and control territory. Unlike speeches made on behalf of AQ, IS spokespersons' references to US political-economic behaviours included insufficient detail for their effective comparison with neo-Marxist and other anti-capitalist commentary on neoliberalism. In general, they were vague, romanticised, and loquacious in specifying IS's political-economic strategy. The examined cases do indicate, however, that IS projected its territorial ambitions onto its political-economic criticism.

In stark contrast to the textual and rhetorical nature of AQ propaganda, the majority of IS's public communications have consisted of audiovisual media. In consideration of this, the following discussion reflects on how US administrations' capitalist and territorial logics are addressed in IS magazines and online videos, with reference to ideas regarding neoliberalism outlined in the previous chapters. With the exception of one example, these media were produced in English by the

Al Hayat IS media department, which primarily created and distributed material in European languages targeted at Western audiences.

IS audiovisual media

IS's most explicit engagement with neoliberalism in audiovisual media was 'The rise of the Khilafah: Return of the gold dinar' (Al Hayat 2015a), a documentary-style production released on 29 August 2015, which advocated replacing the US fractional-reserve banking system with a form of economic sharia predicated on a new form of currency, the Islamic dinar. Throughout a narrative characteristically interspersed with footage of raids, bombings and executions, the narrator advocates an attack on aspects of the US-led international financial system that might be broadly described in terms of Clark's (2005) theory of petro-dollar warfare, as explained in Chapter 2. Comparable with AQ's post-9/11 propaganda, this video also provides an explanation of the monetary characteristics of the US-led international financial system and the international political-economic conditions that allow for the proliferation of neoliberal outcomes in 'economic and non-economic domains' (Peck 2010, 24). In so doing, the spokesperson in this video, following Naji's advice, appeals to social, cultural, and symbolic capital in a layered fashion.

Perhaps the most overt example of cultural capital in 'The rise of the Khilafah' is the narrator's analysis of US control over major oil regions in the Middle East, and his exposition of the US dollar via a history of the Federal Reserve banking system. Identified by commentators as North American and therefore likely to possess insight into the US political-economic situation (Mahood and Rane 2017), he refers to an edict of Islamic finance that proscribes *riba*, or the acquisition of monetary interest, explained in more detail in Chapter 5. The narrator then conflates Islamic theological doctrine with anti-capitalist sentiment in a similar manner to Bin Laden's display of cultural capital. This entails a combined emphasis on political Islamism with anti-neo-colonial and anti-globalisation rhetoric, which was likewise apparent in AQ propaganda in the lead up to 9/11. Such statements include the broad-based condemnation of interest payments as 'the most insidious instrument' of the 'satanic usury-based global economic system' (Al Hayat 2015a). Extending AQ's pledge to boycott US money, in a manner more practical (if implausible) than AQ's instructions, the statements promoting the adoption of the Islamic dinar as an alternative to the US dollar explain that it will consist of gold, silver, and copper coins, 'made from the measures of wealth that Allah created' (Al Hayat 2015a).

IS's critique of the US-led international political economy, contextualised by a finance-oriented evaluation of capitalism and US-directed neoliberal industries, extends to the narrator's criticism that 'inflation' is an 'inherent and perpetual part of this evil system' (Al Hayat 2015a) leading to the devaluation of local currencies and the debilitation of national economic systems. In dialectical engagement with Western critical discourse, and demonstrating the importance of cultural capital, the video also incorporates a textual snapshot of US economist Ron Paul's judgement that a 10 per cent devaluation of the US dollar 'robs' the domestic US population of '10 percent of its accumulated wealth' (Al Hayat 2015a).

While intertextually appropriating Western critical commentary, this aspect of the IS video is reminiscent of Bin Laden's conflation of global Islamist theological precedent with contemporary reactions to global capitalism. Further demonstrating this, the narrator asserts that IS, 'built on faith, rises to face this Evil head on, initiating a countdown to bring about the end of the petrodollar system, and the destruction of America itself' (Al Hayat 2015a). As such, and particularly in relation to its personification of 'Evil', this example conveys the ideological reflexivity between IS propaganda and the fundamentalist religious-economic statements of the US government in the aftermath of 9/11. As discussed in Chapter 2, these include former US President George W. Bush's comments about his own 'divine role' in foreign policy and his declaration of war against the unaligned Iranian and North Korean regimes and AQ as an 'axis of Evil' (Bush 2001a, 2001b). For the purposes of this comparison it is worth noting that, while President Obama continued to justify foreign interventions against 'terrorism' with invocations of 'God bless America' (Beauchamp and Obama 2015), US President Donald Trump from 2016 to 2019 more starkly described US efforts against insurgent groups supported by Iran as a 'battle between Good and Evil', alleging that the Iranian government itself was a 'radical regime' (Radio Farda 2019). As has long been observed by spectators of US foreign policy, US political discourse has been characteristically interspersed with a pseudo-religious exceptionalism; as Ali explained of US rhetoric in the GWOT, 'American imperialism' is 'the mother of all fundamentalisms' (2003, 307).

Although the cultural capital of the narrator expressing his understanding of Islamist theological precedent is important for the sensational, propagandised dimensions of 'The rise of the Khilafah', the vision in the video is also heavily laden with historical imagery and themes, an appeal to symbolic capital. These examples also serve to contextualise symbolic accusations of US neoliberal behaviour in terms of IS's own territorial situation. This is apparent, for instance, where the narrator's prose overlays images of armed conflict featuring chariots, cannons, and bows, which discernibly signify battles waged during the post-eleventh-century Christian Crusades. Demonstrating that the video's intertextuality extends to the reflexive, superficially contradictory benefit IS derives from the technological products of US-directed commercial capitalism, the video's depiction of the Crusades was in fact captured from the Hollywood film *Kingdom of heaven* (2005). Illustrative of the structural, technologised, and discursive dialectics of IS's power and resistance, this part of the video also shows how the ongoing material focus in the organisation's political-economic critique is persistently bound by references to land and territory.

Territorial statements in 'The rise of the Khilafah' can be said to echo post-Marxist historical materialist critiques of 'embedded neoliberalism' (Cerny 2008) pertaining to financialisation, neo-colonialism, and the deleterious socio-economic conditions its actions produce for marginalised populations (Peck 2010). This includes the narrator citing 'the dark rise of bank notes, borne out of the Satanic conception of banks, which mutated to a fraudulent and *riba*-based financial system of enslavement, orchestrated by the Federal Reserve in America', which would 'deprive the people of their due' (Al Hayat 2015a). With their indication of social and cultural capital, the populist political-economic style of such statements – their popular twenty-first-century references to neoliberalism as a form of symbolic 'enslavement', owing to its generation of exacerbating wealth inequality and undesirable policy outcomes (Chomsky and Barsamian 2017) – might also hold appeal for IS supporters. Furthermore, references to Manichean and Abrahamic tropes such as 'dark' and 'Satan' signify the fundamentalist religious-economic logic that underlies these statements, in a differentiated (and more brutal) reflection of statements made by religious and political leaders in the US since the 1981–1989 Reagan administration, and including the 1990s PNAC (Tyler 1992), as illustrated in Chapter 2.

IS's critique of US commercial industries, contextualised by implicit and explicit allusions to territoriality, is also apparent in online texts produced by other members of IS, who are not necessarily leaders. One example is Siddhartha Dhar's (aka Abu Rumaysah 'al-Britani's) online ebook, *A brief guide to the Islamic State* (Rumaysah 2015), which concludes with a chapter entitled 'Capitalism is dead'. In this chapter, Rumaysah uses popular political rhetoric to condemn monetarist economic policies stemming from the introduction of neoliberal programmes by the US and UK governments in the early 1980s, stating: 'in the last fifty years or so we have seen developing countries in South America, Africa and Asia feel the brunt of trickledown economics and bad advice, and it has crippled them' (Rumaysah 2015, 40). Reflecting Naji's instruction to encourage migration to the site of battle, Rumaysah uses state-like logic to justify IS's enforcement of the Caliphate, asserting: 'the Islamic State, on the other hand, has stuck to its guns and moved forward with the shariah and made incredible gains' (2015, 40). In doing so, he implicitly compares IS and the territory it controlled with the unsuccessful neoliberal policies and practices of trickle-down economics and bad advice practised and provided by conventional nation states. Indicating continuity in neo-jihadist positioning, this occurs much in the same way as Bin Laden implicitly promoted theocratic governance under AQ by condemning the US's 'democratic capitalism' (Bin Laden 2007).

IS's dialectical emphasis on territory and the merits of centralised, non-liberal governance is also reflected in the organisation's critique of US neoliberal-neo-conservative politics and its extension to military industries. In 'No respite', for example, a March 2016 video IS released following its bombings of an airport and metro station in Brussels, the narrator cites 'hard facts' about US Army suicides and the overall rising costs of war in the Middle East (Al Hayat 2015b). He accuses the US-led counterterrorist coalition of excessive expenditure and financial waste, declaring: 'in addition to the 6 trillion-dollar price tag on your war against the Muslims, you are now too weak to put boots on the ground'; and 'you opt instead to attack us from the air with missiles, each worth US$250,000, while we send your proxies to hell with 50 cent bullets'. Contextualising these arguments with allusions to geography, the narrator concludes by mentioning IS's improvised Islamist eschatological prophecy that 'the flames of war' will burn the international coalition 'on the hills of Dabiq' (Al Hayat 2015b), a northern town in Syria IS once controlled but forfeited to opposing military forces in 2016.

Extending 'No respite''s broad-based condemnation of US military industries (and the impact of economic incentives for the military–industrial complex in international conflicts), the narrator's demonstration of cultural capital manifests as educational awareness. This includes, for example, his assertion of his knowledge of the 'hard facts' about military conflict, likewise demonstrating the multidimensional themes evoked in this medium. Passages such as these also indicate how for IS meaning is produced in a dialectical, neo-Marxist sense, by the reproduction of historical events, or 'inherited history' (Bourdieu 1977), rather than through explicit reference to contemporary political-economic conditions (Reuten 2000). In a Bourdieusian framework this, in turn, indicates how, distinct from AQ's evolving 'idealism' focus, IS propaganda maintained a discernible focus on what can be described as 'historical materialism', albeit with divergent emphases on 'history' and 'materialism'.

From an overarching perspective, history is important for the habitus of IS, and for neo-jihadism generally, particularly in terms of the medieval and twentieth- and twenty-first-century historical behaviours of US and (primarily) Western military forces in the Middle East. The importance to IS of its related dialectical relationship with the US is signified in 'No respite' not only by history regarding 'the West' versus 'Islam', extending back to the eleventh-century Crusades, but by the inclusion of detailed economic accounts of US expenditure and the military–industrial complex. Dialectically and chronologically, this connects with the allusions to historical behaviour on the part of the US and the West in *The management of savagery* (Naji 2006). As we have seen, in 'No respite' the narrator's contemporary economic-materialist critique is contextualised through reference to IS's occupation of the Syrian city of Dabiq, the site of IS's anticipated future apocalypse (Al Hayat 2015b).

Other IS media that emphasises land in relation to capitalism, particularly in its material aspect, include a 2014 Al Hayat video, 'There is no life without jihad' (Al Hayat 2014a), in which a UK IS recruit, Abu Dujana al Hindi, asks the viewer: 'look around you while you sit in comfort and ask yourself is this how you want to die? …. Do you wish to be resurrected with the dust from [the land of] kuffar still in your lungs?' (Al Hayat 2014a). Another example from 2014 is 'The end of Sykes Picot' (Al Hayat 2014b), in which a Chilean IS recruit, Abu Safiyya, discusses IS's alleged dissolution of the colonial border between Iraq and Syria. Safiyya exhibits trucks and artillery vehicles originally provided by the US to the Iraqi administration after the war that began in 2003, which were subsequently seized by IS militants. He comments:

> Look how much money America spends to fight Islam and it just ends up just being in our pockets … look at this car … American Ford … you spent millions, up until now America spent up to, I read in the news, 20 billion of dollars, now they [are] bankrupt, they cannot enter back into Iraq, they lost in Iraq, they lost in Afghanistan, they're going to lose in Syria also inshallah when they come. (Al Hayat 2014b)

Collectively, these statements connect IS's introspective concern with territory to its overarching critique of the US, predicated on anti-capitalism, economic condescension regarding US military industries, and IS's own claim of theocratic legitimacy, entailing alleged historical precedent. To a greater extent than AQ propaganda, they demonstrate IS's preoccupation with the power of history to shape the self, both individually and as a collective (for the philosophical context, see Latour 2012). Although IS speeches might differentially appeal to collective and individual notions of habitus, the organisation's symbolic and pseudo-educational remarks about Western intervention in the Middle East in its audiovisual media signify its reliance upon a shared habitus, which has developed, according to IS's representation, by virtue of international Muslim populations' inherited history of political and economic oppression (Devji 2008). To this end, they also epitomise the attempted neo-jihadist transformation of this condition, from AQ to IS, into a practical enactment of resistance. As with Naji's text and the IS speeches previously examined, this represents a more active and applied example of modern ideations about terrorism than that apparent in AQ propaganda.

The historical and practical elements of IS propaganda are also evident in media that outline its prophecy of defeating US-led forces in Syria. The organisation's repeated reference to defeating the US, and Western forces in general (Atwan 2015; Zelin 2015), typically entail metaphorical allusions to the 'armies of Rome'. Beyond audiovisual media, this is also apparent in the Al Hayat magazine, *Dabiq*, which, in addition to being a town that IS occupied until 2016–17, was named after the alleged Syrian site of Armageddon (McCants 2015). In a mirror of statements made by IS's fundamentalist US government and military counterparts, the *Dabiq* publications are the most overt example of IS's civilisational rhetoric. In *Dabiq*, as with certain of the organisation's audiovisual media, IS writers refer at length to 'Armageddon', the 'Caliphate', and the 'Crusades'. Like former US President George W. Bush's statements about the US's 'crusade against the Axis of Evil' (2001a), these propaganda examples recall a history of 'civilisational' battles that goes back further than that evident in Bin laden and Zawahiri's propagandised targeting of US-directed neo-colonialism during the twentieth century.

To this end, the habitus that IS audiovisual media speaks to is constituted by 'embodied history, internalised as second nature and so forgotten as history' (Bourdieu 1990, 56), rather than a 'strategy generating principle' (Bourdieu 1977, 72), as was the case with AQ. IS attempts to make contemporary a history of religious conflicts, through thematic and discursive means, by emphasising the material conditions that provided for the emergence of its leaders' twenty-first-century neo-jihadist perspective. In *Dabiq*'s third issue, 'The call to hijrah' (Al Hayat 2014c), for example, the author of a chapter entitled 'Foley's blood is on Obama's hands' petitions followers to travel to the Caliphate by explaining IS's ideological motivations for war, and by a comparative discussion of political-economic conditions in the Caliphate and in the US. Specifically, the author highlights the effects of US support for Israel, arguing that by engaging in repeated military action in the Middle East, former

US President Obama, who oversaw a tenfold increase in the number of drone strikes in the Middle East relative to his predecessor (Purkiss and Serle 2017), 'sacrifices the welfare of the American public for the sake of the "chosen few" benefitting from Zionism and capitalism' (Al Hayat 2014c, 38). In IS media more broadly, accusations such as these are often paired with the organisation's exposition of what its adherents argue to be the machinations of the US-led petrodollar system. In the sixth issue of *Dabiq*, for instance, John Cantlie, a UK journalist held captive by IS and forced against his will to produce propaganda for the organisation, referred to the role of both petrodollar warfare and military industries in sustaining US economic hegemony internationally. Cantlie wrote:

> In return for using dollars only as the trade currency for oil and investing billions in US bonds, America would provide [Saudi Arabia] military support and protect their oil fields. At Saudi's bidding, the other OPEC countries fell into line, and the petrodollar was born. The dollar had been pinned to gold, now it was pinned to oil. (Al Hayat 2014d, 59)

This example further represents a territorial and resource-oriented critique of neoliberalism and US military activity, which remained prevalent in other IS media after *Dabiq* was discontinued following the organisation's expulsion from the Syrian city of Dabiq in October 2016. In September, the magazine was replaced with another online publication, *Rumiyah*. The name, translating literally as 'Rome', refers to a Hadith prophesy in which the Prophet Muhammad declared that the 'armies of Islam' will conquer Constantinople and Rome. In terrorism scholars' interpretations, the magazine's title represents a metaphorical allusion to the organisation's offensive against anti-IS nation states (Reed and Ingram 2016; Monaci 2017); for this investigation, it also demonstrates the importance of symbolism for IS. Following its loss of territory in 2016 and 2017, and its eventual retreat from its last Syrian territory in 2019, these statements in *Rumiyah* were early harbingers of what might become IS's de-territorialised ideology, comparable with the decentralised and non-material ideology of AQ, as opposed to IS's territorial characteristics. To the extent that this shift is apparent in *Rumiyah*, however, symbolism is incorporated in such a manner as to be historically situated and non-contemporary, unlike the symbolism of the World Trade Center evoked by AQ on 9/11.

Throughout the thirteen issues of *Rumiyah* produced in 2016 and 2017, IS authors detail the organisation's strategy for destabilising governance in countries that deploy forces against IS, by executing terrorist attacks and provoking disproportionate and oppressive domestic security responses. To justify the targeting of civilians, the anonymous author of a chapter in the magazine's second issue asserts, for instance, that 'the huge costs associated with bombs dropped by these aircrafts and drones are largely financed through the tax money generated from the so-called "innocent civilians" of these democratic nations' (Al Hayat 2016, 9). In one way, this contrasts with sympathetic statements Zawahiri made on behalf of AQ to US civilians following the 2008 GFC. Moreover, it contradicts Al Hayat's discussion in 'The rise of the Khilafah' (Al Hayat 2015a) of US elites 'robbing' domestic citizens, suggesting that this publication targeted a narrower anti-US demographic than those disenfranchised following the GFC. In another way, this statement highlights the state-oriented and state-centric logic to IS's neo-jihadist orientation, indicating reflexivity with the organisation's own territorial aspirations. Once more, the author implicitly promotes the Caliphate relative to the US through his condemnatory reference to the social harms caused by economic policies embraced by 'democratic nations' (Al Hayat 2016, 9).

In line with IS's critique of the *taghut* (unbelievers), highlighted in *Dabiq* and *The management of savagery* (Naji 2006), a final, distinctive anti-capitalist characteristic of IS media that demonstrates its self-reflective comparison with Western countries is the critique of capitalist desires and innovations. As with IS's projection of its territorial interests, it is the nature of the contrast with and the relationship between IS and its political opposition that constitutes the organisation's process of ideological identification. As Peck (2010) highlights, neoliberal paradigms and their descendants cannot exist without ongoing political-economic antagonism. IS, like AQ, is dialectically constituted on a structural level by a process of engagement with its material and ideological US-led neoliberal opponents. To this end, the organisation projects its own geo-economic and geopolitical interests into its stated anti-capitalist positioning.

As was the case with AQ, IS's anti-capitalism is reminiscent of the disgust expressed by Sayyid Qut'b and Ali Shari'ate following their respective periods of residence in the US and France (Tripp 2006). Similar to Bin Laden's assertion following 9/11 regarding those he terms 'the gang of criminals in the White House ... whose idiotic leader claims we despise their way of life' (Bin Laden 2005, 193), a chapter in the second issue of *Rumiyah* states: 'you can continue to believe that those "despicable terrorists" hate you because of your lattes and your Timberlands ... or you can accept reality and recognize that we will never stop hating you until you embrace Islam' (Al Hayat 2016, 33). This phrase features an implicit allusion to the popular term 'latte liberals' (and also the more recent variant of 'latte socialists'), used in the first instance to denote popular political groups that benefit from the inequality brought about by late modern capitalism while professing to observe egalitarian values (Anderson 2007). Statements such as this typify the broad focus of neo-jihadist propaganda directed at Western audiences, which rejects the neoliberal modern philosophies of commodification and individualism. It also evinces neo-jihadist organisations' awareness of the multilayered contradiction that results from a comparison between the justification of neoliberal ideas and the impact of actual neoliberal philosophies, instantiated, as Chapter 2 explained, in cases of deleterious economic policies.

Although there is insufficient space to explore in more detail how IS's criticism of 'worldly pleasures' dominates much of its ideological messaging, it is worth noting that, as with the organisation's emphasis on military industries, such criticisms are often inextricable from IS spokespersons' petitions for supporters to travel to the Caliphate and the organisation's pervasive emphasis on geo-economic and territorial reasoning. In addition to overt comparisons between IS-held territories and Western nations, this includes its repeated dichotomous associations of the Caliphate with *Dar al-Islam* (the Abode of Peace), and all 'apostate' countries with *Dar al-Harb* (the Abode of War). Although there is contention among scholars of Islam about the concept's contemporary application, the reference is sometimes interpreted as the 'house', 'domain', or 'abode' of Islam, versus the 'house', 'domain', or 'abode' of war. At other times, Dar al-Islam is taken to mean 'the Abode/Domain/ House of Peace' (McCants 2015); and in a geo-political context, 'territories' governed differentially by Islamic or non-Islamic governance or jurisprudence are in question (Ayoub 2012). In line with Peck's (2010) explanation of neoliberal reasoning, and with Qut'b (1966) and Bush's (2001a, 2001b, 2003) civilisational statements, elaborated notably by Ali (2003), this ideology indicates how IS and its ideological opponents self-identify through binary, dichotomising means of comparison. From a strategic perspective, and in line with Naji's direction for the Mujahideen to appeal to both well- and less-educated audiences, framing 'neo-jihadism' on the part of AQ and IS in this way grounds what might be an abstract political-economic circumstance in a more easily comprehensible spatial and material reality.

Where AQ propaganda over time focused on the non-territorial pursuits of US military and economic industries, IS persistently (from 2014 to 2017) located its anti-capitalist critique within the context of its own territorial ambitions. Examples that recall a shared logic in AQ media, and in historical Islamism, indicate that IS engaged with the political-economic circumstances and rationalities prevalent following major political-economic events. Where AQ responded to the Cold War, 9/11, and the GFC, IS has been for the most part concerned with geopolitical alliances and situations that arose in relation to the initial George W. Bush administration's GWOT. Its attention to contemporary circumstances is furthermore embedded with thematic references to ancient historical competitions between western European forces, 'the armies of Rome', and what IS terms the 'armies of Islam' (Al Hayat 2014c), rather than exclusively referencing the political-economic actions of the US during the twentieth and twenty-first centuries.

The way that IS and ideologues such as Naji interpolate critique of the US and the West's historical economic behaviour into its directions for contemporary IS followers' political-economic strategies can thus be illuminated with reference to neo-Marxist, rather than Hegelian, tenets of the Bourdieusian framework, witness Jacques Bidet's description of historical materialism in Bourdieu's theory as:

> The 'productive forces' [that] comprise both technical knowledge (in its dialectical link with various sciences), as the art of arranging mechanisms in nature, and social know-how, cooperative knowledge. In this sense, market and organisation pertain to the productive forces – 'limited' rationality, which equally qualifies these forces as 'destructive'. In as much as it is social, this rational know-how is inseparable from rules. (Bidet 2008, 600)

To this end, the rules set by IS's focus on material events in its constructed history correspond to the rules that would govern its future activity, oriented as they are around organisation, shared identity, and political economy, including in relation to neoliberal markets. Extending upon these insights, and those on AQ propaganda set out in the previous chapter, Chapters 5 and 6 reflect on the seeming paradox that arises from AQ and IS's financial practices when these are considered in relation to their political-economic propaganda. They also examine underlying structural connections between these organisations' management of finance and broader dimensions of neoliberal financial relationships and systems, drawing on ideas in Chapters 1 and 2.

5

Al Qaeda's financial practices

Further to its utility for attracting recruits, justifying attacks, and generating public support for neo-jihadism, the political-economic propaganda of AQ and IS is significant in the extent to which it works coterminously with these organisations' financial practices. Through their combined propaganda and finance, AQ and IS exist in a circular causative relationship with US-led counterterrorist and military activity (Falleti and Lynch 2009). Here, risk-based approaches to counterterrorism in the GWOT, including in pre-emptive wars in the Middle East and predictive counterterrorist policing, are pursued through performative and profitable pre-crime technologies, generating self-fulling national-security prophesies (Amoore 2013; McCulloch and Wilson 2016). On the one hand, they generate criminogenic risk by inflicting social and economic exclusion on those who might support neo-jihadist ideologies (Young 2011). On the other, they protect and promote open technologised-economic borders and transnational flows of finance, such that these borders and flows ultimately become intersectional with the practical and ideological dimensions of neo-jihadism (Reid 2004; Barkawi and Laffey 2006; Larner 2008). As explored in previous chapters, in response to US actions neo-jihadist organisations through their propaganda reflexively exploit international anti-capitalist and anti-US perspectives to raise political capital in its social, symbolic, and cultural forms.

This and the following chapter collectively argue that an ultimate effect of AQ and IS's economic interdependence with neoliberalism is their followers' constitution as terroristic 'power and resistance' subjects. Via their communicative and organisational practices, AQ and IS reinforce the dominance of neoliberal political-economic systems, both logistically, with regard to finance, and ideologically, by legitimising their comparatively 'rational' opponents' political position. As Gray (2003), Barber (1995), and Ali (2003) elaborated, these counter/terrorism dialectics in part result from shared philosophical histories between 'Eastern' and 'Western' 'terrorists' and 'counterterrorists', including their Enlightenment origins and 'reason'-oriented thinking, as well as their inherent use of positivism, religion, and pseudo-scientific fundamentalism. As Slavoj Žižek articulated, albeit in a somewhat Eurocentric way, 'the problem is not cultural difference (their effort to preserve their identity), but the opposite fact that they already like us, that, secretly, they have already internalized our standards and measure themselves by them' (2014).

Though differing from Žižek's civilisational perspective, I extend existing comparative analyses to demonstrate that neoliberal methods of financial management by AQ and IS not only sustain their violence: they also contribute to the continuation of neoliberal political-economic systems and hence the structural violence neo-jihadist entities claim to resist. Where Chapters 3 and 4 explored how propaganda on the part of AQ and IS reflect a changing field of anti-capitalism over time, this and the following chapter consider that their financial activity occurred via a doxa of expectation that neoliberalism will persist, and where its international dominance is uncritically taken as self-evident (Bourdieu 1998a, 1998b). Following Bourdieu (1986), economic capital in its most autonomous and directive form is interpreted as having tangible and profound effects on the entirety of human sociality. While, as previous discussions showed, extra-economic forms of capital in neo-jihadist propaganda correspond to histories of inequitable economic capital distribution in the Middle East and internationally, financially AQ and IS persist via their participation in capitalism's 'mercantile exchange' (Bourdieu 1986), within a wider field of neoliberal political-economic relations.

This investigation does not, however, interpret AQ and IS as wholly neoliberal. The extent of their capitalist financial practices is, rather, interpreted as noteworthy given its apparent contradiction with their propaganda, and its impact on the underlying economic structures that contribute to the perpetuation of both neoliberalism and the phenomenon of neo-jihadism. In line with Peck's (2010) explanation of neoliberal political economy, AQ and IS's financial practices are here interpreted as a series of 'layers', where policies and programmes adopted by the organisations build upon pre-existing political-economic conditions. The cases I draw from demonstrate that their behaviour developed in response to the historical outsourcing of state functions to private institutions in the region, as with state violence outsourced to private mercenaries and non-state terrorism. Ontological connections between neo-jihadism and neoliberalism are empirically evidenced by the effects that actions on the part of neoliberal nation states and their private partners have on the political-economic environments in which these terrorist organisations operate (Young 2007; Amoore and De Goede 2008; Heath-Kelly 2013).

Reflecting AQ's diverse approach to governance, the organisation has, since its inception, differentially and recurrently interacted with precepts of neoliberalism. The organisation's exploitation of global financial networks within the international financial system from its establishment in 1988 was foundational, and prominent AQ actors have exploited public–private economic partnerships with individuals close to governments that are strategically and economically allied with the US. Over the course of its history, AQ has also engaged with licit and illicit economic managerial mechanisms available within the neoliberal financial systems. These engagements have in part been facilitated by the US's counterterrorist targeting of alternative remittance systems that to a certain extent lie outside the formal neoliberal political economy (or the 'international financial system'). In other respects, they correlate with AQ's extra- and non-territorial strategic ambition, including its transnational orientation after 2001.

This chapter begins by reflecting on AQ's early history, including its emergence from the MAK bureau, funded and supported by the US and its allies in the Afghan–Soviet War (1979–89). Following this, it considers that since the 1990s AQ has benefited from neoliberal partnerships between the US, wealthy Gulf states, and government-aligned individuals. Herein, it explores how the reality of these funding sources for AQ was obscured by the US-directed counterterrorist targeting of alternative remittance. In an account of AQ's commercial activities, it emphasises the organisation's exploitation of financial apparatus available in neoliberal environments. There is then a brief account of Islamic-finance principles, which run counter to the philosophies, policies, and practices of neoliberalism. I consider how, in combination with AQ's anti-capitalist propaganda, these principles illustrate tension in the outward ideological orientation of AQ as a neo-jihadist organisation.

The discussion begins from the premise that AQ's engagement with neoliberalism, both in terms of its reliance on partnerships with the US, and its direct benefit from neoliberal dimensions of international finance, is related to its geopolitical evolution. Although characteristics of this evolution are contentious, here they are taken to include AQ's emergence in 1988, its leadership and organisational 'base' in Sudan and Afghanistan during the 1990s, and its decentralisation following 9/11 to a contemporary rhizomatic, 'outsourced' orientation (Deleuze and Guattari 1988; Kuronen and Huhtinen 2017). I argue that this changing organisational structure in part determined AQ's financial governance, given that prior to 2001 AQ was reliant upon funds raised and distributed by central leadership (later, AQ branches and cells engaged in independent fundraising and expenditure). At the beginning of the analysis, I explore the financial practices of AQ and its affiliates, beginning with an exposition of the organisation's origins during the Afghan–Soviet conflict.

Maktab al-Khidamat (MAK)

The first major intersection of AQ finance with neoliberal structures and actors occurred at the inception of the organisation in 1988, when it was supported by nation states allied with the US. In this situation, AQ's collective habitus can, in line with Bourdieusian theory, be interpreted as a product of US military and economic 'reason':

> Economic coercion is often dressed up in juridical reasons. Imperialism drapes itself in the legitimacy of international bodies. And, through the very hypocrisy of the rationalizations intended to mask its double standards, it tends to provoke or justify, among the Arab, South American or African peoples, a very profound revolt against the reason which cannot be separated from the abuses of power which are armed or justified by reason (economic, scientific or any other). (Bourdieu 1998b, 20)

Seen through this lens, the 'rational' intervention of US-led forces in Afghanistan during the closing stages of the Cold War, ostensibly to liberate the Afghan people from Soviet occupation, can be seen to have reflexively catalysed the creation of a military and economic condition fundamental to the emergence of AQ. Social and cultural capital was important to the propagandised identity of AQ from the 1990s onwards, and so too was economic capital, in the form of material support provided by the US and its allies to the Mujahideen forerunners to AQ. Networks and interlinkages dependent on the international financial system and leveraged by the Mujahideen during the war provided for AQ's subsequent political-economic development (Burke 2004; Jones 2014). Attention to events that occurred during this period can help to illuminate the causative and layered nature of early dialectical engagements between AQ and its US-directed opposition.

Political-economic connections between AQ and the US during the Afghan–Soviet conflict include the financial and military assistance that the US and its allies provided to the Mujahideen for the purpose of engaging and debilitating Soviet armed forces, before and during Ronald Reagan's presidency. This activity developed further with the introduction of neoliberal US policies under Reagan and their gradual adoption worldwide during the Cold War (Harvey 2005; Peck 2010). It also extended to the imminent symbolic and strategic triumph of US and US-led pro-capitalist forces over the 'communist' USSR. As discussed in

Chapter 2, the enduring influence of neoliberal policy reasoning in the Reagan administration on contemporary US military history, and wider trends in global political economy, is indicated in several high-profile think-tank reports. In one report, notable PNAC members (who came to office in the neoliberal-neo-conservative George W. Bush administration at the commencement of the GWOT) called for the protection of US hegemony via 'a Reaganite policy of military strength and moral clarity' (Abrams et al. 1997). Moreover, such examples echoed a political environment in which US policymakers widely conflated communism with terrorism before the collapse of the USSR at the end of the Cold War (Zulaika 2009, 143).

Although the US is popularly believed to have provided aid to the Afghan people during this period in response to the USSR's aggression, figures close to the Jimmy Carter administration acknowledged that the US in fact sought to lure the Soviet forces into a protracted campaign for the purpose of bleeding the USSR financially, undermining confidence in the Soviet empire, and entrapping their forces in a demoralising quagmire. This knowledge became public through ex-CIA director Robert Gates' 1996 memoir, *From the shadows: The ultimate insider's story of five presidents and how they won the Cold War*, which revealed that US intelligence agencies began providing finance and arms to the Mujahideen six months before the first Soviet troops arrived, including an explicit directive to channel US$500 million to anti-government insurgents in Kabul (Gates 2011). Also, in a 1998 interview with *Le Nouvel Observateur*, Zbigniew Brzezinski, who was National Security Advisor to President Carter during the Afghan–Soviet war, confirmed that the above directive was signed on 3 July 1979 and, further, that he had advised President Carter this was likely to provoke a Soviet military response. Later, in 2016, US foreign-policy critic William Blum famously cited a declassified US Department of State cable that proved 'US foreign service officers had been meeting with Moujahedeen leaders to determine their needs at least as early as April 1979' (Blum 2016).

During the Afghan–Soviet conflict, the Mujahideen were assisted collectively and in individual units by the US and Gulf monarchies, principally Saudi Arabia, through a US Central Intelligence Agency (CIA) venture called Operation Cyclone (Girardet 2012). According to US State Department documents, the operation entailed the provision of funds, weapons, and training for the Mujahideen through Pakistan's Inter-Services Intelligence (ISI) agency. Training was conducted by Americans, Egyptians, Chinese, and Iranians, primarily in Pakistan and China to maintain the 'anonymity' of US support, and Soviet-style weaponry was provided to the Mujahideen after purchase by the CIA from Israel, Poland, Egypt, and

China (Blum 1995, 345). This supply of weapons, including Stinger anti-aircraft missiles capable of bringing down Soviet helicopters, contributed immensely to the loss of Soviet troops and the USSR's military expenditure. An unknown number of these missiles and other sophisticated weaponry are believed to be in current circulation among anti-Western 'rebel militias, narco-criminals, and terrorist groups' in the region, as acknowledged in a US State Department Bureau of Diplomatic Security report during the Clinton administration (Silverstein 2001).

Throughout the nine-year war, the local Afghan Mujahideen were joined by approximately 20,000 to 35,000 foreign fighters, often referred to as 'Afghan-Arabs' (Tarrow 2002). They were comprised of predominantly Sunni Islamist fighters that travelled from Pakistan, Saudi Arabia, and Iran. Among these was Osama Bin Laden, the Saudi heir to a billion-dollar construction-industry fortune and future leader of AQ. Also among the Afghan-Arabs was Palestinian cleric Abdullah Yusuf Azzam, who convinced Bin Laden to join the 'jihad' effort in Afghanistan, and who would later assist him in forming AQ. During the war, Azzam and Bin Laden provided funding and facilitation for arms and equipment, and for recruits to join the Mujahideen in Afghanistan. These efforts were coordinated via their MAK financial bureau, which would later be instrumental in funding and facilitating recruitment for AQ (Roth et al. 2004).

The MAK's provision of around US$1 million financial assistance to the Mujahideen was nominal in comparison with the US$20 billion provided by the US alliance (Lynch et al. 2013, 219). Of strategic significance regarding the MAK was its negotiation of international recruitment and donations; it was in effect the first expression of a truly 'global jihad', possessing many of the transnational characteristics of AQ and IS as neo-jihadist organisations today. In dialectical fashion, the MAK was established during a time in which the effects of neoliberal globalisation were materialising around the world, including global flows of people, goods, and services, cultural commodification, the homogenisation of McWorld (Barber 1995), and intensifying international capital mobility, sustained by deregulatory policy conditions promoted by the US and IFIs (Harvey 2005). Bourdieu's investigation of the role that nation states play in sustaining neoliberalism, and at the same time promoting dialectical engagements between politically violent entities, is useful in understanding this aspect of AQ's early history.

In 'The globalisation myth' chapter of *Acts of resistance Against the new myths of our time* (1998b), Bourdieu explains financial markets, as opposed to social and cultural services, to be the primary setting in which economic globalisation produced tangible, deleterious outcomes for civilian populations in the 1980s and 1990s, during the period of

AQ's emergence. As discussed in Chapters 1 and 2, he emphasises that since the 1980s, financial networks have been skewed in favour of public–private partnerships between elites, via the support of dominant nations (Bourdieu 1998b, 38; Brenner and Theodore 2002; Peck 2010). Summarising the wider political-economic environment in which this occurred, Bourdieu cites former neo-conservative Francis Fukuyama's (2007) theory that the neoliberal Washington Consensus would constitute a final and enduring political-economic model, asserting: 'it is by arming itself with mathematics (and power over the media) that neo-liberalism has become the supreme form of the conservative sociodicy which started to appear some thirty years ago as "the end of ideology", or more recently, as "the end of history"' (Bourdieu 1998b, 35). Although, as elaborated in Chapter 3, Bin Laden's *Declaration* (1996) of a terrorist campaign against the US rejected at first instance the Washington Consensus and New World Order, as this chapter shows, from its inception AQ as an organisation was deeply implicated in neoliberal flows of international finance.

With multiple offices in Europe, the UK, and the US, the MAK was a part of international financial networks sustained with the support of the US and its Cold War allies. The MAK's financial activities during this period, albeit on a relatively small scale, were both influenced by and constitutive of a transnational neoliberal 'whole' (Peck 2010, 22; Clarke 2008). This broader neoliberal environment included the Mujahideen's political and economic relationships with US-affiliated individuals and organisations internationally. As elaborated below, in the twenty-first century these extended to AQ's ties to US-affiliated energy interests.

Although scant available evidence confirms that Bin Laden, as the inaugural leader of AQ, received immediate assistance from the US during the organisation's early years, or that he met directly with US government employees, his leadership role in the MAK meant that he was likely separated from US influence by only one or two strategic connections (Posner 2009). This proximity corresponds in particular to the CIA's support for the Mujahideen through Pakistan, and Bin Laden's Cold War affiliations with Pakistani officials. According to investigative reporter Gerald Posner (2009), Bin Laden regularly met with General Akhtar Abdur Rahman, the Pakistani ISI head from 1980 to 1987, to organise for a mutually beneficial 'tax' to be imposed upon the opium networks of tribal warlords. Other sources confirm that Bin Laden was closely connected to and indeed worked with the Mujahideen commander Gulbuddin Hekmatyar (Bergen 2002), who received the greatest allocation of US funds via the ISI and commanded the most violent and fundamentalist of the resistance groups. Indicating interpersonal connections between politically violent individuals and neoliberal entities during this period, for his dedication to the anti-Soviet cause Hekmatyar was flown to the UK to meet with Prime Minister Margaret Thatcher (Pilger 2015).

Statements by retired ISI military and intelligence officers confirm that through international networks the CIA in fact 'nurtured' Bin Laden's MAK (Dreyfuss 2006, 279–280; Moran 1998), and de-classified CIA and US Department of State reports show that MAK fundraising offices operated internationally under the supervision of US and UK intelligence agencies (Holmes and Dixon 2001, 51; Gates 2011, 349). Following the dissolution of the MAK in 1989, the 'rationality' of US-led political-economic intervention during the Cold War period was reflected in the 'irrationalism' of AQ's subsequent political-economic activity (Bourdieu 1998b, 20). A cyclical and causative political-economic dialectic between the US and the Mujahideen subsequently extended to AQ partnerships with individuals close to US-allied governments in the Middle East, which often had originated in the Afghan–Soviet conflict. The following section of this chapter explores how these partnerships with donors, sometimes facilitated via 'Islamic charities', were integral to AQ's early political-economic habitus, through its financial behaviour. Exploring the dialectical nature of AQ's actions in a neoliberal field of economic capital relations, it also reflects on how entities financially supporting AQ were connected to the US via trading and commercial relationships.

Donors and charities

Donors and charities that facilitated financial support for AQ in the 1990s reflected the organisation's geo-economic orientation and behaviour. In line with the territorial characteristics of the early AQ, under the leadership of Bin Laden its efforts at fundraising and financial governance were guided by the direction of central authorities, prior to 1996 from Sudan and following 1996 from Afghanistan and then Pakistan (Hoffman 2004). After 9/11 and the commencement of the US military assault on Afghanistan, AQ divided into branches, sometimes described as 'franchises', via which it would coordinate the individualised management of finance (Farrall 2011). While Bin Laden and then Zawahiri retained command over the finance of AQ Central from 1988 until this book's time of writing, as indicated in US Department of State documents (Levitt 2014), AQ branches and AQ Central have consistently relied on donations from wealthy benefactors often aligned with governments that shared economic and strategic partnerships with the US (De Goede 2008).

Two aspects of AQ's financial behaviour related to its organisational evolution might in particular be said to characterise its dialectical relationship with US-directed neoliberalism. First, as outlined in the Introduction, AQ's decentralisation was catalysed by the US invasion of Afghanistan and assassination of its leaders in Afghanistan and Pakistan, following AQ's targeting of symbols of neoliberalism – the Pentagon and World Trade Center – in the attacks of 9/11. This decentralisation facilitated AQ's adoption of a model of governance that some have compared to the privatised, outsourced, and networked governance of venture capitalist corporations (Basile 2004; Burke 2004; Charette 2007; Hubbard 2014). Moreover, as the discussion of AQ's commercial activities below demonstrates, the extent of AQ's decentralised outsourcing suggests a form of mirroring between AQ and licit commercial entities within their shared neoliberal financial environments. As discussed in this section, Gulf-state-affiliated donations to AQ franchises and AQ Central, continuing from the US sponsorship of the Mujahideen, are evidence of neoliberal layering in the region (Peck 2010). While the description of the origins of AQ donations as neoliberal is not without contention, to the extent to which these sources share political-economic connections with the US and its political-economic allies, AQ benefited from public–private partnerships locally that were both intersectional with neoliberal finance and predicated on US energy interests.

The extent of US petrodollar donations to AQ in particular demonstrates the pervasive influence that long-standing neoliberal trading relationships have had on political violence in the Middle East, though these have changed over time. As Harvey (2003, 20) summarised in *The new imperialism*, after the Vietnam War 'the US chose to use the surrogate states of Iran and Saudi Arabia to look after its proliferating interests in the region'. It also struck billion-dollar oil and gas deals, establishing the Gulf Cooperation Council (GCC) with the UAE, Saudi Arabia, Kuwait, Qatar, and others, while providing military wares to the GCC with which it would support US forces (Harvey 2003, 22). While the US use of proxy governments to maintain its satellite influence internationally is well known (Lewis 2003; Hanieh 2008; Cooper 2012), the criminogenic impacts of this are less often acknowledged, including in particular the effect of such actions on the emergence of AQ and IS. In an exception, 'oil crusade' critics explored how the 2001 Afghanistan War protected the proposed US–EU Union Oil Company of California (UNOCAL) pipeline, and the 2003 destabilisation of Iraq alleviated US concerns about Saddam Hussein's unpredictable plans for energy export (Le Billon and El Khatib 2004, 122; Fouskas and Gökay 2005, 23, 157). In addition, in the wake of the 2011 Syrian civil conflict, others considered how US support for the GCC's manoeuvring to destabilise the Assad regime reflected the interests of long-standing neoliberal trade agreements between the US, EU, and Gulf State sponsors of jihadism (Bichler and Nitzan 2014). As Jessop (2006, 162) explains, US capital accumulation in neoliberal settings demands a 'regional structural coherence' constituted by state and non-state alliances to defend shared economic interests.

These alliances and the financial networks they correspond to were justified in the eyes of AQ supporters (and potentially for supporters of the US) through the propagandising and obfuscatory effect of 'symbolic power' during the GWOT, which can be understood in Bourdieusian terms as 'the process whereby power relations are perceived not for what they objectively are but in a form which renders them legitimate in the eyes of the beholder' (Bourdieu 1977, 8). In the GWOT, signifying AQ's transformation from a resistance movement to one of domination, symbolic power was evident in the organisation's political-economic activity, and on the part of the US and AQ in their narratives. AQ propaganda here served to mask for its followers US relationships with donors in Gulf states. Indicating the recursive nature of this situation, then, the economic interrelationships of the US and regional supporters of neo-jihadism, including Saudi Arabia and Qatar, were for several decades under-acknowledged by both proponents and opponents of US foreign policy (Hanieh 2016).

Symbolism also played a significant role in influencing the habitus that justified AQ's violent actions on religious grounds (Bourdieu 1984; Rehbein 2011), while concealing the strategic-ideological contradiction of the sources and destinations of economic capital used by AQ (and then IS). The opacity of power and finance in this case was often related to the 'Islamic' and 'charitable' source of the funds donated to AQ. Despite their ostensibly religious institutional origins and humanitarian destinations, economic capital donated by powerful entities to AQ was often initially aggregated via the US-led petrodollar system (Clark 2005). Contrary to the official statements of some fundraising institutions, they were also not destined for humanitarian purposes but for violent ones (Bokhari et al. 2014).

Critics of US links to AQ's financiers and the obscuring of sources of funding for political violence in the Middle East have highlighted 2009 WikiLeaks cables originally authored by former US Secretary of State Hillary Clinton. In the transcript of the cables, Clinton announced that 'donors in Saudi Arabia constitute the most significant source of funding to Sunni terrorist groups worldwide' (WikiLeaks 2017; see also Walsh 2010), and that Saudi Arabia 'remains a critical financial support base for al-Qa'ida, the Taliban, [Lashkar-e-Taiba], and other terrorist groups' (WikiLeaks 2017). In 2014 and 2016, further leaks of documents authored by Clinton revealed that repressive theocratic states in the region (including Saudi Arabia, Qatar, and Kuwait) 'exported' extremist ideologies through terrorism finance and educational and charitable organisations, and that state officials from these countries were lax in addressing this as a strategic priority (WikiLeaks 2017). Moreover, when considered in relation to the civilisational narratives of the George W. Bush administration following 9/11, and Robert Zoellick's pledge to 'counter terror with trade' (Zoellick 2001; Juhasz 2006), the origins of AQ funding from individuals close to US-allied states evince a reflexive and dialectical intersection of market and religious fundamentalism on the part of both AQ and the US.

The symbolism that allowed for the continuation of donations to AQ, both for supporters and opponents of the US, corresponded to its contextualisation in religious charities. As revealed in Paul Thompson's *The terror timeline* (2004) and Michael Ruppert's *Crossing the Rubicon: The decline of the American empire in the age of oil* (2004, 127), in April 1999 an audit by the Saudi government allegedly revealed that five Saudi billionaires transferred tens of millions of dollars via Saudi Arabia's largest financial institution, the National Commercial Bank (NCB), in funding for charities in London and New York that serve as fronts for AQ, though the existence of the audit was denied by the NCB. US$3 million was also transferred from a Saudi pension fund (Ruppert 2004, 127). The only response by the Saudi government to the audit was the house arrest of Khalid bin Mahfouz, heir to the NCB, before he sold his shares to the Saudi government in the late 1990s. Deepening the nature of the neoliberal connection in this case was Mahfouz's personal business history. In 1999, it was reported in *USA Today* and the *Boston Herald* that from 1989 Mahfouz had invested in a number of George W. Bush's businesses, including through the secretive US private equity company The Carlyle Group (Ruppert 2004). Both Mahfouz and Bush were also historically implicated in the Bank of Commerce International case, in which the institution was revealed as engaging in extensive unlawful banking practices and hosting the finance of terrorism and organized crime (Ruppert 2004; see also Brisard and Dasquie 2002). For the purposes of this analysis, such connections, and the symbolic (and material) power that disguised them, were signposted in Bin Laden's statement cited in Chapter 3: 'many of America's policies have come under the influence of the Mujahideen … even if our interests overlap with the interests of the major corporations and also with those of the neoconservatives' (Bin Laden 2007).

Charitable sources of funding for AQ from Saudi Arabia also extend to the proceeds of large-scale commercial activity, as revealed during a US and Saudi investigation into the Al Haramain Islamic Foundation, which ceased operation in 2004. Between 2002 and 2004, the US designated 13 Al Haramain offices around the world as providing material support for terrorism, allegedly including funding the 1998 bombings in Kenya and

Tanzania and bankrolling the AQ-affiliate Jemaah Islamiyaah in the 2002 Bali bombings (Bokhari et al. 2014; US Department of the Treasury 2020). The sources of donations to Al Haramain for these purposes included Saudi benefactors with stakes in private industry, such as a wholesale fish business (Rosenberg 2004). In another example, Mustafa Ahmed al-Hasnawi, a Saudi national and contractual Bin Laden 'money man', received US$15,000 from the 9/11 hijackers in unused funds before 11 September 2001, when he was provided with a safe haven by the UAE government following the attacks (Levitt 2002b). Diplomatic and economic arrangements between the UAE and the US, deriving from the UAE's founding membership of the GCC, allegedly meant that Hasnawi was never extradited or tried for his role in 9/11. US government officials have also said that the wealthy Jedda businessman Yasin al-Qadi, who created the Muwafaq Foundation, provided funds to front organisations for Hamas, and that the Foundation has been used internationally to channel millions of dollars to AQ (Levitt 2002b).

There are other powerful individuals in Saudi Arabia who maintain financial and trading interdependencies with the US and who are believed to be sponsors of AQ. Their names appear as 'Golden Chain' donors and beneficiaries, a list seized in a March 2002 raid by Bosnian police on the Benevolence International Foundation (BIF), an organisation designated as supporting terrorism by the US and UN in November 2002. This designation related to evidence from the BIF's Chief Executive Officer Enaam Arnaout's alleged close personal association with Bin Laden from the 1980s, and the BIF's alleged logistical support provided to AQ actors including Mamdouh Mahmud Salim and Mohammed Loay Bayazid. When US District Judge Suzanne Conlon found insufficient evidence for terrorism charges, however, Arnaout pled guilty to using BIF for the purposes of racketeering, chanelling money without donors' consent to Islamist militants in Bosnia, and began a 136-month sentence in 2003 (US Department of the Treasury 2020), which on appeal was lowered to 120 months.

The Golden Chain document is broadly significant in that it indicates neoliberal layering in the region and its impact on AQ's evolution. According to the US Senate's *9/11 Commission Report* (2004), the financiers it lists funded AQ's establishment in Afghanistan in 1996 following the confiscation of Bin Laden's financial assets by Sudan prior to his deportation. This funding contributed to the organisational restructuring of AQ and the political-ideological environment in which Bin Laden's 1996 *Declaration* was written. As discussed in Chapter 3, the *Declaration* (Bin Laden 1996) was published following Bin Laden's interview with Robert Fisk, in which he spoke about his business interests in Sudan and made the first explicit announcement of AQ's intentions for violence against the US.

As a Council on Foreign Relations report highlighted, social and financial ties between individuals listed in the Golden Chain document dated back to Bin Laden and Azzam's fundraising activities during the Afghan–Soviet War (Bruno 2010). These ties might, as such, be taken not only to indicate evidence of development and trade-related layering in the region but a process of 'part–whole doubling' (Clark 2005; Peck 2010) between AQ and its Mujahideen forebears, who were sustained by the US and US-allied governments. Connections between the financial interests of US-affiliated political-economic entities and AQ were once more legitimised and excused via symbolic representational methods. Golden Chain cases also demonstrate that AQ emerged within a political-economic field constituted by US-directed neoliberal intervention. While the petrodollar origins of the funds have been examined elsewhere (Cooper 2012), the commercial capitalist activities and connections of individuals listed on the document, as detailed below, demonstrate that a doxa of expected neoliberal financial relations was widespread in the region.

Individuals named in the Golden Chain document include Bin Laden brothers (though their first names are not given), Adel Batterjee, the founder of BIF; Saleh Abdullah Kamel, the majority shareholder of the Dallah al-Baraka (the third largest commercial entity in Saudi Arabia, based in Jeddah); Saudi billionaire, banker, and philanthropist Suleiman Abdul Aziz al-Rajhi; Khalid bin Mahfouz, though he admitted to contributing only a small amount of money to the Mujahideen in the 1980s; and Wa'el Hamza Julaidan, who was under a UN embargo for terrorism finance from 2002 to 2014 (Brisard 2003; US Department of the Treasury 2004; Illahi 2018). Also named, and one of the few who has not been prosecuted, was Ahmad Turki Zaki Yamani (Illahi 2018), son of a previous Chief Justice of Saudi Arabia, and former Director of Saudi Arabian Oil Company (otherwise known as ARAMCO), former Saudi Minister of Petroleum and Mineral Resources, and the founder of the financial firm Investcorp. In 2017, under the leadership of Crown Prince Mohammed bin Salman, the Saudi government arrested individuals implicated in terrorism and high finance (Kirkpatrick 2017). Whether long-standing regional and international acceptance of US neoliberal connections with GCC energy interests associated with terrorism-financing is reformed, however, remains to be seen.

Businessmen affiliated with Gulf-state allies of the US who are not listed in the Golden Chain document but who have been linked to AQ finance include powerful Qatari nationals close to that country's government. Strategic-economic connections between the business interests of these individuals, their ties to government, and the Qatari government's economic alliance with the US once again might be said to evidence dialectical, mutually financially beneficial relationships between these entities, including specifically in their neoliberal dimensions. Since the 1990–1991 Gulf War, US companies including Mobil, Penzoil, Enron, and Bechtal have had major stakes in the extraction of Qatar's oil and gas reserves (Prados 1999). AQ's benefit from these energy holdings is apparent in its receipt of donations from government-aligned individuals.

One case in which AQ received support from individuals linked to both government and high finance in Qatar concerns the notorious 9/11 coordinator Khalid Sheikh Mohammed, or KSM, who received and channelled funds from Khalifa Muhammad Turki al-Subaiy (a former employee of the state-owned Qatar Central Bank and at the time of writing an employee of the Barwa Group, a real-estate company in Doha) (US Department of the Treasury 2008b). Another pertains to a former employee of Qatar University and President of the Qatar Football Association, Abdulrahman al-Nuaimi, who, according to the US Department of the Treasury, donated large sums of money to AQ in Syria (as Jabhat al-Nusra) during the ongoing civil war (Dorsey 2015); US intelligence agencies in fact alleged that in 2001 al-Nuaimi had sent US$2 million per month to AQ for one year (Al-Arabiya 2017b). Other connections include Abd al-Latif al-Kawari, who worked for Qatar's Ministry of Municipality and Urban Planning, and according to the US Department of the Treasury also 'worked … to coordinate the delivery of funding from Qatari financiers intended to support Al Qaeda and to deliver receipts confirming that al-Qaeda received foreign donor funding from Qatar-based extremists' (US Department of the Treasury 2008a; Al-Arabiya 2017a). There is also Salim Hasan Khalifa Rashid al-Kuwari who was employed by the Qatari Ministry of the Interior until at least 2011, and accused of providing AQ with hundreds of thousands of dollars (US Department of the Treasury 2011a); and, notably, fifty-nine individuals and twelve institutions designated by the UAE, Egypt, Bahrain, and Saudi Arabia as financing terrorism, partly through commercial businesses, while receiving support from the Qatari government (Al Arabiya 2017b).

As Clark (2005) and Anderson (2014) highlight, although this is infrequently reported in mainstream Western news media, discernible organisational connections between the commercial activity of some individuals, US oil lobby groups, and members of national governments correspond to US reliance upon energy reserves mined in and by Qatar, and the fact that US trade with the Qatari government, primarily in Qatari oil, is brokered in US dollars.

Though such connections are often under-reported, the extent and breadth of US connections to suspected financiers of terrorism in Gulf territories has been acknowledged by US politicians beyond Clinton's leaked statements. For example, Joe Biden, Vice President during the

Obama administration and US Presidential candidate at the time of writing, stated in 2013 at Harvard University's Kennedy School of Government that Saudi Arabia and Turkey were 'so determined to take down' the Assad regime in Syria that they 'poured hundreds of millions of dollars and tens of tons of weapons into anyone who would fight against Assad – except that the people who were being supplied were al-Nusra, and al-Qaida, and the extremist elements of jihadis who were coming from other parts of the world', adding: 'we could not convince our colleagues to stop supplying them' (Brull 2017).

Reflecting the Bourdieusian habitus of AQ discussed in Chapter 3, US agents, Gulf-state financiers, and the neo-jihadist organisation itself in effect acted as 'a structuring structure, which organises practices and the perception of practices' (Bourdieu 1984, 170). With the perception of charitable origins and humanitarian destinations for these funds, the practice of acquiring funding from US-affiliated entities was justified for AQ and international spectators of neo-jihadism on symbolic and religious grounds. It was also sanctioned by a doxa of neoliberal relations in the region, under conditions of US political and economic influence.

The international dimension of AQ's fundraising through donations, and its ties to international finance acquired through neoliberal methods, can also be explained by Peck's (2010) contention that political-economic layering takes place in specific geographies characterised by regulatory tendencies favourable to capital accumulation. Further to general US influence in the Middle East, this extends more specifically to the role of neoliberal finance for government-allied 'charitable' entities in the Middle East, facilitated by the US's close political-economic ally the UK. In its presentation of evidence against the Golden Chain, for instance, a 2012 US Senate report revealed alleged money-laundering and terrorism-financing offences committed by the UK bank HSBC. According to the US Senate Committee, HSBC maintained strong ties to the Al Rajhi Bank until 2005, of which Golden Chain member and alleged terrorism financier Sulaiman al-Rajhi was a founder (Permanent Subcommittee on Investigations 2012). This was despite the fact that al-Rajhi's connection to the bank had been reported in mainstream international media, including the *Guardian* and the *Independent*, since 2004, while direct evidence had been heard in government hearings and civil lawsuits since the recovery of the BIF documents in 2002 (Ryle et al. 2015).

Perhaps recalling Stiglitz's famous (2011) doctrine of the 1 per cent, and broader recognition in the twenty-first century of the exacerbation of global wealth inequality (Piketty 2014), in 2012 al-Rajhi was awarded the King Faisal International Prize for donating half of his fortune to charity; this fortune was estimated by *Forbes* to be US$4.7 billion, making him the

120th richest person in the world (Khalife 2017). The estimated total economic capital of those listed in the BIF documents and benefactors close to US-allied regimes, and the amount of funds they hold in HSBC (in 2012 the Al Rajhi bank held US$59 billion) (Lopez 2012), puts each of these individuals among the most prosperous beneficiaries of US petrodollar activity. When considered in relation to the AQ spokesperson Adam Gadahn's petition for AQ supporters to stand up for the 'exploitation of the weak and impoverished' against 'rampant Crusader globalization' (AQIS 2014, 53), the financial constitution and involvement of such entities in terrorism financing indicates a strategic-ideological paradox in the behaviour of AQ. Furthermore, the organisation's dependence on large donations from wealthy US and UK donors demonstrates the nature of the power-and-resistance dialectic in question, where 'those at the bottom ... hang on the arbitrary decision of a power responsible for the "continued creation of their existence"' (Bourdieu 1998b, 99). In this case, extending to the organisation's propagandised narratives, AQ's exploitation of and benefit from US trading activity in the region operates in a reflexive dialectic with the rampant globalisation of hegemonic US economic activity.

Elsewhere in the Middle East, Islamic charities themselves have been accused by the US Department of State of financing AQ-affiliated terrorism. Once more, these examples explicate ideological tension in AQ's donated finance, given its stated rejection of US economic influence, including historical US financial activity. Two high-profile cases include the Global Relief Foundation, based in the US (Jacobson 2010), and Interpal, based in the UK (De Goede 2008). The Commission for the EU froze the assets of the Global Relief Foundation in 2006, and Interpal was accused by the US Department of the Treasury of financing AQ and its affiliates in 2003, though, in part owing to the UK's hesitation to prosecute the company, and a 2003 Charity Commission inquiry that highlighted a lack of evidence brought by US authorities, Interpal continues to operate. The Global Relief Foundation's case was characterised by tangible connections between its Chief Executive Rabih Haddad and AQ, stemming back to the MAK. Interpal's case concerns its alleged provision of support for political violence in the Gaza Strip against Israel (Delmar-Morgan and Osborne 2014). Further to the protection of its economic interests, US opposition to Interpal reflects the religious-fundamentalist tenets of the country's foreign policy, extending to the 'Christian-Zionist' Congressional alliance discussed in Chapter 2, and US President Donald Trump's 2017 designation of Jerusalem as the capital of Israel (Tawfik 2017). Such cases might be said to indicate 'religious-economic' recursivity between AQ and its US-directed neoliberal opposition.

The involvement of wealthy fundamentalist-religious entities is not the only means by which financiers have facilitated transfers of public funds to AQ. Indicating the importance of symbolic power in facilitating AQ's fundraising, in several cases non-government organisations and Islamic charities that were not specifically established for the purpose of terrorist financing were infiltrated and influenced by supporters of AQ through a manipulation of *zakat* (Byman 2015) and *sadaqah*. While the Islamic tradition of *zakat* stipulates that 2.5 per cent of a Muslim person's wealth should be donated to charity, voluntary charitable giving, *sadaqah*, is not obligatory but is encouraged culturally (Atwan 2008). Supporters of AQ have exploited these traditions, petitioning imams sympathetic to AQ's cause to collect *zakat* and *sadaqah* from Islamic congregations, which are then channelled through religious charities and donated to AQ. At other times, imams have been misinformed that the money was not destined for AQ (Moghadam 2008).

Although AQ has infiltrated and exploited charities throughout its history, and this source of funding was important for AQ in the 1990s, terrorism financing was heavily policed and regulated by the US in the aftermath of 9/11. As the American Civil Liberties Union (ACLU) high-lighted, however, in many cases where charities were prosecuted and pursued via provisions in the Patriot Act, convictions of 'terrorist financing entities' failed or were overturned due to insufficient evidence (Deflem and McDonough 2015). Several of the previously discussed wealthy individuals who were alleged to control or contribute to flows of finance to AQ went unprosecuted, in part because a primary target of investigation following 9/11 existed outside the formal international financial system in forms of alternative remittance.

The following discussion, building on the previous analysis of the doxa of normalised and tolerated financial connections between AQ and US-aligned states and individuals in the Middle East, explores how high-profile US counterterrorist financing targeting of alternative remittance systems has allowed material networks implicating AQ in neoliberal systems of high finance to continue relatively unrestricted.

Alternative remittance systems

In targeting alternative remittance, neoliberal actors ensured that broader financial systems often went unimpeded and that powerful and wealthy actors were unpursued and unprosecuted by counterterrorist financing efforts. This targeting was justified in part by counterterrorism strategists who emphasised that donations to AQ through charities and on the part of wealthy benefactors are often at one point in the transfer process facilitated by alternative remittance (Levitt and Jacobson 2010). This has been the case because alternative remittance companies and their systems exist outside of or are peripherally integrated into the formal international financial system, such that they leave minimal transaction paper trails and are therefore very difficult to monitor. The relationship between neoliberal elites in the international system and the agents of alternative remittance is hereby 'performative' (Castañeda 2010), to the extent that 'it produces the effect that it names' (Amoore and De Goede 2008, 9). By attributing blame for terrorism financing to alternative remittance companies, neoliberal economic authorities whose purview is traditionally the international financial system dictate performatively to these companies what services they should provide and how they should behave. The nature of this risk-based targeting corresponds, in turn, to a causative dimension of the dialectical engagements that exist between neo-jihadism, in its recruitment efforts, and the behaviour of neoliberal companies and nation states. The targeting through US-led counterterrorist financing measures of LDCs that rely on alternative remittance has at times produced the very disaster situations in which terrorism is often generated (Klein 2007).

Building on the previous discussion of neoliberal reasoning, Bourdieu's understanding of a 'theory effect' is useful in explaining performativity in US counterterrorist actions towards neo-jihadist targets. Defined by Bourdieu as 'the words, the names, which construct social reality as much as they express it' (1989, 21), the theory effect in particular characterises the criminogenic and otherwise harmful social effects of powerful actors designating low socio-economic status populations, who may often be reliant on alternative remittance systems, as risky.

Reflecting neoliberalism's contradictory engagements with philosophical notions of 'modernity', proponents of counterterrorist financing policies with neoliberal agendas have the power, through the effect of remittance theories, to make pseudo-scientific predictions that generate pre-ordained economic outcomes (Springer 2015). Just as communicating 'expertise' about financial systems by promoting neo-classical macroeconomic theories enables powerful actors to reaffirm the inevitability of neoliberalism as a doxa and reinforce its perceived relevance, remittance systems become counterproductively co-opted by neoliberal authorities as part of a 'neoliberal developmental discourse' (Castañeda 2010, 22; see also Ong 2006). As outlined in Ostry et al.'s (2016) report for the IMF, this discourse has historically dismissed the role of IFIs in creating deleterious socio-economic outcomes for targeted populations, and transferred accountability for the development of LDCs to the disadvantaged populations in question, as 'rational' economic agents (Bourdieu 1998b, 20). It has also served to resource conflict situations, drawing as it does on the neoliberal principles of open markets, responsibilisation, and individualisation (see also De Goede 2003).

As we have seen, due to their separation from the international financial system, and usage by some politically violent actors, remittance systems are often deemed legitimate targets by neoliberal actors who seek to avoid undermining confidence in formal streams of international finance. This was apparent after 9/11, when *hawala* systems, meaning 'transfer' in Arabic, were publicly associated with neo-jihadist terrorism. In Maryam Razavy's explanation:

> An example of a contemporary hawala transfer might look like the following: the hawala agent takes the money from a client (together with a commission fee of roughly 5 percent) and gives the client a code, which is often a random word or phrase from the Koran. The intermediary then contacts one of his partners in the area where the funds are destined and notifies the dealer there of the code as well as the amount being transferred. The receiving agent of the fund then contacts the hawala dealer in his area, and having passed on the code, accepts the payment. At this time, all parties destroy any paper records indicating codes or monetary amounts (less often parties may retain a paper record, but it is in a code that only the dealer will understand), leaving no paper-trail of the transactions. (2005, 279)

From 1996 until 2001, during which time AQ Central principally operated out of Afghanistan, there were scant alternatives apart from *hawala* systems for the organisation to access funding. This was due to a lack of financial infrastructure in the country and residents' lack of access to formal banking, despite the existence of social and physical networks facilitating transfers of money, dating to the MAK in the 1980s (Schweitzer and Oreg 2014). The use of *hawala* by AQ and some militant Islamist entities since this time has also been relatively prevalent in the Indian Subcontinent, Southeast Asia, and Africa (Tomolya and White 2015). As part of the neoliberal co-optation of alternative remittance, on the other hand, these systems were also extensively used beyond AQ to deliver much needed aid to LDCs. From 1986, for example, the *hawala* organisation Al Barakaat facilitated transfers of money into Somalia, with even the UN using it to deliver aid (Roth et al. 2004, 67). On 7 November 2001, under provisions of the Patriot Act, and in response to Federal Bureau of Investigation (FBI) speculation that Al Barakaat had ties to AQ that went as far back as the US presence in Somalia during the 1992–1994 Operation Restore Hope, the US government froze the assets of all Al Barakaat offices in the US and pressured other countries around the world to follow suit. Although in 2002 Al Barakaat was absolved of any connection with AQ, asset seizures forced the company into bank-ruptcy and provoked an economic crisis in Somalia (Passas 2006). In the following decade, the AQ-allied Somalian organisation Al Shabaab became a prominent presence in the country.

Further to their harmful impacts on basic services provision and development, US-led actions in targeting remittance served to redirect attention away from US energy and trading partners, who remained a significant source of support for AQ, to the end-scale recipients of remittance finance in LDCs. Despite a lack of evidence implicating some remittance networks in terrorism financing, at times they were reasonably interpreted as important for AQ and other organisations' access to money. Afghanistan's largest *hawala* network, The New Ansari Exchange, was under investigation in January 2010, for exam-ple, for its facilitation of the transfer of proceeds from the country's opium trade to the Taliban and AQ (US Department of the Treasury 2011b). Despite Bin Laden's alleged historical donations to Al Barakaat, however, most of its assets were unfrozen from UN sanction interna-tionally, and domestically in the US, after US-based Al Barakaat money remitters challenged the government action of seizing its books and freezing its assets (Roth et al. 2004).

While such examples signify AQ's possible usage of *hawala* networks to *move* money, they do not account for the origins of funds that reached the organisation. Moreover, the difference between alternative remittance systems and neoliberal institutions (such as banks) does not necessarily indicate empirical separation or an absence of dialectical connections. Rather, remittance systems are often co-opted and targeted by neoliberal entities by virtue of the fact that they remain relatively unintegrated into mainstream flows of economic capital. The importance of remittance sys-tems such as *hawala* for the success of AQ finance should thus be criti-cally considered in light of the broader neoliberal field in which financing for terrorism and political violence occurs. The origins of funding for AQ have historically not been related to grass-roots economic activity in LDCs but, rather, have corresponded primarily to donations from wealthy individuals and the exploitation of financial networks tied to old trading routes and weapons smuggling, as well as financial partnerships between the US, AQ, and wealthy individuals and nation states.

With an awareness of the role of remittance systems for facilitating transfers of proceeds to AQ from licit and illicit financial activity, the next section of this chapter explores AQ's broader engagement in inter-national commerce. Specifically, it focuses on how AQ participated in commercial activity constituted by financial mechanisms and managerial measures available in neoliberal environments.

Commercial activity

AQ has profited in many ways from international flows of commerce. Adding credence to Burke's (2004) (and Mossad's) description of the organisation as 'jihadi international', its business interests are facilitated by the neoliberal architecture of the international financial system, including its deregulatory economic environments and commercial capitalist financial apparatus. AQ's commercial activity can be understood to echo Bourdieu's explanation that neoliberalism, as a new kind of 'conservative revolution', is governed by the 'law of the market':

> It ratifies and glorifies the reign of what are called the financial markets, in other words the return to a kind of radical capitalism, with no other law than that of maximum profit, an unfettered capitalism without any disguise, but rationalized, pushed to the limit of its economic efficacy by the introduction of modern forms of domination, such as 'business administration', and techniques of manipulation, such as market research and advertising.
> (Bourdieu 1998b, 35)

In this state of affairs, AQ's expression of habitus is constituted by its engagement with neoliberal finance, extending to commercial, business activity, while it is supported by a doxa in which widespread usage of late modern capitalist mechanisms is accepted as self-evident. Its own neo-jihadist 'radicalism' is here in certain respects reflective of fundamentalist neoliberal approaches to social policy, explored in Chapter 2 through reference to high-profile international cases.

The decentralised and de-territorial characteristics of AQ's commercial activity might also again be interpreted with reference to Jessop's (2006, 168) assertion that 'capitalist', as opposed to 'territorial', entities are concerned with the 'geo-economics of capital flows, emergent spatial monopolies' and the 'production of new scales'. Differing from the territoriality of IS, which is discussed in the following chapter, in its commercial activity AQ exploits the 'uneven geographical conditions' and 'asymmetries' (Jessop 2006, 158) of diverse political-economic settings. These include environments characterised by lax regulation and taxation favourable to neoliberal business, which collectively extend the possibilities for perpetual capital accumulation (Harvey 2003; Peck 2010). AQ's management of finance within these environments, moreover, demonstrates its dialectical, mutually beneficial relationship with the broader systems of neoliberal finance it purports to oppose and resist. AQ's 'rhizomatic' orientation (Deleuze and Guattari 1988), including its decentralised leadership and governance, is in many ways comparable with the organisational structure of neoliberal businesses (Venn 2009). This is first apparent in its outsourcing of commercial activity from which it would benefit.

One case of AQ's commercial outsourcing was highlighted in testimony from UN representatives that Al Itihaad al Islamiyah, an Islamist militant organisation that sought to overthrow the Somalian government, was affiliated with AQ while it collected money for AQ, cooperated on the terrorist bombings in Somalia and Ethiopia, and established training centres for AQ recruits (Loewenstein 2010). Al Itihaad's commercial activity included the operation of coal mines transporting output to the Middle East, the provision of telecommunications, protection, and security services, the integrated operation of alternative remittance systems, agricultural, and hospitality investments, and the distribution of fishing rights. Through the modern capitalist financial practice of price fixing, Al Itihaad held monopolies on a number of these services and used its position to engineer large profit margins by manipulating supply and demand (UN 2006; Del Cid Gómez 2010). As US and UK firms did in the Middle East and elsewhere after 9/11, AQ might be said to have benefited intrinsically from a co-occurring market and religious fundamentalism within a field of neoliberal industry.

Other cases of outsourcing associated with AQ extended to smaller operations. In one situation, a senior FBI official revealed that a plumbing and construction company run by members of an AQ cell in Europe provided funds to hire 'Mujahideen' to fight in conflict areas, including in Bosnia (Levitt 2002c). Cell members then engaged in money-laundering practices made possible by neoliberal characteristics of the EU banking system. In addition to proceeds from a business buying, fixing, and reselling used cars, they would deposit licit 'salaries, government subsidies, supplemental income from family members, and funds received by cash or wire transfer into the same one or two accounts' and use these funds to coordinate activities under the name of AQ (Levitt 2002c).

As will be discussed in Chapter 6 in relation to IS, examples of outsourced financial activity signify neo-jihadist organisations' regular co-opting of diverse economic and military actors. Moreover, this aspect of contemporary neo-jihadism might be critically considered in light of the US government's historical employment of private military companies and mercenaries (Singer 2007). As they were for the US, such practices were strategically important for AQ in protecting organisational leaders and ensuring that branches (or franchises), cells, and supporters of the organisation had the means to act independently, as others may have for IS from 2020. Extending the earlier discussion of symbolic violence on the part of AQ, these cases indicate the organisation's direct financial benefit from commercial partnerships made possible by opaque reporting requirements in neoliberal financial environments.

Further to its benefit from outsourced activity, licit and illicit commerce was integral to the symbolic heart and origins of AQ. As discussed in Chapter 3, Bin Laden himself had a history of large-scale investment in commercial industries, and during his time as AQ leader he used this expertise to establish fronts, networks, and governance infrastructure that would provide for AQ's entry into legitimate banking systems (Basile 2004). Although early speculations that Bin Laden's personal wealth was immense and that he used early private businesses to siphon cash to AQ have been disputed (De Goede 2003), he does appear to have maintained a number of offices in business centres such as London and held a number of incorporated entities that provided finance for AQ (Atwan 2013). The *New York Times*, for instance, reported Bin Laden's ownership of a series of honey outlets throughout the Middle East and Pakistan, the revenue from and transport infrastructure for which was used to facilitate the transfer of money and weapons to AQ (Miller and Gerth 2001). As indicated in Bin Laden's interview with Robert Fisk in 1993, owing to his overriding business interests in Sudan he did not outwardly prioritise violent jihad during the nascent stages of AQ's development and was known to have lived a life of affluence and luxury in his youth (Bodansky 2011).

Where Bin Laden's private financial activity in Sudan prior to AQ's movement into Afghanistan did pertain to the organisation, it indicates the extent of its reliance upon neoliberal public–private partnerships in the region. From the time of his arrival in Sudan from Afghanistan, in 1991, Bin Laden opened several businesses, including the construction and farming businesses of Al Hajira and Wadi al-Aqiq. According to Gutbi el-Mahdi, the country's former head of intelligence services, his initial investment in Sudan through formal banking networks was around UK£10 million (Astill 2001). Owing to these connections, and in response to AQ's bombing of the USS Cole less than one year prior to 9/11, fifteen injured sailors and three surviving spouses of deceased victims of the attack lodged a 2010 federal lawsuit against the Republic of Sudan, alleging that the government in effect provided funding and training for AQ prior to the attack. They sought remuneration from the government and Sudanese banks, and in 2017 the US federal appeals court ordered Sudan to pay US$2.1 billion in damages to the families of the victims (Wilson 2017).

Also indicating AQ's dependence on institutions of high finance was its management of proceeds from licit and illicit commercial activities using neoliberal financial mechanisms, such as tax evasion and the concealment of ownership and financial holdings. In several cases, AQ representatives established fictitious, offshore fiduciary 'shell' companies to conceal the origins, purpose, and destinations of funds, typically in the form of international business corporations (IBCs). As Juan Del Cid Gómez (2010) observed regarding AQ's strategic ambition, IBCs are suitable for AQ's purposes, given that they typically have 'complex financial structures' that 'can be established using bearer shares', and do not have a legal obligation to make information about their accounts publicly available. Local residents and managers of the accounts can also act as directors, effectively concealing the legal identity of the entities that dictate business behaviour (Mirowski 2013). Though this activity was probably justified for AQ by the neo-jihadist philosophy that behaving in a 'sacrilegious' way, from their perspective, is acceptable for the purposes of engaging in what they argue to be a holy war (Ignatieff 2004), the use of offshoring, the financialisation of the money trail, and the obfuscatory mechanisms designed to conceal the origins and destinations of AQ funds were arguably neoliberal in their design.

The practices of financialisation and offshoring might be said to recall and resemble the neoliberal behaviour of investing in tax havens and evading financial regulations frequently practised by transnational corporations and the wealthy elite of the US, UK, and elsewhere. While this activity has been widespread for some time, notorious cases were highlighted by document leaks known as the Panama Papers and Paradise Papers (Tombs 2016; Poynting and Whyte 2017). Not only did the managerial measures used to transfer and store capital enable proprietors in these cases to avoid regulation and tax, they perpetuated an environment in which illegal activities associated with the funds, such as human trafficking and drug trading, were concealed from regulatory authorities (Saviano 2017).

As Del Cid Gómez (2010) highlighted, the 'Fiscalia' of the High Court in Spain revealed one case in which AQ's fiduciary management of funds resembled the investments of transnational corporations. According to the Court, a group previously known as the Salafist Group for Preaching and Combat, which was subsequently absorbed into Al Qaeda in the Islamic Maghreb (AQIM), used companies located in tax havens in Delaware and the Bahamas that were either in the process of liquidation or inactive to send money to AQ fighters in Syria and Algeria (Del Cid Gómez 2010). The investigation revealed that more than US$200,000 was transferred by an Algerian citizen in Spain who held accounts in Palma de Mallorca, in the name of a US company based in Delaware, for the alleged purposes of paying an invoice for information-technology services from a company based in the Netherlands and Germany. The company denied issuing the invoices, casting into question the legitimacy of the reported transaction. The money trail indicated that the funds subsequently travelled to Syria and Algeria to fund fighting in these areas through AQ front men (Del Cid Gómez 2010). While indicative of the international, decentralised scale of AQ's financial activity, this case also illustrates the complex nature of the financial assets with which its violent acts are facilitated. Moreover, AQ's endorsement of these assets might be said once more to contradict its propagandised condemnation of financialised high finance, including AQ commentary on the conditions that preceded the 2008 GFC.

Insofar as actions associated with AQ were not directed by its centralised governance and funded from the branches of organisational coffers, as was the case with Al Itihaad, independent cells and individuals financed their activities by means that were in other ways intersectional with the neoliberal instruments of international finance. Although there are many examples of this, the bombings on the London underground on the 7 July 2005 (7/7) and the *Charlie Hebdo* attacks in Paris in 2015 are particularly illustrative. A UK House of Commons inquiry revealed that although the perpetrators of the bombings were initially trained by AQ Central in Pakistan, they were funded by credit-based products of the international financial system. After working in London for three years in full-time employment, Mohammad Sidique Khan financed the attacks using money obtained from credit cards and loan overdrafts (UK House of Commons 2006). Cherif Kouachi, one of the perpetrators of the 2015 shooting at the French satirical magazine *Charlie Hebdo*, which left 12 people dead, told BFM-TV while in hiding following the event that Al Qaeda of Yemen (AQY) via Anwar al Awlaki had provided resources for the attack (Rayner 2015). Though this, and Al Qaeda in the Arabian Peninsula's (AQAP) tactical support for the attack has not been verified, Said Kouachi, Cherif's brother, is widely thought to have received weapons training in Yemen (Al Jazeera 2015) – and the attack is alleged to have been financed by a EUR6000 consumer loan, the proceeds of a car sale, and 'cash transfers linked to the sale of counterfeit goods' (FATF 2015a, 11). To the extent to which AQY resourced or in other ways provided support for the attack, it is also relevant that this AQ branch has a long history of profiting from oil smuggling in the region (Browning et al. 2016). Indeed, the international and decentralised nature of both cases demonstrates how AQ's layered political-economic history, both materially and ideologically, is intersectional with neoliberal interventions, while it relies upon neoliberal debt-based monetary mechanisms.

Perhaps in light of connections between AQ, US-allied actors, and institutions of high finance, including relationships with Gulf states and the Cold War origins of AQ, there has been concerted effort on the part of US governments to downplay the organisation's integration into the international financial system. This has been evident not only in the ongoing US targeting of alternative remittance systems and neglect of the ultimate origins of funding sources, but also in the counterterrorist financing measures adopted by the US after AQ's move to Afghanistan in 1996 (see, for example, Roth et al. 2004). Despite these efforts, AQ's separation from the formal economy has been contested by prominent terrorism academics (Basile 2004; Mishal and Rosenthal 2005; Gurulé 2010). Loretta Napoleoni (2004), an expert on AQ finance, notes that in addition to its licit financial activity, illicit practices AQ uses to garner funds have included kidnapping, extortion, and the sale of drugs, the proceeds of which were laundered and processed in recognised banking systems. It has also been widely noted that AQ historically maintained strong financial ties with the Taliban and that the two have jointly been involved in weapons- and heroin-smuggling. The United Nations Office of Drugs and Crime (UNODC) estimated in 2011 that 83 per cent of the international opiate share derived from the AQ, Taliban, and allied drug trafficking in Afghanistan, constituting a US$61 billion market (FATF 2014). Bearing in mind AQ's political ties in the region, association between the Taliban and the US further indicates how mutually beneficial financial partnerships remain prevalent between US and AQ actors.

Such evidence of political-economic connections between the US and the Taliban is apparent in their history of mutual support, dating back to the Afghan–Soviet War and meetings between Taliban representatives and US energy companies. The best known of these after the Cold War occurred in Sugarland, Texas in 1997 between the Taliban and a US-based company, UNOCAL (Bezhan 2020). The meeting was part of UNOCAL's efforts to outbid an Argentinian firm, Bridas, for the rights to construct a gas pipeline from Turkmenistan through Afghanistan and into Pakistan (Williams 2004, 86). Indicating the strategic importance of such connections, some have speculated that money from AQ's narcotics trade with the Taliban in Afghanistan and Pakistan was used to fund AQ attacks (Hamm 2007; Peters 2009). Although these assertions have been contested by US governments (Roth et al. 2004), the case of *Charlie Hebdo* provides a useful illustration of associations between AQ's on-the-ground attacks and neoliberal institutions of high finance that have strategic partnerships with the US. In this case, in contrast with the FATF's citation of the Kouachi brothers' independent fundraising activity (FATF 2015a), it has been alleged that in addition to AQY's supposed training of Said Kouachi, AQAP wired the perpetrators US$20,000 to finance the attack (Clarke 2016). In any case, the former possibility would illustrate the perpetrators' exploitation of formal banking channels and usage of debt-based apparatus from banks, while the latter would illustrate the attackers' connection to an international drug trade, coordinated by AQ and the Taliban.

Aside from its large-scale fundraising and exploitation of neoliberal environments for the purposes of facilitating attacks, in its ongoing, day-to-day operations AQ actors make significant use of consumer capitalist technological products available in late modern, neoliberal settings. Such products are used by AQ, for instance, to finance wages and the maintenance of AQ members and their families. Del Cid Gómez (2010) explained how in one case AQ used pre-paid mobile-telephone cards to transfer cash internationally; and, according to Interpol, AQ profited from criminal activity related to intellectual property (Moneyval 2008). A transnational investigation by Denmark, UK, and US law-enforcement agencies revealed, among other things, that an AQ member sent counterfeit goods from Dubai to Denmark, including shampoos, creams, cologne, and perfume (Elias 2004). It has also been demonstrated that AQ raised funds through tax fraud in Italy, financial crimes in Switzerland, and the theft of credit cards and digital credit-card details (Del Cid Gómez 2010). As Rukmini Callimachi (2014) notes, kidnapping ransoms paid to AQ by the governments of western European countries also result in a circumstance whereby these states 'inadvertently act as underwriters' to AQ. AQ's small- and large-scale fundraising and financial expenditure in this manner demonstrate how a field constituted by conditions of neoliberalism has created opportunities for the organisation to benefit significantly from both existing financial structures and organised crime, contravening AQ's outward petition for its supporters to boycott US finance.

One final example of AQ's illicit management of funding garnered through a variety of means within the international financial system highlights how the system itself is foundational to AQ's financial governance strategy. The Al Taqwa Trade, Property and Industry Company Limited allegedly provided significant assistance to AQ in the 1990s (Baker 2005). Although in 2010 Al Taqwa was removed from the UN's 'Al Qaida entities' list, counterterrorist financing strategists over the years have cited the bank in connection with AQ (Levitt 2002a). They highlight that six members of the Bin Laden family are contributors to the Bahama branch, while Ahmad Huber, the director of the bank, displays a portrait of Bin Laden (next to one of Adolf Hitler) in his office. In January 2001, Huber was quoted as saying that AQ leaders are 'very discreet, well-educated and very intelligent people' (Baker 2005).

On a technical level, the complex financial structure of Huber's bank and its incorporation in Liechtenstein mean that the neoliberal managerial mechanisms of money laundering, tax evasion, and opaque fiduciary relationships are at the core of its business model. As Raymond Baker, the author of *Capitalism's Achilles heel* (2005), notes, the financial infrastructure to facilitate activity such as Al Taqwa's was not created by AQ or other entities who were its beneficiaries; the architecture that enables the practices of tax evasion, money laundering, and the usage of complex financialised entities was already in place. As discussed in Chapter 2, mechanisms of deregulation, privatisation, and financialisation are protected and prevalent in neoliberal policy environments and in US-led international banking systems. At the least, AQ built its model of financial governance off the back of long-standing expectations and operations within conditions of late modern finance, exploiting as it did so a history of neoliberal layering.

Although the magnitude of AQ's involvement in legal and illegal activities and the exact scale of the resources accumulated through such activities is difficult to quantify, in 2009 Financial Action Task Force (FATF) experts estimated that more than roughly 3.6 per cent of global GDP represented proceeds of crime, and roughly 2.7 per cent of global GDP (at that time US$1.6 trillion) represented laundered capital (FATF 2009). Given this, it is probable that AQ-affiliated entities' financial activity constitutes a measurable percentage of economic capital in the global financial system. This is also likely to be the case given AQ's decentralised structure, its inherent transnational orientation, and the fact that entities with limited tangible connections to Bin Laden, Zawahiri, or other 'official' organisers of AQ can in the eyes of international politicians and news media claim the 'Al Qaeda name' (Heath-Kelly 2013; Jackson 2018). With this situation in mind, and given their association with AQ Central in international governments' policy statements, it is reasonable to conclude that such entities might be interpreted as AQ-affiliated financial actors.

Indeed, despite AQ's changing organisational structure over time, examples in this chapter demonstrate that the organisation has had ongoing and variegated engagements with the international financial system, including some cases with discernible neoliberal dimensions. These include financial partnerships with government-sponsored entities, neoliberal financial managerial measures, and a reliance upon the neoliberal affordances of the international financial system to manage and conduct licit and illicit commercial activity. AQ's offshoring and broader reliance upon the international economic apparatus of high finance also demonstrate that, reflecting its shifting (de-)territorial interests over time, AQ's commercial activities have corresponded to its geo-economic orientation.

Drawing on these insights, in particular AQ's reliance upon donations and commercial activity, its integration into legitimate banking networks, and its intermediary usage of alternative remittance systems, in the final section of this chapter I explore evidence of tension between AQ's political-economic propaganda and its financial practices. An overview is provided of the precepts of Islamic finance that organisations such as AQ and IS profess to observe and which run counter to neoliberal philosophies, policies, and practices.

Islamic finance

Three primary surface-level contradictions between sharia banking, or Islamic finance, and the policies and precepts of neoliberalism are directly apparent. In different respects, they each derive from an order of Islamic finance that prohibits the institution of interest, referred to in the Qur'an and Hadith as *riba*. There has, though, been some contention as to what constitutes *riba* in the religious context. Some have asserted that it refers to usury charged by crash-finance lenders and not to more moderate interest charged by official banks, while others have argued that interest (although not *riba*) is allowed in sharia banking when it derives or occurs in conjunction with mutually profitable investment (Roy 1994; Khan 2013). Historically, the principle of *riba* has been understood as interchangeable with all forms of monetary interest that are prohibited in Islamic finance.

The first primary rule of Islamic finance that contrasts with neoliberal financialisation is that money not linked to a material asset is not permitted to generate more money. According to this rule, only exchanges of tangible goods and services should yield a profit. Money loaned from one entity to another must therefore not generate interest for one party and accordingly should not produce disadvantage for the other (Khan and Masih 2014). Given that the majority of international banks and other financial institutions that AQ has shared ties with rely on profits accrued through the exchange of interest, its activity in this regard contradicts a key dimension of Islamic finance. This is despite the fact that some banks have, since the 1990s, developed Islamic finance sections, as AQ's interest in explicitly monetarist and financialised tenets of high finance evinces 'non-Islamic' examples of neoliberalism.

The second rule in Islamic finance that is inconsistent with the financialising tendencies of neoliberalism, extending to AQ's commercial management of finance, is *gharar*, the proscription of high levels of risk in financial investment. According to this principle, all known risks must be disclosed to the investor by the broker and only absolutely necessary risks may be taken (Chapra 2008). The result of this rule, in conjunction with the prohibition of interest, is that Islamic banking institutions should not invest in financial products such as derivatives or bundled debt packages (Hasan and Didri 2010), which were characteristic of the neoliberal conditions that led to the GFC.

The third principle of Islamic finance antithetical to neoliberalism is that one should invest only in ethical causes and projects. According to Islamic finance tenets, investment in what are considered unethical projects such as weapons, pornography, and gambling are strictly prohibited (Khan 2013). This has several implications for the subjects under focus here. It clearly contradicts AQ and IS's investment in and ownership of weapons (including their usage of weapons to stage attacks and their participation in weapons-smuggling rings (Sanderson 2004; Weiss and Hassan 2016)), and it might also be considered in relation to US military–industrial interests and the country's privatised outsourcing of military activity in the Middle East. The growth of the military–industrial complex in the Syrian and Iraqi region and insurgent organisations' access to related weapons production have been a central focus of Western counterterrorist entities, from the CIA's arming of AQ against the Soviet invasion of Afghanistan (Byman 2003) to the US arming of IS-linked forces in Syria from 2011 (Barrett 2014). Financial investment in weapons and the related privatisation of military apparatus on the part of IS and AQ, as on the part of US counterterrorist and military entities, are inconsistent with the guiding ethical principle of Islamic finance.

While certain pillars of Islamic finance, including *mudaraba* and *musharaka* partnerships, do operate within and approve some late modern capitalist, neoliberal behaviours, these are less relevant to this book's research interest in tension and underlying socio-structural connections between AQ and IS's propaganda and their financial practices. The other practices I have examined indicate to a greater degree evidence of discordance between spoken and performed neo-jihadist expressions of habitus. They show that, although neo-jihadist organisations such as AQ profess to oppose US-led capitalism and to observe religious guidance, they are in fact constituted in and via these neoliberal environments.

Through cases and examples, this chapter demonstrated that AQ's organisational model has historically been sustained by its reliance upon financial systems, networks, and practices that can be described as neoliberal. Drawing on Bourdieu's analytical framework, these cases reveal two primary political-economic dynamics in AQ's habitus tendencies: first, the organisation's fundraising through US economic partnerships and the global political economy, such that it is in effect materially reliant upon neoliberal dimensions of this economy for its financial survival; and, second, financial activity on the part of AQ actors that reflects and resembles those of the neoliberal, commercial entities they profess to oppose and resist. Indicating the correlation between AQ propaganda and finance, as Bloom highlights, 'the discipline of the market is matched with a "safe" discursive history of power and resistance' (2016, 135).

AQ's dialectical relationship with the US has therefore persisted, despite its usage of alternative remittance. It is also in part by preferentially and somewhat exclusively targeting alternative remittance systems that proponents and protectors of neoliberal financial networks have allowed international capital flows, which also sustain AQ, to continue relatively unchecked. While the application of Bourdieu's ideas helped to demonstrate the performative nature of this situation, it also showed that a dialectic between strategically opposed actors arises from the imposition of 'rational' political-economic decision-making, while the political-economic habitus of AQ is sustained by its relationship with the field of neoliberalism in which it operates. When considered in relation to the earlier discussions of neo-jihadist propaganda, this state of affairs reinforces the interrelationship between AQ's social, political, and symbolic capital, and its engagement with an ideological doxa in which the economic capital characteristics of neoliberalism are expected, normalised, and tolerated.

Drawing on Peck's (2010) and Jessop's (2006) theories, this chapter also highlighted that certain financial characteristics of AQ are reflective of the organisation's decentralised political orientation and have been empirically intersectional with political-economic activities of US-directed entities from the Cold War until 2020, almost two decades after 9/11 (later historical examples of terrorism finance are examined with more rigour in Chapter 6). AQ's activities derive from the MAK's provision of funds for combat in the Afghan–Soviet War, right through to its contemporary trading in narcotics and financial ties to insurgent groups in East Africa, the Middle East, Southeast Asia, and the Indian Subcontinent. Moreover, the contradiction between the proposed designation of AQ funding for charitable, humanitarian activities and its real usage to support political violence indicates how AQ's behaviour is at odds with key precepts of Islamic finance. Other surface-level contradictions include AQ's general reliance upon donations from the proceeds of an interest-based, US-led petrodollar system, contravening the Islamic prohibition on *riba*, and upon the investment yields of licit and illicit commercial financial activity. Collectively, AQ finance might in several ways also be said to contravene Islamic finance's proscription of risk, the financialisation of economic capital, and profits garnered through risky financial practices and the generation of profit through interest.

The collective application of cases and theory revealed that the dialectic between AQ finance and US-directed neoliberalism has entailed elements of causation, reflexivity, and mirroring. Where causation is evident in Mujahideen, MAK, Taliban, and Cold War connections with AQ, reflexivity emerges in AQ and US-allied entities' mutual reliance upon the formal international financial system. Financial connections were demonstrated to exist between wealthy Gulf-state benefactors of major US energy industries and AQ, particularly in Qatar, the UAE, and Saudi Arabia. AQ's usage of offshore fiduciary accounts and its investment in tax havens also indicate mirroring between AQ and late modern capitalist corporations. Although the origins of AQ funds are sometimes obscured through symbolic means, the organisation is very much a part of the international financial system it condemns.

Extending this investigation, in the following chapter I explore how, differing from the financial practices of AQ, those of IS have in large part entailed its reliance upon centralised, territorial control of resources, and its geopolitical orientation. In comparison with the relatively de-territorialised financial behaviour of AQ, the analysis reflects on how IS differentially and dialectically interacts with political-economic environments and practices that can be described as neoliberal.

6

Islamic State's financial practices

Significant effort has been dedicated to defining the organisational identity and behaviour of IS since its emergence in 2013. Some have argued that IS is a religiously motivated terrorist group (McCants 2015; Stern and Berger 2015), and others emphasise its continuity with the modern and technologised aspects of contemporary political movements (Armstrong 2014). As highlighted in the Introduction, in light of their institutional arrangements and quasi-capitalist financial practices, IS and AQ for some resemble modern post-industrial corporations (Gray 2003; Daragahi and Solomon 2014). While there has been a lack of in-depth investigation of aspects of neo-jihadism that interact with, reflect, and in some cases embody characteristics of neoliberalism, some research has broadly investigated ubiquitous ideological and material conditions that have in various measures become part of neo-jihadism. There is, for example, a relative consensus that from its June 2014 declaration of a Caliphate until 2017 IS relied upon its acquisition and retention of territory to self-finance (Lister 2014; Solomon et al. 2016). In response to its extensive exploitation of the oil and gas trade in the Middle East, and its dependence on the dominance of the US dollar, Nafeez Ahmed (2015) presciently described IS as the 'cancer of modern capitalism'. Owing to its declaration of a Caliphate, paramilitary operations, and state-building practices, IS was until 2017 sometimes described as a quasi-nation state (Cronin 2015), in contrast to the widely recognised networked and global geo-economic orientation of AQ.

Building upon these existing explanations of neo-jihadism, in this chapter I illustrate that a political-economic interpretation of IS can account in a holistic way for its multidimensional organisational characteristics. Through a lens of neo-Marxist commentary on political economy, and drawing on Bourdieusian theory, this chapter seeks to develop an empirically grounded interpretation of IS, focusing on its dialectical engagements with the political-economic paradigm of neoliberalism and its US-directed military and counterterrorist opposition.

In five sections the chapter investigates key IS fundraising and financial governance practices from 2014 to 2017, paying attention to their neo-liberal dimensions. Before commencing an empirical analysis, it provides an overview of US-directed interventions in Iraq and the political-economic foundations upon which subsequent neoliberal 'layering' (Peck 2010), prior to and after the emergence of IS, took place. Following this, cases of IS finance are analysed for their neoliberal features through a neo-Marxist lens and in relation to the political-economic frame outlined in Chapters 1 and 2. Different examples pertain to IS's engagement with financial institutions, its oil and gas interests, exploitation of natural resources in the region, and its administration of finance in managing the Caliphate at its peak between 2014 and 2017, prior to the eventual dissolution of the Caliphate in 2019. Continuing the discussion of AQ finance in Chapter 5, the final section of the chapter considers how financial practices on the part of IS contradict core principles of Islamic finance.

Contradictions between IS's financial practices, its claims of religious precedent, and its anti-US and anti-capitalist propaganda are again explored in this chapter for the extent to which they indicate tension between IS's neo-jihadism and its US-affiliated strategic opposition. Following the discussion in previous chapters, these tensions are not interpreted as evidence of the ontological or structural dissimilarity of the politically violent actors in question. Rather, they are taken to signify IS's connection with a history of peaceable and violent resistance movements founded in opposition to dominant structures and systems. Like these movements, IS and AQ articulate resistance while exploiting the apparatus of these systems to attain power and legitimacy. When considered together, Chapters 3 through 6 in this book therefore extend Bloom's (2016) perspective on how this has occurred in Western history. As elaborated in Chapters 1 and 2 through philosophical and policy examples, with regard to neoliberalism's example of the 'hegemony of power and resistance', 'if the Enlightenment was its catalyst, colonialism its internalization, then capitalism represents its materialization' (Bloom 2016, 88). Building on this assessment to consider the empirical circumstances of neo-jihadism, the cases on which I draw demonstrate how the phenomenon is ideologically founded in anti-capitalist resistance discourses communicated by AQ and IS, while it is also dependent in practice upon their exploitation of the financial historical (materialist) apparatus of neoliberal capitalism.

This chapter therefore extends *Neoliberalism and neo-jihadism*'s investigation of how contemporary neo-jihadism is constituted in and via the political-economic system of neoliberalism. Following a history of resistance, the analysis implicitly reflects on the extent to which AQ and IS propaganda in limited ways imitate forms of *détournement* and 'culture jamming' characteristic of non-state social movements, as exemplified since the Situationist International in 1967–1968 by, for instance, the Billboard Liberation Front (founded 1977) and contemporary anti-fascist activists in Germany (Ferrell 2019). Financially, it considers how neo-jihadist organisations could be understood to use commercial boycotting, as practised by the Industrial Workers of the World (IWW) labour union (Ferrell 2019). Distinguishing AQ and IS from progressive movements, on the other hand, the analysis emphasises Ferrell's (2019) insight that social movements lacking 'analytical resistance' end up 'reproducing the existing logic of power in the process of confronting it'. In line with this manner of thinking, AQ and IS's comparatively insecure resistance can be seen in many ways to contribute to the continued international dominance and influence of US-driven neoliberal conditions. This chapter shows that, in contrast with the emancipatory potential of non-state anarchist and socialist movements, in its efforts at state-building in particular IS resembles many forms of sovereign struggle that began as 'resistance' and became corrupt once they achieved power and access to government. These include, for instance, the aftermath of the 1917 Russian Revolution, several 'communism' failures during the Cold War period, and US-backed revolutions in Iraq, Ukraine, and Kyrgyzstan in the 2000s (DeFronzo 2018).

Collectively, Chapters 3 to 6 demonstrate that, unlike progressivist social movements, the appropriation and repurposing of technological, discursive, and financial affordances of neoliberalism by AQ and IS is not undertaken with the conscious incentive to 'decode' or 'reverse' the apparatuses of power that provide for the subjugation of neo-jihadism's target audience. Rather than destabilising neoliberalism, AQ and IS's violent activism in fact serves to reconstitute the paradigm's violent characteristics (Giroux 2004; Springer 2015).

Following the discussion of AQ finance in Chapter 5, this chapter explores the financial practices IS used to resource and coordinate its activities and to govern residents in its territory. Peck (2010), Jessop (2006), and Harvey's (2003) interpretations of the role of place and territory in processes of neoliberal capital accumulation are called upon to explain how IS's territorial geo-economic orientation correlates with its financial practices, in comparison with the relatively de-territorialised AQ after 2001. Bourdieusian theory is then applied to examine how political-economic mirroring between 'rational' counterterrorists and 'irrational' terrorists in a field and doxa of neoliberalism highlights the causative effects of US-directed restructuring in the Middle East on the political economy of IS. In comparison with AQ, for which social, cultural, and symbolic capital were important, I argue that in its efforts at state-building IS appeals to these forms of capital but also to what Bourdieu termed 'metacapital' (1998a). In a manner consistent with IS propaganda, this is demonstrated to entail a focus on materiality and land in contrast to AQ's intensified emphasis on symbolism and idealism over the course of its historical development.

To conceptualise the symbolic and material significance of territory for IS finance, and the political-economic environment in which the organisation emerged, the discussion begins with an explanation of the neoliberal economic reforms that took place in Iraq prior to the formation of IS in 2013. I elaborate on a history of neoliberal political-economic interventions in Iraq that had regional effects preceding the formation of the Caliphate in 2014, and, as with US intervention in Afghanistan during the Cold War, provided the political-economic foundations upon which subsequent neoliberal 'layering' occurred (Peck 2010). Recognising that political and economic reforms in the Middle East since 2001 have been extensive, the discussion foregrounds those that were US-directed and that occurred in Iraq both prior to and after the 2003 US invasion.

US-led interventions

Contemporary political violence in the Middle East arguably cannot be understood without reference to historical Western interventions and conflicts in the region, extending beyond the 1928 Red Line agreement back to the eleventh-century Christian Crusades (Richman 1991; Le Billon and El Khatib 2004; Fouskas and Gökay 2005). While this history is exploited in IS propaganda (Al Hayat 2015a), three US-directed interventions in Iraq are pertinent for understanding the political-economic development of IS. These are the sanctions led by the US against Saddam Hussein's government during the Iran–Iraq War, the UN-directed Oil-for-Food Programme, and the economic reforms introduced in the country following the 2003 Iraq War.

Iraqi sanctions from 1990 were enacted under provisions of UN Security Council Resolution 661, imposing a near total financial and trade embargo. They were implemented four days after Iraq's invasion of Kuwait despite evidence that the US was aware of Hussein's plans and indicated that it did not consider the matter to be of US concern (Atwan 2015), these plans remaining for the most part unaltered until the US-led invasion of the country in 2003 (Woods and Stout 2010). After the end of the Persian Gulf War in 1991, sanctions were extended under UN Security Council Resolution 687 to include the removal of weapons of mass destruction. Their wide-ranging nature produced a number of devastating situations for Iraqi citizens, including malnutrition and disease exacerbated by a lack of clean water and medical supplies. Certain chemicals that could be used to clean water, for instance, were on the sanctions list for their potential dual-use of producing chemical weapons (Gordon 2010). The Hussein administration had established expertise in manufacturing chemicals weapons, leading to their use in the Iran–Iraq War (1980–1988) with US support (Blight et al. 2012; SBS 2015), and the sanctions were an example of more direct US political-economic influence in the country.

The implementation of the UN-directed Oil-for-Food Programme for Iraq on 14 April 1995, under UN Security Council Resolution 986, was an extension of US influence (Jeong and Weiner 2012). The programme was intended to mitigate the damaging effects of the former sanctions by allowing the Iraqi government to sell a percentage of its oil in exchange for humanitarian supplies. It was beset by controversy, including allegations that Hussein received kickbacks of US$1.7 billion and that the regime received further proceeds of US$10.9 billion from selling oil to friends of the government at below-market prices and from illegal oil smuggling (Otterman 2005), implicating UN officials (Usborne 2005). A 22 April 2004 inquiry headed by the former United Nations Association of the United States of America Director and US Federal Reserve Chairman Paul Volcker revealed that Oil-for-Food Programme head Benon Sevan allegedly solicited illegal allocations of oil in the interests of a trading company registered in Panama, African Middle East Petroleum Co (Volcker et al. 2005).

In the aftermath of the Oil-for-Food Programme, there were allegations that large discrepancies existed between valuations of humanitarian goods and contracts paid for with Iraqi oil money by Cotecna inspectors and overseers from the UN Security Council (Otterman 2005). A report by Charles Duelfer, former Special Advisor to the Director of Central Intelligence for Iraqi weapons of mass destruction and leader of the Iraq Survey group, alleged that Chinese, Russian, Polish, Indian, and French military industries were paid with funds from the scheme to supply Iraq with weapons, including a tank carrier, missile-fuel-processing plant, a propulsion system, and missile guidance systems (Duelfer and CIA 2004; Otterman 2005). Although the programme allowed Iraq to improve its domestic economic situation and strengthened Hussein's command economy, in practice it was intersectional with what this book interprets as neoliberal mechanisms of profit generation engaged in by the US- and UN-directed individuals and organisations.

Following the sanctions and Oil-for-Food Programme, the US-led assault on Baghdad, Basra, Kirkuk, and Mosul on 19 March 2003 lasted approximately six weeks (Atwan 2015). The US-directed restructuring of Iraq's economy through neoliberal and territorial means resulted from events during the war, including US military targeting of government entities and organisations located in civilian centres; entire villages were destroyed and the infrastructure of public services was devastated (Mearsheimer and Walt 2003). After the assault, a US- and UK-led Coalition Provisional Authority (CPA) assumed temporary control over governance in the country, including responsibility for the management of domestic Iraqi assets acquired through the extraction and sale of oil and natural gas. The CPA also ran the Development Fund for Iraq (DFI) from 21 April 2003 until the CPA was disbanded on 28 June 2004. The programme was designed to replace the UN's Oil-for-Food Programme and once more, to offset the harm caused to Iraqi civilians by economic sanctions and continuous war (Halchin 2005).

The DFI enabled Iraq's currency exchange, wheat purchase, electricity and oil infrastructure-renewal programmes, as well as facilitating equipment for Iraqi security forces, regulating civil-service salaries, and maintaining various government departments (KPMG Bahrain 2004). Although the Iraqi Governing Council (IGC), established on 22 July 2003, maintained some responsibilities for governing the country, the CPA was the primary authority on all judicial, administrative, and legislative matters until it finally transferred power to the interim Iraqi government on 28 June 2004 (Crocker 2004). During the time it was in power, the CPA engaged in a radical reconstruction of Iraq's domestic economy along neoliberal lines. Economic reforms during this period have been criticised for rendering the country vulnerable to exploitation by major corporations and of fuelling support for the violent mobilisation of a disillusioned and disenfranchised citizenry (Le Billon 2005). As the discussion of Abu Bakr Naji's text in Chapter 4 illustrated, the disaster conditions created by US actions were exploited in propaganda influential to the evolution of neo-jihadist ideologies during IS's organisational development.

Criticisms from international commentators of the laws introduced by the CPA relate primarily to its privatisation of Iraq's domestic assets and poor management of finances allocated to the DFI. Both of these factors created conditions that allowed major US and UK multinationals to expropriate US$20 billion in the first years following the invasion (Whyte 2007) and that debilitated what was left of the country's public services. Under the direction of Paul Bremer, former Managing Director of the transnational corporation Kissinger Associates, the CPA introduced 100 legally binding orders, some of which were intended to reform Iraq's 'command economy', which was centrally controlled by government, with major services nationalised (Halchin 2005). Order 17 granted foreign corporations with economic interests in the country immunity from Iraq's domestic legal process, while Order 12 removed all tariffs on imported goods, eradicating any advantage that Iraqi producers had. Order 49 provided a tax cut for foreign corporations from a possible maximum of 40 per cent to 15 per cent; it also included a caveat that entities working with the CPA would be exempt from paying tax altogether. Order 57 stipulated the inauguration of Inspectors General to investigate corruption in the Iraqi ministry, a measure criticised for the likelihood that it would ensure ongoing US influence in the country after the transfer of sovereignty to the Iraqi government (Halchin 2005). With their privatising and deregulatory agenda, the reforms were patent examples of neoliberalism in action.

Indicating the territorial, neo-colonial, and resource-intensive origins of the funds administered by the CPA, in the initial year after the invasion (2004), it spent only US$400 million of the US Congress Iraq Relief and Reconstruction Fund (IRRF), which had provided US$18.4 billion for development projects, in comparison with expenditure of US$17.7 billion from funding for the DFI as of 24 June (Richter et al. 2004, 10). Critics of this action assert that the US government's preference for the DFI was likely due both to the lesser degree of oversight to which it was subject in comparison with IRRF funds (Richter et al. 2004) and a US political preference for spending money garnered through the sale of Iraqi oil. Often cited is Rumsfeld's assertion in relation to the post-war period: 'if you think we're going to spend a billion dollars of our money over there, you are sadly mistaken' (Frick 2008). Others emphasise close political-economic connections between the private corporations who benefited from DFI funding for the projects and the US policymakers who authored the policies for Iraq's reconstruction (Duncan 2006). It is often noted, for example, that in the years directly preceding his election to office US Vice President Dick Cheney was CEO of Halliburton, the beneficiary of US$18 billion in reconstruction contracts during the war (Bollyn 2004).

Although it is not the primary focus here, neoliberal collusions between US and UK public and private entities during the period of Iraq's postwar economic reconstruction provide the context for the emergence and early success of IS, given the economic and ideological conditions that such relationships created in Iraq following 2003. As Chapter 4 explained, these were exploited extensively in IS propaganda and in Naji's (2006) directions for building a society in the aftermath of the 'savagery' and 'chaos' wrought by political violence. For this reason, it is useful to analyse the political-economic ideologies, rhetoric, and case studies that evidence the US-led coalition's interest in Iraq in 2003, and the long-term effects of the CPA reforms.

Beyond the explicit protections for private financial interests stipulated in CPA Orders 12, 17, and 29, directives for a broader neoliberalisation of the Iraqi economy were implicit in US government statements made in relation to Iraq, and in a number of documents that informed the writing of CPA policies. Statements made by Paul Bremer, Donald Rumsfeld, and George W. Bush confirm that in certain unambiguous respects neoliberal economic reform in Iraq took precedence over successful democratic elections. Such statements are indicative of US strategic attitudes towards Iraq and neighbouring Arab states, which were subsequently exploited in the propaganda of IS.

Bremer, the head of the CPA from May 2003 until June 2004, stated that 'a free economy and a free people go hand in hand' (Dower 2010, 413), that 'history tells us that substantial and broadly held resources, protected by private property rights, are the best protection of political freedom' (cited in Wilson 2003; see also Looney 2003, 57), and that 'everybody knows we cannot wait until there is an elected government to start economic reform' (cited in Reuters 2003). International acceptance of such rationales for the US occupation and the restructuring of Iraq's economy from 2003 indicate that the economic 'shock and awe' (Klein 2007) tactics employed by the US government and contracted entities were deemed both necessary and viable to ensure the country's post-war re-stabilisation. The quality of infrastructure rebuilt by US and UK organisations was often appalling, and neither the proceeds of funds from natural resources nor many of the benefits of renewed public services went to Iraqi citizens (Tiefer 2007). Indicating the causative nature of the dialectical relationship in question, these actions also fuelled anti-US (and likely anti-capitalist) sentiment in the country and contributed to the conditions of chaos Naji (2006) described.

Despite the apparent lack of success of US political and economic actions in Iraq shortly after 2003, this activity continued to be supported by long-standing political contentions that neoliberal reforms were the optimal developmental path for the country. Indicating a strategic perspective directly preceding the invasion in February 2003, George W. Bush indicated that the measures undertaken in Iraq were not only justified and necessary, they were also intended to serve as a prototype for the economic liberalisation of Arab nation states generally. He asserted that Iraq's reform would bring about 'a new Arab charter that champions internal reform, greater political participation, economic openness and free trade', and that Iraq 'would serve as a dramatic and inspiring example of freedom for other nations in the region' (Bush 2003). Indicating the broader field at play, this perspective was reinforced by submissions to the US government by think tanks and academic institutions (including the William David Institute, the Adam Smith Institute, and the Royal Institute of International Affairs), of which a paper published by the Heritage Foundation in Washington was the most influential.

The Heritage Foundation's *The road to economic prosperity for a post-Saddam Iraq* (Cohen and O'Driscoll 2002) laid out guidelines for Iraq's neoliberal reform, with the country's long-term prosperity being a primary matter of concern. Although brief, the report includes directives that were reiterated by US policymakers at the initiation of the Iraqi campaign. The following has often been noted:

> A new federal Iraqi Government must take steps to create a modern legal environment that recognizes property rights and is conducive to privatization through a public information campaign; deregulate prices internally, including the utilities and energy sector; prepare state assets, including industries, utilities, transportation, ports and airports, pipelines, and the energy sector, for privatization; keep the budget balanced and inflation, taxes, and tariffs low; and liberalize and expand trade, and launch an effort for Iraq to join the World Trade Organization. (Cohen and O'Driscoll 2002)

The recommendations in the Heritage Foundation's report correlated with the policy statements previously mentioned and influenced instructions for Iraq's reform outlined in the US government document *Moving the Iraqi economy from recovery to growth* (King, Jr 2003). This document, which remains officially classified, was a collaboration between USAID and the US Department of the Treasury, with substantive input from financial consulting firm Bearing Point (a subsidiary of accounting firm KPMG), and was described as 'a blueprint for prospective contractors' (Laursen 2003). Key aspects leaked to Neil King of the *Wall Street Journal* and Greg Palast of the *Guardian* in 2003 detailed a model for the privatisation of Iraq's financial institutions, community organisations, and state-run services for exploitation by foreign investors. In the aftermath of the reforms introduced in 2003 and 2004, it became apparent that explicit directions for the 'privatization of state-owned enterprises', the 'modernizing of the Baghdad stock exchange', the 'reforming of the central Bank', 'jump-starting the private sector with fresh credit and training', and 'rewriting' the Iraqi tax code had been part of the plan of policymakers with respect to Iraq for some years before 2003 (King, Jr 2003). While Chapter 4 explored how such directives and the neoliberal agendas they signify are reflected in the anti-capitalist rhetoric of IS, the following section of this chapter considers how Iraq's political-economic environment provided the material and ideological foundation for IS finance.

Financial institutions

One characteristic of IS finance reminiscent of US institution building in Iraq from 2003, and broader US-directed neoliberal activity in the Middle East, was the organisation's combined exploitation of financial institutions and energy resources in the region. This example of neoliberal 'mirroring' occurred both empirically and ideologically, again epitomising Bourdieu's (1998b, 20) observation that neo-colonial subjects refer to the rationality of the forces that suppress them as 'inert violence of the powers which invoke reason'. In much the same way that AQ's financial behaviour in the years following the Afghan–Soviet War incorporated networks and alliances established during the war through material support provided by the US, IS's engagement with financial institutions, gas, and oil was facilitated by the economic infrastructure and political conditions in Iraq and the Middle East that developed under US-led influence.

From mid-2014, within the field of post-war 'disaster capitalism' (Klein 2007) in Iraq, IS was widely recognised for its immediate acquisition of vast sums of money (Levitt 2015; Fanusie and Heid 2016). The amount of economic capital IS earned from its control of financial institutions has, however, been a point of contention. Many reported in June 2014 that IS received US$425–450 million in cash from its looting of the Iraqi Central Bank in Mosul (McCoy 2014; Tait 2014). This was corroborated at the time by exile Ahmed Chalabi's testimony, and by the Governor of the Province of Nineveh, Atheel al-Nujaifi, who confirmed that IS had stolen millions from banks in the region. Then, in July 2017, Bourzou Daraghi of the *Financial Times* reported al-Nujaifi's refutation of his story about the seizure, and an executive director of the private Union Bank of Iraq, Talal Ibrahim, stated: 'not a single center [*sic*] has been stolen from the bank. Isis never put a hand on the money' (Bender 2014). As a later discussion will elaborate, early estimates of IS's oil revenue at the end of 2014 also varied widely, from US$400 million to over US$1 billion. Despite these differing accounts, in the years following 2014 it became apparent that IS's engagement with financial institutions and its involvement in the energy trade were a formative aspect of the organisation's early political-economic behaviour. For some critics, they indicated the organisation's nascent imitation of a modern capitalist nation state, holding large capital reserves in banks and engaging in taxation, trade, and currency exchange (Goodwin 2015; Tsvetkova and Kelly 2015).

Insofar as IS's looting of the Iraqi Central Bank did take place, it would have added to the existing capital IS already held in Iraq's banks, with the financial statements of these institutions revealing that the organisation's financial reserves were in excess of US$1 billion at the end of 2013 (Brisard and Martinez 2014, 6). Following IS's movement into Syria in 2015, it also controlled financial institutions in Raqqa and Deir ez-Zor, including the Popular Credit Bank, which it used to facilitate tax administration (Bindner and Poirot 2016). US$360 million of IS's annual wealth was estimated to have derived from taxes and extortion imposed on residents in its territories and on those passing through (Swanson 2015). These included a protection tax for Christians and other religious minorities (often referred to as a 'racket'), as well as taxes for all goods and services, resource distribution, the discovery of antiquities and other cultural items to be sold, travel privileges, and cash withdrawals from banks (Solomon and Jones 2015). In Iraq and Syria, IS controlled around 125 bank branches in 2014, and 115 in 2015 (Bindner and Poirot 2016, 23). By the end of 2015, the US Department of the Treasury estimated that it had assumed control of state-owned banks in Kirkuk, Al Anbar, Ninevah, and Salah Din (FATF 2015b). As discussed further below, this provided IS with the means to negotiate financially with the Syrian Bashar al Assad regime through intermediaries (Bindner and Poirot 2016). Given international sanctions on trade and currency distribution in the region, however, money deposited in Syrian and Iraqi banks could not be floated in the international financial system, and it was primarily denominated in local currencies (the Iraqi dinar and Syrian pound), limiting its usage outside IS-held territories (Solomon 2017). These sanctions were enforced by various measures, primarily directed by the US.

As with US and US-led efforts to target *hawalas* that operated separately from the international financial system after 9/11, IS's isolation from the financial system despite its control of financial institutions occurred as a result of US-led sanctions imposed by the UN on both a regional basis and on IS specifically (Nichols and Irish 2015). In 2015, for example, the US pressured the Iraqi government to cease paying salaries to employees residing within IS-held territory. It then spearheaded multilateral efforts to counter IS finance at the UN Security Council, establishing the Iraq–US Committee to Counter Terrorist Financing, and the thirty-six-member Counter-ISIL Finance Group (56 members in 2019) (US Department of the Treasury 2016a). UN Security Council Resolution 2253, enacted 17 December 2015, extends the sanctions applied to AQ to IS, 'calls upon' states to 'improve … information sharing … to enhance engagement with the private sector' to adhere more rigorously to standards set by the FATF, and cites major sources of IS revenue as 'oil smuggling, extortion, taxation, robbery, kidnapping for ransom, foreign donations, trade in antiquities and human trafficking' (UN 2017; see also Bindner and Poirot 2016). Resolution 2170 (2014) proscribes commercial activity with IS, targeting oil trades in particular. Resolution 2199 (2015) pertains to the prevention of IS's trade in oil and in antiquities, stipulating that IS financial assets in banks incorporated in member states should be frozen (UN 2017). Given these and other measures, IS's early management of finance was to a large extent non-monetary (unlike the monetary characteristics of AQ's 'offshoring'); the banks effectively acted as repositories for proceeds acquired through physical activity involving the collection of cash.

Despite IS's initial reliance upon non-monetary, on-the-ground methods of fundraising, and its early usage of banks for 'warehousing', the organisation's subsequent management of proceeds garnered through territorial fundraising methods did make use of neoliberal mechanisms of 'financialising', although the detail of this is often unrecognised and under-reported in terrorism financing scholarship (see, for instance, Solomon and Jones 2015).

These characteristics of IS's activity indicate the organisation's observance of a neoliberal doxa in the region, whereby such methods and modes of economic managerialism were accepted as both 'inevitable' and 'self-evident' (Bourdieu 1998a, 1998b). To the extent to which this is a fair assessment of capitalist state-like entities including IS, it reflects Bourdieu's assessment that the 'desocialised and dehistoricised "theory"' of neoliberalism has 'the means of making itself true, empirically falsifiable' (1998b, 95), or that such financial practices were uncritically accepted. In relation to the discussion in Chapter 5 of alternative remittance and the Bourdieusian 'theory effect' (Bourdieu 1991), neoliberal policies and practices in the Iraq–Syria region following successive years of US-led intervention were entrenched and expected, such that they became imperative to IS's economic success. Although in 2014 IS was relatively unintegrated into the international financial system, the organisation adhered to a neoliberal economic order, in particular through its engagement in monetary practices such as currency speculation, manipulation, and arbitrage, and, like AQ, in its public–private collusion with exploitative governments.

Although US sanctions prevented IS from trading in the Middle East, the organisation circumnavigated them by combining Western commercial and *hawala* banking, and through monetary means. For example, according to the UK Foreign Affairs Sub-Committee Chairman, John Baron MP, IS could bid in Iraq's central-bank auctions for foreign currency, primarily the US dollar (Freeman 2016), through the use of *hawaladars* (*hawala* brokers). Baron alleged that IS sent money from bank looting and siphoned-off pensions in its territories to Jordan, where it was used to play the stock market. According to his testimony, the money then re-entered the system in Baghdad, where IS would 'take a turn (profit) on the foreign currency actions, and siphon that cash back' (Freeman 2016), before it returned to IS reserves through *hawaladars*. As Stephen Kalin of Reuters notes (Kalin 2016), once inside IS territory, brokers who worked for the organisation fixed the rate of currency exchange and traded the US dollar to local brokers for dinar at margins of up to 20 per cent (see also Homeland Security Committee 2016).

Further indicating the breadth of IS's economic reliance upon the neoliberal US Federal Reserve system, the organisation empirically depends upon the regional dominance of the US dollar; all fines and taxes must be paid to IS in US dollars, while it pays its employees in dinar (Keating 2016). In response to these activities, the US halted shipments of Federal Reserve dollars to Iraq between July and August 2015 and took action to bring the Iraqi banking sector into the international regulatory system (Coles 2015). As a related measure, the Iraqi government banned the sale of hard currency to areas controlled by IS (Coles 2015). Despite this, neoliberal monetary practices on the part of IS remained ongoing until the middle of 2017 (Haid 2017), while a lack of integrated analysis of the value chain meant that the scale and implications of this behaviour remained obfuscated.

The second characteristic of IS's engagement with financial institutions that might be considered neoliberal entails the organisation's multifaceted engagement with regional governments. As with AQ's intergovernmental arrangements, IS's behaviour recalls Bourdieu's (1998b, 20) theory that dialectics of economic and military neo-colonialism can produce conditions in which the 'rational' actions of nation states produce and sustain 'irrational' politically violent situations. This extends to the compound effects of neoliberal layering in post-conflict disaster situations that were explored in Naji's (2006) text and Klein's (2007) well-known 'shock and awe' maxim.

IS's capitalising on disaster situations through forming collective partnerships with local governments and engaging with neoliberal finance was overtly apparent in its usage of financial institutions in Syria from 2014 to 2016 to facilitate economic dealings with the Assad regime (Bindner and Poirot 2016). In this situation, IS used banks inside Syria to broker deals through middlemen to raise funds for its operations, at the same time providing resources to meet the Syrian regime's oil and gas needs. This was revealed in a 2015 declassified CIA report detailing how US forces used bank records to identify IS-held oil facilities in the region, in preparation for targeted strikes on oil infrastructure in its Operation Tidal Wave II campaign (Torbati and Wolf 2015).

While Operation Tidal Wave II, which began on 21 October 2015, entailed airstrikes targeting wellheads, pump jacks, and drilling rigs, it was also directed at IS intermediaries. One of these was George Haswani, a broker who facilitated trades using his construction firm HESCO, which became subject to sanctions for providing material support to terrorism in 2015 by the US Office of Foreign Assets Control (OFAC) (US Department of the Treasury 2015). Also designated as finance for terrorism by OFAC were the business holdings of Faysal Ahmad Bin Ali al-Zahrani, a former associate of the now deceased IS 'finance minister' Abu Sayyaf, who funnelled tens of millions of dollars to IS from Syria and Iraq from oil and gas revenues (US Department of the Treasury 2016b). In 2017, Amos Hochstein of the US Department of State, supported by European intelligence officials, announced to the *Wall Street Journal* that sales to the regime constituted the largest source of funding for IS (Faucon and Al Omran 2017). In comparison with AQ, which relied upon donations from government-allied individuals, IS relied on broad-based public–private partnerships with government employees and their affiliates, in a manner perhaps comparable with the collusive, resource-oriented behaviour of US forces and contractors in Iraq following the US assault in 2003.

Although its relations with the Assad government are an overt example of the organisation's neoliberal partnerships, IS, like AQ, maintained overt and covert patronage networks with governments from the Gulf region and their strategic allies. Former US Vice President Biden's statement that 'we could not convince our colleagues to stop supplying them' (Brull 2017) indicates US governments' inadvertent support for IS and its affiliates, through IS ties to US allies and through the US's overt and covert arming of 'moderate' rebels in Syria via proxies and local governments. As widely observed after 2014, these rebels comprised an AQ branch and other groups, which were often subjugated by IS forces, who acquired their funding and artillery (Ackerman 2015; Safadi 2015). As Chapter 4 highlighted, IS boasted about its benefit from this and its acquisition of US armaments provided to Iraqi forces. Further exacerbating the strategic gravity of the situation was the fact that successive Iraqi governments until this book's time of writing were reticent to adopt measures that would tangibly undermine IS's financial capabilities and thereby harm other aspects of the country's economy. One noteworthy example was the Iraqi government's December 2016 ban on 142 currency houses trading on the Baghdad exchange, which was widely criticised for its delayed implementation (Freeman 2016).

In addition to the factors listed above, ineffective local government responses to IS resulted in part from the success of the organisation's covert espionage tactics, whereby it infiltrated, bribed, and extorted government entities prior to its invasion and takeover of territory, such that the highest levels of the Iraqi armed forces deserted their responsibilities and otherwise sabotaged Iraq's military efforts. These were, interestingly, often the same individuals put in power by the US and trained by US forces (Hendawi and Abdul-Zahra 2015). The dialectical relationship between IS and US neoliberal entities in question here entails both mirroring and causation, extending to revolving-door relationships characteristic of neoliberalism, whereby alliances are based on economic capital exchange rather than on non- or extra-economic social and political values. Demonstrating this, the intelligence and covert governance structures of IS consist of unemployed ex-Baathist officials who were trained by the CIA in the Iran–Iraq War and rendered unemployed during the US-led 'de-Baathification' programme in 2003 (Atwan 2015; Kilcullen 2016). Herein neoliberalism operated in a quintessential way as a doxa: the logic of economic productivity was favoured over human interests and social concerns (Bourdieu 2000; Brenner and Theodore 2005), while neoliberal entities exhibited a reluctance to interrupt global flows of economic capital, despite their access by IS.

One high-profile accusation of international governments' support for IS, combined with assertions regarding the organisation's connection with the international financial system, was made by Russian President Vladimir Putin at the 2015 G20 summit (Druzhinin 2015). Although Putin's list was not made public, he declared that forty countries were involved in financing IS, including G20 states and US allies that had otherwise announced their dedication to 'degrading and destroying' the organisation (Walker 2015).

While no clear and credible evidence substantiates Putin's claims, or those of US foreign-policy sceptics regarding IS finance, there is evidence that the scale, magnitude, and intricacies of IS's financial behaviour were operative within the US-controlled international petrodollar system that Clarke (2005) described. In line with Nicholas Fogle's (2011, 73) take on Bourdieu, the dialectical relationship between these entities is constituted by 'a self-perpetuating loop, wherein the outputs are fed back into the system as inputs', such that they become 'reflexive, self-referential', and 'self-organizing'. In this way, money expended by the US on military industries, and local government sponsorship of IS, both directly and indirectly, produce reflexive economic benefits for both IS and US-affiliated (and strategically unaligned) powers in the region. The US moreover benefits from the reinforcement of its satellite control in the Middle East and the profits accrued through military industries themselves, further to IS's destabilisation of anti-US regimes such as the Assad government in Syria. There is, in short, extensive money to be made in the conflict, as there were profits to be gained by US and UK industries from Iraqi reconstruction contracts after 2003.

Recalling AQ's usage of financial networks established via the MAK, certain oil- and gas-trading routes used by IS originated from black-market channels established during the 1990s sanctions on Iraq and the Oil-for-Food Programme (Soergel 2015). In the following part of this chapter, I explore how IS managed oil and gas trades through these routes, using neoliberal monetary managerial measures, and via its collusion with local governments, including some who were strategically allied with the US. Once again, IS is not defined here as 'neoliberal'. Rather, financial behaviours on the part of the organisation are taken to signify its contribution to and reliance upon the US-led petrodollar system it condemns (Clark 2005; Naji 2006; Cowell 2013; Al Hayat 2014d, 2015a).

Oil and gas

In addition to the previously discussed ambiguity surrounding IS funds held in financial institutions, estimates of the organisation's revenue raised via oil from 2014 to 2017 vary considerably, owing to a dearth of information regarding the price per barrel of oil in Iraqi and Syrian territories, the level of production, and the absence of a publicly available centralised bookkeeping system (Hawramy et al. 2014). This uncertainty was also contributed to by the restructuring of IS's business model. A report by CAT (Bindner and Poirot 2016) revealed that although the revenue IS received from oil was, in the organisation's early years, contingent upon its control of territory, the organisation and its fundraising became increasingly decentralised over time. IS had initially controlled the beginning-to-end-scale processes of extraction, refinement, and distribution of oil within its territory, but from 2015 it determined a fixed price at which crude oil would be sold to members of its distribution network and a corresponding transport tax; those driving the trucks were at liberty to determine the most profitable and easiest route and recipient for resale (Solomon and Jones 2015). This might be interpreted in some respects as comparable with AQ's 'venture capitalist franchising' (Charette 2007; see also Ronfeldt 2005) and the organisation's decentralisation into independent cells after 9/11 (Burke 2004). To a greater extent than AQ, however, IS resembled a nation state in several ways. To the extent to which its decentralisation revealed characteristics of a political-economic orientation or identity, they might be interpreted alongside neoliberal states' outsourcing of state-run public industries.

According to a Reuters report, IS might have made as much as US$730–1460 million from oil sales in 2014 (Brisard and Martinez 2014, 7), while the ICSR at King's College places an estimate for this time period in the much more modest range of US$150–450 million (Heißner et al. 2017). What can be established, despite this variation, is that IS's revenue from oil was significantly reduced in the aftermath of Operation Tidal Wave II. Researchers at the ICSR observed that IS's income from natural resources has consistently correlated with the organisation's ability to retain control over territory; by November 2016, following almost a year of Operation Tidal Wave II airstrikes, it had lost 62 per cent of its peak holdings in mid-2014, debilitating its capacity for earning (Heißner et al. 2016). According to this report, which drew from a variety of leaked IS documents, congressional testimonies, government reports, media articles, and studies commissioned by think tanks, the net takings of oil trade for IS in 2015 was US$435–550 million, and for 2016 it was US$200–250 million (Heißner et al. 2016). Despite its decentralised operations, like a neoliberal nation state IS relied upon its acquisition and retention of territory to ensure capital accumulation in its favour. Although IS may not be unproblematically described as 'neoliberal', the practices and habitus of IS members were influenced by 'geo-politics of territorial strategies of states and empires to accumulate control over territories' (Jessop 2006, 158) and the geographical and political-economic field in which years of neoliberal layering took place (Peck 2010).

As mentioned, a patent example of this layering occurred prior to and following the emergence of IS in 2013 when US forces were pre-occupied with garnering control over oil in Iraq (Whyte 2007). Other examples include potential US incentives to prevent the establishment of a Russian–Chinese pipeline through Syria, which would effectively provide EU states with oil, the trades of which would not be denominated in US currency (Bichler and Nitzan 2014). Dialectically, the significance of IS's reliance upon energy resources has been apparent throughout the organisation's history. Despite the organisation's declining revenue from oil since 2014, until 2017 it remained one of its largest sources of funding, and was to this end reflected in its strategic messaging, representing its external political-economic identity. As discussed in Chapter 4, the scale of profits IS garnered through hydrocarbon trade and the number of energy and gas facilities under its control were exploited extensively in its propaganda.

The significant economic importance of hydrocarbon trading to IS, and its corresponding reliance upon territory, was particularly apparent in the year prior to the coalition air strikes of 2015, during which time

IS was estimated to earn around US$1.5 million per day from the sale of oil in Syria (Tokmajyan and The Aleppo Project 2016). The al-Tanak and al-Omar fields constituted the largest revenue streams at, on average, $40 for 11,000–12,000 barrels per day (bpd), and $45 for 6,000–9,000 bpd respectively (Bindner and Poirot 2016, 9). These fields are situated in the conflict areas of northern and eastern Syria, and until 2017 IS maintained a virtual monopoly on the market, while the price and production levels to this time remained more or less consistent. Elsewhere in Syria, including in al-Tabqa, al-Kharata, al-Shoula, Deiro, al-Taim, and al-Rashid, prices ranged from $20 to $40 per barrel depending on oil quality and demand, while bpd ranged from 200 to 3000 (Solomon et al. 2016). Following the commencement of the strikes, IS adjusted its oil production and distribution line by having independent traders who drive trucks, known as truckers, register outside fields and giving them a time and place at which they could return to fill up their tanks from the IS wells of crude, in order to avoid obvious queues. This ensured efficiency in the trading process and diminished the likelihood that the distribution infrastructure would be identified and targeted by airstrikes. Despite the relative successes of Operation Tidal Wave II, in 2017 IS controlled 160 oil and gas fields in Syria and 13 oil fields in Iraq (Gerges 2017).

IS's exercise of neoliberal economic managerialism was also apparent in its coordination of oil trades. These were broadly reminiscent of brokerage partnerships between the US government and US and UK commercial entities in Iraq following 2003, and the general neoliberal practice of endorsing and relying upon revolving-door relationships and public–private economic partnerships, discussed in Chapters 1 and 2. Following the beginning of Operation Tidal Wave II, for example, IS began offering traders 'licenses' that would enable them to avoid queues and obtain 1,000 barrels of oil at a time, if they could pay the entire cost upfront. This not only signified the importance of preferential trading for IS, it was also a means of using price fixing to ensure that the organisation made a guaranteed profit (Solomon et al. 2016).

The mutual significance of oil trading in the region for IS and its US-led opposition, and a contiguity in their economic interests, is apparent in the manner in which Operation Tidal Wave II was executed. Despite the debilitating effects of airstrikes on IS trades, Russian bombers targeted their vehicles and the oil wells to a greater extent than the US-led coalition. US defense secretary Ashton Carter confirmed to a House of Representatives panel in 2015 that the US was avoiding strikes that would debilitate Syria's energy infrastructure (Argus 2015). Government, academic, and other research reports also indicate that US-led forces targeted areas around the wells and the oil field facilities, as well as IS vehicles, rather than the specific extraction infrastructure (Opsal 2015). It is possible that these activities indicate US and coalition mindfulness of preserving energy reserves in order to avoid a resource or financial crisis. On the other hand, they might be taken to signify the US and its coalition partners' interest in profiting from future oil mining in the Middle East. Either way, the pattern of targeting demonstrates the US and IS's shared economic interests.

Another neoliberal characteristic of IS's hydrocarbon trade beyond its reliance upon trading revenue was the organisation's fiduciary management of end-stage trading processes. IS's methods in this respect might in many ways be said to resemble the outsourcing practices of AQ and of late modern capitalist corporations. These methods included the increasingly decentralised sale and purchase of oil, and an outsourcing of refinement processes during the course of changing refinery ownership and control (Hawramy et al. 2014). While IS had previously held a number of prefabricated mobile refineries, for example, several of these were destroyed in 2015 by the US. As the writers of 'Inside ISIS Inc: The journey of a barrel of oil' reported in 2016, since the middle of 2015 IS had again purchased five refineries (Solomon et al. 2016). In these cases, the original owner of an IS refining plant would remain on as a front man while IS managed the process covertly. IS would then supply the crude oil to the refinery and the proceeds from the petrol production would be split between the original owner and IS, and IS would take the entire proceeds of the *mazout* production, a heavy form of diesel in high demand for use in electricity generators (Solomon et al. 2016). By the time the refined oil was sold in local markets, IS was almost entirely disengaged from the process. From this point, it profited only from taxes imposed upon the trade in IS-controlled markets, which in Syria in 2015 was around US$0.67 per barrel (Solomon et al. 2016).

IS's management of oil trading in the region not only affected those resident in its territories, it was also more broadly influential in that it entailed public–private collaboration with companies and local-government-affiliated entities. Like AQ, and capitalising on the privatising, neoliberal tenets of the international financial system, IS dealt extensively with US economic and strategic allies that are very much a part of the US-directed petrodollar system IS outwardly condemns. One example is the Putin administration's accusation that the Turkish government tacitly facilitated IS oil trades across its border and that relatives of Turkish President Recep Tayyip Erdogan financially benefited from these transactions (Tsvetkova and Kelly 2015). Turkey, in kind, asserted that Russia profited from IS oil trades in light of Russia and IS's support for and collusion with the Assad regime (Brookes-Pollock 2015; Delaney 2015). There was limited evidence to substantiate the latter claim; however, the former was supported by statements from US Treasury officials and the Vice President of Research at the Foundation for the Defense of Democracies (Schanzer and Tahiroglu 2014). Both sources affirm that IS oil until 2017 was sold in Turkey through middlemen acting on behalf of prominent business and state interests (Fanusie and Entz 2017), as mentioned in relation to Naji's propagandised statements in Chapter 4. In this situation, demonstrating evidence of a doxa constituted by neoliberal reason (Peck 2010), social and political concerns were sublimated beneath the economic logic of capital accumulation.

This logic was also indicated by the fact that the scale of the sale of oil through Turkey demonstrated the government to be systematically implicated in this trade, despite Turkey's NATO status and strategic alliance with the US. Indeed, just as the Saudi Arabian and Qatari regimes are economically tied through hydrocarbon trade to the US, Turkey has a long history of both strategic and economic partnerships with non-regional states. Notwithstanding its enactment of anti-democratic policies, including summarily incarcerating political prisoners in 2016 (Arango and Yeginsu 2016), the Erdogan administration has often been praised by international communities for its progressive governance in comparison with some of its regional neighbours, while its mode of economic managerialism is sometimes termed 'Islamic capitalism' (Madi 2014; Ahmed 2015).

Turkey's political status as 'capitalist' and also, selectively, 'Islamic' is especially relevant given some Turkish government officials' support of IS. As writers for the *International Business Times* note, former CIA Director Mike Morrell announced in September 2015 that during the previous year IS had sold around 100,000 bpd from Iraq and Syria to Turkey that cost on average US$20 when sold outside IS territory (Masi 2015). This was less than half the market price of oil in the region, and even less on average internationally. Moreover, some speculated that price fixing and oil monopolies in regions such as this area of the Middle East rendered the risk of conducting business with IS financially worthwhile for some commercial entities (Ahmed 2015). Here, affirming Bourdieu, 'maximum growth, and therefore productivity and competitiveness' were represented as 'the ultimate and sole goal of human actions' (1998b, 31), such that human interests including safety and security became secondary to economic concerns.

Business partnerships with IS and the widespread adoption of market-fundamentalist ideologies were apparent, then, in situations where the economic interdependency of IS and representatives of regional governments was antithetical to their erstwhile strategic interests. In another example, previously mentioned, the Syrian government and its private affiliates benefited from partnerships established following IS's acquisition of oil facilities, despite their military opposition to the organisation (Bindner and Poirot 2016). Correspondingly, its private affiliates provided large injections of water to ensure the continued running of dilapidated oil facilities when IS workers did not possess the requisite engineering expertise to perform this operation (FATF 2015b). Following such actions, certain fields, including those IS acquired in late 2012, were sold back at a price favourable to affiliates of the government (Butter 2016). As mentioned, members of the Assad government were also variously alleged to be recipients of discounted petrol and *mazout* (Solomon et al. 2016).

Indicating the breadth of neoliberal economic arrangements in the region, extending to the suppression of strategic interests to defeat IS, government representatives from Iraqi Kurdistan, Jordan, and Iran have been oil customers of IS. All were implicated, for example, in one deal in which Kurdish traders purchased IS oil for '"half its international price"' (Hawramy et al. 2014) and paid US$1,500 per unit for the tankers to travel through checkpoints in Kirkuk, Makhmour, Daquq, and Tuz Khormato under Peshmerga control. IS oil smugglers were here paid double the usual amount for the oil, and it was subsequently sold on to Turkish and Iranian traders (Hawramy et al. 2014). Demonstrating evidence of neoliberal layering, the smuggling routes IS used through Iraq went as least as far back as the Oil-for-Food Programme (Simpson and Philips 2015). The relevant Trans-Saharan and Turkish trading and migration routes dated back centuries, and the now prevalent IS branch, Islamic State Khorasan Province (ISKP), used networks in the Pachir wa Agam district developed by non-state militants from the Afghan–Soviet war (Sarban 2016).

Despite the importance of such financial activity for IS and its regional partners, it is necessary to note the existence of strategic-military motivations for such partnerships. While long-standing economic partnerships existed between the US and Turkey, Saudi Arabia, and other Gulf states, and Turkey has been a long-standing member of the US-led NATO alliance, Turkey and Saudi Arabia have also, in various ways, provided tacit and more active support to IS and other regional Islamist organisations. During IS's strategic peak, some highlighted, for example, how Turkey became 'a revolving door through which foreign fighters enter and exit Syria' (Rubin 2017), while others noted how IS fighters made 1,000-mile journeys to Turkish hospitals in order to receive medical treatment and were exempt from having to answer questions from

Turkish officials about their activities afterwards (Phillips 2014). From 2014 to 2017, high-ranking government officials within the House of Saud were also accused of providing material support in the form of armaments and funding to IS, while IS itself used Saudi educational text-books in its so-called classrooms (Olidort and Sheff 2016).

Support for IS on the part of regional governments and individuals close to these governments also correlated with Turkish, Saudi Arabian, and US strategic and military opposition to Iran, Russia, and Syria, although the relationship between Turkey and Saudi Arabia has histori-cally been tense. Political factors underpinning opposition to the Assad government within the region are many and far-ranging, despite the fact that control over energy resources remains significant. As highlighted by 'blood for oil' critics (Bichler and Nitzan 2014), Turkey and the US opposed the establishment of an oil pipeline to be funded by Russia and Iran that would allegedly run through the top of Iraq, through Iran and Syria, and eventually provide western Europe with oil not tied to US currency. Perhaps to protect the pipeline, protect persecuted Sunni Mus-lim people in Syria, and suppress the Assad government's interests, rep-resentatives of Turkey, Saudi Arabia, the US, and elsewhere supported forces opposed to the government in the country, despite the fact that these forces have variously included future IS fighters, and fighters sub-sequently dispossessed and subjugated by IS (Castner 2017).

While Turkey, the US, and other states have in a number of ways tac-itly and actively provided support to IS, the organisation's financial activity has also in some respects resembled and reflected the neoliberal management of energy resources by government and private entities. Further to IS's trade of oil, its usage of neoliberal managerial behaviours of brokering supply and demand and its investment in technological expertise were also discernible in IS's trading and management of natu-ral gas. Indicating the importance of this resource, a 2014 Reuters report stated that 'gas plants under IS control could generate as much as 1,360MMcf/d' (M is a thousand, and Mcf/d is the volume of 1,000 cubic feet of natural gas per day), with a market value of US$81,600,000 million in that year. Factoring in the assumed discounted price of US$2/Mcf and a reduction in trading rates of 50 per cent, the total trade of gas by IS would have amounted to US$489 million in 2014 (Brisard and Martinez 2014, 8). In a subsequent report, Bindner and Poirot (2016, 11) revealed that the organisation controlled at least twelve natural gas fields in 2015 and cited the US Energy Information Administration's June 2015 findings that gas production in Syria was 40 per cent lower than it had been prior to the beginning of the conflict. Douglas Lovelace, the Director of the Strategic Studies Institute and author of *The evolution of Islamic State*

(2016), similarly put this figure at 32 per cent down from levels in 2011–2013 (Lovelace 2016, 109). As it had with oil, IS relied upon stable control of territory to profit from its sale of gas. It was, on the other hand, capable of generating profit from gas ventures by embracing neoliberal partnerships with private industry and government administrations.

In other cases, IS dealt with Syrian-government and affiliated private entities in treating and transporting gas, IS lacking the necessary knowledge and skills to do this (Bindner and Poirot 2016, 12). This interdependence was contributed to by US coalition airstrikes that after 2015 targeted transformation infrastructure used to extract and chemically process the gas, controlled by IS at gas facilities, rather than the pipelines themselves (Bindner and Poirot 2016, 12). Given its volatility and difficulty in handling, the only means by which to move gas, unlike oil, was through these existing transportation systems (Lovelace 2016). Private Syrian-government-affiliated entities would hence provide the equipment and personnel with which IS would oversee the completion of the gas extraction, processing, and distribution. Once again, the proceeds of raw sale or (more often) the electricity produced by the gas was itself divided between the regime and IS. An exemplar case is the Twinan gas facilities southwest of Raqqa, which in 2016 and 2017 were conjointly managed by IS and affiliates of the Syrian government (Bindner and Poirot 2016, 12).

Again, this example illustrates both the combined importance of territoriality and capital for IS and a practical political-economic dialectic between IS and governments who are either allied with or opposed to its US-led opposition. In its state-like political-economic identity, gas was required by both IS and the Syrian government to support their mutual military activity and to service their territories with electricity.

Minerals and agricultural resources

Another major source of revenue for IS was its territorial exploitation of minerals and agricultural resources, in part facilitated by its usage of neoliberal monetary mechanisms. Although this constituted a lesser percentage of IS net revenue in comparison with the money it made from oil and gas, these resources vastly outweighed the sum of sponsorship IS garnered from outside donors. Leaked IS internal documents obtained by US intelligence agencies indicate that prior to 2015, external donations to the organisation comprised on average only about US$50 million per year (Brisard and Martinez 2014; Bindner and Poirot 2016). Also, according to Brisard and Martinez (2014, 4), independence and the diversification of funding sources, including through natural resources, was vital to IS's early successes after 2014, as it is to conventional commercial start-ups. With independence of funding, IS was not beholden to the wishes or instructions of its benefactors, and was free to pursue its ruthless 'management of savagery' campaign (Naji 2006). With diversification, the organisation was in a position to respond flexibly to efforts at inhibiting its fundraising on the part of the UN and its US-led international opposition. Furthermore, although minerals and agricultural resources were relatively less vital to IS's continued operations, they remained strategically significant to the organisation given the control they afforded IS over territory, and their symbolic quasi-nation-state representation.

Various characteristics of IS's management of non-energy resources might be considered neoliberal, including its commercial, flexible approach to management (Harvey 1989) and state-like engagement in 'accumulation by dispossession' (Harvey 2003), wherein 'resources are expropriated once and for all from a "commons" that has been built up over many years and/or where the rate of economic exploitation of a given resource exceeds its natural rate of renewal' (Jessop 2006, 151). From a philosophical perspective, IS's behaviour in this regard also reflects the Bourdieusian premise that in conditions of neoliberalism, a '"flexible" company in a sense deliberately exploits a situation of insecurity which it helps to reinforce' (1998a, 29, 1998b, 84; see also Harvey 1989). Such economic tactics to manage natural resources on the part of IS again entailed its establishment of economic partnerships with its otherwise military-strategic opponents, in this case including Western countries and US-allied Gulf states, combined with the tandem usage of monetary economic managerial measures. In this situation, IS manipulated supply and demand, exploited military and resource-crisis situations, and engaged in deceitful monopolistic economic managerial measures such as price fixing. Its flexible management of non-energy resources was, in the first instance, perhaps most apparent in its mining and processing of essential minerals.

Minerals exploited by IS include predominantly phosphate and sulphur as well as the derivative products of phosphoric acid and sulphuric acid (Sherlock 2015). In one noteworthy case, the Iraqi Ministry of Human Rights reported on Al-Arabiya News that IS had assumed control over the al-Qaem facility and was 'transferring raw material of phosphate to Raqqa in Syria' (Al-Arabiya 2014). This plant is located 400km northwest of Baghdad and has provided Iraq with its primary source of fertiliser. It belongs to the same public company as Akashat, another mine formerly under IS control near Rutba in the al-Anbar province (Sherlock 2015). Indicating the strategic significance of such reserve controls, the *Financial Times* reported in 2011 on behalf of an NGO working to bring international attention to the humanitarian situation in Syria that a US geological survey claimed Iraq had 'world-class' phosphate reserves only second to Morocco's (Raqqa Is Being Slaughtered Silently 2017). Other sources recorded that the mines in Iraq constituted '1.6 per cent of the world's supply of phosphate rock' (Napoleoni 2015), and that they were ranked ninth globally for phosphate rock production. Meanwhile, Reuters researchers estimated that in 2015 the potential revenue from phosphate extraction for IS from Syria was approximately US$50 million (Swanson 2015), while other accounts show that prior to the beginning of the 2011 Syrian civil war, the revenue on phosphate exported from Syria was on average US$60 million (Vovcul 2015; Bindner and Poirot 2016). In 2015 in Syria, IS also acquired control of the Palmyra and Khnaifess mines, which are situated alongside the main highway between Damascus and Palmyra (Swanson 2015).

Given the scale of mineral wealth in the region, control over mineral-rich areas had political-economic and strategic implications for IS. These included the primary market for these minerals being Western countries allied with the US, and the minerals' potential dual-use in the manufacture of weapons. In relation to the first situation, Shiloach (2015) noted that historically a significant percentage of Syria's phosphate had been purchased by the EU; during 2012, it bought 40 per cent of the country's exports (Reuters 2012). Others observed that the potential revenues from sulphuric and phosphoric acid generated at these mines was estimated at US$300 million per annum (Brisard and Martinez 2014, 8).

The fact that facilities at mines in Iraq and Syria have been used extensively to make sulphuric and phosphoric acid perhaps add credence to claims that IS, its Syrian opponents, and outside government proxies in the region prior to 2017 possessed the requisite resources to create chemical weapons (Johnston et al. 2016). This is, moreover, a primary reason why these mines have historically been under the control of state-affiliated entities. This fact notwithstanding, the political-economic environment in Syria fomented support for oppositional groups and was underwritten by exclusivist and exclusionary political ideas of statehood in Syria, influential to the development of IS. Once again, public–private partnerships between IS and Syrian government entities to manage resource facilities were common and reflect evidence of historically 'embedded neoliberalism' in the country during this period (Cerny 2008). IS's production of cement from minerals, on the other hand, was typically conducted either by IS independently or in concert with non-government, private entities.

While the control of cement factories was privatised and strategically significant for IS, its approach to this industry was flexible, given that the strategic benefits of destroying, seizing, or debilitating cement factories at times outweighed the possible financial benefit of maintaining production levels (Johnston et al. 2016). For example, in preparation for the commencement of 2015 coalition attacks on Mosul, IS moved several of these factories to Syria. Then, in April 2016, the organisation released a statement saying that it had seized control of a cement factory in Syria and executed twenty 'regime supporters' (Dearden 2016). Although Russian state media reported that 175 workers had been massacred in the event, this was later proven inaccurate (Dearden 2016). In 2017, IS also set fire to the Badush cement plant in western Mosul to prevent Iraqi forces retaking the region, though the prevention of this ultimately failed (Adel 2017). Moreover, in 2015 cement was estimated to represent around 4 per cent of the organisation's revenue, at US$100 million, while in 2014 IS earned US$300 million from cement (Bindner and Poirot 2016). In addition to IS's destruction of the factories themselves, this reduction was once more attributed to IS's loss of territory; where it previously controlled the Lafarge al-Jalabiya plant in Ayn al-Arabin, the al-Raqqah Guris Cement plant in Fallujah, and the Kubaisa and al-Qa'im plants in Iraq, IS lost control of the Kubaisa and al-Jalabiya plants fighting with coalition forces in 2015 (Bindner and Poirot 2016). Collectively, these cases show that, although IS's profits from this resource declined with its loss of territory, these assets remained symbolically and strategically significant for IS, as it capitalised on its flexible approach to their economic management and the related insecurity in the region its actions helped to reinforce.

Perhaps most revealing in terms of the neoliberal characteristics of IS's handling of cement firms was its collaboration with powerful private commercial entities incorporated in countries involved in military actions against IS. A high-profile 2017 case was brought against the French cement firm LaFarge for paying 'taxes' and lump-sum bribes to IS to protect its business in Syria. The case, lodged by 11 former employees of LaFarge in Syria, and Sherpa, the European Center for Constitutional and Human Rights, claimed that the company maintained 'business relations' with militant groups in Syria in order to keep its cement mines open (Atkins et al. 2017). The investigation furthermore revealed that the company had established intermediary partnerships with entities transferring funds to IS and other proscribed groups in Syria to ensure the safe passage of workers to the facilities and the continuation of its operations. These actions were primarily undertaken following the commencement of fighting near IS's al-Jalabiyeh plant in northern Syria in 2013 for control of the border. They also occurred prior to the 2015 Lafarge–Holcim merger of Swiss and French companies, the latter being particularly relevant to the fiduciary characteristic of neoliberal finance, given its potential to obscure the origins of proceeds that resulted from economic activity with IS, and the safeguarding of the company's Syrian business. While prosecutors from Paris opened a preliminary inquiry into the company's dealings in Syria in 2016, the Swiss federal prosecutor stated in 2017 that it was 'not concerned with this matter at the moment' (Atkins et al. 2017). At the time of this book's writing, the Swiss authorities have not pursued the firm, but in Paris the company has been charged with complicity in crimes against humanity and financing terrorism.

IS's flexible approach to resource management, extending to its exploitation of resource crises for economic ends, was also apparent in its handling of agriculture. As US Department of State sources in 2017 confirmed, between 2014 and 2017 IS seized the most fertile lands in Iraq and Syria (Eklund et al. 2017). Researchers at CAT also observed that IS's agricultural revenue derived from processes of both production and distribution, as well as profit acquired through 'taxes levied at various points on the value chain' (Bindner and Poirot 2016, 13–14).

One detailed account of IS's funding from the production and sale of wheat, barley, and cotton is Hadi Jaafar and Eckart Woertz's (2016) satellite-imagery and remote-sensing analysis. Jaafar and Woertz revealed that wheat and barley production was maintained at high levels throughout the Syrian and Iraqi civil conflicts from 2011–2017, while irrigated summer crops, including cotton, were significantly debilitated. They also found that the total value of IS wheat production in these territories, at 2.45 million tons in 2015, could equal that of IS's oil production during its peak in late 2014 and early 2015. Agricultural resources were thus of great magnitude and importance for IS despite this being infrequently reported in critical research and international news media during the time of the Caliphate, from 2014 to 2019.

Jaafar and Woertz's (2016) study also intimates a relevant comparison between IS's management of resources and the activity of neoliberal nation states and late modern capitalist corporations. In ways reminiscent of US-directed organisations and multinational corporations, IS manipulated supply, demand, and resources to garner profits, and used agricultural resources as a weapon of war. To explain the nature of this situation, questions posed by Ehtesham Shahid (2016) in relation to Jaafar and Woertz's research are relevant. Shahid (2016) asked, pertinently: if it is possible for academic researchers to conduct such studies, why can't powerful governments do the same? To answer this, it is initially worth reflecting on the role that food security, which since the 1980s has been exploited by monopolistic agricultural industries (see, for instance, Van Horn 2009), plays in IS governance.

In theory, agriculture for IS has been a potentially sustainable income stream, unlike the extractive sources of hydrocarbons, which can be limited in terms of accessibility. Maintaining agricultural production was also important for the organisation as it allowed IS to reinforce its theocratic legitimacy by showing the organisation's ability to feed its 'citizens'. Scholars of (neo-)jihadism, for example, have extensively argued that IS required successful territory, food, and service provision to substantiate its claim that the Caliphate is Allah's blessed nation (Armstrong 2014). The methods that IS used to provide agricultural goods, however, along with its allocation of resources, indicates its leverage of these resources to exploit people in the Caliphate. This occurred via its control over flows of goods to specific areas, a practice that might be interpreted in relation to controls over supply and demand exercised by late modern capitalist states and neoliberal 'agribusiness' organisations (Murray 2002).

Demonstrating the gravity of the food-security issue in previously IS-held territory, the Food and Agriculture Organization of the United Nations (FAO) raised concerns from 2014 that the displacement of populations, IS's monopoly on agriculture, and the suspension of the former Iraqi government's subsidy for food in regional areas could lead to food scarcity (FAO 2014), a reality that became manifest in popularised media images of starving Syrian citizens. This occurred in part as a result of regional conflict generally, but also as a result of IS's manipulation of supply and demand through its control of resource yield, access, and distribution. Despite surplus crop yields during 2015 and 2016, for example (which were in large part a result of the declining local population), inadequate provision of wheat and flour in Iraq and Syria allowed IS to drive the price of wheat higher (Fick 2014). When considered in relation to Jaafar and Woertz's study (2016), which highlighted wheat surpluses in the region, it is likely that IS engaged in this form of price fixing while still drawing a profit by smuggling wheat, wheat-based products, and other grains to government-affiliated entities in Syria, which were then distributed to specific populations at the discretion of the regime (Georgy and El Dahan 2017). Indicative of sublimated social, political, and strategic concerns beneath economic interests, this case also signifies the importance of a 'destabilised habitus' for IS and supporters of neoliberalism generally (Bourdieu 1998b, 98), where civilians living in IS territory experienced insecurity, and IS reinforced this insecurity for the purpose of raising funds and securing territory.

Although IS did not engage to the same extent in a for-profit extortion with water as it did with wheat, the organisation has wielded this resource as a weapon of war. This behavioural characteristic of IS is similar in some ways to political-economic strategies used by the US, as blocking and jeopardising water supplies was not an uncommon practice for the US government and US-affiliated industries in conflicts throughout the twentieth and twenty-first centuries (Gleick 1993; Gleick et al. 2014). During the Korean War, for example, US forces destroyed dams in North Korea, causing a drought for local farmers and catalysing widespread conditions of starvation and malnutrition (Chomsky 2004). Similar behaviour was also undertaken for economic gain in neoliberal settings, as, for instance, when US companies withheld loans for clean-water projects in Haiti during the 1980s (Lacey 2008). For different political and economic reasons, though similarly for strategic gain, following the commencement of the Iraqi and US-led offensive in November 2016 to retake Mosul from IS, the latter deliberately cut water supplies to neighbourhoods near the front line of the fighting in order to force civilians to withdraw with the troops, so that they could be used as human shields (Dearden 2016; Blanche 2017).

Exploitative and flexible mechanisms of agricultural control indicate therefore that IS engaged in the 'dispossession' of people for strategic ends (Harvey 2001, 2003), broadly recalling the neoliberal practice of manipulating markets at the expense of starving populations. This practice has been criticised in international reports about 'dumping scandals', where product surpluses that could be used to feed starving populations around the world (such as Californian oranges) were disposed of at sea in order to sustain high pricing (US Environmental Protection Agency 2017). In relation to the Iraqi and Syrian context, international communities have recognised the historical and cyclical nature of resource exploitation producing poverty, malnutrition, and disease. The understated though implicit recognition of this situation in institutional arenas is also evidenced by commentaries likening issues of food and water scarcity in Iraq to such examples of neoliberal layering as the 1980s sanctions regime against the Saddam Hussein administration, the Oil-for-Food Programme, and the outcomes of CPA orders introduced following the 2003 Iraq invasion (Woertz 2014, 2017).

IS administration of finance

IS's management of resources and other financial assets in its territory comprises applied examples of its overall political-economic governance. Like its management of financial assets, IS's administration of finance reflects the behaviours of US-associated entities in the Middle East, and neoliberal economic circumstances in the wider international financial system. Extending the previous sections' exploration of IS finance and the importance of territory for IS, in this section I elaborate on how IS's administration of finance exemplifies its state-like geo-economic ambitions. In particular, these practices might be interpreted as signifying the organisation's reliance upon 'metacapital' (Bourdieu 1998a), wherein its exercise of extra-economic and economic capital combined with its retention of territory sustain its perceived theocratic legitimacy. As Bourdieu explained, this constitutes 'the culmination of a process of concentration of different species of capital: capital of physical force or instruments of coercion (army, police), economic capital, cultural capital or (better) informational capital, and symbolic capital' (1998a, 41). This is first apparent in IS's use of a two-tiered management system, through which profits for the Caliphate were garnered through the exploitation of local citizens and through the promotion of competitive market activity.

At the head of IS's two-tiered system from 2014 to 2017 (and perhaps continuing in some ways after 2020) was the Commander in Chief, the Caliph Abu Bakr al-Baghdadi, who was advised by a Cabinet, including a Shura Council and Executive Branch, below which sat a Deputy of Iraq and a Deputy of Syria. In each of the two tiers of Iraq and Syria, there were twelve Governors who variously oversaw the operations of 'Councils for Finance (weapons, financing)', 'Military (defense)', 'Leadership (laws, policies)', 'Legal (executions and recruitment)', 'Fighters Assistance (foreign fighters)', 'Security (policing)', 'Intelligence (information on IS enemies)', and 'Media (social and other)' (TRAC 2015). Although Baghdadi and IS refuted the territorial division of Iraq and Syria created by the Sykes–Picot agreement, exemplified directly in the Al Hayat video 'The end of Sykes Picot' (2014b), for pragmatic reasons, within the field of neoliberalism, the organisation managed and coordinated finance in each of these territories independently.

IS's coordination of finance was illuminated in a cache of 1,200 documents uncovered by US marines in a routine patrol in Anbar province during January 2007 (in a town called Tuzliyah al Gharbiyah, situated along the Euphrates) and delivered to US-government-sponsored think tank the National Defense Research Institute of the Rand Corporation (Rand). In their report, Rand researchers likened Islamic State of Iraq's decentralised management structure to a 'multidivisional-hierarchy form' of management, sometimes termed 'M-form', which first became operational in the Western corporate setting of Alfred Sloan's 1920s General Motors (Bahney et al. 2010; Simpson 2014). (The cache also revealed that a similar governance model was used by the precursor to IS, Islamic

State of Iraq (Simpson 2014).) The benefits of this form of management are that 'firms' or sectors are semi-autonomous, and they are as such responsible for overseeing their own production and maximising profit levels. This represents a form of decentralisation and 'rhizomatic' assemblage (Deleuze and Guattari 1988) characteristic of mainstream neoliberal corporations (Lazzarato 2009). IS's adoption of this model to a degree indicates both contiguity between the organisation and its stated Western capitalist opponents, as well as the ongoing, layered effects of political-economic restructuring in the region. In addition to the macro Western commercial origins of its organisational infrastructure, IS's administration of finance on a micro level was designed to facilitate the perpetuation and growth of economic capital in the organisation's territories. While the Finance Council regulated and oversaw the activities and enterprise discussed previously (such as taxes and trade), other councils exhibited operational characteristics typical of a neoliberal nation state in several dimensions.

In one example, the Military and Fighters Assistance Councils oversaw wages paid to those fighting for IS, which from 2014 to 2017 vastly superseded those from other readily available employment in the region. In 2014, fighters were paid between US$400 and US$1,200 monthly depending on whether they were local or foreign and their level of weapons training and tactical knowledge (Al-Tamimi 2016). These wages were more competitive than those for most non-violent labour following the beginning of the Syrian civil conflict and the de-Ba'athification programme in Iraq, after 2003. According to the US Congressional Research Service, in 2016 IS fighters were paid US$25 for each child and US$50 for their wives (Pagliery 2016). Also significant in this respect was IS's 'privatisation', or outsourcing, of combat to mercenaries. Based on the Geneva Convention definition that a mercenary 'is motivated to take part in the hostilities essentially by the desire for private gain and, in fact, is promised, by or on behalf of a party to the conflict, material compensation substantially in excess of that promised or paid to combatants of similar rank and functions in the armed forces of that party' (UN General Assembly 1989), all of IS's foreign fighters – 31,000 from 86 countries before the end of 2015, some of whom were highly skilled (Westcott 2015) – could be considered mercenaries. Not only does this situation destabilise the 'holy warrior' narrative communicated through IS's evocation of social, cultural, and symbolic capital in its propagandised media, it also indicates a monetary strategy for recruitment ideologically resembling the ruthless profit incentives that underlie neoliberal industry.

As Chapter 2 elaborated, the neoliberal practice of outsourcing state functions has been connected with a growth of private military industries and revolving-door relationships between the US government and heads of private military contractors (Smart 2016). Successive US governments' employment of mercenaries to perform military actions in the Middle East has in particular been well documented (Scahill 2008; Isenberg 2009). Examples of the neoliberal outsourcing of combat to private entities in Iraq included contractual partnerships with firms such as the (now re-branded) Blackwater, along with DynCorp International, and Triple Canopy Incorporated (Lovewine 2014). Given this history, IS's outsourcing of its operations to private, hire-to-kill mercenaries is significant in revealing its political-economic identity. Not only do IS and the US exploit financial incentives for war through private military industries, they also mutually justify this activity by exploiting 'religious' fundamentalism. As we saw in Chapter 2, religious American exceptionalism both before and after the Bush administration has been sustained by the civilisational rhetoric of terrorist and counterterrorist forces since 9/11 (Jackson 2018).

Further to its neoliberal governance of violent activities, the IS Leadership Council enforced governance that might be interpreted as neoliberal of certain non-violent financial activities within the Caliphate. In 2015, for example, the IS media team published a photograph of the head of a Consumer Protection Authority in Raqqa in its propaganda magazine, the *Islamic State Report*, and quoted one of its restaurant inspectors: 'it's an office that's concerned with protecting shoppers by inspecting the goods being sold in shops, markets, shopping centers, and wholesale outlets, discovering goods that are spoiled or not suitable for sale and taking those responsible to account' (Alexander and Alexander 2015, 112; Al Hayat 2015c, 5). This 'office' comprised a board of inspectors who monitored quality and fair pricing in the Caliphate for the purpose of safeguarding competition between businesses. Although characteristic of classical liberal economics as opposed to those that might be considered strictly 'neoliberal', this practice in effect served to reinforce IS fundraising through taxation, price fixing, and its complex financialised participation in resource and currency manipulation, previously outlined.

Reflecting tensions and transfers between different forms of social, symbolic, and economic capital in state-like entities' expression of meta-capital, certain measures IS imposed on its residents, largely resulting from its loss of territory over time, undermined its stated aim of promoting successful commerce in the Caliphate. For example, to compensate for its loss of territory in 2015 and 2016 and the resulting loss of revenue, IS augmented profit ratios in its resource-price-fixing activities and amplified the scale and rapidity of its activity in oil and gas exploitation

(European Parliament 2017). It also reduced spending on public services and significantly cut public salaries. A leaked document published by Aymenn Jawad al-Tamimi revealed, for example, that in late 2015 IS cut salaries 'paid to all mujahideen by half, and it is not allowed for anyone to be exempted from this decision, whatever his position' (Beauchamp 2016). It also reduced access to a restricted internet and resource rations (Al-Tamimi 2016) in ways that perhaps, reflect neoliberal austerity measures imposed in developed Western nations after the GFC, analysed critically by the IMF in 2016 (Ostry et al. 2016).

In combination with the already aggressive taxation system for trades and services within the Caliphate, and in IS's activity generally, reduced financial support and services for citizens in the Caliphate rendered its domestic economic circumstance unsustainable. The erratic imposition of taxes by IS created an uncertain regulatory environment that impeded the growth of private business; moreover, with less money, people did not have the surplus income to spend or invest. Wes Cooper (2017) suggested that, because IS is first and foremost an 'extractive state', its loss of territory and failing economic confidence in the Caliphate beyond 2017 means further engagement in international criminal activity and the formal international financial system are the only reliable mechanisms by which the organisation would be able to generate the economic capital necessary for its survival. This prediction may indeed appear to have been correct, given IS's loss of all major territory by 2019 and the fact that the organisation appears in 2020 to be restructuring its organisational model to the decentralised support of IS-aligned organisations internationally, although before his death in October 2019 Baghdadi reasserted his leadership of 'IS Central' (Williams 2019). Potentially, it was IS's former 'non-neoliberal' financial behaviour, including its usage of taxation, combined with its military defeat that prevented IS's immediate survival post-2017 in a field of neoliberal economic relations.

To the extent that IS finance has not relied upon the literal retention and exploitation of land and territory, it has to some degree engaged with international flows of finance. Although these flows have typically existed outside of the formal international economy, they have often been facilitated by modern capitalist technologies, as they were for AQ. Examples facilitated via the internet include IS's solicitation of donations through PayPal and CASHU, and crowdsourcing sites such as GoFundMe (Homeland Security Committee 2016). At the organisation's peak, donors and fighters were also most often identified and recruited via social media such as Facebook, Twitter, and Skype before they were transitioned for more secure (end-to-end encrypted) communications networks such as WhatsApp, Telegram, and Kik Messenger. IS and its intermediaries have auctioned off local antiquities on eBay, (Maremont and Stewart 2015), which the UN Educational, Scientific and Cultural Organization (UNESCO) warned in 2015 was occurring on an 'industrial scale', with many of the antiquities likely to end up on licit and illicit markets in London (Osborn 2015). Other sources of capital for IS have included its usage of pre-paid money cards and experiments with cryptocurrency. To 2020, though, there is scant evidence that these measures comprised a significant source of fundraising for IS. Nevertheless, as was the case with AQ, independent fundraising measures adopted by foreign fighters and those who have independently supported the organisation have been facilitated by their engagement with the international financial system, including, for example, US and UK fighters who used credit-based and student-loan systems to finance their travel to the Caliphate.

Though this chapter has not sought to quantify the exact scale, division, or implications of IS finance, it has explained how IS fundraising and financial management was facilitated by the neoliberal dimensions of the international financial system. Drawing on Bourdieusian and neo-Marxist ideas, I argued that IS engaged in a number of fundraising and financial governance practices that are differentially continuous with and reflexive of neoliberal situations and actions extant in the Middle East prior to its announcement of a Caliphate.

The application of Jessop's (2006) theory demonstrated how, in a manner comparable with neoliberal nation states as opposed to de-territorialised financial entities, IS was until 2017 concerned with the geo-economic dimensions of fundraising and finance, particularly regarding its handling of trade, taxation, and local resource management. Peck's notion of neoliberal layering (2010) was of practical use in explaining how in these practices the organisation often made use of routes, networks, and connections that derived from US-led invasions in Iraq in the 1990s and 2003, including the Oil-for-Food Programme and ISKP's use of networks from the MAK in the 1980s. Drawing on Harvey's (2003) theory, the investigation then demonstrated how this situation was in large part predicated on IS's engagement with resource exploitation in conditions of neoliberalism that may be understood as 'accumulation by dispossession'. Bourdieu's theory aided the analysis by allowing for the elaboration of IS financial practices that were dialectical and referential, given the political-economic history and character of the region. Through the usage of this political-economic framework, I sought to emphasise the multifaceted nature of the dialectic in question, determined by the organisation's appeal to different forms of capital. This dialectic was broadly determined by capital, particularly when considered in the light of IS's anti-capitalist campaigning. Where social, cultural, and symbolic capital were important for IS between 2014 and 2017, including as metacapital in the organisation's administration of a Caliphate, cases of IS finance demonstrate the sustained importance of economic capital for IS, as part of its political-economic habitus expression. This was shown to occur in a neoliberal economic environment characterised by adherence to a competitive and action-oriented political-economic paradigm, which was also upheld by IS. Support for IS actions was then reinforced by a political situation in which neoliberal concerns for profit, competition, and capitalist managerialism are experienced by powerful actors as a doxa and uncritically accepted as self-evident.

The 'rational' imposition of US intervention in Iraq and the region broadly since the 1980s, contributing to the entrenchment of disaster-predicated political-economic development, comprised a series of political-economic layers generative of the political-economic environment in which IS emerged. Though broader strategic and military concerns in the Middle East were also in part responsible for nation states providing tacit and overt support to IS and for opposing the Assad government, IS was demonstrated to mirror and reflexively respond to the neoliberal incentives and behaviours of its strategic opposition. Collectively, the analytical framework in this and earlier chapters demonstrated the interdependent importance of territory to IS from 2014 to 2017, in comparison with the relatively decentralised, de-territorialised neo-jihadist organisation of AQ.

Beyond their different geo-economic orientations, I sought in these chapters to reveal a number of key discernible differences between the financial practices of AQ and IS. These include IS's close ties to regional governments and their organisational proxies, whereas AQ relied to a greater extent on donations from wealthy government-aligned individuals. Whereas AQ was more comprehensively integrated into the international financial system, IS engaged in neoliberal economic managerial practices through hybrid and opaque interactions with formal systems in a localised context, again dependent on territory, such as the manipulation of supply and demand, and currency speculation. As was the case with AQ's de-territorialised financial practices, IS's practices are antithetical to Islamic finance because in a number of respects they depend upon neoliberal financial environments, which survive via the exploitation of interest and risk, and because the proceeds from IS's financial activity (like AQ's) are used to fund political violence. As will be elaborated in the following, final chapter, this violence, in turn, signified these organisations' exploitation of power and the consequent destabilisation of their combined 'resistance' ethic, particularly in the extent to which they might be considered to constitute terrorism. Further disrupting AQ and IS's ostensible theological elements, several of their practices such as currency trading and investment in tax havens are predicated on 'making money from nothing' – the religiously forbidden practice of *riba* – while they are generally reliant upon the broad-based exploitation of Syrian and Iraqi citizens, in contravention of the ethical dimensions of Islamic finance.

Drawing on the insights thus far set out, in the final chapter of this book I reflect on how the political-economic behaviour of AQ and IS signifies dialectical engagements between neo-jihadism and neoliberalism, in particular those that entail aspects of causation, reflexivity, and mirroring. Examining these insights in relation to the broader political-economic paradigm of neoliberalism, and the impact of the GWOT, I also reflect on likely future directions for the politically violent phenomena in question.

Conclusion

The cases in *Neoliberalism and neo-jihadism* have revealed ideological and material ways in which AQ and IS engage with the political-economic paradigm of neoliberalism. While campaigning on the basis of culturally prevalent anti-capitalist sentiments, these organisations raise and manage funds by exploiting the apparatus and affordances of neoliberal political-economic systems. Although AQ and IS are exclusive examples of the (r)evolutionary phenomenon of neo-jihadism, they are both characteristic of the mutually constitutive nature of power and resistance. Just as many resistance movements throughout modern history, from the Enlightenment to (anti-)colonialism, communism, and late modern capitalism, have ended up resembling the forms of power they sought to overthrow, so too have AQ and IS ended up resembling and reconstituting the dominant political-economic paradigm of neoliberalism they, in part, mobilised in response to.

Dialectics of resistance

Differing from other, strategic analyses of these groups, in this book I argued that the various ways in which these organisations re-purpose and reconstitute neoliberalism are in certain respects unsurprising. In their state and institution building, AQ and IS reconstruct elitist and oppressive political-economic hierarchies in a similar manner to historical examples of power-cum-resistance – for instance, the 1917 Russian Revolution, Mao Zedong's China in the 1930s, and the US-backed 'Purple', 'Orange', 'Cedar', and 'Rose' revolutions in Iraq, Ukraine, Lebanon, and Georgia in the 2000s (DeFronzo 2018). In their use of finance and technology for military ends, AQ and IS tactically appropriate the weapons of their enemies, following a long-standing tradition of warfare first popularised by Sun Tzu (Griffith 1963). In some ways resembling contemporary non-state social movements, including labour unions and left-wing agitprop groups, AQ and IS re-purpose the apparatus of late capitalism to highlight its deleterious effects (Ferrell 2019).

Unlike contemporary and historical examples of progressive resistance, on the other hand, as neo-jihadist organisations, AQ and IS lack what Ferrell (2019) termed 'analytical resistance', whereby the machineries of power are seized for the purpose of their eventual subversion. In their efforts to mobilise resistance sentiments and realise power, both AQ and IS uncritically exploit the affordances of neoliberalism to the effect that they ultimately contribute to its continued existence. Further to their logistical support for neoliberal dimensions of the international financial system, this occurs ideologically via essentialised, propagandised representations of neoliberalism in neo-jihadist propaganda, which reinforce the competitive philosophical premises of neoliberalism and fortify the political-ideological antagonism on which neoliberalism depends (Peck 2010). Discourses of resistance evident in AQ and IS propaganda promote limited attention to the repressive characteristics of neoliberalism and, in so doing, allow pervasive and widespread manifestations of neoliberalism in finance and politics internationally to persist relatively unrestricted. By broadly endorsing what Bloom (2016) terms the 'social ontology of power and resistance', AQ and IS are, in a political-economic sense, wholly constituted in and via the structures and systems they superficially contest.

As the examples of neo-jihadist propaganda and finance demonstrate, in their quest for power through violent acts of terrorism AQ and IS in many ways, in fact, extend beyond the limits of resistance. The limits of these organisations' resistance efforts are particularly apparent in their course towards the attainment of power, wherein they inflict financial and physical exploitation, generating neo-jihadism's own resistance opposition. One noteworthy case not accounted for in this book are efforts on the part of the People's Protection Units (YPG), Women's Protection Units (YPJ), and Kurdistan Workers' Party (PKK) to defend Kurdish territories and communities from IS between 2014 and 2019 (Gerges 2017). These forces used violence to protect residents of Kurdish and neighbouring Syrian and Iraqi areas in resistance to IS's extreme violence and oppression, including its commencement of the perpetration of genocide in the Iraqi Sinjar province on 3 August 2014, where 5000 Kurdish people were murdered, up to 10,000 were injured or captured, and 500,000 became refugees.

To conceptualise the impact of politically violent entities such as AQ and IS, it is therefore necessary to recognise how their various exercise of power reflects epistemological debates on mutable, politicised, and subjective 'resistance' or 'terrorism' definitions. Contextualised by Richard

Jackson's (2010, 123) understanding of terrorism as 'the violence or its threat intended as a symbolically communicative act in which the direct victims of the action are instrumentalized as a means to creating a psychological effect of intimidation and fear in a target audience for a political objective', a comparison of IS and Kurdish forces exemplifies this tension. Where IS has been widely designated as a terrorist organisation, though it mobilises on the basis of resistance to the exploitation of power by the West, the PKK has been designated as a terrorist organisation by the NATO military alliance but not by Russia, China, Brazil, Switzerland, India, Egypt, and the UN (Sentas 2018).

To elaborate briefly: various perspectives on the political actions of Kurdish organisations correspond to their history of perpetrating and (in some cases allegedly) planning attacks on Turkish law-enforcement and military organisations, as well as government-affiliated schools, civilians, and infrastructure. Since its establishment in 1978, the PKK has also been interpreted by some as a resistance movement in its efforts at self-determination and defence against Turkish state forces that inflicted physical violence, forced displacement, mass imprisonment, execution, and food embargoes against Kurdish people while refusing their rights to political representation from the commencement of the 1978 Turkish–Kurdish conflict (Gunes 2013). In another illustration, the Patriotic Union of Kurdistan's (PUK) Peshmerga forces have been considered terrorist actors by Turkey, though, unlike the PKK, they are not often labelled as such by many other states. Also in resistance to state oppression, the PUK historically opposed the Hussein administration, including as a response to the administration's murder of 180,000 Kurds in chemical warfare during the Al-Anfal Campaign (1986–1989) (Izady 2015). IS, by contrast with both Kurdish organisations, is typically interpreted as a terrorist actor in respect of its wide and in some ways indiscriminate persecution of Muslim, Christian, other-faith, and secular civilians, ostensibly, and unlike most liberatory movements, in the service of its own very selective interpretation of religion.

The case of Kurdish military activity in the region therefore indicates a noteworthy contrast with neo-jihadism. Differences between these movements can also be highlighted through comparison of the ideology of neo-jihadism and that of the political philosophy of anarchism. Despite its definition as terrorism by some, the PKK in fact claims inspiration from the principles of anarchism, and the Kurdish territory of Rojava is sometimes described as a quasi-anarchist municipality (Izady 2015). Deepening the dialectical nature of the above-stated classifications, anarchism has, perhaps, historically provided the most direct and tangible alternative to state-based logics of 'power and resistance'

(Graeber 2004; Bloom 2016; Ferrell 2019). Nineteenth-century assassinations and bombings of political elites by anarchists (sometimes termed 'propaganda of the deed') were a temporary phenomenon, with the bulk of anarchist activity dedicated to establishing egalitarian, non-hierarchical forms of collective democracy, as exemplified in the Paris Commune of 1871, the 1918–1921 Ukrainian 'Free State' of Nester Makhno, Catalonia in the 1930s, and individual 'colonies' in the UK and US in the twenty-first century (Williams 2017; Woodcock 2018). The sublimation of anarchism within the political logics of international counterterrorism variously served to re-enshrine and politically legitimise its sovereign opposition. Also, as with the violence associated with various social movements, violence perpetrated by allegedly anarchist actors, despite often targeting elites rather than civilians, has for provisional supporters in history served to undermine those actors' emancipatory commitment.

Kurdish revolutionary forces, then, compared with neo-jihadists in the Middle East, and with consideration of the Erdogan administration's support for IS, might be said to destabilise artificially dichotomising, Manichean logics often used to describe terrorism (Richards 2017). Indeed, as *Neoliberalism and neo-jihadism* demonstrated, cultural essentialism can explain fewer characteristics of the GWOT than paying attention to the broader strategic-military game, which, within the market at least, extends conspicuously to the field of neoliberalism.

Drawing on the example of neo-jihadism, a primary aim of this book has therefore been to shed light not only on the ontology of AQ and IS but also on the limits of possibility for resistance to neoliberalism. In doing so it extended Bloom's (2016) perspective that the logics of power and their resistance opposition were incubated during the Enlightenment, developed in response to international colonialism, and enshrined as a material and ideological reality with the birth of late modern capitalism. As Bloom explained (2016, 88), and as I explored in this book, the emergence of capitalism constituted 'the transformation of power and resistance from the discursive foundation for establishing truth and subjectivity into the very material and ideological conditions for sustaining human existence'. Neoliberalism, on the one hand, represented the hegemonic relations of power AQ and IS sought to challenge, while, on the other, it comprised the dominant structural environment through which their insecure resistance was articulated.

Lessons on neo-jihadism

The application of Bourdieusian ideas to interpret AQ and IS's engagements with neoliberalism had important implications for the discussion.

Initially, Bourdieu's perspective in *Acts of resistance* (1998b) was useful in elaborating a core contention of this book: that by virtue of its philosophical and practical dimensions, neoliberalism has often been naturalised as 'self-evident' (Jessop 1982; Brenner and Theodore 2002; Peck 2010; Crouch 2011). The early discussion elaborated that although neoliberalism and neo-classical economics are promoted as an inviolable science (Gray 2003), in reality they derive historical inspiration from the scientific-spiritual fanaticism of early positivists, including Auguste Comte and Henri de Saint-Simon (Peck 2010; Gray 2014). While these positivist belief systems were perpetuated in the 1920s Vienna Circle and the 1950s and 1960s Chicago and Austrian schools of thought, they promoted an external, ostensible 'de-linking' of economic theory from its social and historical contingents (Thorsen and Lie 2006; Rodrik 2011). As the analysis of contemporary neoliberal policies illustrated, the tangible social effects of neoliberal policies are apparent in the various deprivation they have caused, including in the GFC. Such policies, moreover, produce reflexive effects for the economy which cannot be accounted for in purely 'scientific', ahistorical, and asocial models.

In his explanation of the different forms of capital, Bourdieu recognised this situation, arguing that the pseudo-science of neoliberalism became entrenched through discourses related to deregulation, privatisation, and flexibility, which collectively facilitated a 'utopia of exploitation' (1998a; 1998b). In *Neoliberalism and neo-jihadism*, Bourdieu's (1986) 'forms of capital' provided for a holistic consideration of AQ and IS's political-economic strategy, wherein their appeal to symbolic, cultural, and social forms of capital was interpreted as correlative with neoliberal economic capital distribution.

Drawing on Bourdieu, the first part of the analysis revealed that the anti-capitalist discourses of AQ and IS reflected internationally prevalent anti-capitalist sentiments during the time of neo-jihadist propaganda distribution. In the 1960s and 1970s, for example, literature that influenced AQ was replete with Cold War, quasi-socialist references to a 'revolutionary vanguard' (Qut'b 1981), as well as to individualisation and commodification. These influences were reflected in the 1980s statements of Osama Bin Laden's early second-in-command, Abdullah Azzam, and in the contemporaneous quasi-socialist proselytising of the early AQ deputy, Ayman al-Zawahiri. During the 1990s, after AQ's official inception in 1988, the organisational leader, Osama Bin Laden, posited an anti-globalisation argument for waging jihad against the US, which echoed dominant neo-colonial critiques of anti-globalisation movements active at the time (Holzapfel and König 2009). After 2001, AQ propaganda assumed a broad-based anti-capitalist critique that targeted financialised, non-territorial capital, and relatedly sought to capitalise on the symbolic act of targeting the World Trade Center on 9/11. Immediately after the GFC, Zawahiri and Bin Laden emphasised the domestic US and international effects of the crisis, paying attention to its non-territorial, monetary dimensions.

The analysis also revealed that developments in AQ propaganda over time occurred in a manner that reflected the organisation's own de-territorialisation, while incorporating rhetorically sophisticated techniques. These included Bin Laden's display of his education as cultural capital, Zawahiri's appeal to collectivisation and social capital, and both leaders' overarching reference to the ideals of anti-capitalist disenfranchisement as a 'subjugated habitus' (Bourdieu 1984, 1986). The analysis explored how, despite its reductive qualities, AQ's long-form prose incorporated sophisticated rhetoric with extensive use of reinforcement, self-inclusive prefixes, metaphors, and direct address. I also highlighted AQ's intensifying usage of symbolism, which was likewise interpreted in relation to the 'rhizomatic' (Deleuze and Guattari 1988), decentralised spread of the organisation following the US-directed invasion of Afghanistan in 2001. Through reference to the political-economic theory of Harvey (2003) and Peck (2010), these characteristics of AQ propaganda were argued to reflect in various ways dominant critiques of neoliberalism.

The next part of the analysis began with the supposition that, like AQ, IS's territorial ambition would be reflected in its political-economic propaganda. Like the investigation into AQ, this began with an account of ideologues that influenced the organisation, in addition to those discussed in relation to AQ, such as the pseudonymous author of *The management of savagery* (2006), Abu Bakr Naji. Where the early quasi-socialist proselytising of Qut'b and Azzam were demonstrated to have been influential to AQ at its emergence, Naji's petition for the Mujahideen (as he termed the neo-jihadists) to engage in petrodollar warfare (Clark 2005; Naji 2006) demonstrated a preoccupation on the part of neo-jihadism and its strongest proponents with US control over oil and currency in the Middle Eastern region. Reflecting Zawahiri and Gadahn's explicit targeting of the US petrodollar (AQAP 2013), this propaganda indicated contiguity between IS at its origins and AQ in 2013 and 2014.

Despite certain similarities between AQ and IS, the period of propaganda distribution examined in the case of IS extended only from the organisation's declaration of a Caliphate in 2014 to 2017, a significantly shorter duration than that in which the examined AQ propaganda was published. Clear trends in IS's anti-capitalist propaganda that corresponded to global political-economic developments were therefore less apparent than was the case with AQ. My analysis of IS propaganda did, however, reveal a number of ways in which Naji's instructions were demonstrably influential to the propaganda and strategies of IS. Both Naji's text and IS's propaganda recalled the 'civilisational' rhetoric and actions of counterterrorist and military efforts during and after the George W. Bush administration – for example, Naji's direct citation of Donald Rumsfeld (2006, 69, 104).

Where AQ's long-form explanations of its political-economic orientation were explained as featuring distinct chronological appeals to social and cultural capital, as well as sophisticated rhetorical techniques, IS propaganda regularly took long and short-forms, and its appeals to divergent forms of capital took place simultaneously. IS propaganda included speeches made by then IS leader Abu Bakr al-Baghdadi and spokesman Abu Muhammad al-Adnani, combined with audiovisual media that often featured simple though symbolic rhetoric with sophisticated editing techniques. In line with Naji's instruction to produce and disseminate media that is accessible to the 'masses' as well as the intellectual 'elite' (2006, 110), IS apparently sought to target a broader audience than AQ since 2014.

While the geo-economic aspect of AQ's propaganda was most prominently reflected in its shift from a neo-colonial critique of US-directed industries towards an increasingly symbolic, de-territorialised propaganda focus following 9/11 and the 2008 GFC, IS more plainly endorsed the 'land' and 'territory' of the Caliphate through a propagandised discussion of neo-colonial borders in the Middle East and an ongoing rhetorical comparison between the Caliphate and the US. Harvey (2003) and Peck (2010) were useful in revealing the symbolic and at-times opaque orientation of AQ's propaganda, and Jessop's (2006) neo-Marxist discussion of the interdependencies between capitalism and territoriality was useful in illuminating the ongoing territoriality of IS propaganda, given its subjective positioning as a quasi-nation state.

Substantive differences between AQ and IS's propaganda were thus explored in the first part of the book with reference to Bourdieusian and neo-Marxist theory. In addition to the organisations' divergent displays of capital in their propaganda, the discussion revealed that, correlative with their respective geo-strategic interests, AQ throughout its history became more preoccupied with the symbolic 'idealism' of anti-capitalism, whereas IS was more interested in the 'material' realities of its own anti-US and anti-capitalist ambition, such as exploiting the destruction in Iraq and controlling oil fields. In the case of IS, this propaganda focus reflected Naji's instruction to capitalise on 'disaster situations' (2006), which itself was reminiscent of Naomi Klein and Alex Dupuy's treatises on 'disaster capitalism' (Klein 2007, 2010; Dupuy 2010). It also indicates the divergent applicability of Bourdieu's manifold idealism–materialism dialectic, a confluence of Hegelian and Marxist traditions, to explain the extrinsic political-economic identities of AQ and IS respectively.

In the next section, I explored the extent to which the financial practices of these organisations could be interpreted through a neoliberal framework as quasi-capitalist. As such, the analysis considered how the fundamental political-economic identities of these organisations, as represented through their financial behaviour, might be antithetical to their external, anti-capitalist credos. This subject of enquiry was addressed with reference to similar political-economic theory applied in the earlier discussion; however, the analysis more directly emphasised a comparison of AQ and IS with neoliberal economic policies, rather than with the philosophical tenets of neoliberalism per se. In doing so, it emphasised fundraising and financial governance practices that entailed late modern capitalist dimensions and that intersected with broader neoliberal financial systems.

The analysis here did not assert that either AQ or IS may be interpreted as simply neoliberal. Rather, I argued that, to the extent to which these organisations materially benefit from practices that are a part of the broad political-economic paradigms they purport to condemn, such practices are critically significant, particularly when considered in relation to the anti-capitalist propaganda these organisations disseminate. This remains the case even if the scope and specifically neoliberal dimensions of such behaviours are small in relation to the organisation's entire strategic financial operations. With this understanding in mind, the investigation emphasised the scope and scale of AQ and IS's quasi-capitalist operations, which were neither small nor insignificant. Evidencing this, the behaviours examined in each case constituted a major source of revenue for these organisations, and they were facilitated or directed by AQ and IS's central structures of governance.

In a section between the accounts of AQ and IS finance, the discussion outlined precepts of Islamic finance, sometimes referred to as sharia banking, to highlight superficial contradictions between AQ and IS's propaganda and practice and further problematise these organisations' claims of theological precedent. Three primary contradictions between Islamic finance and the version of neoliberalism reflected on in this book were evident. These are, first, neoliberal finance's reliance on interest, otherwise referred to as usury, or *riba*, often entailing processes by which money becomes detached from material assets and can thus generate more money by itself, as in the neoliberal process of financialisation, the creation of purely financial assets (Roy 1994). Second, Islamic finance proscribes large financial risks such as the neoliberal supports for the broad debt-based economy and mortgage-backed securities market that preceded the GFC (Chapra 2008). Third, according to Islamic finance, financial actors should only invest in ethical causes and projects, not in weapons, drugs, and gambling (Byman 2003). While AQ and IS's breach of this third condition is patent in their various investments in weapons, and in AQ's historical benefit from narcotics trafficking (primarily with the Pakistani Taliban (Napoleoni 2004)), I revealed that the organisations contravened other tenets of Islamic finance via their engagement in financial practices that might, in one way or another, be described as neoliberal.

The neo-jihadist financial practices discussed were again interpreted within a framework of Bourdieusian theory. In particular, the analysis considered Bourdieu's interpretation of neoliberalism as both a political and social paradigm, and the role that economic capital, as 'mercantile exchange' (Bourdieu 1986), played therein. I also drew on neo-Marxist interpretations of neoliberal policies related to Bourdieu's philosophy. These include Peck's (2010) account of neoliberal 'layering', where the historical installation of capitalist and neoliberal restructuring in specific geographies has ongoing, recursive, and cumulative effects, Jessop's (2006) interpretation of the importance of territoriality for modern neoliberal nations, and Harvey's (2003) theory of 'accumulation by dispossession'. Examples of AQ and IS finance were taken to represent their observance of differential pro- and anti-capitalist doxas, in which neoliberal financial practices that engender various deleterious social and political impacts were widespread internationally and accepted as 'self-evident' (Bourdieu 1998a, 1998b).

In line with Peck's theory of neoliberal layering, AQ was shown, from its inception in 1988, to have used several of the physical networks and connections with donors that were originally facilitated by the MAK bureau, with the sponsorship and support of the US and its allies in the Afghan–Soviet War (1979–1989). I then argued that a history of neoliberal layering in the Iraqi region, including through the Oil-for-Food Programme and the CPA's neoliberal restructuring of Iraq after 2003, provided the disaster conditions in which IS thrived, much in the manner of the 'vexation and exhaustion' campaign promoted by the early IS ideologue Abu Bakr Naji (2006). In relation to the exploitation of residents in the Caliphate, such behaviour was explained as contradictory to the humanitarian edicts of Islamic finance. With reference to the account of neo-jihadist propaganda, my analysis of neo-jihadist finance also explored the extent to which US energy interests in the region were reflexively apparent in the territorial and resource-oriented behaviour of AQ and IS. Despite its erstwhile reliance upon networks and regional alliances established via the MAK, I argued that AQ relies less on terri-tory for funding than IS. This is likely to remain strategically significant, given IS's exploitation of residents in its territories, and the propagan-dised promise of a Caliphate, which will in future be used by both organ-isations to incentivise acts of terrorism.

A major strategic point of difference between AQ and IS is the latter's financial independence from exogenous support groups such as donors, whereas AQ has been in large part reliant upon external sources of fund-ing throughout its history. This reliance upon foreign donations by nation states that were allied with the US was explained through reference to Bourdieu's perspective that 'terrorist violence, through the irrationalism of the despair which is almost always at its root, refers back to the inert violence of the powers which invoke reason' (1998b, 20). A prominent example was support for AQ that originated with US intervention in the Afghan–Soviet conflict. The discussion revealed that following the close of the Cold War, from the 1990s onwards, AQ relied upon donations facilitated via charities and the informal money transfer systems of *hawalas* to sustain its operations. Following 9/11 and its decentralisation, the organisation established 'franchises' (Hubbard 2014) and outsourced its efforts at financing to licit and illicit commercial enterprises.

As a part of its commercial behaviour, AQ and AQ funding entities engaged in neoliberal practices that were contradictory to the principles of Islamic finance, including establishing offshore fiduciary funds such as IBCs situated in tax havens (Del Cid Gómez 2010). Although not emphasised in the analysis, they also capitalised on credit-based prod-ucts of the international financial system, such as student loans and loan overdrafts. Finally, I demonstrated that AQ made use of late modern capitalist technology and expanded on historical public–private connec-tions, such as that which existed between the US-based oil company UNOCAL and the Taliban. AQ also used funds garnered via kidnapping, extortion, and drugs, the proceeds of which were laundered and pro-cessed in formal banking systems (Napoleoni 2004; Levitt and Jacobson 2010), although I explored these in less detail than AQ's previously dis-cussed financial characteristics.

IS's primary means of fundraising, which it practised to a greater extent than AQ, was revealed to be underwritten by a history of US-di-rected economic restructuring in the region, including the 1990s sanc-tions against the Hussein regime, the UN installation of the Oil-for-Food Programme, and the US-directed neoliberal reconstruction of Iraq after 2003 with the introduction of CPA policies. The discussion of IS's financial practices demonstrated that the interpersonal and physical-geographical networks it used for resource trade in part stemmed from routes established during the corrupt Oil-for-Food Programme and, as AQ did, IS forces in Afghanistan used routes dating back to the MAK. Other practices, such as IS's manipulation of supply and demand in exploiting the essential resources of water and wheat, were shown to be reminiscent of a regional and US military history of exploiting civilians as a weapon of war, as well as of the broader neoliberal practice of exploiting the resource needs of citizens for the benefit of transnational corporations (Bakker 2007; Spronk and Webber 2007).

The investigation of IS revealed other quasi-neoliberal methods of fundraising practised by the organisation: its usage of late modern economic managerial measures, such as currency manipulation and arbitrage, and its public–private engagement with government entities from the Syrian administration and neighbouring territories including the Kurdish lands, Iran, Iraq, and Turkey. As was the case with AQ, the behaviours of IS were interpreted in relation to Bourdieu's understanding of US neoliberalism in its neo-colonial aspect as provoking an 'irrational' backlash of violence and terrorism against the 'rational' imposition of imperial powers in conflict territories (Bourdieu 1998b).

In reflecting on IS's state-like identity, I also explored financial governance measures imposed by IS, in comparison with the brief discussion of governance on the part of AQ, regarding its organisational devolution and use of outsourcing following 9/11. These discussions revealed that while AQ's funding comes from a multitude of sources, and is distributed as living wages and provisions for attacks, from 2014 to 2017 IS practised a complex form of state-like governance to maintain its territory and to fund ongoing militaristic activity. IS's two-tiered, 'multidivisional-hierarchy form' of management derived from the organisational business model originally conceptualised by the US transnational company General Motors (Bahney et al. 2010; Simpson 2014). As the analysis also explained, IS relied upon methods of financial governance and administration to sustain its acquisition of territory and to fortify its display of capital. The concept of 'metacapital' (Bourdieu 1977) as a form of capital unique to state-like entities was applied for the purpose of conceptualising the importance of IS's capitalist government administration, such as its efforts to promote growth and ensure competitive marketisation within its territory, including, for instance, the installation of a Consumer Protection Bureau (Alexander and Alexander 2015, 112; Al Hayat 2015c).

In combination with findings from the investigation of AQ and IS propaganda, the discussion of these organisations' methods of financial governance revealed various ways in which neo-jihadist organisations differentially interact with the precepts of neoliberalism. Although no model of late modern capitalism perfectly characterises these organisations, I maintained that AQ may be aptly interpreted in relation to a financialised and transnational corporation, whereas IS, during the period examined, exhibited behaviours similar to and recursive of those engaged in by neoliberal nation states. While this distinction is not absolute, it is useful in demarcating AQ and IS's divergent engagement with financial practices that might be deemed neoliberal. As previously mentioned, this situation carries strategic and critical theoretical implications given the impact of these organisations' anti-capitalist propaganda, and twenty-first-century geopolitical developments in the state of neo-jihadism in the Middle East.

Bourdieu and neoliberalism

Although Bourdieu's interpretation of modern political economy might seem speculative or conjectural to some, by virtue of its ability to take account of the extra- and non-economic effects of neoliberalism I suggest that it is an apt framework through which to interpret these forms of political violence. Despite AQ and IS's reference to neoliberalism's deleterious effects, the scientific rigour of neo-classical economics is not under question in these organisations' propaganda, and critical reflections on neoliberalism are no more evident in AQ and IS's financial practices than they are in the ongoing crises that have befallen US-directed multinationals. As a 'messy hybrid' of 'philosophies, policies, and practices' (Peck 2010, 7), neoliberalism is intersectional with AQ and IS's performance of neo-jihadism, and the aspect of comparison in *Neoliberalism and neo-jihadism* was illustrative in revealing AQ and IS's political-economic dimensions.

While neither AQ nor IS can be described as plainly neoliberal, their dialectical engagements with the ideological and material exigencies of neoliberalism warrant strategic and scholarly attention. As I have demonstrated in this book, this remains the case, not least because the violent, social effects of neoliberal economic policies, extending to seemingly ever increasing global wealth inequality (Piketty 2014), are themselves propagative of the conflicts and political tensions that foment support for this form of terrorism.

The findings of the analysis indicate that the geo-economic concerns of AQ and IS, with respect to neoliberalism, are expressed reflexively in their propaganda and financial practices. Where AQ following 9/11 emphasised the non-territorial practices of US-directed neoliberal entities, IS has consistently communicated an anti-capitalist critique that is substantiated with reference to land. Reflecting the theoretical vein of this book, the manner in which these organisations share a dialectical relationship with the paradigm of neoliberalism can further be understood when considered in relation to the tenets of Bourdieusian and neo-Marxist theory that challenge long-standing social-science tendencies towards reductionism and determinism.

In applying Bourdieusian and neo-Marxist frames to interpret neo-jihadism, this book also advocated for a rejection of intellectual exercises that employ linear cause-and-effect models to explain the impact of political and economic behaviours upon social entities and systems (Fuchs 2014). Indeed, such exercises would fall outside the purview of an interdisciplinary sociological, criminological, and political-economic enquiry. *Neoliberalism and neo-jihadism* rather sought to interpolate critical theory's recognition of circular causality (Falleti and Lynch 2009) and its emphasis on the subjective and metaphysical undercurrents that influence contemporary political-economic thinking. In line with the book's interpretivist and inductive approach, I argued that evidence of intersections and oppositions between neoliberalism and neo-jihadism can reveal broader truths about the nature of modern political economy and political violence.

This entailed paying attention not only to the cyclical, self-referential, and self-perpetuating nature of power and resistance, but to broader flows of power that often go unrecognised. Despite prevalent structuralist constructionist approaches to sociological phenomena (including through Bourdieusian 'capital' theory), observers of terrorism can overlook the inherent interdependencies that exist between monetary power, cultural and formal education, social status, and symbolic resonance within a community, and that collectively constitute a person's 'class'. By relying on the widespread socio-political obscuration of such interdependence, changeability, and transfer between social, cultural, symbolic, and economic capital, organisations such as AQ and IS can sustain their operational strength via fundraising while recruiting supporters to their cause without revealing the paradoxical nature of their external political-economic orientations. The manner in which these organisations wield non-economic forms of capital is therefore critically relevant as well as practically and ideologically significant.

Although it was not my primary aim in writing this book to delineate insights about the phenomenon of neo-jihadism that might be used to optimise efforts at terrorism prevention, it therefore goes some way towards redressing a prevailing 'epistemological crisis' in contemporary counterterrorism (Jackson 2015). As highlighted in the Introduction, since 9/11 this crisis has been characterised by an 'expert ignorance' in Western counterterrorism (Zulaika 2012; Stampnitzsky 2013), extending to the racialisation and securitisation of 'suspect communities' predicated on a reductive Cartesian logic of us versus them. Although critical and comparative analyses of terrorism have long been recognised for their merit, these often preclude consideration of the 'subjugated knowledges' of terrorism (Jackson 2012), lest the critical researcher be accused of 'moral equivalence', legitimising terroristic narratives, or, dare it be suggested, 'apologising for terrorism' (Hynek and Chandler 2013; Lindahl 2017).

One aspect of these knowledges set out in *Neoliberalism and neo-jihadism* is that the symbolic, political, and interpersonal violence of terrorism extends to the structural violence perpetrated by those powerful entities that supporters of terrorism (and non-supporters) so fervently condemn. Another is that the philosophical orientation of contemporary political movements derives fundamentally from the beliefs and actions of their political-economic opposition. Demonstrating this, beyond neoliberalism and neo-jihadism, causation, reflexivity, and mirroring are apparent in the dialectics that sustain contemporary far-right actors, the GWOT coalition, and AQ and IS.

The far-right and the GWOT

After twenty years of US-directed military and counterterrorist action undertaken in response to 9/11, combined with regional conflicts and environmental devastation, there occurred a mass displacement of people from Africa and the Middle East, which former Under-Secretary-General of the UN Stephen O'Brien described as 'the largest humanitarian crisis since the creation of the United Nations [in 1945]' (UN News 2017). With more than 70 million people displaced worldwide in 2020, far-right-wing entities in Australia, Europe, and the US have targeted Muslim populations, and migrants, often citing intensified flows of international migration and the post-9/11 GWOT as their primary ideological justification.

Like AQ and IS, far-right individuals and organisations often express violent opposition to the (left-liberal) democratic governance standards of equality, freedom, and human rights; also in a manner similar to neo-jihadist groups, they consider the social and economic impacts of (neoliberal) globalisation to be undesirable (Pisoiu 2015; Holt et al. 2017). Many far-right and neo-jihadist actors mutually reject increasing global wealth inequality leading to a lack of ready access to goods and services, including employment and education (Ansari 2017). Despite their often anti-democratic politics and archetypal rejection of progressive socialism, proponents of these movements outwardly criticise the transference to corporate elites of power and influence formerly, at least to some extent, in the hands of democratically accountable politicians (Post 2015; Koehler 2016; Shaffer 2016).

Perhaps unsurprisingly in light of the pervasive influence of neoliberal capitalism, far-right entities and neo-jihadists also mutually articulate their eschatological worldviews, anti-Semitism, and extreme social conservatism through late capitalist technology and media (Pupcenoks and McCabe 2013; Abbas 2017), often using these media to facilitate commercial fundraising. Echoing AQ and IS's mirroring of neoliberal corporations and capitalist nation states, neo-fascist movements, including the 'identitarians' in Europe, 'patriots' in Australia, and 'alt-right' in the US, often syncretically and dialectically imitate their left-wing opposition. In a well-known example, Generation Identity (GI) between 2015 and 2020 used the slogans 'White Lives Matter' and 'British Girls Matter' as a rejoinder to progressive pluralist initiatives, while exploiting a propagandised image of its membership as middle-class, digitally literate, and countercultural, with 'hipster' hairstyles and clothing (Heim 2017; Richards 2019b). In its first Defend Europe mission, GI's method of disrupting humanitarian rescue boats for asylum seekers on the Mediterranean Sea logistically resembled the long-standing tactics of Greenpeace and the Sea Shepherd (Wildman 2017).

The dialectics of far-right extremists and other political movements are multifaceted, though, also incorporating symbolic mirroring between the far-right and the GWOT. In GI's second Defend Europe mission, for example, it established a simulated border in the Swiss Alps to deter would-be migrants from entering Europe. The organisation displayed large banners visible from the mountains and branded a rented helicopter with the slogan 'No Way ... You Will Not Make Europa Home' (@GID_UKIRE 2018). In an interview with RT News, a leader of GI's Austrian branch and co-founder of the movement, Martin Sellner, acknowledged that these tactics were derived from the Australian government's 2014 YouTube Border Force video advertisement 'No Way: You Will Not Make Australia Home', part of a multi-language campaign designed to deter asylum seekers from coming to Australia by sea (ABF TV 2014; RT Producers 2017).

Indicating the relevance of the GWOT in this case, offshore asylum-seeker processing and a militarisation of the country's border policy was originally promoted by the 2001 Liberal–National Coalition government, supported by Australian voters, as an implicit response to 9/11. The Liberal party under John Howard in fact campaigned successfully in the 2001 Australian federal election on the basis of fallacious newsmedia reporting about asylum seekers throwing their children overboard on the Tampa vessel moored off of Christmas Island. As Australian troops boarded the vessel, the Coalition signposted perceived security risks associated with refugees from the Middle East in light of the events of 9/11 (McAllister 2003; McCulloch 2004; Grewcock 2007; McKay et al. 2011; Martin 2015).

Political developments

Given its harmful social, economic, and political effects, including human rights abuses inflicted on 'suspect communities' (Aradau and Van Munster 2007), counterterrorist securitisation in the GWOT was recognised internationally in the two decades after 9/11 as propagative of political violence and terrorism (Amoore 2013; McCulloch and Wilson 2016; Mythen and Walklate 2016). On the one hand, the GWOT contributed to a significant increase in attacks perpetrated by far-right and white-supremacist terrorist actors, who cite a perceived threat of the 'Islamisation' of Western countries and express hatred towards Muslim people (Wodak et al. 2013). Demonstrating this increase, 71 per cent of the 387 'extremist related fatalities in the US' from 2008 to 2017 were committed by far-right and white-supremacist groups, while 'Islamic extremists' were responsible for only 26 per cent (Cullen 2019). As the National Consortium for the Study of Terrorism and Responses to Terrorism at the University of Maryland revealed, there were nearly 350 white-supremacist attacks across Australia, Europe, and the US from 2011 to 2017; one quarter of these attacks in Europe targeted Muslims and mosques, and 86 attacks in Europe in 2015 alone targeted refugee shelters and migrants (Cai and Landon 2019). Indicating the enduring prevalence of neo-jihadism during this period, despite the GWOT, the Center for Strategic and International Studies estimated there to be approximately 230,000 people across the world supporting IS and AQ in 2018, an increase of 400 per cent since 2001 (Jones et al. 2018).

However, as a result of the efforts of the US military coalition and Kurdish forces, IS did experience a significant loss of territory in Iraq and Syria after 2017. Between July and October 2017, the organisation was driven from Raqqa in the Deir ez-Zour province of Syria, the 'capital' of its Caliphate; and in July 2017, former Iraqi Prime Minister Haider al-Abadi announced that IS had been ejected from the strategically important city of Mosul, in Iraq, after a nine-month battle (Hamzah and Al-Attabi 2017). Following Operation Tidal Wave II, IS was also driven from major oil-producing areas, predominantly those in northeastern Syria (Foundation for the Defense of Democracies 2019). Then, in March 2019, the Syrian Democratic Forces announced that the organisation had lost its final stronghold in the region, bringing an end to the Caliphate that once spanned an area from Baghdad to western Syria greater than the size of the UK (Wedeman and Said-Moorhouse 2019).

From 2001 to 2020, the GWOT cost the US US$6.4 trillion (Costs of War 2020). By 2019, AQ had extended its influence and presence beyond Afghanistan and regional states to East Asia, Central Asia, the Gulf States, Yemen, and West Africa, while it increasingly worked in support of regional governments (Taylor 2019). From 2013 to 2019, IS and its supporters, via eight branches and two-dozen networks established across four continents, were responsible for perpetrating more than 143 non-regional attacks in 29 countries (Lister et al. 2018), and, according to the organisation, despite its recent loss of territory, for 3,670 attacks in 2018 (al-Lami 2019). As a 2019 UN report revealed, between US$50 and $300 million in revenue had remained in IS hands since the dissolution of the Caliphate (UNSCR 2019). In 2017, Baghdadi issued a statement incentivising IS 'soldiers' to perpetrate attacks internationally, despite 'the feeling of defeat' (Wright 2019). Following the murder of 259 people in churches and hotels around Sri Lanka by IS supporters on 21 April 2019 (Easter Sunday), he released another statement, warning of 'more to come' and declaring 'global jihad is a fact' (Williams 2019). Despite the ultimate erasure of IS's self-proclaimed Caliphate in Iraq and Syria in 2019, neo-jihadism, as signified through the actions of AQ and IS, is an ongoing politically violent phenomenon.

As the discussion in *Neoliberalism and neo-jihadism* demonstrated, actions in the GWOT that have contributed to sympathy and support for neo-jihadist groups include US-led interventions in the Middle East, such as drone strikes on leaders in Afghanistan and Pakistan, proxy wars in the Middle East and East Africa, and direct wars in Afghanistan and Iraq in 2001 and 2003. They also include post-war economic reconstructive projects in Iraq, outsourced to US and UK contractors, that led to the direct dispossession of Iraqi civilians (Whyte 2007). Coalition support to forces opposing the Assad administration in Syria after the commencement of the civil war there in 2011 also materially benefited AQ and IS. The oppositional forces in question were at times associated with or led by AQ's Syrian branch, Jabhat Fatah al-Sham (active until January 2017), and at others they were subjugated by IS (Safadi 2015).

Researchers of neo-jihadism have, since IS's loss of territory from 2015 to 2017, recognised that a shift in the organisation's geo-economic strategy towards transnational idealism, intangibility, and the 'Virtual Caliphate' would in some respects recall AQ's post-9/11 decentralisation and its adoption of a 'franchise' institutional model (Rao 2019). Given this state of affairs, it is worth reflecting on the geo-economic orientation of IS at its inception, and the extent to which this orientation changed throughout its development, including in the cases examined in this book, between 2014 and 2017. IS's shift in process during and after this period indicates strategically significant continuities between neo-jihadist organisations that have wider implications for the phenomenon of neo-jihadism and its political-economic aspects. An emerging pattern of de-territorialisation in neo-jihadism corresponds dialectically to the global, financialising tendencies of neoliberalism, and the centrifugal, privatised, and outsourced behaviour of US and US-directed military and counterterrorist organisations. The chronological and practical aspects of AQ and IS propaganda and finance demonstrate that neo-jihadism, as a globalised form of political-economic expression, has taken root at the heart of late modern capitalism.

Future research directions

By applying Bourdieu's theory of dialectics, through a lens of power and resistance, this book provides an inroad for destabilising reductive and dualistic accounts of terrorism and establishing an empirically grounded theory of political violence capable of explaining more than the simple binary logic of us versus them. To the extent that a 'law of science' should be applied to the study of sociological phenomena such as terrorism, this dialectical approach accords empirically with the essentialist Newtonian (meta-)physical principle that every action produces an equal and opposite reaction. If it were to become widespread, such a shift in counterterrorist thinking would be strategically significant given that, insofar as we remain cognisant of the 'field' of constraints that influence human behaviour, we are primarily able to control events that correspond to our own behaviour and thereby effect change via our own expressions of agency.

Although some might argue that this work undermines the persuasive powers of counterterrorist agencies, challenging reductive and dualistic explanations of political violence in fact empowers genuine anti-terrorism agents by affording them an avenue through which to influence the course of events within situations of political violence and devastation. In the case of neo-jihadism, this would involve recognising the political-economic dimensions of its violence and beginning to openly question the underlying assumptions that sustain the field of conditions in which such violence operates.

In an increasingly interconnected world of cultural and economic globalisation, comparative investigations such as this one are vital for ensuring the continued relevance of disciplinary insights from, for instance, international relations, sociology, and criminology, including the translation of community activism. This is particularly true of investigations that seek to explore the developments of political violence that exist at the interstice of domestic law enforcement and international security (Bigo 2016). As this book promotes and advances a neo-Marxist understanding of the world, these developments extend beyond their effects on the market. Violence and its political-economic correlates can certainly be understood to have had widespread effects in political and social domains, irrespective of whether neo-jihadism is directly relevant.

With the continuous nature of such political-economic paradigms in mind, a number of future directions for research are discernible. The first of these relates to the fact that neoliberalism is not static (Peck 2015); furthermore, at the time of this book's writing, neoliberalism has been recognised by critical political-economists to have morphed and changed in ways which preclude a fixed definition (Cook 2016). To address this, the analysis in *Neoliberalism and neo-jihadism* emphasised the philosophical as well as the specific economic policies promoted within conditions of neoliberalism, which broadly correlate with late modern capitalism, rather than specific and strict interpretations of monetary policies related to financialisation and deregulation. This might be extended or amended in future studies, such that the political-economic philosophies and policies analysed reflect the tangible and dominant political-economic conditions most relevant to neo-jihadism.

A second possible future direction for research on the political economy of neo-jihadism might be to amend or vary the method of data selection for the materials examined. It is important to recognise that extensive data on neo-jihadist finance, and indeed the financial practices of the US, is not available in open sources. In this book, I purposefully used material that is open-source and available to a general public with internet access, also because widely available material is most relevant to the vein of inquiry concerned with assessing the strategic implications of propaganda, politics, and practices. Future investigations of neo-jihadist finance might seek to draw from new and potentially broader datasets, incorporate advanced methods to a greater extent, or draw from examples and measures of terrorist and counterterrorist finance that can be demonstrated to be materially connected.

Lastly, future research in this area might elaborate on and explore the nature of the contradiction between neo-jihadist organisations' engagements with neoliberalism by investigating neo-jihadist finance in quantitative detail, to the extent to which this information becomes available. One could, for instance, pursue a more rigorous theological exploration of the manner in which edicts of Islamic finance are contradictory to neoliberalism, and how this is relevant to the behaviours of neo-jihadist organisations. If this investigation were conducted and synthesised with extensive data about neo-jihadist finance and propaganda, it might be operationalised to dispel the resistance mythology that renders the neo-jihadist ideology attractive to susceptible individuals. Similar investigations might develop insights set out in this book about the underlying premises of neoliberal power and alternatives for resistance. Such a broad approach to analysis would indeed represent a pioneering contribution to critical and strategic 'terrorism' scholarship. For this to be possible, however, it is necessary for critics to address the grievance that politically violent individuals have in response to the deleterious impacts of neoliberalism, and how this grievance is accessed by proponents of neo-jihadism.

References

@GID_UKIRE 2018, Twitter, "Generation Identity: 'You will not make Europe home! Back to your homeland!@DefendEuropeID won't allow migrants to invade France through the Alps any longer.Activists are taking a stand by constructing a fence and patrolling it day and night both on theground and in the air. #StopMigrantAlpes', viewed 10 May 2018, https://twitter.com/gid_ukire/status/987721967703904256?lang=en

Abbas, T. 2017, 'Ethnicity and politics in contextualising far right and Islamist extremism', *Perspectives on Terrorism*, vol. 11, no. 3, pp. 54–61.

ABF TV 2014, 'No way. You will not make Australia home – English', YouTube, 15 April, viewed 29 December 2019, www.youtube.com/watch?v=rT12WH4a92w

Aboufadel, L. 2017, 'ISIS member filmed burning Turkish soldiers alive in Syria was imprisoned by Turkey in 2012: Report', *AMN*, 21 January, viewed 10 February 2017, www.almasdarnews.com/article/ISIS-member-filmed-burning-turkish-soldiers-alive-syria-imprisoned-turkey-2012-report/

Abrams, E., Bauer, G., Bennett, W., Bush, J., Cheney, D., Cohen, E., Decter, M., Dobrianksy, P., Forbes, S., Friedberg, A., Fukuyama, F., Gaffney, F., Ikle, F., Kagan, D., Khalilzad, Z., Libby, I., Podhoretz, N., Quayle, D., Rodman, P., Rosen, S., Rowen, H., Rumsfeld, D., Weber, V., Weigel G. and Wolfowitz P. 1997, *Project for a New American Century: Statement of principles*, 3 June, viewed 10 May 2017, www.rrojasdatabank.info/pfpc/PNAC---statement%20of%20principles.pdf

Ackerman, S. 2015, 'US has trained only "four or five" Syrian fighters against ISIS, top general testifies', *Guardian*, 17 September, viewed 21 July 2017, www.theguardian.com/us-news/2015/sep/16/us-military-syrian-isis-fighters

Adel, L. 2017, 'Iraqi forces liberate Badush cement plan in Western Mosul', *Iraqi News*, 26 March, viewed 10 May 2017, www.iraqinews.com/iraq-war/iraqi-forces-liberate-badush-cement-plant-western-mosul/

Adnani, A. 2014, 'Indeed your Lord is ever watchful', 21 September, viewed 10 May 2017, https://archive.org/details/IndeedYourLordIsEverWatchful

Adnani, A. and Al Furqan 2016, 'That they live by proof', 11 May, viewed 10 May 2017, https://archive.org/stream/ANewSpeechByAbuMuhammadAlAdnani/A%20New%20Speech%20by%20Abu%20Muhammad%20al-%27Adnani_ djvu.txt

Adnani, A. and Al Hayat 2015, 'Say to those who disbelieve, you will be overcome', 18 October, viewed 10 May 2017, https://ansaaar1.wordpress.com/2015/10/18/you-will-be-overcome-by-shaykh-abu-muhammad-al-adnani/

Ahmed, N. 2015, 'Islamic State is the cancer of modern capitalism'. *Middle East Eye*, 27 March, viewed 10 May 2017, www.middleeasteye.net/columns/cancer-modern-capitalism-1323585268

Al Hayat 2014a, 'There is no life without jihad', 19 June, viewed 10 May 2017, https://archive.org/details/ThereIsNoLifeWithoutJihad

Al Hayat 2014b, 'The end of Sykes Picot', 29 June, viewed 10 May 2017, http://jihadology.net/2014/06/29/al-%E1%B8%A5ayat-media-center-presents-a-new-video-message-from-the-islamic-state-of-iraq-and-al-sham-the-end-of-sykes-picot/

Al Hayat 2014c, 'The call to hijrah', *Dabiq*, no. 3, viewed 10 January 2017, https://clarionproject.org/docs/ISIS-isil-islamic-state-magazine-Issue-3-the-call-to-hijrah.pdf

Al Hayat 2014d, 'Al-Qa'idah of Waziristan: A testimony from within', *Dabiq*, no. 6, viewed 10 May 2017, https://clarionproject.org/docs/ISIS-isil-islamic-state-magazine-issue-6-al-qaeda-of-waziristan.pdf

Al Hayat 2015a, 'The rise of the Khilafah: Return of the gold dinar', 29 August, viewed 10 February 2016, https://archive.org/details/TheRiseOfTheKhilafah AndTheReturnOfTheGoldDinar

Al Hayat 2015b, 'No respite', 24 November, viewed 10 May 2016, http://heavy.com/news/2015/11/new-ISIS-islamic-state-news-pictures-videos-no-respite-englishlanguage-propaganda-full-uncensored-youtube-daesh/

Al Hayat 2015c, 'Islamic State report: An insight into the Islamic State: Issue 1', Al Hayat, viewed 10 February 2017, https://azelin.files.wordpress.com/2014/06/islamic-state-of-iraq-and-al-shc481m-22islamic-state-report-122.pdf

Al Hayat 2016, *Rumiyah*, no. 2, viewed 10 May 2017, https://clarionproject.org/factsheets-files/Rumiyh-ISIS-Magazine-2nd-issue.pdf

Al Jazeera 2015, 'Kouachi brothers had weapons training in Yemen', 11 January, viewed 10 May 2017, http://america.aljazeera.com/articles/2015/1/11/kouachi-france.html

Al Qaeda 1988, 'The solid base', *Al-Jihad*, no. 41, in J. Burke (ed.), *Al-Qaeda: The true story of radical Islam* (2004), Macmillan, London.

Al-Arabiya 2014, 'Iraq says ISIS transferring phosphate to Syria's Raqqa', *Al-Arabiya: English*, 1 December, viewed 10 May 2017, http://english.alarabiya.net/en/News/middle-east/2014/12/01/Iraqi-says-ISIS-transferring-phosphate-to-Syria-s-Raqqa.html

Al-Arabiya 2017a, 'These are the most prominent Qataris accused of financing terrorism', *Al Arabiya: English*, 1 June, viewed 10 August 2017, http://english.alarabiya.net/en/features/2017/06/01/These-are-the-most-prominent-Qataris-accused-of-financing-terrorism.html

Al Arabiya 2017b, 'Arab powers list 59 individuals as Qatar-linked terrorism supporters', viewed 10 August 2017, https://english.alarabiya.net/en/News/

gulf/2017/06/09/Arab-countries-release-list-of-terrorist-financiers-sup-ported-by-Qatar.html

Al-Lami, M. 2019, 'Where is the Islamic State group still active around the world?', *BBC News*, 27 March, viewed 29 December 2019, www.bbc.com/news/world-middle-east-47691006

Al-Madkhalee, R. 1995, *Al-Awaasim Mimmaa Fee Kutub Sayyid Qutb Min al-Qawaasim*, Islamic Board, viewed 10 May 2017, www.islamicboard.com/archive/index.php/t-35198.html

Al-Tamimi, A. 2016, 'Archive of Islamic State administrative documents (cont.)', 11 January, viewed 10 May 2017, www.aymennjawad.org/2016/01/archive-of-islamic-state-administrative-documents-1

Albrecht, H. and Schlumberger, O. 2004, '"Waiting for Godot": Regime change without democratization in the Middle East', *International Political Science Review*, vol. 25, no. 4, pp. 371–392.

Alexander, Y. and Alexander, D. 2015, *The Islamic State: Combating the Caliphate without borders*, Lexington Books, Lanham.

Ali, T. 2003, *The clash of fundamentalisms: Crusades, jihads and modernity*, Verso, London.

ALR 2016, 'Under pressure: A report on labour conditions in Korean factories in Myanmar by Action Labor Rights', Business & Human Rights Resource Centre, 28 March, viewed 29 December 2019, www.business-humanrights. org/en/under-pressure-a-report-on-labour-conditions-in-korean-factories-in-myanmar-by-action-labor-rights

Althusser, L. 2003, *The humanist controversy and other writings (1966–67)*, ed. F. Matheron, trans. G. M. Goshgarian, Verso, London.

Arnett, P. 2001, 'Transcript of Osama Bin Laden interview by Peter Arnett', *Information Clearing House: News You Won't Find on CNN*, viewed 10 January 2017, www.informationclearinghouse.info/article7204.htm

Amoore, L. 2013, *The politics of possibility: Risk and security beyond probability*, Duke University Press, Durham.

Amoore, L. and De Goede, M. (eds) 2008, *Risk and the war on terror*, Routledge, London.

Anderson, G. 2007, 'Media's impact on educational policies and practices: Political spectacle and social control', *Peabody Journal of Education*, vol. 82, no. 1, pp. 103–120.

Anderson, I. 2014, *Aramco, the United States, and Saudi Arabia: A study of the dynamics of foreign oil policy, 1933–1950*, Princeton University Press, New Jersey.

Ansar, B. 2017, '2017 is the year global terror became mainstream. This is what we're doing to tackle it', *Independent*, 30 December, viewed 29 December 2019, www.independent.co.uk/voices/radicalisation-online-twitter-extremism-isis-far-right-international-efforts-a8134606.html

AQAP 2013, *Inspire*, no 10, viewed 10 January 2017, https://azelin.files.wordpress.com/2013/03/inspire-magazine-issue-10.pdf

AQIS 2014, *Resurgence*, no. 1, viewed 10 January 2017, https://azelin.files.wordpress.com/2015/04/resurgence-1.pdf

Aradau, C. and Van Munster, R. 2007, 'Governing terrorism through risk: Taking precautions (un) knowing the future', *European Journal of International Relations*, vol. 13, no. 1, pp. 89–115.

Arango, T. and Yeginsu, C. 2016, 'Turkey to release tens of thousands of prisoners to make room for coup suspects', *New York Times*, 17 August, viewed 10 May 2017, www.nytimes.com/2016/08/18/world/europe/turkey-prisoners-erdogan.html

Argus, 2015, 'US strikes to spare Iraq, Syria oil capacity', 2 December, viewed 10 May 2017, www.argusmedia.com/en/news/1146754-us-strikes-to-spare-iraq-syria-oil-capacity

Armstrong, K. 2014, 'The deep roots of Islamic State: Wahhabism – and how Saudi Arabia exported the main source of global terrorism', *New Statesman*, vol. 143, no. 5237, viewed 10 January 2018, www.newstatesman.com/world-affairs/2014/11/wahhabism-ISIS-how-saudi-arabia-exported-main- source-global-terrorism

Astill, J. 2001, 'Osama: The Sudan years', *Guardian*, 17 October, viewed 10 May 2017, www.theguardian.com/world/2001/oct/17/afghanistan.terrorism3

Atkins, R., Solomon, E. and Stothard, M. 2017, 'LafargeHolcim's reputation at risk over alleged links with ISIS', *Financial Times*, viewed 10 May 2017, www.ft.com/content/406b06fe-05b6–11e7-aa5b-6bb07f5c8e12

Atwan, A. 2008, *The secret history of al Qaeda*, University of California Press, California.

Atwan, A. 2013, *After Bin Laden: Al Qaeda, the next generation*, The New Press, New York.

Atwan, A. 2015, *Islamic State: The digital caliphate*, University of California Press, Oakland.

Awan, A. 2014, 'Terrorism craves an audience and we are playing into Islamic State's hands by watching', *New Internationalist*, viewed 10 May 2017, http://works.bepress.com/akil_awan/15

Ayer, A. 1966, *Logical positivism*, Simon and Schuster, New York.

Azzam, A. 1979, *Defence of the Muslim lands: The first obligation after faith*, trans. M. Taqi-ud-Oin Al-Hilali and M. Khan (1993), viewed 10 January 2017, http://johnclamoreaux.org/smu/islam-west/s/azzam-def.pdf

Azzam, A. 1987, 'Join the caravan', in G. Kepel, J. P. Milelli and P. Ghazaleh (eds), trans. P. Ghazaleh, *Al Qaeda in its own words* (2008), Harvard University Press, Cambridge, pp. 151–165.

Baghdadi, A. 2014, 'Translation of the Khutbah of Commander of the faithful, Caliph of the muslims, Abu Bakr al-Husayni al-Qurayshi al-Baghdadi (may Allah protect him) Ramadan 6th 1435 in Mosul, Iraq', trans. Amreeki Witness and Mujahid4Life, *Azelin*, viewed 10 May 2017, https://azelin.files.wordpress.com/2014/07/abc5ab-bakr-al-e1b8a5ussaync4ab-al-quraysh-c4ab-al-baghdc481dc4ab-22khue1b9adbah-and-jumah-prayer-in-the-grand-mosque-of-mc5abe1b9a3ul-mosul22-en.pdf

Baghdadi, A. 2015, 'Read: Full English translation of ISIS "Caliph" Abu Bakr al-Baghdadi's new speech', trans. S. Prince, *Heavy*, 28 December, viewed 5

June 2016. http://heavy.com/news/2015/12/new-ISIS-islamic-state-news-pic-tures-videos-so-wait-indeed-we-along-with-you-arewaiting-abu-bakr-al-baghdadi-speech-english-translation/

Baghdadi, A. and Al Hayat 2016, 'This is what Allah and his messenger prom-ised us', *Rumiyah*, no. 3, 2 November, viewed 10 January 2017, https://azelin.files.wordpress.com/2016/11/rome-magazine-3.pdf

Bahney, B., Shatz, H., Ganier, C., McPherson, R. and Sude, B. 2010, *An eco-nomic analysis of the financial records of Al-Qaida in Iraq*, Rand Corpora-tion, viewed 10 May 2017, www.rand.org/content/dam/rand/pubs/monographs/ 2010/RAND_MG1026.pdf

Baker, R. 2005, *Capitalism's Achilles heel: Dirty money and how to renew the free-market system*, John Wiley & Sons, New York.

Bakker, K. 2007, 'The "commons" versus the "commodity": Alter-globalization, anti-privatization and the human right to water in the global south', *Anti-pode*, vol. 39, no. 3, pp. 430–455.

Ball, L., Furceri, D., Leigh, D. and Loungani, P. 2013, 'The distributional effects of fiscal austerity', UN-DESA Working Paper 129, United Nations.

Barber, B. 1995, *Jihad vs Mcworld*, Random House, New York.

Barkawi, T. and Laffey, M. 2006, 'The postcolonial moment in security studies', *Review of International Studies*, vol. 32, no. 2, pp. 329–352.

Barrett, R. 2014, 'Foreign fighters in Syria', *Soufan Group*, December, viewed 11 November 2017, http://soufangroup.com/wp-content/uploads/2015/12/TSG_ForeignFightersUpdate3.pdf

Basile, M. 2004, 'Going to the source: Why Al Qaeda's financial network is likely to withstand the current war on terrorist financing', *Studies in Conflict & Terrorism*, vol. 27, no. 3, no. 169–185.

Baudrillard, J. 2003, *The spirit of terrorism and other essays*, Verso, London.

Beatty, J. 2003, 'In the name of go', *Atlantic*, 5 March, viewed 5 June 2016, www.theatlantic.com/past/docs/unbound/polipro/pp2003–03–05.htm.

Beauchamp, Z. 2016, 'Leaked ISIS document: We're cutting fighter salaries in half', *Vox*, 20 January viewed 10 May 2017, www.vox.com/2016/1/20/10798476/ISIS-salary-cut

Beauchamp, Z. and Obama, B. 2015, 'Full text: Obama's oval office address on San Bernardino and ISIS', *Vox*, 6 December, viewed 5 June 2016, www.vox.com/2015/12/6/9857270/obama-speech-address-transcript-san-bernardino-ISIS.

Becchio, G. and Leghissa, G. 2016, *The origins of neoliberalism: Insights from economics and philosophy*, Routledge, London.

Bender, J. 2014, 'Iraqi bankers say ISIS never stole $US430 million from Mosul banks', *Business Insider*, 18 July, viewed 10 May 2017, www.businessinsider.com.au/ISIS-never-stole-430-million-from-banks-2014–7?r=US&IR=T

Bergen, P. 2002, *Holy war, inc.: Inside the secret world of Osama bin Laden*, New York: Simon and Schuster.

Bergen, P. 2006, *The Osama bin Laden I know: An oral history of al Qaeda's leader*, Simon and Schuster, New York.

Bergen, P. 2012, *Manhunt: The ten-year search for Bin Laden: From 9/11 to Abbottabad*, Random House, New York.

Berger, P. and Luckmann, T. 1991, *The social construction of reality: A treatise in the sociology of knowledge*, Penguin, London.

Bezhan, F. 2020, 'How the Taliban went from international pariah to U.S. peace partner in Afghanistan', *RadioFreeEurope: RadioLiberty*, viewed 21 July 2020, www.rferl.org/a/how-the-taliban-went-from-international-pariah-to-u-s-peace-partner-in-afghanistan/30502909.html

Bichler, S. and Nitzan, J. 2014, 'The weapondollar-petrodollar coalition: Still about oil?', *Philosophers for Change*, viewed 10 January 2017, https://philosophersforchange.org/2014/12/16/the-weapondollar-petrodollar-coalition-still-about-oil/

Bidder, S. and Nitzan, J. 1996, 'Putting the state in its place: US foreign policy and differential capital accumulation in Middle East "energy conflicts"', *Review of International Political Economy*, vol. 3, no. 4, pp. 608–661.

Bidet, J. 2008, 'Bourdieu and historical materialism', in J. Bidet and S. Kouvelakis (eds), *Critical Companion to Contemporary Marxism*, Brill, Netherlands, pp. 587–603.

Biersteker, T. and Eckert, S. 2007, *Countering the financing of terrorism*, Routledge, London.

Bigo, D. 2016, 'Rethinking security at the crossroad of international relations and criminology', *British Journal of Criminology*, vol. 56, no. 6, pp. 1068–1086.

Bin Laden, O. 1996, *Declaration of jihad against the Americans occupying the land of the two holiest sites*, Combating Terrorism Center, Westpoint, viewed 10 May 2017, https://ctc.usma.edu/wp-content/uploads/2013/10/Declaration-of-Jihad-against-the-Americans-Occupying-the-Land-of-the-Two-Holiest-Sites-Translation.pdf

Bin Laden, O. 2005, *Messages to the world: The statements of Osama Bin Laden*, trans. J. Howart and B. Lawrence (eds), Verso, London.

Bin Laden, O. 2007, 'Translation of Osama bin Laden video', trans. SITE Intelligence Group, *Daily News*, 12 September 2007, viewed 10 January 2017, www.nydailynews.com/news/world/translation-osama-bin-laden-video-article-1.247087

Bin Laden, O. 2009, *Bin Laden's bookshelf: Letter to the American people*, Office of the Director of National Intelligence, viewed 10 May 2017, www.dni.gov/files/documents/ubl2016/english/To%20the%20American%20people.pdf

Bin Laden, O. and Alouni, T. 2002, 'Transcript of Bin Laden's October interview', CNN.com: *World*, 5 February, viewed 10 January 2017, http://edition.cnn.com/2002/WORLD/asiapcf/south/02/05/binladen.transcript/

Bin Laden, O., al-Zawahiri, A., Taha, A. R., Hamzah, M. and Rahman, F. 1998, *World Islamic front for jihad on the Jews and crusaders*, ed. Storer, C, DIA, trans. CIA, Investigative Project, viewed 10 May 2017, www.investigative-project.org/documents/180-text-of-world-islamic-front-statement-urging.pdf

Bindner, L. and Poirot, G. 2016, *ISIS financing: 2015*, Center for the Analysis of Terrorism, J.-C. Brisard and D. Martinez (eds), May, viewed 10 May 2017, www.cat-int.org/wp-content/uploads/2016/06/ISIS-Financing-2015-Report.pdf

Bird, K. 2010, *Crossing Mandelbaum gate: Coming of age between the Arabs and Israelis, 1956–1978*, Simon and Schuster, New York.

Blanchard, C. 2007, *Al Qaeda: Statements and evolving ideology*, Library of Congress Washington DC Congressional Research Service, 9 July, viewed 10 May 2017, www.dtic.mil/docs/citations/ADA470199

Blanche, E. 2017, 'In Syria, everyone uses water as a weapon of war', *The Arab Weekly: News & Analysis*, 2 April, viewed 10 May 2017, www. thearabweekly.com/pdf/2017/04/02–04/p04.pdf

Blight, J., Banai, H., Byrne, M. and Tirman, J. 2012, *Becoming enemies: US–Iran relations and the Iran–Iraq War, 1979–1988*, Rowman & Littlefield, Lanham.

Bloom, P. 2016, *Beyond power and resistance: Politics at the radical limits*, Rowman & Littlefield, Lanham.

Blum, W. 1995, *Killing hope: U.S. military and CIA interventions since World War II*, Common Courage Press, Monroe.

Blum, W. 2016, 'Afghanistan, 1979–1992: America's jihad', *William Blum: Blog*, viewed 10 May 2017, https://williamblum.org/chapters/killing-hope/afghanistan

Boal, I., Clark, T., Matthews, J. and Watts, M. 2005, *Afflicted powers: Capital and spectacle in a new age of war*, Verso, New York.

Bodansky, Y. 2011, *Bin Laden: The man who declared war on America*, Prima Lifestyles, Placer County.

Bohnsack, R. 2010, 'Documentary method and group discussions', in R. Bohnsack, N. Pfaff and W. Weller (eds), *Qualitative Analysis and Documentary Method in International Educational Research*, Barbara Budrich, Opladen, pp. 99–124.

Bokhari, Y., Chowdhury, N. and Lacey, R. 2014, 'A good day to bury a bad charity: The rise and fall of the Al-Haramain Islamic Foundation', in R. Lacey and J. Benthall (eds), *Gulf charities and Islamic philanthropy in the 'age of terror' and beyond*, Gerlach Press, Berlin, pp. 199–230.

Bollyn, C. 2004, 'Halliburton and Cheney in middle of Iraq oil money controversy', July, viewed 10 May 2017, http://hugequestions.com/Eric/TFC/Bollyn-Halliburton-Cheney.html

Bookchin, M. 1995, *Social anarchism or lifestyle anarchism: An unbridgeable chasm*, ak Press, Edinburgh.

Bourdieu, P. 1977, *Outline of a theory of practice*, trans. R. Nice, Cambridge University Press, Cambridge.

Bourdieu, P. 1982, *Language and symbolic power*, J. Thompson (ed.), trans. G. Raymond and M. Adamson (1991), Harvard University Press, Cambridge.

Bourdieu, P. 1984, *Distinction: A social critique of the judgment of taste*, trans. R. Nice, Harvard University Press, Cambridge.

Bourdieu, P. 1985a, 'The genesis of the concepts of habitus and field', *Sociocriticism*, vol. 2, no. 2, pp. 11–24.

Bourdieu, P. 1985b, 'The social space and the genesis of groups', *Theory and Society*, vol. 14, no. 6, pp. 723–744.

Bourdieu, P. 1986, 'The forms of capital', in J. Richardson (ed.), trans. R. Nice, *Handbook of theory and research for the sociology of education*, Greenwood, Westport, pp. 241–258.

Bourdieu, P. 1989. 'Social space and symbolic power', *Sociological theory*, vol. 7, no. 1, pp. 14–25.

Bourdieu, P. 1990, *The logic of practice*, trans. R. Nice, Stanford University Press, Redwood City.

Bourdieu, P. 1993, *The field of cultural production*, trans. R. Nice, Polity Press, Cambridge.

Bourdieu, P. 1998a, *Practical reason: On the theory of action*, trans. R. Johnson, Stanford University Press, Redwood City.

Bourdieu, P. 1998b, *Acts of resistance: Against the new myths of our time*, trans. R. Nice, Polity Press, Cambridge.

Bourdieu, P. 2000, *Pascalian Meditations*, Polity Press, Cambridge.

Bourdieu, P. 2005, *The social structures of the economy*, trans. C. Turner, Polity Press, Cambridge.

Bourdieu, P. and Wacquant, L. 1992, *An invitation to reflexive sociology*, University of Chicago Press, Chicago.

Bowles, W. 2003, '"Frauds-R-Us": The Bush Family Saga: Arbusto Oil and the Bin Laden Connection', *Information Clearing House*, 11 May, viewed 1 May 2017, www.informationclearinghouse.info/article3332.htm

Brachman, J. 2008, *Global jihadism: Theory and practice*, Routledge, London.

Braedley, S. and Luxton, M. 2010, *Neoliberalism and everyday life*, McGill-Queen's Press-MQUP, Ontario.

Brauer, J. 1999, 'An economic perspective on mercenaries, military companies, and the privatisation of force', *Cambridge Review of International Affairs*, vol. 13, no. 1, pp. 130–146.

Brenner, N. and Theodore N. 2002, 'Cities and the geographies of "actually existing neoliberalism"', *Antipode*, vol. 34, no. 3, pp. 349–379.

Brenner, N. and Theodore, N. 2005, 'Neoliberalism and the urban condition', *City*, vol. 9, no. 1, pp. 101–107.

Brenner, N., Jessop, B., Jones, M. and Macleod, G. 2008, *State/space: A reader*, John Wiley & Sons, New York.

Brenner, N, Peck, J. and Theodore, N. 2010, 'Variegated neoliberalization: Geographies, modalities, pathways', *Global Networks*, vol. 10, no. 2, pp. 182–222.

Breton, A., Galeotti, G., Salmon, P., and Wintrobe, R. (eds) 2002, *Political extremism and rationality*, Cambridge University Press, Cambridge.

Brisard, J.-C. 2003, Written testimony of Jean-Charles Brisard: International expert on terrorism financing: Lead investigator, 911 Lawsuit: CEO, Jcb Consulting International: Before the Committee on Banking, Housing and Urban Affairs: United States Senate, viewed 10 May 2017, www.banking. senate.gov/download/brisard-october-22-2003

Brisard, J.-C. and Dasquie, G., 2002. *Forbidden truth: US-Taliban secret oil diplomacy and the failed hunt for Bin Laden*. Nation Books, New York.

Brisard, J.-C. and Martinez, D. 2014, *Islamic State: The economy-based terrorist funding*, Reuters, Center for the Analysis of Terrorism, October, viewed 10 May 2017, http://cat-int.org/wp-content/uploads/2016/06/White-Paper-IS-Funding_Final.pdf

Bronner, S. 2019, *Socialism unbound*, Routledge, London.

Brookes-Pollock, T. 2015, 'Russia unveils "proof" Turkey's Erdogan is smuggling ISIS oil across border from Syria', *Independent*, 4 December, viewed 10 May 2017, www.independent.co.uk/news/world/europe/russia-releases-proof-turkey-is-smuggling-ISIS-oil-over-its-border-a6757651.html

Brown, K. 2013, 'Agitprop in Soviet Russia', *Constructing the Past*, vol. 14, no. 1.

Brown, W. 2009, *Edgework: Critical essays on knowledge and politics*, Princeton University Press, Princeton.

Browning, N., Saul, J. and Ghobari, M. 2016, 'Al Qaeda still reaping oil profits in Yemen despite battlefield reverses', Reuters, 27 May, viewed 10 May 2017, www.reuters.com/article/us-yemen-security-smuggling/al-qaeda-still-reaping-oil-profits-in-yemen-despite-battlefield-reverses-idUSKCN0YI0Q2

Bruenig, M. 2019, 'Top 1% up $21 trillion. Bottom 50% down $900 billion', People's Policy Project, 14 June, viewed 29 December 2019, www.peoplespolicyproject.org/2019/06/14/top-1-up-21-trillion-bottom-50-down-900-billion/

Brull, M. 2017, 'Weak on terrorism, strong on supporting genocide: Four lessons from Trump's speech in Saudi Arabia', *New Matilda*, 18 June, viewed 10 August 2017, https://newmatilda.com/2017/06/18/weak-terrorism-strong-supporting-genocide-four-lessons-trumps-speech-saudi-arabia/

Brunnermeier, M. 2009, 'Deciphering the liquidity and credit crunch 2007–08', *Journal of Economic Perspectives*, vol. 23, no. 1, pp. 77–100.

Bruno, G. 2010, *Al-Qaeda's financial pressures*, Council on Foreign Relations, 1 February, viewed 10 May 2017, www.cfr.org/backgrounder/al-qaedas-financial-pressures

Brzezinski, Z. 1998, 'Les Révélations d'un Ancien Conseiller de Carter: 'Oui, la CIA est Entrée en Afghanistan avant les Russes…'." *Le Nouvel Observateur: Le Nouvel Observateur*, 15 January, viewed 10 May 2017, www.voltairenet.org/article165889.html

Buckley, P. and Clegg, J. 2016, *Multinational enterprises in less developed countries*, Springer, New York.

Burke, J. 2003, 'What is Al Qaeda?', *Guardian*, 13 July, viewed 10 May 2017, www.theguardian.com/world/2003/jul/13/alqaida.bookextracts

Burke, J. 2004, *Al-Qaeda: The true story of radical Islam*, Macmillan, London.

Bush, G. W. 2001a, 'Transcript of President Bush's address', CNN, 21 September, viewed 11 November 2016, http://edition.cnn.com/2001/US/09/20/gen.bush.transcript/

Bush, G. W. 2001b, *Address to a joint session of congress and the American people*, US Government: Department of State, 20 September, viewed 10 May 2017, https://2001–2009.state.gov/coalition/cr/rm/2001/5025.htm

Bush, G. W. 2003, 'Full text: George Bush's speech to the American Enterprise Institute', *Guardian*, 23 February, viewed 10 May 2017, www.theguardian.com/world/2003/feb/27/usa.iraq2

Butter, D. 2016, *ISIL financing*, UK House of Commons Foreign Affairs Sub-Committee, 2 February, viewed 10 May 2017, parliamentlive.tv/Event/Index/86b56bdc-76b7–462c-9519-df9d10a90803

Byman, D. 2003, 'Al-Qaeda as an adversary: Do we understand our enemy?', *World Politics*, vol. 56, no. 1, pp. 139–163.

Byman, D. 2015, *Al Qaeda, the Islamic State, and the global jihadist movement: What everyone needs to know*, Oxford University Press, New York.

Cai, W. and Landon, S. 2019, 'Attacks by white extremists are growing. So are their connections', *New York Times*, 3 April, viewed 29 December 2019, www.nytimes.com/interactive/2019/04/03/world/white-extremist-terrorism-christchurch.html?fbclid=IwAR1tDZdL4FeO1gqonH1njT7HKlMiIRD-DrrdgFtcsIUhPbh GxnTAQMlIoI4E

Callimachi, R. 2014, 'Paying ransoms, Europe bankrolls Qaeda terror', *New York Times*, 29 July, viewed 10 May 2017, www.nytimes.com/2014/07/30/world/africa/ransoming-citizens-europe-becomes-al-qaedas-patron.html

Canto, V., Joines, D. and Laffer, A 2014, *Foundations of supply-side economics: Theory and evidence*, Academic Press, Cambridge.

Caplan, M. and Ricciardelli, L. 2016, 'Institutionalizing neoliberalism: 21st-century capitalism, market sprawl, and social policy in the United States', *Poverty & Public Policy*, vol. 8, no. 1, pp. 20–38.

Castañeda, E. 2010, 'Creating authority over remittances: Development experts and the framing of remittances as a development tool', draft paper, viewed 10 May 2017, https://faculty.utep.edu/Portals/1858/Castaneda%20Authority%20Remittances.pdf

Castells, M. 1996, *The rise of the network society*, Blackwell, Oxford.

Castner, B. 2017, 'Exclusive: Tracing ISIS' weapons supply chain – back to the US', *Wired*, 12 December, viewed 1 May 2018, www.wired.com/story/terror-industrial-complex-isis-munitions-supply-chain/

CAT 2017, *Centre d'analyse du terrorisme*, viewed 10 May 2017, http://cat-int.org/index.php/accueil/about-us/?lang=en

Celso, A. 2015, 'The "caliphate" in the digital age: The Islamic state's challenge to the global liberal order', *International Journal of Interdisciplinary Global Studies*, vo. 10, pp. 1–26.

Cerny, P. 2008, 'Embedding neoliberalism: The evolution of a hegemonic paradigm', *Journal of International Trade and Diplomacy*, vol. 2, no. 1, pp. 1–46.

Chambliss, W., Michalowski, R. and Kramer, R. (eds) 2013, *State crime in the global age*, Willan Publishing, Collumpton.

Chapra, M. 2008, *The Global Financial Crisis: Can Islamic Finance help minimize the severity and frequency of such a crisis in the future?* Forum on the Global Financial Crisis at the Islamic Development Bank, 21 October, viewed 10 May 2017, www.unctad.info/EpiSecured/239581/5-M_Umer_Chapra.pdf

Charette, R. 2007, 'Al-Qaeda: Venture capitalists of terror: A Q&A with Lawrence Husick on how insurgents spread their message via the web', *Spectrum*, 1 November, viewed 10 May 2017, http://spectrum.ieee.org/telecom/security/alqaeda-venture-capitalists-of-terror

Chomsky, N. 1998, *The common good*, Odinian Press, New York.

Chomsky, N. 1999, *Profit over people: Neoliberalism and global order*, Seven Stories Press, New York.

Chomsky, N. 2003, *Middle East illusions: Including peace in the Middle East: Reflections on justice and nationhood*, Rowman & Littlefield, New York.

Chomsky, N. 2004, *At war with Asia*, AK Press, Oakland.

Chomsky, N. and Barsamian, D. 2010, *Imperial ambitions: Conversations on the post-9/11 world*, Macmillan, New York.

Chomsky, N. and Barsamian, D. 2017, *Global discontents: Conversations on the rising threats to democracy*, Metropolitan Books, New York.

Chughtai, A. 2018, 'Understanding US military aid to Israel', Al Jazeera, 8 March, viewed 29 December 2019, www.aljazeera.com/indepth/interactive/2018/03/understanding-military-aid-israel-180305092533077.html

Clark, W. 2005, *Petrodollar warfare: Oil, Iraq and the future of the dollar*, New Society Publishers, Gabriola Island.

Clarke, C. 2016, 'Drugs & thugs: Funding terrorism through narcotics trafficking', *Journal of Strategic Security*, vol. 9, no. 3, pp. 1–15.

Clarke, J. 2008, 'Living with/in and without neo-liberalism', *Focaal*, no. 51, pp. 135–147.

Clarkwest, A. 2008, 'Neo-materialist theory and the temporal relationship between income inequality and longevity change', *Social Science & Medicine*, vol. 66, no. 9, pp. 1871–1881.

Clifton, E. 2011, 'Meet an Islamophobia network 'expert': Steven Emerson', *Think Progress*, 31 August, viewed 10 May 2017, https://thinkprogress.org/meet-an-islamophobia-network-expert-steven-emerson-52f4dad98b29/

Cohen, A. and O'Driscoll, G. 2002, *The road to economic prosperity for a post-Saddam Iraq*, The Heritage Foundation, 24 September, viewed 10 May 2017, http://s3.amazonaws.com/thf_media/2002/pdf/bg1594.pdf

Cohen, G. 2009, *Why not socialism?* Princeton University Press, New Jersey.

Coles, I. 2015, *Despair, hardship as Iraq cuts off wages in Islamic State cities*, Reuters, 2 October, viewed 10 May 2017, www.reuters.com/article/us-mideast-crisis-iraq-salaries/despair-hardship-as-iraq-cuts-off-wages-in-islamic-state-cities-idUSKCN0RW0V620151002

Comte, A. 1858, *The catechism of positive religion*, trans. R. Congreve, John Chapman, London.

Connell, R. and Dados, N. 2014, 'Where in the world does neoliberalism come from?', *Theory and Society*, vol. 43, no. 2, pp. 117–138.

Cook, D. 2015, *Understanding jihad*, University of California Press, Oakland.

Cook, E. 2016, 'The neoclassical club: Iriving Fisher and the progressive origins of neoliberalism', *Journal of the Gilded Age and Progressive Era*, vol. 15, no. 3, pp. 246–262.

Cooper, A. 2012, *The oil kings: How the US, Iran, and Saudi Arabia changed the balance of power in the Middle East*, Simon and Schuster, New York.

Cooper, W. 2017, 'The dark side of the economy: A comparative analysis of the Islamic State's revenue streams', *Journal of Terrorism Research*, vol. 8, no. 1.

Costs of War 2020, 'Estimate of the U.S. War on Terror spending in $ billions FY2001–2020', viewed 21 July 2020, https://watson.brown.edu/costsofwar/figures/2019/budgetary-costs-post-911-wars-through-fy2020-64-trillion

Cowell, A. 2013, 'Attack U.S., Qaeda chief tells Muslims in a speech', *New York Times*, 13 September, viewed 10 January 2017, www.nytimes.com/2013/09/14/world/al-qaeda-leader-ayman-al-zawahiri-urges-muslims-to-attack-america.html

Crawford, N. 2016, *US budgetary costs of wars through 2016: $4.79 trillion and counting: summary of costs of the US wars in Iraq, Syria, Afghanistan and Pakistan and homeland security*, Brown University, Watson Institute of International & Public Affairs: Costs of War, September 2016, viewed 10 May 2017, http://watson.brown.edu/costsofwar/files/cow/imce/papers/2016/Costs%20of%20War%20through%202016%20FINAL%20final%20v2.pdf

Crocker, B. 2004, 'Reconstructing Iraq's economy', *Washington Quarterly*, vol. 27, no. 4, pp. 73–93.

Cronin, A. 2015, 'ISIS is not a terrorist group: Why counterterrorism won't stop the latest jihadist threat', *Foreign Affairs*, vol. 94, no. 2, pp. 87–98.

Crothers, L. 2012, *Globalization and American popular culture*, Rowman & Littlefield, Lanham.

Crouch, C. 2011, *The strange non-death of neo-liberalism*, Polity, London.

Cullen, T. 2019, 'The grave threats of white supremacy and far-right extremism', *New York Times*, 22 February, viewed 29 December 2019, www.nytimes.com/2019/02/22/opinion/christopher-hasson-extremism.html

Currie, E. 1998, *Crime and punishment in America*, Henry Holt & Co, New York.

Daragahi, B. and Solomon, E. 2014, 'Fuelling ISIS Inc.', *Financial Times*, 21 September, viewed 10 May 2017, www.relooney.com/NS3040/000_New_1556.pdf

Day, M. 2018, 'Democratic socialism, explained by a democratic socialist', *Vox*, 1 August, viewed 29 December 2019, www.vox.com/first-person/2018/8/1/17637028/bernie-sanders-alexandria-ocasio-cortez-cynthia-nixon-democratic- socialism-jacobin-dsa

De Goede, M. 2003, 'Hawala discourses and the war on terrorist finance', *Environment and Planning D: Society and Space*, vol. 21, no. 5, pp. 513–532.

De Goede, M. 2008, 'Money, media and the anti-politics of terrorist finance', *European Journal of Cultural Studies*, vol. 11, no. 3, pp. 289–310.

Dearden, L. 2016, 'ISIS announces masacre of captives from Syrian cement factory after majority of 300 workers "released"', *Independent*, 9 April, viewed 10 May 2017, www.independent.co.uk/news/world/middle-east/ISIS-announces-massacre-of-captives-from-syrian-cement-factory-after-majority-of-300-workers-a6976121.html

Deflem, M. and McDonough, S. 2015, 'The fear of counterterrorism: Surveillance and civil liberties since 9/11', *Society*, vol. 52, no. 1, pp. 70–79.

DeFronzo, J. 2018, *Revolutions and revolutionary movements*, Routledge, London.

Del Cid Gómez, J. 2010, 'A financial profile of the terrorism of Al-Qaeda and its affiliates', *Perspectives on Terrorism*, vol. 4, no. 4, viewed 10 May 2017, www.terrorismanalysts.com/pt/index.php/pot/article/view/113/html

Delany, M. 2015, 'Turkey accuses Russia of profiting from ISIS oil', Arutz Sheva, viewed 10 May 2017, www.israelnationalnews.com/News/News.aspx/204369

Deleuze, G. and Guattari, F. 1988, *A thousand plateaus: Capitalism and schizophrenia*, trans. B. Massumi, Bloomsbury Publishing, London.

Delmar-Morgan, A. and Oborne, P. 2014, 'Why is the Muslim charity Interpal being blacklisted as a terrorist organization', *Telegraph*, 26 November, viewed 10 May 2017, www.telegraph.co.uk/news/religion/11255294/Why-is-the-Muslim-charity-Interpal-being-blacklisted-as-a-terrorist-organisation.html

Devji, F. 2008, *The terrorist in search of humanity: Militant Islam and global politics*, Columbia University Press, New York.

Dhiman, Col S. C. 2015, *Islamic State of Iraq and Syria (ISIS) reconciliation, democracy and terror*, Neha Publishers and Distributors, New Delhi.

Dorrien, G. 2010, *Economy, difference, empire: Social ethics for social justice.* Columbia University Press, New York.

Dorsey, J. 2015, 'How Qatar is its own worst enemy', *The International Journal of the History of Sport*, vol. 32, no. 3, pp. 422–439.

Dower, J. 2010, *Cultures of war: Pearl Harbour/Hiroshima/9–11/Iraq*, WW Norton & Company, New York.

Drake, P.W. and Frank, V.K. 2004, *Victims of the Chilean miracle: Workers and neoliberalism in the Pinochet era, 1973–2002*, Duke University Press, Durham.

Dreyfuss, R. 2006, *Devil's game: How the United States helped unleash fundamentalist Islam*, Macmillan, London.

Druzhinin, A. 2015, 'Russia, Egypt support forming anti-ISIS coalition in Syria – Putin', *RT*, 26 August, viewed 10 May 2017, www.rt.com/news/313537-russia-egypt-putin-meeting/

Duelfer, C. and CIA 2004, *Testimony by Charles Duelfer on Iraqi WMD Programs*, Central Intelligence Agency, 30 March, viewed 10 May 2017, www.cia.gov/news-information/speeches-testimony/2004/tenet_testimony_03302004.html

Duggan, L. 2012, *The twilight of equality? Neoliberalism, cultural politics, and the attack on democracy*, Beacon Press, Boston.

Duncan, H. 2006, *Bush and Cheney's war*, Trafford Publishing, London.

Duncan, T. and Coyne, C. 2015, 'The revolving door and the entrenchment of the permanent war economy', *Peace Economics, Peace Science and Public Policy*, vol. 21, no. 3, pp. 391–413.

Dupuy, A. 2010, 'Disaster capitalism to the rescue: The international community and Haiti after the earthquake', *NACLA Report on the Americas*, vol. 43, no. 4, pp. 14–19.

Dupuy, A. 2011, 'Wesleyan Professor Alex Dupuy: Haiti transformed into the "republic of the NGOs"', *Democracy Now!* 12 January, viewed 10 May 2017, www.democracynow.org/2011/1/12/alex_dupuy_foreign_aid_keeps_haiti

Durkheim, E. 2008, *The elementary forms of the religious life*, trans. J. Swain, Courier Corporation, New York.

Durkheim, E. 2013, *The evolution of educational thought: Lectures on the formation and development of secondary education in France*, trans. P. Collins, Routledge, New York.

Durkheim, E., Mauss, M. and Needham, R. 1963, *Primitive classification: Vol. 273*, University of Chicago Press, Chicago.

Easterly, W. 2006, 'Haiti's eternal crisis', *The globalist: Rethinking globalization*, 3 April, viewed 10 May 2017, www.theglobalist.com/haitis-eternal-crisis/

Edgerton, J. and Roberts, L. 2014, 'Cultural capital or habitus? Bourdieu and beyond in the explanation of enduring educational inequality', *Theory and Research in Education*, vol. 12, no. 2, pp. 193–220.

Eklund, L., Degerald, M., Brandt, M., Prishchepov, A. and Pilesjö, P. 2017, 'How conflict affects land use: Agricultural activity in areas seized by the Islamic State', *Environmental Research Letters*, vol. 12, no. 5, pp. 1–10.

Elias, D. 2004, 'How illicit labels may fund terror', *The Age*, 20 November, viewed 10 May 2017, www.theage.com.au/news/National/How-illicit-labels-may-fund-terror/2004/11/19/1100838223880.html

Epstein, G. 2005, *Financialization and the world economy*, Edward Elgar Publishing, Cheltenham.

Eschle, C. 2004, 'Constructing "the anti-globalisation movement"', *International Journal of Peace Studies*, vol. 9, no. 1, pp. 61–84.

Eschle, C. and Maiguashca, B. 2005, *Critical theories, IR and 'the anti-globalisation movement': The politics of global resistance*, Routledge, London.

Escobar, A. 2004, 'Beyond the third world: Imperial globality, global coloniality and anti-globalisation social movements', *Third World Quarterly*, vol. 25, no. 1, pp. 207–230.

Escobar, A. 2005, 'Other worlds are (already) possible', in R. H. Savyasaachi (ed.), *Social movements: Transformative shifts and turning points*, Routledge, London.

European Parliament 2017, *In-depth analysis: The financial of the 'Islamic state' in Iraq and Syria (ISIS)*, Directorate-general for External Policies; Policy Department, viewed 10 May 2017, www.europarl.europa.eu/RegData/etudes/IDAN/2017/603835/EXPO_IDA(2017)603835_EN.pdf

Faksh, M. 1997, *The future of Islam in the Middle East: Fundamentalism in Egypt, Algeria, and Saudi Arabia*, Greenwood Publishing Group, Westport.

Falleti, T. and Lynch, J. 2009, 'Context and causal mechanisms in political analysis', *Comparative Political Studies*, vol. 42, no. 9, pp. 1143–1166.

Fanusie, Y. and Entz, A. 2017, *Islamic State: Financial assessment*, Foundation for Defense of Democracies: Center on Sanctions & Illicit Finance, March, viewed 10 May 2017, www.defenddemocracy.org/content/uploads/documents/Islamic_State_Terror_Finance.pdf

Fanusie, Y. and Heid, L. 2016, 'What ISIS is banking on', *Forbes*, viewed 10 May 2017, 17 June, www.forbes.com/sites/realspin/2016/06/17/what-ISIS-is-banking-on/#778587f81651

FAO 2014, *Serious food security cocnerns following escalation of conflict*, Global Information and Early Warning System on Food and Agriculture (GIEWS), Special Alert n°332, 25 June, viewed 10 May 2017, www.fao.org/3/a-i3898e.pdf

Faraj, M. 1986, 'The neglected duty', in W. Laqueur (ed.), *Voices of terror* (2004), Reed Press, New York, pp. 401–403.

Farrall, L. 2011, 'How Al Qaeda works – what the organization's subsidiaries say about its strength', *Foreign Affairs*, no. 90, p. 128.

FATF 2009, *History of the FATF*, Financial Action Task Force, viewed 10 May 2017, www.fatf-gafi.org/faq/moneylaundering/

FATF 2014, *Financial flows linked to the production and trafficking of Afghan opiates*, Financial Action Task Force, viewed 10 May 2017, www.fatf-gafi.org/publications/methodsandtrends/documents/financial-flows-afghan-opiates.html

FATF 2015a, *Emerging terrorist financing risks*, October, Financial Action Task Force, viewed 10 May 2017, www.fatf-gafi.org/media/fatf/documents/reports/Emerging-Terrorist-Financing-Risks.pdf

FATF 2015b, *Financing of the terrorist organisation Islamic State in Iraq and the Levant (ISIL)*, Financial Action Task Force, February, viewed 10 May 2017, www.fatf-gafi.org/media/fatf/documents/reports/Financing-of-the-terrorist-organisation-ISIL.pdf

Faucon, B. and Al Omran, A. 2017, 'Islamic State steps up oil and gas sales to the Assad regime', *Wall Street Journal*, 19 January, viewed 10 May 2017, www.wsj.com/articles/islamic-state-steps-up-oil-and-gas-sales-to-assad-regime-1484835563

Ferrell, J. 2019, 'In defense of resistance', *Critical Criminology*, https://doi.org/10.1007/s10612–019–09456–6

Fick, M. 2014, *Special report: Islamic State uses grain to tighten grip in Iraq*, Reuters, 30 September, viewed 10 May 2017, www.reuters.com/article/us-mideast-crisis-wheat/special-report-islamic-state-uses-grain-to-tighten-grip-in-iraq-idUSKCN0HP12J20140930

Fisk, R. 1993, 'Anti-Soviet warrior puts his army on the road to peace: The Saudi businessman who recruited mujahedin now uses them for large-scale building projects in Sudan. Robert Fisk met him in Almatig', *Independent*, 6

December, viewed 10 January 2017 www.independent.co.uk/news/world/anti-soviet-warrior-puts-his-army-on-the-road-to-peace-the-saudi-businessman-who-recruited-mujahedin-1465715.html

Fitzpatrick, M. 2014, 'ISIS, Al Qaeda and the wretched of the earth', *Flinders Journal of the History of Philosophy*, vol. 30, no. 21, pp. 21–34.

Flannery, F. 2015, *Understanding apocalyptic terrorism: Countering the radical mindset*, Routledge, London.

Flick, U. 2009, *An introduction to qualitative research*, Sage, London.

Fogle, N. 2011, *The spatial logic of social struggle: A Bourdieuian topology*, Lexington Books, Washington.

Foray, D. and Lundvall, B. 1996, *The knowledge-based economy*, OECD, viewed 10 May 2017, www.oecd.org/sti/sci-tech/1913021.pdf

Foreign Broadcast Information Service 2004, 'Compilation of Usama Bin Ladin statements: 1994- January 2004', United States Government, January, viewed 10 May 2017, https://fas.org/irp/world/para/ubl-fbis.pdf

Foundation for the Defense of Democracies 2019, *Economic defeat of the Islamic State: Behind the scenes of Operation Tidal Wave II*, Conference, 10 May, viewed 29 December 2019, www.fdd.org/events/2019/05/10/economic-defeat-of-the-islamic-state-behind-the-scenes-of-operation-tidal-wave-ii/

Fouskas, V. and Gökay, B. 2005, *The new American imperialism: Bush's war on terror and blood for oil*, Greenwood Publishing Group, Santa Barbara.

Freeman, C. 2016, 'Islamic State "earning millions by playing the stock market"', *Telegraph*, 2 March, viewed 10 May 2017, www.telegraph.co.uk/news/worldnews/middleeast/iraq/12180652/Islamic-State-earning-millions-by-playing-the-stock-market.html

Frick, A. 2008, 'Rumsfeld on eve of Iraq war: "If you think we're going to spend $1 billion in Iraq, you're sadly mistaken"', *ThinkProgress*, 14 December, viewed 10 May 2017, https://archive.thinkprogress.org/rumsfeld-on-eve-of-iraq-war-if-you-think-were-going-to-spend-1-billion-in-iraq-you-re-sadly-mistaken-f168bc524b85/

Friedman, M. 1962, *Capitalism and freedom*, University of Chicago Press, Chicago.

Friedman, M. 1983, 'Monetarism in rhetoric and in practice', *Bank of Japan Monetary and Economic Studies*, vol. 1, no. 2, pp. 1–14.

Friedman, M. 1998, 'Reviving Japan', *Hoover Digest*, no. 2, viewed 10 May 2017, http://unpan1.un.org/intradoc/groups/public/documents/APCITY/UNPAN 014771.pdf

Fromson, J. and Simon, S. 2015, 'ISIS: The dubious paradise of apocalypse now', *Survival*, vol. 57, no. 3, pp. 7–56.

Fuchs, C. 2009, 'A contribution to the critique of the political economy of transnational informational capitalism', *Rethinking Marxism*, vol. 21, no. 3, pp. 387–402.

Fuchs, C. 2014, *Digital labour and Karl Marx*, Routledge, London.

Fukuyama, F. 2007, *America at the crossroads: Democracy, power, and the neoconservative legacy*, Yale University Press, New Haven.

Garfinkel, H. 1972, Remarks on ethnomethodology, in J. Gumperz and D. Hymes (eds), *Directions in sociolinguistics*, Holt, Rinehart & Winston, New York, pp. 301–309.

Gates, R. 2011, *From the shadows: The ultimate insider's story of five presidents*, Simon and Schuster, New York.

Gendzier, I. L. 2015, *Dying to forget: Oil, power, Palestine, and the foundations of US policy in the Middle East*. Columbia University Press, New York.

George, A. 1991, *Western state terrorism*, Polity Press, Cambridge.

George, S. 1999, 'A short history of neoliberalism', in *Conference on Economic Sovereignty in a Globalising World*, vol. 24, p. 26, viewed 10 May 2017, www.tni.org/en/article/short-history-neoliberalism

Georgy, M. and El Dahan M. 2017, *How a businessman struck a deal with Islamic State to help Assad feed Syria*, Reuters, 11 October, viewed 10 May 2017, www.reuters.com/article/us-mideast-crisis-syria-wheat-islamic-st/how-a-businessman-struck-a-deal-with-islamic-state-to-help-assad-feed-syrians-idUSKBN1CG0EL

Gerges, F. 2017, *ISIS: A history*, Princeton University Press, New Jersey.

Ghosh, A., Ostry, J. and Qureshi, M. 2016, 'When do capital inflow surges end in tears?', *American Economic Review*, vol. 106, no. 5, pp. 581–585.

Gibbs, D. 2006, 'Reassessing Soviet motives for invading Afghanistan: A declassified history', *Critical Asian Studies*, vol. 38, no. 2, pp. 239–263.

Gilligan, J. 2001, *Preventing violence*, Thames & Hudson, New York.

Girardet, E. 2012, *Afghanistan: The Soviet War*, Routledge, London.

Giroux, H. 2004, *The terror of neoliberalism: Authoritarianism and the eclipse of democracy*, Paradigm Publishers, Colorado.

Giroux, H. 2012, 'Disturbing pleasures: Murderous images and the aesthetics of depravity', *Third Text*, vol. 26, no. 3, pp. 259–273.

Giroux, H. 2014, 'ISIS and the spectacle of terrorism: Resisting mainstream workstations of fear', *Truthout*, 30 September, viewed 10 May 2017, www.truth-out.org/news/item/26519-ISIS-and-the-spectacle-of-terrorism-resisting-mainstream-workstations-of-fear

Gleick, P. 1993, 'Water and conflict: Fresh water resources and international security', *International security*, vol. 18, no. 1, pp. 79–112.

Gleick, P. H., Pacific Institute, Ajami, N., Christian-Smith, J., Cooley, H., Donnelly, K., Fulton, J., Ha, M.-L., Heberger, M., Moore, E., Morrison, J., Orr, S., Schulte, P. and Srinivasan, V. 2014, *The world's water: The biennial report on freshwater resources: Volume 8*, Island Press, Washington.

Gonzalez, C. 2004, 'Trade liberalization, food security and the environment: The neoliberal threat to sustainable rural development', *Transnational Law and Contemporary Problems*, vol. 14, pp. 419, viewed 10 May 2017, https://papers.ssrn.com/Sol3/papers.cfm?abstract_id=987150

Goodstein, L. 2003, 'Top Evangelicals critical of colleagues over Islam', *New York Times*, 8 May, viewed 10 May 2017, www.nytimes.com/2003/05/08/us/top-evangelicals-critical-of-colleagues-over-islam.html

Goodwin, C. 2015, '"We have to understand that ISIS is a country now"', *The Times*, 4 January, viewed 10 May 2017, www.thetimes.co.uk/article/we-have-to-understand-that-ISIS-is-a-country-now-rhvthgpwtpq.

Gordon, J. 2010, *Invisible war: The United States and the Iraq sanctions*, Harvard University Press, Cambridge.

Gould, E. and Fitzgerald, P. 2011, *Crossing zero: The AfPak war at the turning point of American empire*, City Lights Books, San Francisco.

Graeber, D. 2004, *Fragments of an anarchist anthropology*, Prickly Paradigm Press, Cambridge.

Gray, J. 2003, *Al Qaeda and what it means to be modern*, Faber & Faber, London.

Gray, J. 2014, 'A point of view: ISIS and what it means to be modern', *BBC News*, 11 July, viewed 10 May 2017, www.bbc.com/news/magazine- 28246732

Green, E. 2016, 'Why does the United States give so much money to Israel?', *Atlantic*, 15 September, 15 September, viewed 10 May 2017, www.theatlantic.com/international/archive/2016/09/united-states-israel-memorandum-of-understanding-military-aid/500192/

Grenfell, M. and Lebaron, F. 2014, *Bourdieu and data analysis: Methodological principles and practice*, Peter Lang, Pieterlen.

Grewcock, M. 2007, 'Shooting the passenger: Australia's war on illicit migrants', in M. Lee (ed.), *Human trafficking*, Willan Publishing, Cullompton, pp. 178–200.

Griffith, S. 1963, *Sun Tzu: The art of war* (Vol. 39), Oxford University Press, London.

Griswold, E. 2015, 'Is this the end of Christianity in the Middle East?', *New York Times*, 22 July, viewed 10 May 2017, www.nytimes.com/2015/07/26/magazine/is-this-the-end-of-christianity-in-the-middle-east.html?_r=0

Gunes, C. 2013, *The Kurdish national movement in Turkey: From protest to resistance*. Routledge, London.

Gunning, J. and Jackson, R. 2011, 'What's so "religious" about "religious terrorism"?', *Critical Studies on Terrorism*, vol. 4, no. 3, pp. 369–388.

Gurulé, J. 2010, *Unfunding terror: The legal response to the financing of global terrorism*, Edward Elgar Publishing, Cheltenham.

Habermas, J. 1990, 'What does socialism mean today? The rectifying revolution and the need for new thinking on the left', *New Left Review*, no. 183, p. 3, viewed 10 May 2017, https://newleftreview.org/I/183/jurgen-habermas-what-does-socialism-mean-today-the-rectifying-revolution-and-the-need-for-new-thinking-on-the-left

Hafiz, Y. 2013, 'Syria conflict indicates Armageddon, say one third of Americans', *Huffington Post*, 14 September, viewed 10 May 2017, www.huffingtonpost.com.au/entry/syria-conflict-armageddon_n_3923123

Haid, H. 2017, 'How the economic model of ISIS evolves post-caliphate', *ND: Syria Deeply*, 17 July, viewed 10 May 2017, www.newsdeeply.com/syria/community/2017/07/17/how-the-economic-model-of-ISIS-evolves-post- caliphate

Halchin, E. 2005, *The Coalition Provisional Authority (CPA): Origin, characteristics, and institutional authorities*, June, Washington DC Congressional Research Service: Library of Congress.

Hall, S. 2011, 'The neo-liberal revolution', *Cultural Studies*, vol. 25, no. 6, pp. 705–728.

Hall, S., Massey, D. and Rustin, M. 2015, *After neoliberalism?* Lawrence & Wishart, London.

Halliday, F. 1978, 'Revolution in Afghanistan', *New Left Review*, no. 112, p. 3.

Halliday, F. 1980, 'The war and revolution in Afghanistan', *New Left Review*, no. 119, p. 20.

Halliday, F. and Alavi, H. (eds) 1988, *State and ideology in the Middle East and Pakistan*, Macmillan Education, London.

Hallward, P. 2007, *Damming the flood: Haiti, Aristide, and the politics of containment*, Verso, New York.

Hamm, M. 2007, *Terrorism as crime: From Oklahoma City to Al-Qaeda and beyond*, NYU Press, New York.

Hamzah, W. and Al-Attabi, K. 2017, 'Islamic State loses territory in last strongholds in Syria and Iraq', *DPA: International*, 3 November, viewed 10 May 2017, www.dpa-international.com/topic/islamic-state-loses-territory-last-strongholds-syria-iraq-171103–99–716415

Hanieh, A. 2008, 'Palestine in the Middle East: Opposing neoliberalism and US power', *Monthly Review*, 19 July, viewed 10 May 2017, https://mronline.org/2008/07/19/palestine-in-the-middle-east-opposing-neoliberalism-and-us-powerpart-1/

Hanieh, A. 2016, *Capitalism and class in the Gulf Arab states*, Springer, New York.

Harris, L. 2002, 'Al Qaeda's fantasy ideology', *Policy Review*, no. 114, p. 19.

Harvey, D. 1989, *The condition of postmodernity*, Blackwell, Oxford.

Harvey, D. 1995, 'Globalization in question', *Rethinking Marxism*, vol. 8, no. 4, pp. 1–17.

Harvey, D. 2001, *Spaces of capital: Towards a critical geography*, Routledge, New York.

Harvey, D. 2003, *The new imperialism*, Oxford University Press, Oxford.

Harvey, D. 2005, *A brief history of neoliberalism*, Oxford University Press, Oxford.

Harvey, D. 2007, 'Neoliberalism as creative destruction', *The ANNALS of the American Academy of Political and Social Science*, vol. 610, no. 1, pp. 21–44.

Hasan, M. and Dridi, J. 2010, 'The effects of the global crisis on Islamic and conventional banks: A comparative study', IMF Working Papers, pp. 1–46, September, viewed 10 May 2017, www.imf.org/external/pubs/ft/wp/2010/wp10201.pdf

Hashim, A. 2014, 'The Islamic State: From Al-Qaeda affiliate to caliphate', *Middle East Policy*, vol. 21, no. 4, pp. 69–83.

Hawramy, F., Mohammed, S. and Harding, L. 2014, 'Inside Islamic State's oil empire: How captured oilfields fuel ISIS insurgency', *Guardian*, 20 November, viewed 10 May 2017, www.theguardian.com/world/2014/nov/19/-sp-islamic-state-oil-empire-iraq-isis

Hayek, F. 1937, 'Economics and knowledge', *Economica*, vol. 4, no. 13, pp. 33–54.

Haykel, B. 2009, 'On the nature of Salafi thought and action', in R. Meijer (ed.), *Global Salafism: Islam's new religious movement*, Taylor & Francis, Abingdon, pp. 33–57.

Hayward, K. and Schuilenburg, M. 2014, 'To resist = To create? Some thoughts on the concept of resistance in cultural criminology', *Cultuur & Criminaliteit*, vol. 4, no. 1, pp. 22–36.

Heath-Kelly, C. 2013, 'Counter-Terrorism and the counterfactual: Producing the "radicalisation" discourse and the UK Prevent strategy', *The British Journal of Politics & International Relations*, vol. 15, no. 3, pp. 394–415.

Hegel, G. 1901, *Philosophy of history: Vol. 12*, trans. J. Sibree, PF Collier and Son, New York.

Hegel, G. 1969, *Science of logic*, trans. A Miller, Humanities Press International, New Jersey.

Heißner, S., Neumann P., Holland-McCown, J. and Basra, R. 2017, *Caliphate in decline: An estimate of Islamic State's financial fortunes*, The International Centre for the Study of Radicalisation and Political Violence, King's College, London, viewed 10 December 2017, http://icsr.info/wp-content/uploads/2017/02/ICSR-Report-Caliphate-in-Decline-An-Estimate-of-Islamic-States-Financial-Fortunes.pdf

Heim, J. 2017, 'Recounting a day of rage, hate, violence and death', 14 August, viewed 29 December 2019, www.washingtonpost.com/graphics/2017/local/charlottesville-timeline/?utm_term=.40631f2f8ae3&tid=a_inl_manual&tid-loc=9

Hellmich, C. 2011, *Al-Qaeda: From global network to local franchise*, Zed Books, London.

Hendawi, H. and Abdul-Zahra, Q. 2015, 'ISIS top brass is Iraq army's former best and brightest', *Haaretz*, 8 August, viewed 10 May 2017, www.haaretz.com/israel-news/1.670177

Herman, E. and Chomsky, N. 2010, *Manufacturing consent: The political economy of the mass media*, Random House, New York.

Hijzen, A. and Swaim, P. 2010, 'Offshoring, labour market institutions and the elasticity of labour demand', *European Economic Review*, vol. 54, no. 8, pp. 1016–1034.

Hitchings-Hales, J. 2018, 'Hundreds of H&M and gap factory workers abused daily, report says', *Global Citizen*, 5 June, viewed 29 December 2019, www.globalcitizen.org/en/content/hm-gap-factory-abuse-fast-fashion-workers/

Hobsbawm, E. 2010, *Age of capital: 1848–1875*, Hachette, New York.

Hoffman, B. 2003, 'Al Qaeda, trends in terrorism, and future potentialities: An assessment', *Studies in Conflict & Terrorism*, vol. 26, no. 6, pp. 429–442.

Hoffman, B. 2004, 'The changing face of Al Qaeda and the global war on terrorism', *Studies in Conflict & Terrorism*, vol. 27, no. 6, pp. 549–560.

Hoffman, B. 2008, 'The myth of grass-roots terrorism – why Osama bin Laden still matters', *Foreign Affairs*, vol. 87, no. 3, pp. 133–138.

Hoffman, B. 2013, *Inside terrorism*, Columbia University Press, New York.

Hoffman, B. and Reinares, F. 2014, *The evolution of the global terrorist threat: From 9/11 to Osama Bin Laden's death*, Columbia University Press, New York.

Holbrook, D. 2015, 'Al-Qaeda and the rise of ISIS', *Survival* vol. 57, no. 2, pp. 93–104.

Hollander, P. 1992, *Anti-Americanism: Critiques at home and abroad, 1965–1990*, Oxford University Press, Oxford.

Holmes, D. and Dixon, N. 2001, *Behind the US war on Afghanistan*, Resistance Books, Broadway.

Holt, T., Freilich, J. and Chermak, S. 2017, 'Internet-based radicalization as enculturation to violent deviant subcultures', *Deviant Behavior*, vol. 38, no. 8, pp. 855–869.

Holzapfel, M. and König, K. 2009, *A brief history of the anti-globalisation protests*, viewed 10 May 2017, www.eurozine.com/articles/2002–04–05-holzapfel-en.html

Homeland Security Committee 2016, *Cash to chaos: Dismantling ISIS' financial infrastructure*, United State Government, House Homeland Security Committee Majority Staff Report, October, viewed 10 May 2017, https://homeland.house.gov/wp-content/uploads/2016/10/Dismantling-ISIS-Financial-Infrastructure.pdf

Hubbard, B. 2014, 'The franchising of Al-Qaeda', *New York Times*, 25 January, viewed 10 May 2017, www.nytimes.com/2014/01/26/sunday-review/the-franchising-of-al-qaeda.html?_r=0

Hudson, M., 2012, 'The road to debt deflation, debt peonage, and neofeudalism', *Levy Economics Institute of Bard College*, Working Paper, no. 708, viewed 29 December 2019, https://papers.ssrn.com/sol3/papers.cfm?abstract_id=2007284

Huliaras, A. 2006, 'Evangelists, oil companies, and terrorists: The Bush administration's policy towards Sudan', *Orbis*, vol. 50, no. 4, pp. 709–724.

Huntington, S. 1993, 'The clash of civilizations?', *Foreign Affairs*, vol. 72, no. 3, pp. 22–49.

Huntington, S. 1996, *The clash of civilizations and the remaking of world order*, Penguin Books India, New Delhi.

Husserl, E. 1973, *Experience and judgement: Investigations in a Genealogy of Logic*, ed. L. Landgrebe, trans. J. Churchill and K. Ameriks, RKP, London.

Husserl, E. 1989, *Ideas pertaining to a pure phenomenology and to a phenomenological philosophy*, Second Book, in *Studies in the Phenomenology of Constitution* series, trans. R. Rojecwicz and A Schuwer, Kluwer Academic Publishers, London.

Hynek, N. and Chandler, D. 2013, 'No emancipatory alternative, no critical security studies', *Critical Studies on Security*, vol. 1, no. 1, pp. 46–63.

Iellatchitch, A., Mayrhofer, W. and Meyer, M. 2003, 'Career fields: A small step towards a grand career theory?', *International Journal of Human Resource Management*, vol. 14, no. 5, pp. 728–750.

Ignatieff, M. 2004, 'The terrorist as auteur', *New York Times Magazine*, 14 November, viewed 10 May 2017, www.nytimes.com/2004/11/14/movies/the-terrorist-as-auteur.html

Ignatius, D. 2014, 'The manual that chillingly foreshadows the Islamic State', *Washington Post*, 25 September, viewed 10 May 2017, www.washingtonpost.com/opinions/david-ignatius-the-mein-kampf-of-jihad/2014/09/25/4adbfc1a-44e8–11e4–9a15–137aa0153527_story.html?utm_term=.a8be28f36318

IISA 2014, 'IISA Launches a new programme: "Neo-jihadism; the study of changing jihadists landscape and its global and Islamic-world implications"', *Institute for Islamic Strategic Affairs*, 17 July, viewed 1 June 2015, http://iisablog.org/

Illahi, M. 2018, *Doctrine of terror: Saudi Salafi religion*. FriesenPress, Altona.

Investigative Project on Terrorism 2018, *About the investigative project on terrorism*, viewed 10 January 2018, www.investigativeproject.org/about.php

Ip, G. 2017, 'Trump, Brexit, Le Pen: West's anti-globalism backlash', *The Australian*, 12 January, viewed 10 May 2017, www.theaustralian.com.au/business/wall-street-journal/trump-brexit-le-pen-wests-antiglobalism-backlash/news-story/e4c5cbb15ccb582b930579295b5a5dc4

Isenberg, D. 2009, *Private military contractors and US grand strategy*, International Peace Research Institute (PRIO), viewed 10 May 2017, www.files.ethz.ch/isn/109297/Isenberg%20Private%20Military%20Contractors%20PRIO%20Report%201–2009.pdf

Izady, M. 2015, *Kurds: A concise handbook*, Routledge, London.

Jaafar, H. and Woertz, E. 2016, 'Agriculture as a funding source of ISIS: A GIS and remote sensing analysis', *Food Policy*, vol. 64, pp. 14–25.

Jabareen, Y. 2015, 'The emerging Islamic State: Terror, territoriality, and the agenda of social transformation', *Geoforum*, vol. 58, pp. 51–55.

Jackson, R. 2005, *Writing the war on terrorism: Language, politics and counter-terrorism*, Manchester University Press, Manchester.

Jackson, R. 2006, 'Genealogy, ideology, and counter-terrorism: Writing wars on terrorism from Ronald Reagan to George W. Bush Jr', *Studies in Lanugage & Capitalism*, vol. 1, no. 1, pp. 163–193.

Jackson, R. 2010, 'In defence of "terrorism": Finding a way through a forest of misconceptions', *Behavioral Sciences of Terrorism and Political Aggression*, vol. 3, no. 2, pp. 116–130.

Jackson, R. 2011, 'Culture, identity and hegemony: Continuity and (the lack of) change in US counterterrorism policy from Bush to Obama', *International Politics*, vol. 48, no. 2–3, pp. 390–411.

Jackson, R. 2012, 'Unknown knowns: The subjugated knowledge of terrorism studies', *Critical Studies on Terrorism*, vol. 5, no. 1, pp. 11–29.

Jackson, R. 2015, 'On how to be a collective intellectual', in *Security Expertise: Practice, Power, Responsibility*, p. 186, viewed 10 May 2017, http://cast.ku.dk/papers_security_expertise/Jackson_2011.pdf

Jackson, R. 2018, *Writing the war on terrorism: Language, politics and counter-terrorism*, Manchester University Press, Manchester.

Jacobson, M. 2010, 'Terrorist financing and the Internet', *Studies in Conflict & Terrorism*, vol. 33, no. 4, pp. 353–363.

Jahan, S. and Papageorgiou, C. 2014, 'What is monetarism?', *Finance & Development*, vol. 51, no. 1, pp. 38–39.

Jawitz, J. 2009, 'Learning in the academic workplace: The harmonization of the collective and the individual habitus', *Studies in Higher Education*, vol. 34, no. 6, pp. 601–614.

Jenkins, B. 2015, *The continuing lure of violent jihad*, Committee on Homeland Security House of Representatives, Rand Corporation, 24 May, viewed 10

May 2017, www.rand.org/content/dam/rand/pubs/testimonies/CT400/CT429/RAND_CT429.pdf

Jeong, Y. and Weiner, R. 2012, 'Who bribes? Evidence from the United Nations' oil-for-food program', *Strategic Management Journal*, vol. 33, no. 12, pp. 1363–1383.

Jessop, B. 1982, *The capitalist state*, New York University Press, New York.

Jessop, B. 2000, 'The crisis of the national spatio-temporal fix and the tendential ecological dominance of globalizing capitalism', *International Journal of Urban and Regional Research*, vol. 24, no. 2, pp. 323–360.

Jessop, B. 2002, 'Liberalism, neoliberalism, and urban governance: A state–theoretical perspective', *Antipode*, vol. 34, no. 3, pp. 452–472.

Jessop, B. 2006, 'Spatial fixes, temporal fixes and spatio-temporal fixes', in N. Castree and D. Gregory (eds), *David Harvey: A Critical Reader*, Blackwell, Oxford, pp. 142–166.

Jessop, B. 2011, 'Constructions of neoliberal reason – by Jamie Peck', *British Journal of Sociology*, vol. 62, no. 4, pp. 750–752.

Johnson, S. 2009, 'The quiet coup', *Atlantic*, May, viewed 10 May 2017, www.theatlantic.com/magazine/archive/2009/05/the-quiet-coup/307364/

Johnston, P., Shapiro, J., Shatz, H., Bahney, B., Jung, D., Ryan, P. and Wallace, J. 2016, *Foundations of the Islamic State: Management, money, and terror in Iraq, 2005–2010*, Rand Corporation, 16 February, viewed 10 May 2017, www.rand.org/content/dam/rand/pubs/research_reports/RR1100/RR1192/RAND_RR1192.pdf

Jones, S. G. 2014, *A persistent threat: The evolution of Al Qa'ida and other Salafi jihadists*, Rand Corporation, 14 March, viewed 10 May 2017, www.rand.org/content/dam/rand/pubs/research_reports/RR600/RR637/RAND_RR637.pdf

Jones, S. G., Newlee, D., Harrington, N., Sharb, C. and Byrne, H. 2018, *The evolution of the Salafi-Jihadist threat: Current and future challenges from the Islamic State, al Qaeda, and other groups*, Center for Strategic and International Studies, 20 November, viewed 29 December 2019, www.csis.org/analysis/evolution-salafi- jihadist-threat

Juhasz, A. 2006, 'Trading on terror to profit a few', *Los Angeles Times*, 26 June, viewed 10 May 2017, http://articles.latimes.com/2006/jun/26/opinion/oe-juhasz26

Kaiser Jr, W. 2010, *History of Israel*, B&H Publishing Group, Nashville.

Kalin, S. 2016, '*Islamic State rigs currency rates in Mosul to prop up finances*', Reuters, 23 February, viewed 10 May 2017, www.reuters.com/article/us-mideast-crisis-iraq-mosul/islamic-state-rigs-currency-rates-in-mosul-to-prop-up-finances-idUSKCN0VV1FO

Keating, J. 2016, 'The official currency of ISIS's Caliphate: The U.S. dollar', *Slate*, 16 February, viewed 10 May 2017, www.slate.com/blogs/the_slatest/2016/02/16/ISIS_will_only_accept_payment_in_u_s_dollars.html

Keohane, R. 1980, *The theory of hegemonic stability and changes in international economic regimes, 1967–1977*, Center for International and Strategic Affairs, University of California, Oakland.

Keohane, R. 2005, *After hegemony: Cooperation and discord in the world political economy*, Princeton University Press, New Jersey.

Keynes, J. 1936, *The general theory of employment, interest, and money*, Palgrave Macmillan, London.

Khalife, L. 2017, 'This Saudi man went on Snapchat to say he's given $16bn to charity', *Step Feed*, 18 April, viewed 10 May 2017, https://stepfeed.com/this-saudi-man-went-on-snapchat-to-say-he-s-given-usd16bn-to-charity-7691

Khan, A. and Masih, M. 2014, *Correlation between Islamic stock and commodity markets: An investigation into the impact of financial crisis and financialization of commodity markets*, 15th Malaysian Finance Association Conference, 3–5 June, Kualar Lumpur, viewed 10 January 2018, https://mpra.ub.uni-muenchen.de/56979/1/MPRA_paper_56979.pdf

Khan, M. 2013, *What is wrong with Islamic economics? Analysing the present state and future agenda*, Edward Elgar Publishing, Cheltenham.

Kilcullen, D. 2016, *Blood year: Islamic State and the failures of the war on terror*, Black Inc., Melbourne.

King, Jr, N. 2003, 'Bush officials devise a broad plan for free-market economy in Iraq', *Wall Street Journal*, 1 May, viewed 10 May 2017, www.wsj.com/articles/SB105174142750007600

Kingdom of Heaven 2005, motion picture, Scott Free Productions. Distributed by 20th Century Fox, and starring Orlando Bloom and Eva Green.

Kirkpatrick, D. 2006, 'For evangelicals, supporting Israel is "God's foreign policy"', *New York Times*, 14 November, viewed 10 May 2017, www.nytimes.com/2006/11/14/washington/14israel.html

Kirkpatrick, D. 2017, 'Saudi Arabia arrests 11 princes, including billionaire Alwaleed bin Talal', *New York Times*, 4 November, viewed 10 May 2017, www.nytimes.com/2017/11/04/world/middleeast/saudi-arabia-waleed-bin-talal.html

Klein, N. 2002, 'Between Mcworld and jihad', *Development*, vol. 45, no. 2, pp. 6–10.

Klein, N. 2007, *The shock doctrine: The rise of disaster capitalism*, Macmillan, London.

Klein, N. 2010, *Fences and windows: Dispatches from the front lines of the globalization debate*, Vintage Canada, Toronto.

Kleiner, J. 2006, 'Diplomacy with fundamentalists: The United States and the Taliban', *The Hague Journal of Diplomacy*, vol. 1, no. 3, pp. 209–234.

Koehler, D. 2016, 'Right-wing extremism and terrorism in Europe: current developments and issues for the future', *Prism: A Journal of the Center for Complex Operations*, vol. 6, no. 2, pp. 84–105.

KPMG Bahrain 2004, *Development fund for Iraq: Report of factual findings in connection with disbursements for the period from 1 January 2004 to 28 June 2004*, Baghdad: International Advisory and Monitoring Board of the Development Fund for Iraq and the Project and Contracting Office, KPMG, September 2004, viewed 10 May 2017, www.iamb.info/auditrep/disburse101204.pdf

Kramer, R. and Michalowski, R. 2005, 'War, aggression and state crime: A criminological analysis of the invasion and occupation of Iraq', *British Journal of Criminology*, vol. 45, no. 4, pp. 446–469.

Kramer, R. and Michalowski, R. 2011, 'Empire and exceptionalism: The bush administration's criminal war against Iraq', in M. Bassiouni, W. Chambliss, G. Barak, D. Bohlander, R. Haveman and K. Hoofnagle (eds), *State Crime: Current Perspectives*, Rutgers University Press, New Brunswick.

Krassó, N. and Mandel, E. 1968, *Trotsky's Marxism*, DB Young.

Kristol, I. 1972, 'An urban civilization without Cities', *Horizon*, vol. 14, no. 4, pp. 36–41.

Kristol, I. 1978, *Two cheers for capitalism*, Basic Books, New York.

Kristol, W. and Kagan, R. 1996, 'Toward a neo-Reaganite foreign policy', *Foreign Affairs*, vol. 75, p. 18.

Krugman, P. 1987, 'Is free trade passé?', *Journal of Economic Perspectives*, vol. 1, no. 2., pp. 131–144.

Krugman, P. 2009, *The conscience of a liberal*, WW Norton & Company, New York.

Kuronen, T. and Huhtinen, A. 2017, 'Organizing conflict: The rhizome of jihad', *Journal of Management Inquiry*, vol. 26, no. 1, pp. 47–61.

Kurtulus, E. 2012, 'The new counterterrorism: Contemporary counterterrorism trends in the United States and Israel', *Studies in Conflict & Terrorism*, vol. 35, no. 1, pp. 37–58.

Lacey, M. 2008, 'Across globe, empty bellies bring rising anger', *New York Times*, 18 April, viewed 10 May 2017, www.nytimes.com/2008/04/18/world/americas/18food.html

LaHaye, T. and Jenkins, J. 2011, *Left behind: A novel of the Earth's last days*, Tyndale House Publishers, Inc, Carol Stream.

Laqueur, W. 2000, *The new terrorism: Fanaticism and the arms of mass destruction*, Oxford University Press, Oxford.

Laqueur, W., Lewis, B. and Carter, A. 2002, *New terrorism*, WW Norton & Company, New York.

Larner, W. 2000, 'Neo-liberalism: Policy, ideology, governmentality', *Studies in Political Economy*, vol. 63, pp. 5–25.

Larner, W. 2008, 'Spatial imaginaries: Economic globalization and the war on terror', in L. Amoore and M. De Goede (eds), *Risk and the war on terror*, Routledge, London, pp. 41–56.

Latour, B. 2012, *We have never been modern*, Harvard University Press, Cambridge.

Lau, R. 2004, 'Habitus and the practical logic of practice: An interpretation', *Sociology*, vol. 38, no. 2, pp. 369–387.

Laub, Z. 2018, 'Yemen's spiraling crisis', Council on Foreign Relations, 31 October, viewed 29 December 2019, www.cfr.org/article/yemens-spiraling-crisis

Laub, Z. and Masters, J. 2014, *Islamic State in Iraq and greater Syria*, Council on Foreign Relations, vol. 12, viewed 10 June 2017, www.cfr.org/iraq/islamic- state/p14811.

Laursen, E. 2003, 'The Bush administration's neoliberal blueprint for the post-Saddam state', *In These Times*, 23 June, viewed 10 May 2017, http://inthese-times.com/article/325/privatizing_iraq

Lazzarato, M. 2009, 'Neoliberalism in action inequality, insecurity and the reconstitution of the social', *Theory, Culture & Society*, vol. 26, no. 6, pp. 109–133.

Le Billon, P. 2005, 'Corruption, reconstruction and oil governance in Iraq', *Third World Quarterly*, vol. 26, nos 4–5, pp. 685–703.

Le Billon, P. and El Khatib, F. 2004, 'From free oil to "freedom oil": Terrorism, war and US geopolitics in the Persian Gulf', *Geopolitics*, vol. 9, no. 1, pp. 109–137.

Lentini, P. 2008, 'The transference of neojihadism: Towards a process theory of transnational radicalisation', *Radicalisation Crossing Borders: New Directions in Islamist and Jihadist Political, Intellectual, and Theological Thought in Practice*, 2009, Global Terrorism Research Centre, Monash University, Melbourne, Refereed Proceedings from the GTReC International Conference.

Lentini, P. 2013, *Neojihadism: Towards a new understanding of terrorism and extremism?* Edward Elgar Publishing, Cheltenham.

Levi-Strauss, C. 1963, *Structural anthropology, Vol. 1*, Basic Books, New York.

Levin, C. and Coburn, T. 2013, *Wall Street and the financial crisis: Anatomy of a financial collapse*, United States Senate: Permanent Subcommittee on Investigations: Committee on Homeland Security and Governmental Affairs, 13 April, viewed 10 May 2017, www.hsgac.senate.gov//imo/media/doc/Financial_Crisis/FinancialCrisisReport.pdf?attempt=2

Levitt, M. 2002a, 'Untangling the terror web: Al-Qaeda is not the only element', The Washington Institute: Improving the Quality of U.S. Middle East Policy, 28 October, viewed 10 May 2017, www.washingtoninstitute.org/policy-analysis/view/untangling-the-terror-web-al-qaeda-is-not-the-only-element

Levitt, M. 2002b, 'Charitable and humanitarian organizations in the network of international terrorist financing', The Washington Institute for Near East Policy, 1 August, viewed 10 May 2017, www.washingtoninstitute.org/policy-analysis/view/charitable-and-humanitarian-organizations-in-the-network-of-international-t

Levitt, M. 2002c, 'The role of charities and NGOs in the financing of terrorist activities', *Hearing before the Subcommittee on International Trade and Finance of the Committee on Banking, Housing, and Urban Affairs, United States Senate*, viewed 10 May 2017, www.govinfo.gov/content/pkg/CHRG-107shrg89957/html/CHRG-107shrg89957.htm

Levitt, M. 2003, 'Stemming the flow of terrorist financing: Practical and conceptual challenges', *Fletcher Forum of World Affairs*, vol. 27, no. 1, pp. 59–71.

Levitt, M. 2014, 'Terrorist financing and the Islamic State', in *Testimony to the House Committee on Financial Services*, edited by The Washington Institute for Near East Policy.

Levitt, M. 2015, 'Here's how ISIS still has access to the global financial system', The Washington Institute for Near East Policy, *Business Insider*, 24 March, viewed 10 May 2017, www.businessinsider.com/heres-how-ISIS-keeps-up-its-access-to-the-global-financial-system-2015–3?IR=T

Levitt, M. and Jacobson, M. 2010, *Continuity and change: Reshaping the fight against terrorism*, The Washington Institute: Improving the Quality of U.S.

Middle East Policy, vol. 3, April, viewed 10 May 2016, www.washington institute.org/policy-analysis/view/continuity-and-change-reshaping-the-fight-against-terrorism

Lewis, B. 2003, *What went wrong? The clash between Islam and modernity in the Middle East*, Harper Collins, New York.

Lia, B. 2010, 'Al-Qaida's appeal: Understanding its unique selling points', *Perspectives on Terrorism*, vol. 2, no. 8.

Lindahl, S. 2017, 'A CTS model of counterterrorism', *Critical Studies on Terrorism*, vol. 10, no. 3, pp. 1–19.

Lister, C. 2014, *Profiling the Islamic State*, in Foreign Policy, edited by Brookings Doha Center, Brookings Institute, Doha.

Lister, C. 2015, *The Islamic State: A brief introduction*, Brookings Institution Press, Washington.

Lister, T., Sanches, R., Bixler, M., O'Key, S., Hogenmiller, M. and Tawfeeq, M. 2018, 'ISIS goes global: 143 attacks in 29 countries have killed 2,043', CNN, 12 February, viewed 29 December 2019, https://edition.cnn.com/2015/12/17/world/mapping-isis-attacks-around-the-world/index.html

Litwak, R. S. and Litwak, R. 2007, *Regime change: US strategy through the Prism of 9/11*, JHU Press.

Lloyd, J. 2001, *The protest ethic: How the anti-globalisation movement challenges social democracy*, Demos, New York.

Loadenthal, M. 2019, 'Introduction: Studying political violence while indicted–against objectivity and detachment', *Critical Studies on Terrorism*, vol. 12, no. 3, pp. 1–10.

Loewenstein, L. 2010, 'Al-Ittihad al-Islamiyya and Political Islam in Somalia', *Bologna Center Journal of International Affairs*, no. 13.

Looney, R. 2003, 'The neoliberal model's planned role in Iraq's economic transition', *The Middle East Journal*, vol. 57, no. 4, pp.568–586.

Lopez, L. 2012, 'Report shows how HSBC maintained its ties with one of Osama Bin Laden's key benefactors', *Business Insider*, 18 July, viewed 10 May 2017, www.businessinsider.com.au/hsbc-ties-to-al-rajhi-bank-2012–7?r=US&IR=T

Lovelace, D. 2016, *The evolution of the Islamic State*, Oxford University Press, Oxford.

Lovewine, G. 2014, *Outsourcing the global war on terrorism: Private military companies and American intervention in Iraq and Afghanistan*, Springer, New York.

Lubin, J. 2012, 'The occupy movement: Emerging protest forms and contested urban spaces', *Berkeley Planning Journal*, vol. 25, no. 1, pp. 184–197.

Lucarelli, S. and Fumagalli, A. 2008, 'Basic income and productivity in cognitive capitalism', *Review of Social Economy*, vol. 66, no. 1, pp. 71–92.

Lukes, S. 1969, 'Durkheim's "individualism and the intellectuals"', *Political Studies*, vol. 17, no. 1, pp. 14–30.

Lynch, T., Boyer, P., Nichols, C. and Milne, D. 2013, *The Oxford encyclopedia of American military and diplomatic history: 'Cold War (1945–1991): External course'*, Oxford University Press, Cambridge.

McAllister, I. 2003, 'Border protection, the 2001 Australian election and the coalition victory', *Australian Journal of Political Science*, vol. 38, no. 3, pp. 445–463.

McCants, W. 2008, 'Managing savagery in Saudi Arabia', *Jihadica: Documenting the Global Jihad*, 26 June, viewed 10 May 2017, www.jihadica.com/managing-savagery-in-saudi-arabia/

McCants, W. 2015, *The ISIS Apocalypse: The history, strategy, and doomsday vision of the Islamic State*, MacMillan, London.

McCoy, T. 2014, 'ISIS just stole $425 million, Iraqi governor says, and became the "world's richest terrorist group"', *Washington Post*, 12 June, viewed 10 May 2017, www.washingtonpost.com/news/morning-mix/wp/2014/06/12/ISIS-just-stole-425-million-and-became-the-worlds-richest-terrorist-group/?utm_term=.592f7caf95ad

McCulloch, J. and Wilson, D. 2016, *Pre-crime: Pre-emption, precaution and the future*, Routledge, London.

McCulloch, J. 2004, 'National (in) security politics in Australia: Fear and the federal election', *Alternative Law Journal*, vol. 29, no. 2, pp. 87–91.

MacEwan, A. 1999, *Neo-liberalism or democracy? Economic strategy, markets, and alternatives for the 21st century*, Zed Books, London.

McFate, S. 2017, *The modern mercenary: Private armies and what they mean for world order*, Oxford University Press, Oxford.

McGregor, A. 2006, 'Jihad and the rifle alone: Abdullah Azzam and the Islamist revolution', *Journal of Conflict Studies*, vol. 23, no. 2, January 10 2017, https://journals.lib.unb.ca/index.php/JCS/article/view/219/377

McKay, F., Thomas, S. and Warwick Blood, R. 2011, '"Any one of these boat people could be a terrorist for all we know!" Media representations and public perceptions of "boat people" arrivals in Australia', *Journalism*, vol. 12, no. 5, pp. 607–626.

McNair, B. 2009, *News and journalism in the UK*, Routledge, London.

Madi, O. 2014, 'From Islamic radicalism to Islamic capitalism: The promises and predicaments of Turkish-Islamic entrepreneurship in a capitalist system (the case of IGIAD)', *Middle Eastern Studies*, vol. 50, no. 1, pp. 144–161.

Magnus, R. and Naby, E. 2002, *Afghanistan: Mullah, Marx, and mujahid*, Westview Press, Boulder.

Mahood, S. and Rane, H. 2017, 'Islamist narratives in ISIS recruitment propaganda', *Journal of International Communication*, vol. 23, no. 1, pp. 15–35.

Maley, W. 1999, *The foreign policy of the Taliban*, Council on Foreign Relations, 15 February, viewed 10 May 2017, www.cfr.org/report/foreign-policy-taliban

Mankiw, N. G. 2014, *Principles of macroeconomics*, Cengage Learning, Melbourne.

Manne, R. 2016, *The mind of the Islamic State*, Black Inc., Victoria.

Maremont, M. and Stewart, C. 2017, 'FBI says ISIS used eBay to send terror cash to U.S.', *Wall Street Journal*, 10 August, viewed 10 May 2017, www.wsj.com/articles/fbi-says-ISIS-used-ebay-to-send-terror-cash-to-u-s-1502410868

Martin, G. 2015, 'Stop the boats! Moral panic in Australia over asylum seekers', *Continuum*, vol. 29, no. 3, pp. 304–322.

Martinez, E. and Garcia, A. 1998, 'What is "neo-liberalism"?', *Third World Resurgence*, pp. 7–8, viewed 10 May 2017, http://occupydaytona.org/images/pdf/what_is_neo-liberalism.pdf

Marx, K. 1992, *Capital: Volumes I–III*, trans. D. Fernbach, Penguin/*New Left Review*, Harmondsworth.

Masi, A. 2015, 'Turkey, Russia, Iraq and Syria: The black market oil trade that's fueling ISIS and dividing the terrorist group's opponents', *International Business Times*, 12 September, viewed 10 May 2017, www.ibtimes.com/turkey-russia-iraq-syria-black-market-oil-trade-thats-fueling-ISIS-dividing-terrorist-2217476

Mason, P. 2012, *Why it's still kicking off everywhere: The new global revolutions*, Verso Books, New York.

Massumi, B. 1993, *The politics of everyday fear*, University of Minnesota Press, Minneapolis.

Maton, K. 2003, 'Reflexivity, relationism, and research: Pierre Bourdieu and the epistemic conditions of social scientific knowledge', *Space and Culture*, vol. 6, no. 1, pp. 52–65.

Mearsheimer, J. and Walt, S. 2003, 'An unnecessary war', *Foreign Policy*, no. 134, pp. 50–59.

Mearsheimer, J. and Walt, S. 2007, *The Israel lobby and US foreign policy*, Macmillan, London.

Miles, H. 2010, *Al Jazeera: How Arab TV news challenged the world*, Hachette, London.

Miller, J. and Gerth, J. 2001, 'A nation challenged: Al Qaeda; honey trade said to provide funds and cover to Bin Laden', *New York Times*, 11 October, viewed 10 May 2017, www.nytimes.com/2001/10/11/world/nation-challenged-al-qaeda-honey-trade-said-provide-funds-cover-bin-laden.html

Mirowski, P. 2013, *Never let a serious crisis go to waste: How neoliberalism survived the financial meltdown*, Verso Books, London.

Mishal, S. and Rosenthal, M. 2005, 'Al Qaeda as a dune organization: Toward a typology of Islamic terrorist organizations', *Studies in Conflict & Terrorism*, vol. 28, no. 4, pp. 275–293.

Mitchell, W. 2011, *Cloning terror: The war of images, 9/11 to the present*, University of Chicago Press, Chicago.

Moghadam, A. 2008, 'The Salafi-Jihad as a religious ideology', *CTC Sentinel*, vol. 1, no. 3, pp. 14–16.

Monaci, S. 2017, 'Explaining the Islamic State's online media strategy: A transmedia approach', *International Journal of Communication*, vol. 11, pp. 2842–2860.

Moneyval 2008, *Money laundering and counterfeiting, Typology research*, Committee of experts of anti-money laundering measures and the financing of terrorism, Strasbourg, pp. 21–25.

Montgomerie, J. and Williams, K. 2009, 'Financialised capitalism: After the crisis and beyond neoliberalism', *Competition & Change*, vol. 13, no. 2, pp. 99–107.

Moran, M. 1998, 'Bin Laden comes home to roost', *NBCNews.com*, 24 August, viewed 10 May 2017, www.nbcnews.com/id/3340101/t/bin-laden-comes-home-roost/#.WlbncU3VeUk

Moten, A. 2003, 'Maududi and the transformation of Jamaat-E-Islami in Pakistan', *The Muslim World*, vol. 93, no. 3/4, p. 391–413.

Mozaffari, M. 2007, 'What is Islamism? History and definition of a concept', *Totalitarian Movements and Political Religions*, vol. 8, no. 1, pp. 17–33.

Murray, W. 2002, 'The neoliberal inheritance: Agrarian policy and rural differentiation in democratic Chile', *Bulletin of Latin American Research*, vol. 21, no. 3, pp. 425–441.

Myre, G. 2016, 'Osama Bin Laden's will: $29 million that should be spent on "jihad"', NPR, 1 March, viewed 29 December 2019, www.npr.org/sections/parallels/2016/03/01/468692846/osama-bin-ladens-will-29-million-that-should-be-spent-on-jihad

Mythen, G. and Walklate, S. 2006, 'Criminology and terrorism: Which thesis? Risk society or governmentality?', *British Journal of Criminology*, vol. 46, no. 3, pp. 379–398.

Mythen, G. and Walklate, S. 2008, 'Terrorism, risk and international security: The perils of asking "what if?"', *Security Dialogue*, vol. 39, no. 2–3, pp. 221–242.

Mythen, G. and Walklate, S. 2016, 'Counterterrorism and the reconstruction of (in)security: Divisions, dualisms, duplicities', *British Journal of Criminology*, vol. 56, no. 6, pp. 1107–1124.

Mythen, G., Walklate, S. and Khan, F. 2009, '"I'm a Muslim, but I'm not a terrorist": Victimization, risky identities and the performance of safety', *British Journal of Criminology*, vol. 49, no. 6, pp. 736–754.

Mythen, G., Walklate, S. and Khan, F. 2013, '"Why should we have to prove we're alright?": Counter-terrorism, risk and partial securities', *Sociology*, vol. 47, no. 2, pp. 383–398.

Nacos, B. 2003, 'The terrorist calculus behind 9–11: A model for future terrorism?', *Studies in Conflict and Terrorism*, vol. 26, no. 1, pp. 1–16.

Naji, A. 2006, *The management of savagery*, trans. W. McCants, John M. Olin Institute for Strategic Studies at Harvard University, viewed 10 January 2017, https://azelin.files.wordpress.com/2010/08/abu-bakr-naji-the-management-of-savagery-the-most-critical-stage-through-which-the-umma- will-pass.pdf

Napoleoni, L. 2004, *Terror incorporated: Tracing the dollars behind the terror networks*, Seven Stories Press, New York.

Napoleoni, L. 2015, *ISIS: The terror nation*, Seven Stories Press, New York.

Navarro, V. 2007, *Neoliberalism, globalization, and inequalities: Consequences for health and quality of life*, Baywood Publishing Company Inc., Amityville.

Nichols, M. and Irish J. 2015, *U.N. Security Council puts sanctions focus on Islamic State*, Reuters, 18 December, viewed 10 May 2017, www.reuters.com/article/us-mideast-crisis-islamic-state-un/u-n-security-council-puts-sanctions-focus-on-islamic-state-idUSKBN0U030P20151217

Nova, S. 2012, 'Apparel industry outsourcing costs garment workers' lives in Bangladesh', *Guardian*, 14 December, viewed 10 May 2017, www.theguardian.com/commentisfree/2012/dec/13/apparel-industry-outsourcing-garment-workers-bangladesh

O'Brien, R. and Williams, M. 2016, *Global political economy: Evolution and dynamics*, Palgrave Macmillan, London.

Olidort, J. and Sheff, M. 2016, 'Teaching terror: The Islamic State's textbooks, guidance literature, and indoctrination methods', The Washington Institute, 15 July, viewed 10 May 2017, www.washingtoninstitute.org/policy-analysis/view/teaching-terror-the-islamic-states-textbooks-guidance-literature-and-indoct

Ong, A. 2006, *Neoliberalism as exception: Mutations in citizenship and sovereignty*, Duke University Press, Durham.

Opsal, R. 2015, 'Here's why the US is reluctant to bomb ISIS oil fields', *Business Insider*, 3 December, viewed 10 May 2017, www.businessinsider.com/why-us-reluctant-to-bomb-ISIS-oil-fields-2015–12?IR=T

Osborn, A. 2015, *Islamic State looting Syrian, Iraqi sites on industrial scale – UNESCO*, Reuters, 3 July, viewed 10 May 2016, https://uk.reuters.com/article/uk-mideast-crisis-unesco/islamic-state-looting-syrian-iraqi-sites-on-industrial-scale-unesco-idUKKCN0PC1OS20150702

Ostry, J., Loungani, P. and Furceri, D. 2016, 'Neoliberalism: Oversold?', *Finance & Development*, vol. 53, no. 2, pp. 38–41, viewed 10 May 2017, www.imf.org/external/pubs/ft/fandd/2016/06/pdf/ostry.pdf

Otterman, S. 2005, *Iraq: Oil for food scandal*, Council on Foreign Relations, 28 October, viewed 10 May 2017, www.cfr.org/backgrounder/iraq-oil-food-scandal

Oxfam 2017, *Just 8 men own same wealth as half the world*, Oxfam International: The Power of People against Poverty, 16 January, viewed 10 May 2017, www.oxfam.org/en/pressroom/pressreleases/2017–01–16/just-8-men-own-same-wealth-half-world

Pagliery, J. 2016, 'ISIS cuts its fighters' salaries by 50%', CNN: *Business*, 19 January, viewed 10 May 2017, http://money.cnn.com/2016/01/19/news/world/ISIS-salary-cuts/index.html

Palley, T. 2005, 'From Keynesianism to neoliberalism: Shifting paradigms in economics', in A. Saad-Filho and D. Johnston (eds), *Neoliberalism: A critical reader*, pp. 20–29, viewed 10 May 2017, https://pdfs.semanticscholar.org/d013/0f246cbbc55db6f990089a729a00bd27c881.pdf

Panitch, L. and Konings, M. 2009, 'Myths of neoliberal deregulation', *New Left Review*, vol. 57, no. 1, pp. 67–83.

Passas, N. 2006, 'Fighting terror with error: The counter-productive regulation of informal value transfers', *Crime, Law and Social Change*, vol. 45, no. 4, pp. 315–336.

Peck, J. 2008, 'Remaking laissez-faire', *Progress in Human Geography*, vol. 32, no. 1, pp. 3–43.

Peck, J. 2010, *Constructions of neoliberal reason*, Oxford University Press, Oxford.

Percy, S. 2013, *Regulating the private security industry*, Routledge, London.

Perez, M. and Cannella, G. 2011, 'Disaster capitalism as neoliberal instrument for the construction of early childhood education/care policy: Charter schools in post-Katrina New Orleans', *International Critical Childhood Policy Studies Journal*, vol. 4, no. 1, pp. 47–68.

Permanent Subcommittee on Investigations 2012, *U.S. vulnerabilities to money laundering, drugs, and terrorist financing: HSBC case history*, United States Senate, released in conjunction with the permanent subcommittee on investigations July 17, 2012 hearing.

Peters, G. 2009, *Seeds of terror: How heroin is bankrolling the Taliban and al Qaeda*, Macmillan, London.

Phillips, D. 2014, 'Research Paper: ISIS-Turkey Links', Institute for the Study of Human Rights, Columbia University, in *HuffPost*, 8 September 2016, viewed 10 May 2017, www.huffingtonpost.com/david-l-phillips/research-paper-isis-turke_b_6128950.html

Pieterse, J. 2015, *Globalization and culture: Global mélange*, Rowman & Littlefield, Lanham.

Piketty, T. 2014, *Capital in the 21st century*, trans. Arthur Goldhammer, The President and Fellows of Harvard College.

Pilger, J. 2015, 'John Pilger: New threats of war and fascism', *Green Left Weekly*, 13 March, viewed 10 May 2017, www.greenleft.org.au/content/john-pilger-new-threats-war-and-fascism

Pisoiu, D. 2015, 'Subcultural theory applied to jihadi and right-wing radicalization in Germany', *Terrorism and Political Violence*, vol. 27, no. 1, pp. 9–28.

Posner, G. 2009, *Why America slept: The reasons behind our failure to prevent 9/11*, Ballantine Books, New York.

Post, J. 2015, 'Terrorism and right-wing extremism: The changing face of terrorism and political violence in the 21st century: The virtual community of hatred', *International journal of group psychotherapy*, vol. 65, no. 2, pp. 242–271.

Poynting, S. 2015, 'Islamophobia and crime–anti-Muslim demonising and racialised targeting: Guest editor's introduction', *International Journal for Crime, Justice and Social Democracy*, vol. 4, no. 3, pp. 1–3.

Poynting, S. and Whyte, D. (eds) 2012, *Counter-terrorism and state political violence: The 'war on terror' as terror*, Routledge, London.

Poynting, S. and Whyte, D. 2017, 'Special edition: Corruption downunder: Guest editors' introduction', *International Journal for Crime, Justice and Social Democracy*, vol. 6, no. 4.

Prados, A. 1999, 'Qatar: Background and U.S. Relations', *EveryCRSReport. com*, 6 October, viewed 29 December 2019, www.everycrsreport.com/reports/RS20354.html

Pupcenoks, J. and McCabe, R. 2013, 'The rise of the fringe: Right wing populists, Islamists and politics in the UK', *Journal of Muslim Minority Affairs*, vol. 33, no. 2, pp. 171–184.

Purkiss, J. and Serle, J. 2017, 'Obama's covert drone war in numbers: ten times more strikes than Bush', *The Bureau of Investigative Journalism*, 17 January, viewed 29 December 2019, www.thebureauinvestigates.com/stories/2017-01-17/obamas-covert-drone-war-in-numbers-ten-times-more-strikes-than-bush

Pyszczynski, T., Rothschild, Z. and Abdollahi, A. 2008, 'Terrorism, violence, and hope for peace a terror management perspective', *Current Directions in Psychological Science*, vol. 17, no. 5, pp. 318–322.

Qut'b, S. 1962, *Islam and the problems of civilisation*, trans. J. Calvert and V. Shepard (eds), Syracuse University Press, New York.

Qut'b, S. 1981, *Milestones*, trans. S Hasan, International Islamic Publishers, Karachi.

Qut'b, S. 2003, *A child from the village*, trans. J. Calvert and W. Shepard (eds), Syracuse University Press, New York.

Radio Farda 2019, 'Iranian, U.S. leaders vie for the sympathy of the people on New Year', Radio Farda, 21 March, viewed 29 December 2019, https://en.radiofarda.com/a/iranian-u-s-leaders-vie-for-the-sympathy-of-the-people-on-new-year/29833942.html

Rais, R. 1992, 'Afghanistan and regional security after the Cold War', *Problems of Communism*, vol. 41, no. 3, pp. 82–95.

Rao, S. 2019, 'ISIS' "Virtual" Caliphate may be its most bloody yet', *Haaretz*, 24 April, viewed 29 December 2019, www.haaretz.com/world-news/.premium-isis-just-blew-up-trump-s-victory-over-them-1.7163073

Raqqa Is Being Slaughtered Silently 2017, *Iraq says ISIS transferring phosphate to Syria's Raqqa*, Raqqa Is Being Slaughtered Silently, viewed 10 May 2017, www.raqqa-sl.com/en/?p=206

Rayner, G. 2015, '*Charlie Hebdo*: Bloody end to French campaign of terror', *Independent.ie*, 15 January, viewed 10 May 2017, www.independent.ie/world-news/europe/charlie-hebdo-attacks/charlie-hebdo-bloody-end-to-french-campaign-of-terror-30896815.html

Razavy, M. 2005, 'Hawala: An underground haven for terrorists or social phenomenon?', *Crime, Law and Social Change*, vol. 44, no. 3, pp. 277–299.

Reed, A. and Ingram, H. 2016, *Exploring the role of instructional material in AQAP's Inspire and ISIS' Rumiyah*, ICCT, The Hague.

Rehbein, B. 2011, *Bourdieu und die Globalisierung*, in D. Šuber, H. Schäfer and S. Prinz (eds), *Pierre Bourdieu und die Kulturwissenschaften. Zur Aktualität eines undisziplinierten Denkens*, UVK, Konstanz, pp. 303–316.

Reid, J. 2004, 'Architecture, Al-Qaeda, and the World Trade Center: Rethinking relations between war, modernity, and city spaces after 9/11', *Space and Culture*, vol. 7, no. 4, pp. 396–408.

Reitan, E. A. 2003, *The Thatcher revolution: Margaret Thatcher, John Major, Tony Blair, and the transformation of modern Britain, 1979–2001*. Rowman & Littlefield, Lanham.

Reuten, G. 2000, 'The interconnection of systematic dialectics and historical materialism', *Historical Materialism*, vol. 7, no. 1, pp. 137–165.

Reuters 2003, *Bremer touts privatization in Iraq*, Reuters News Service, 9 July.

Reuters 2012, 'UPDATE 1-New Syria sanctions have wide backing in the EU – diplomat', viewed 29 December 2019, www.reuters.com/article/syria-eu-idUSL5E8D88SD20120208

Richards, I. 2016a, '"Flexible" capital accumulation in Islamic State social media', *Critical Studies on Terrorism*, vol. 9, no. 2, pp. 205–225.

Richards, I. 2016b, '"The spirit of terrorism" in Islamic State media', *International Journal of Baudrillard Studies*, vol. 13, no. 2, viewed 29 December 2019, www2.ubishops.ca/baudrillardstudies/vol-13_2/v13-2-richards.html

Richards, I. 2017, '"Good and Evil" narratives in Islamic State media and Western government statements', *Critical Studies on Terrorism*, vol. 10, no. 3, pp. 404–428, viewed 10 May 2017, www.tandfonline.com/doi/full/10.1080/175 39153.2017.1311495?scroll=top&needAccess=true

Richards, I. 2019a, 'A dialectical approach to online propaganda: Australia's United Patriots Front, right-wing politics, and Islamic State', *Studies in Conflict & Terrorism*, vol. 42, no. 1–2, pp. 43–69.

Richards, I. 2019b, 'A philosophical and historical analysis of 'Generation Identity': fascism, online media and the European new right', *Terrorism and Political Violence*, https://doi.org/10.1080/09546553.2019.1662403

Richman, S. 1991, *"Ancient history": US conduct in the Middle East since World War II and the folly of intervention*, CATO Institute, Washington.

Richter, A., Svetlana, T., Khafaji, I. and McCarthy J. 2004, *Disorder, negligence and mismanagement: How the CPA handled Iraq reconstruction funds*, Open Society Institute: Middle East and North Africa Initiatives: Central Eurasia Project, Revenue Watch, Report No. 7, September 2004, viewed 10 May 2017, www.mafhoum.com/press7/210E17.pdf

Rinat, Z. 2013, 'Food for thought: How rich countries exploit the resources of poorer ones – and get away with it', *Haaretz*, 12 September, viewed 10 May 2017, www.haaretz.com/world-news/1.546450

Ritzer, G. 1992, *The McDonaldization of society*, Pine Forge Press, California.

Rodrik, D. 2000, 'Institutions for high-quality growth: What they are and how to acquire them', *Studies in Comparative International Development*, vol. 35, no. 3, pp. 3–31.

Rodrik, D. 2011, *The globalization paradox: Democracy and the future of the world economy*, W. W. Norton, New York.

Ronfeldt, D. 2005, 'Al Qaeda and its affiliates: A global tribe waging segmental warfare?', *First Monday*, vol. 10, no. 3, 7 March, viewed 10 May 2017, http://firstmonday.org/ojs/index.php/fm/article/view/1214/1134

Rosenau, W., Powell, A. and Faber, P. 2017, *Al-Qaeda core: A case study*, Center for Naval Analyses, Arlington.

Rosenberg, M. 2004, 'Al Qaeda skimming charity money', *CBS News*, 7 June, viewed 10 May 2017, www.cbsnews.com/news/al-qaeda-skimming-charity- money/

Roth, J., Greenburg, D., Wille, S. and Falk, A. 2004, *Monograph on terrorist financing: Staff report to the commission*, National Commission on Terrorist Attacks upon the United States, viewed 10 May 2017, www.9–11commission.gov/

Rothbauer, P. 2008, 'Triangulation', in L. Given (ed.), *The SAGE encyclopaedia of qualitative research methods: Vol. 1*, Sage, London, pp. 892–894.

Rowthorn, B. 1980, *Capitalism, conflict and inflation*, Lawrence & Wishart, London.

Roy, O. 1994, *The failure of political Islam*, Harvard University Press, Cambridge.

RT Producers 2017, 'Mo Ansar and Martin Sellner debates on RT International', YouTube, 14 July, www.youtube.com/watch?v=4nG5WEE7m4s

Rubin, M. 2017, 'Is Turkey supporting ISIS?', *Commentary*, 4 May, viewed 10 May 2017, www.commentarymagazine.com/michael-rubin/turkey-active-isis-support/

Ruggie, J. 1982, 'International regimes, transactions, and change: Embedded liberalism in the postwar economic order', *International Organization*, vol. 36, no. 2, pp. 379–415.

Ruiz, J. 2009, 'Sociological discourse analysis: Methods and logic', *Forum: Qualitative Social Research*, vol. 10, no. 2.

Rumaysah, A. 2015, *A brief guide to the Islamic State*, viewed 1 May 2016, http://valasz.hu/data/cikk/11/2761/cikk_112761/A_Brief_Guide_to_Islamic_State_2015.pdf

Ruppert, M. 2004, *Crossing the rubicon: The decline of the American empire at the end of the age of oil*. New Society Publishers, Gabriola Island.

Ryle, G., Fitzgibbon, W., Cabra, M., Carvajal, R., Guevara, M., Hamilton, M. and Stites, T. 2015, 'Banking Giant HSBC Sheltered Murky Cash Linked to Dictators and Arms Dealers', *International Consortium of Investigative Journalists*, 8 February, viewed 10 May 2017, www.icij.org/investigations/swiss-leaks/banking-giant-hsbc-sheltered-murky-cash-linked-dictators-and-arms-dealers/

Safadi, M. 2015, 'Don't rely on Syria's "moderate" fighting force. It doesn't exist', *Guardian*, 17 December, viewed 10 May 2017, www.theguardian.com/commentisfree/2015/dec/16/dont-rely-syria-moderate-fighting-force-anti-ISIS

Sageman, M. 2011, *Leaderless jihad: Terror networks in the twenty-first century*, University of Pennsylvania Press, Pennsylvania.

Sanderson, T. 2004, 'Transnational terror and organized crime: Blurring the lines', *SAIS Review of International Affairs*, vol. 24, no. 1, pp. 49–61.

Sarban, K. 2016, 'Islamic State Khorasan Province: Pakistan's new foreign policy tool?', *The Diplomat*, 15 November, viewed 10 May 2017, thediplomat.com/2016/11/islamic-state-khorasan-province-pakistans-new-foreign-policy-tool/

Sassoon, D. 1997, *Looking left: European socialism after the Cold War*, IB Tauris, London.

Saviano, R. 2017, 'Drug traffickers taught the rich how to hide money in tax havens', *Guardian*, 18 November, viewed 10 January 2018, www. theguardian.com/commentisfree/2017/nov/18/paradise-papers-tax-havens-mafia-roberto-saviano

SBS 2015, 'CIA files prove America helped Saddam as he gassed Iran', 26 February, viewed 10 May 2017, www.sbs.com.au/news/cia-files-prove-america-helped-saddam-as-he-gassed-iran

Scahill, J. 2008, *Blackwater: The rise of the world's most powerful mercenary army*, Hachette, London.

Schanzer, J. and Tahiroglu, M. 2014, *Bordering on terrorism: Turkey's Syria policy and the rise of the Islamic State*, Foundation for Defense of

Democracies: Center on Sanctions & Illicit Finance, November, viewed 10 May 2017, www.defenddemocracy.org/content/uploads/publications/border-ing-on- terrorism.pdf

Scherer, G. 2004, 'Christian-right views are swaying politicians and threatening the environment', *Grist*, 28 October, viewed 10 May 2017, http://grist.org/article/scherer-christian/

Scheuer, M. 2002, *Through our enemies' eyes: Osama Bin Laden, radical Islam, and the future of America*, Potomac Books, Lincoln.

Schmidt, S., Shelley, M. and Bardes, B. 2006, *American government and politics today: 2007–2008*, Cengage Learning, Victoria.

Schumpeter, J. 2010, *Capitalism, socialism and democracy*, Routledge, London.

Schutz, A. 1967, The phenomenology of the social world, Northwestern University Press, Evanston.

Schweitzer, Y. and Oreg, A. 2014, *Al-Qaeda's odyssey to the global jihad*, Institute for National Security Studies (INSS), Tel Aviv.

Scott, J. 2014, *A matter of record: Documentary sources in social research*, John Wiley & Sons, New York.

Seib, P. 2008, 'The Al-Qaeda media machine', *Military Review*, vol. 88, no. 3, pp. 74–80.

Sentas, V. 2018, 'Terrorist organization proscription as counterinsurgency in the Kurdish conflict', *Terrorism and Political Violence*, vol. 30, no. 2, pp. 298–317.

Seymour, G. 1975, *Harry's game*, Collins, London.

Shaffer, R. 2016, 'Jihad and counter-jihad in Europe: Islamic radicals, right-wing extremists, and counter-terrorism responses', *Terrorism and Political Violence*, vol. 28, no. 2, pp. 383–394.

Shahid, E. 2016, 'Agriculture as the new oil for ISIS', *Al-Arabiya: English*, 16 September, viewed 10 May 2017, http://english.alarabiya.net/en/views/news/middle-east/2016/09/16/DNP-Agriculture-as-the-new-oil-for-ISIS.html

Sharp, J. 2010, *US foreign aid to Israel*, Diane Publishing, Collingdale.

Sheppard, E. and Leitner, H. 2010, 'Quo vadis neoliberalism? The remaking of global capitalist governance after the Washington Consensus', *Geoforum*, vol. 41, no. 2, pp. 185–194.

Sherlock, R. 2015, 'ISIS seizes Syrian regime's lucrative phosphate mines', *Telegraph*, 27 May, viewed 10 May 2017, www.telegraph.co.uk/news/world news/middleeast/syria/11633289/Isil-seizes-Syrian-regimes-lucrative-phosphate- mines.html

Shiloach, G. 2015, 'ISIS touts giant mines as new million-dollar funding source', *Vocativ*, 26 May, viewed 10 May 2017, www.vocativ.com/news/195776/ISIS-shows-off-a-new-potential-source-of-funding/index.html

Silverstein, K. 2001, 'Stingers, stingers, who's got the stingers?', *Slate*, 3 October, viewed 10 May 2017, www.slate.com/articles/news_and_politics/the_gist/2001/10/stingers_stingers_whos_got_the_stingers.html

Simonen, K. 2015, 'Economic sanctions leading to human rights violations: Constructing legal argument', in A Marossi and M. Bassett (eds), *Economic sanctions under international law*, TMC Asser Press, The Hague, pp. 179–195.

Simpson, C. 2014, 'The banality of Islamic State', *Bloomberg Business*, 20 November, viewed 10 May 2017, www.bloomberg.com/graphics/2014-the-business-of-ISIS-spreadsheets-annual-reports-and-terror/#/

Simpson, C. and Philips, M. 2015, 'Why U.S. efforts to cut off Islamic State's funds have failed', *Bloomberg Business*, 19 November, viewed 10 May 2017, www.bloomberg.com/news/articles/2015-11-19/why-u-s-efforts-to-cut-off-islamic-state-s-funds-have-failed

Singer, P. 2007, *Corporate warriors: The rise of the privatized military industry*, Cornell University Press, New York.

Slaughter, A. 1997, 'The real new world order', *Foreign Affairs*, vol. 76, pp. 183–197.

Smart, B. 2016, 'Military-industrial complexities, university research and neo-liberal economy', *Journal of Sociology*, vol. 52, no. 3, pp. 455–481.

Smith, A. 1776, *An inquiry into the wealth of naytions*, Strahan and Cadell, London.

Soergel, A. 2015, 'Financing terror', *US News*, viewed 10 May 2017 www.usnews.com/news/the-report/articles/2015/11/23/financing-terror-where-does-the-islamic-state-group-get-its-money

Solomon, E. 2017, 'ISIS finds escape route for the profits of war', *Financial Times*, 23 August, viewed 10 May 2017, http://ig.ft.com/sites/2015/isis-oil/

Solomon, E. and Jones, S. 2015, 'ISIS inc.: Loot and taxes keep jihadi economy churning', *Financial Times*, 15 December, viewed 10 May 2017, www.ft.com/content/aee89a00–9ff1–11e5-beba-5e33e2b79e46

Solomon, E., Kwong, R. and Bernard, S. 2016, 'Inside ISIS inc: The journey of a barrel of oil', *Financial Times*, 16 November, viewed 10 May 2017, https://ig.ft.com/sites/2015/ISIS-oil/

Springer, S. 2015, 'The violence of neoliberalism', in S. Spinger, K. Birch and J. MacLeavy, *The Handbook of Neoliberalism*, Routledge, London, pp. 152–163.

Spronk, S. and Webber, J. 2007, 'Struggles against accumulation by disposses-sion in Bolivia: The political economy of natural resource contention', *Latin American Perspectives*, vol. 34, no. 2, pp. 31–47.

Squires, A. 2009, 'Methodological challenges in cross-language qualitative research: A research review', *International Journal of Nursing Studies*, vol. 46, no. 2, pp. 277–287.

Stampnitzky, L. 2013, *Disciplining terror: How experts invented 'terrorism'*, Cambridge University Press, Cambridge.

Stanger, A. 2014, *One nation under contract: The outsourcing of American power and the future of foreign policy*, Yale University Press, New Haven.

Steger, M. and Roy, R. 2010, *Neoliberalism: A very short introduction*, Oxford University Press, Oxford.

Stenersen, A. 2008, 'The internet: A virtual training camp?', *Terrorism and Polit-ical Violence*, vol. 20, no. 2, pp. 215–233.

Stern, J. and Berger, J. 2015, *ISIS: The state of terror*, William Collins, London.

Stiglitz, J. May 2011, 'Of the 1%, by the 1%, for the 1%', *Vanity Fair*, viewed 10 May 2017, www.vanityfair.com/news/2011/05/top-one-percent-201105

Stohl, M. 1984, *The state as terrorist: The dynamics of governmental violence and repression*, Praeger Pub Text, Santa Barbara.

Stringer, R. 2014, *Knowing victims: Feminism, agency and victim politics in neoliberal times*, Routledge, London.

Strombeck, A. 2006, 'Invest in Jesus: Neoliberalism and the *Left behind* novels', *Cultural Critique*, vol. 64, no. 1, pp. 161–195.

Swanson, A. 2015, 'How the Islamic State makes its money', *Washington Post*, 18 November, viewed 10 May 2017, www.washingtonpost.com/news/wonk/wp/2015/11/18/how-ISIS-makes-its-money/?utm_term=.f184decbadff

Swartz D. 1997, *Culture and power: The sociology of Pierre Bourdieu*, University of Chicago Press, Chicago.

Swartz, D. 2002, 'The sociology of habit: The perspective of Pierre Bourdieu', *OTJR: Occupation, Participation and Health*, vol. 22, pp. 614–695.

Swartz, D. 2008, 'Bringing Bourdieu's master concepts into organizational analysis', *Theory and Society*, vol. 37, no. 1, pp. 45–52.

Swartz, D. 2013, *Symbolic power, politics, and intellectuals: The political sociology of Pierre Bourdieu*, University of Chicago Press, Chicago.

Tait, R. 2014, 'ISIS' half-a-billion-dollar bank heist makes it world's richest terror group', *Telegraph*, 14 June, viewed 10 May 2017, www.telegraph.co.uk/news/worldnews/middleeast/iraq/10899995/ISIS-half-a-billion-dollar-bank-heist-makes-it-worlds-richest-terror-group.html

Tarrow, S. 2002, 'From lumping to splitting: Specifying globalization and resistance', in J. Ayers, B. Caniglia, S. Chabot, M. Giugni and M. Hanagan (eds), *Globalization and resistance: Transnational dimensions of social movements*, Rowman & Littefield, Lanham, pp. 229–249.

Tawfik, N. 2017, 'Jerusalem UN vote: Trump threatens US aid recipients', *BBC News*, 20 December, viewed 10 January 2018, www.bbc.com/news/world-middle-east-42431095

Taylor, C. 2019, 'Al Qaida is stronger today than it was on 9/11', *The Conversation*, 4 July, viewed 29 December 2019, https://theconversation.com/al-qaida-is-stronger-today-than-it-was-on-9–11–117718

Temple, B. 2002, 'Crossed wires: Interpreters, translators, and bilingual workers in cross-language research', *Qualitative Health Research*, vol. 12, no. 6, pp. 844–854.

Temple, B. and Young, A. 2004, 'Qualitative research and translation dilemmas', *Qualitative Research*, vol. 4, no. 2, pp. 161–178.

Thompson, P. 2004. *The terror timeline: Year by year, day by day, minute by minute: A comprehensive chronicle of the road to 9/11 – and America's Response* (no. 13). Harper Collins, New York.

Thorsen, D. and Lie, A. 2006, *What is neoliberalism?*, manuscript, University of Oslo, Department of Political Science, Oslo.

Tiefer, C. 2007, 'The Iraq debacle: The rise and fall of procurement-aided unilateralism as a paradigm of foreign war', *University of Pennsylvania Journal of International Law.*, vol. 29, no. 1, pp. 1–59.

Tokmajan, A. and The Aleppo Project 2016, *The war economy in Northern Syria*, The Aleppo Project, 4 December, viewed 10 May 2017, www.thealeppoproject.com/papers/war-economy-northern-syria/

Tombs, S. 2016, 'What to do with the harmful corporation?', *The Open University*, no. 1, pp. 193–216, viewed 1 January 2018, http://oro.open.ac.uk/47698/

Tomolya, J. and White, L. 2015, 'The rise of Al-Qaida in North Africa: AQIM and its role in the region', in J. Tomolya and L. White (eds), *Terrorist threats in North Africa from a NATO perspective, Vol. 124*, pp. 18–33.

Torbati, Y. and Wolf, B. 2015, *In taking economic war to Islamic State, U.S. developing new tools*, Reuters, 24 November, viewed 10 May 2017, www.reuters.com/article/us-france-shooting-usa-sanctions-insight/in-taking-economic-war-to-islamic-state-u-s-developing-new-tools-idUSKBN0TD0BJ20151124

Tormey, S. 2013, *Anti-capitalism: A beginner's guide*, OneWorld Publications, England.

TRAC 2015, 'Terrorism Research & Analysis Consortium', *TRAC*, viewed 29 December 2019, www.trackingterrorism.org

Tremayne, M. 2013, 'Anatomy of protest in the digital era: A network analysis of Twitter and occupy Wall Street', *Social Movement Studies: Journal of Social, Cultural and Political Protest*, viewed 10 May 2017, http://dx.doi.org/10/1090/14742837.2013.830969

Tripp, C. 2006, *Islam and the moral economy: The challenge of capitalism*, Cambridge University Press, Cambridge.

Tsvetkova, M. and Kelly, L. 2015, *Russia says it has proof Turkey involved in Islamic State oil trade*, Reuters, viewed 10 May 2017, www.reuters.com/article/us-mideast-crisis-russia-turkey/russia-says-it-has-proof-turkey-involved-in-islamic-state-oil-trade-idUSKBN0TL19S20151202

Turley, J. 2014, 'Big money behind war: The military-industrial complex', Al Jazeera, 11 January, viewed 10 May 2017, www.aljazeera.com/indepth/opinion/2014/01/big-money-behind-war-military-industrial-complex-20141473026736533.html

Tyler, P. 1992, 'U.S. strategy plan calls for insuring no rivals develop a one-superpower world', *New York Times*, 8 March, viewed 10 May 2017, www.nytimes.com/1992/03/08/world/us-strategy-plan-calls-for-insuring-no-rivals-develop.html?pagewanted=all

UK House of Commons 2006, *Report of the official account of the bombings in London on 7th July 2005*, House of Parliament: The Stationery Office, Great Britain.

UN 2006, *Fourth report of the analytical support and sanctions monitoring team appointed pursuant to Security Council resolutions 1526 (2004) and 1617 (2005) concerning Al-Qaida and the Taliban and associated individuals and entities*, United Nations Security Council: Subsidiary Organs, New York, pp. 20–21.

UN 2017, 'Unanimously adopting resolution 2368 (2017) Security Council reaffirms its resolve to combat terrorism', United Nations: Meetings Coverage and Press Releases, 8007th meeting, 20 July 2017, viewed 10 May 2017, www.un.org/press/en/2017/sc12917.doc.htm

UN General Assembly 1989, *International convention against the recruitment, use, financing and training of mercenaries*, United Nations: 72nd Plenary Meeting, 4 December, viewed 10 May 2017, www.un.org/documents/ga/res/44/a44r034.htm

UN News 2017, 'UN aid chief urges global action as starvation, famine loom for 20 million across four countries', United Nations, viewed 30 May 2018, https://news.un.org/en/story/2017/03/553152-un-aid-chief-urges-global-action-starvation-famine-loom-20-million-across-four

UNSCR 2019, *Letter dated 15 July 2019 from the Chair of the Security Council Committee pursuant to resolutions 1267 (1999), 1989 (2011) and 2243 (2015) concerning Islamic State in Iraq and the Levant (Da'esh), Al-Qaida and associated individuals, groups, undertakings and entities addressed to the President of the Security Council*, 15 July, viewed 29 December 2019, https://undocs.org/S/2019/570

US Department of the Treasury 2004, *Press center: U.S. Treasury designates two individuals with ties to al Qaida, UBL former BIF leader and al-Qaida associate named under E.O. 13224*, viewed 10 May 2017, www.treasury.gov/press-center/press-releases/Pages/js2164.aspx

US Department of the Treasury 2008a, *Kuwaiti charity designated for bankrolling al Qaida network*, United States Government, 13 June, viewed 10 May 2017, www.treasury.gov/press-center/press-releases/Pages/hp1023.aspx

US Department of the Treasury 2008b, *Press center: Treasury designates Gulf-based al Qaida financiers*, viewed 10 May 2017, www.treasury.gov/press-center/press-releases/Pages/hp1011.aspx

US Department of the Treasury 2011a, *Treasury targets key Al-Qa'ida funding and support network using Iran as a critical transit point*, 28 July, United States Government, viewed 10 May 2017, www.treasury.gov/press-center/press-releases/Pages/tg1261.aspx

US Department of the Treasury 2011b, *Treasury designates new Ansari money exchange*, viewed 10 May 2017, www.treasury.gov/press-center/press-re

US Department of the Treasury 2015, *Treasury sanctions networks providing support to the government of Syria, including for facilitating Syrian government oil purchases from ISIL*, US Government, 25 November, viewed 10 May 2017, www.treasury.gov/press-center/press-releases/Pages/jl0287.aspx

US Department of the Treasury 2016a, *Press center: United States, Italy, and the Kingdom of Saudi Arabia hold fourth plenary of the Counter-ISIL Finance Group in Rome*, 4 November, viewed 10 May 2017, www.treasury.gov/press-center/press-releases/Pages/jl0416.aspx

US Department of the Treasury 2016b, *Treasury sanctions key ISIL leaders and facilitators including a senior oil official*, United States Government, 11 February, viewed 10 May 2017, www.treasury.gov/press-center/press-releases/Pages/jl0351.aspx

US Department of the Treasury 2020, *Resource center: Protecting charitable organizations – A*, viewed 21 July 2020, www.treasury.gov/resource-center/terrorist-illicit-finance/Pages/protecting-charities_execorder_13224-a.aspx

US Environmental Protection Agency 2017, *Managing ocean dumping in EPA region*, viewed 10 May 2017, www.epa.gov/ocean-dumping/managing-ocean-dumping-epa-region-9

US Federal Reserve 2017, *Board of governors of the Federal Reserve System: Reserve requirements*, viewed 10 May 2017, www.federalreserve.gov/monetarypolicy/reservereq.htm

US Senate 2004, *The 9/11 Commission Report*, United States Government, viewed 10 May 2017, www.9–11commission.gov/report/911Report.pdf

Usborne, D. 2005, 'Oil-for-food scandal: UN officials are linked to $64bn fiasco', *Independent*, 30 March, viewed 10 May 2017, www.independent.co.uk/news/world/oil-for-food-scandal-un-officials-are-linked-to-64bn-fiasco-5385391.html

Van Horn, R. 2009, 'Reinventing monopoly and the role of corporation', in P. Mirowski and D. Plehwe (eds), *The road from Mont Pèlerin*, Harvard University Press, Cambridge, pp. 204–234.

Velde, D. W. te 2010, *The global financial crisis and developing countries: What happened and what have we learned?* Shaping Policy for Development, 19 March, viewed 10 May 2017, www.odi.org/comment/4785-global-financial-crisis-and-developing-countries-what-happened-and-what-have-we-learned

Venn, C. 2009, 'Neoliberal political economy, biopolitics and colonialism: A transcolonial genealogy of inequality', *Theory, Culture & Society*, vol. 26, no. 6, pp. 206–233.

Venn, F. 2016. *The oil crisis*, Routledge, London.

Vlahos, M. 2012, 'Counterterrorism and the new American Exceptionalism', *Review of Faith & International Affairs*, vol. 10, no. 2, pp. 67–76.

Volcker, P., Goldstone, R. and Pieth, M. 2005, *Volcker report: Manipulation of the oil-for-food programme by the Iraqi regime*, Independent Committee into the Oil-for-Food Programme, viewed 10 May 2017, www.humanrightsvoices.org/assets/attachments/documents/volcker_report_10–27–05.pdf

Vovcuk, V. 2015, 'ISIS just seized one of the Syrian regime's big sources of income', *Business Insider*, 28 May, viewed 10 May 2017, www.businessinsider.com/isis-just-seized-one-of-the-syrian-regimes-last-big-sources-of-income-2015-5?IR=T

Wacquant, L. 2011, 'Habitus as topic and tool: Reflections on becoming a prizefighter', *Qualitative Research in Psychology*, vol. 8, no. 1, pp. 81–92.

Walker, S. 2015, 'Vladimir Putin accuses US of backing terrorism in Middle East', *Guardian*, 23 October, viewed 10 May 2017, www.theguardian.com/world/2015/oct/22/vladimir-putin-accuses-us-backing-terrorism-middle-east

Wall, D. and Bollier, D. 2015, *Economics after capitalism*, University of Chicago Press Economics Books, Chicago.

Walsh, D. 2010, 'WikiLeaks cables portray Saudi Arabia as a cash machine for terrorists', *Guardian*, 6 December, viewed 10 May 2017, www.theguardian.com/world/2010/dec/05/wikileaks-cables-saudi-terrorist-funding

War on Want 2017, *Join forces with us against the root causes of global poverty, inequality and injustice*, War on Want, viewed 10 May 2017, www. waronwant.org/sweatshops-bangladesh

Wedeman, B. and Said-Moorhouse, L. 2019, 'ISIS has lost its final stronghold in Syria, the Syrian Democratic Forces says', CNN, 23 March, viewed 29 December 2019, https://edition.cnn.com/2019/03/23/middleeast/isis-caliphate-end-intl/index.html

Wedgwood, R. 1999, 'Responding to terrorism: The strikes against Bin Laden', *Yale Journal of International Law*, vol. 24, pp. 559–576.

Weimann, G. 2011, 'Cyber-Fatwas and terrorism', *Studies in Conflict & Terrorism*, vol. 34, no. 10, pp. 765–781.

Weimann, G. 2014, 'New terrorism and new media', in *Research Series*, Wilson Center Common Labs.

Weinberg, D. 2017, *Qatar and terror finance: Part II: Private Funders of Al-Qaeda in Syria*, Foundation for Defense of Democracies, January, viewed 10 May 2017, www.defenddemocracy.org/content/uploads/documents/11717_Weinberg_Qatar_Report.pdf

Weiss, M. and Hassan, H. 2016, *ISIS: Inside the army of terror*, Simon and Schuster, New York.

Welch, M. 2008, 'Ordering Iraq: Reflections on power, discourse, & neocolonialism', *Critical Criminology*, vol. 16, no. 4, pp. 257–269.

Westad, O. 1994, 'Prelude to invasion: The Soviet Union and the Afghan communists, 1978–1979', *International History Review*, vol. 16, no. 1, pp. 49–69.

Westcott, L. 2015, 'Report: Number of foreign fighters in Iraq and Syria double to 31,000', *Newsweek*, 7 December, viewed 10 May 2017, www.newsweek.com/foreign-fighters-syria-and-iraq-double-31000–86-countries-report- 402084

Whitehead, P. and Crawshaw, P. (eds), 2012. *Organising neoliberalism: Markets, privatisation and justice*. Anthem Press, London and New York.

Whyte, D. 2007, 'The crimes of neo-liberal rule in occupied Iraq', *British Journal of Criminology*, vol. 47, no. 2, pp. 177–195.

Whyte, D. 2010, 'Don't mention the motive for war: David Whyte discusses why the Chilcot Inquiry will not hear the most readily available and concrete evidence of British government crimes', *Criminal Justice Matters*, vol. 82, no. 1, pp. 8–9.

Whyte, D. 2014, 'Challenging the legitimate right to violence: David Whyte argues that challenging the violence of public institutions and corporations, means challenging their stategiven right to commit violence with impunity', *Criminal Justice Matters*, vol. 98, no. 1, pp. 4–5.

Whyte, D. 2015, 'The neo-colonial state of exception in occupied Iraq', in F. Cante and H. Quehl (eds), *Handbook of research on transitional justice and peace building in turbulent regions*, IGI Global, Pennsylvania, pp. 298–314.

Wight, C. 2012, 'Riot, why wouldn't you', *Journal of Critical Globalisation Studies*, vol. 5, pp. 161–166.

WikiLeaks 2017, 'Terrorist finance: Action request for senior level engagement on terrorism finance', Public Library of US Diplomacy, 30 December, viewed 10 May 2017, https://wikileaks.org/plusd/cables/09STATE131801_a.html

Wiktorowicz, Q. 2005, 'A genealogy of radical Islam', *Studies in Conflict & Terrorism*, vol. 28, no. 2, pp. 75–97.

Wildman, S. 2017, 'A European alt-right group wants to take to the sea to stop rescuers from saving migrants', Vox, 17 July, viewed 29 December 2019, www.vox.com/world/2017/7/6/15804196/generation-identity-identitarians-altright-migration-islam-refugees-europe (accessed 13 September, 2018).

Wilkinson, R. and Pickett, K. 2010, *The spirit level: Why equality is better for everyone*, Penguin, UK.

Williams, D. M. 2017, *Black flags and social movements: A sociological analysis of movement anarchism*, Manchester University Press, Manchester.

Williams, E. D. 2004, *The puzzle of 9–11: An investigation into the events of September 11, 2001 and why the pieces don't fit together*, www.lulu.com/en/gb/shop/eric-d-williams/the-puzzle-of-9-11-an-investigation-into-the-events-of-september-11-2001-and-why-the-pieces-dont-fit-together/paperback/product-18myykz.html

Williams, J. 2019, 'ISIS leader Abu Bakr al-Baghdadi releases new video, proving he's still alive', *Vox*, 29 April, viewed 29 December 2019, www.vox.com/world/2019/4/29/18522532/isis-leader-abu-bakr-al-baghdadi-new-video-propaganda-sri-lanka-bombings

Williamson, J. 1993, 'Democracy and the "Washington consensus"', *World Development*, vol. 21, no. 8, pp. 1329–1336.

Wilson, M. 2017, 'Court upholds multi-billion dollar judgment against Sudan over embassy bombings', *The Hill*, 28 July, viewed 10 August 2017, http://thehill.com/business-a-lobbying/business-a-lobbying/344423-court-upholds-73b-judgment-against-sudan-over-embassy

Wilson, S. 2003, 'Bremer says order being restored', *Los Angeles Times*, 27 May, viewed 10 May 2017, www.thedailycamera.com/bdc/middle_east/article/0,1713,BDC_10836_1991928,00.html

Winter, C. and Saltman, E. 2014, *Islamic State: The changing face of modern jihadism*, Quilliam Foundation, London.

Wintrobe, R. 2002, 'Leadership and passion in extremist politics', in A. Breton, G. Galeotti, P. Salmon and R. Wintrobe (eds), *Political extremism and rationality*, Cambridge University Press, Cambridge, pp. 23–43.

Wittner, L. 2018, 'Has democratic socialism a future in American politics?', *Australian Socialist*, vol. 24, no. 2, pp. 18–19.

Wodak, R. and Meyer, M. (eds) 2009, *Methods for critical discourse analysis*, Sage, London.

Wodak, R., KhosraviNik, M. and Mral, B. 2013, *Right-wing populism in Europe: Politics and discourse*. A&C Black, London.

Woertz, E. 2014, 'How long will ISIS last economically?', *Notes Internacionales CIDOB*, vol. 98.

Woertz, E. 2017, 'Food security in Iraq: Results from qualitative and quantitative surveys', *Food Security*, vol. 9, no. 3, pp. 511–522.

Wood, G. 2019, 'Why Sri Lanka was probably not retaliation for Christchurch', *Atlantic*, 24 April, viewed 29 December 2019, www.theatlantic.com/ideas/archive/2019/04/were-sri-lanka-bombings-retaliation-christchurch/587836/

Woodcock, G. 2018, *Anarchism: A history of libertarian ideas and movements*, Pickle Partners Publishing.

Woods, K. M. and Stout, M. E. 2010, 'Saddam's perceptions and misperceptions: The case of "Desert Storm"', *Journal of Strategic Studies*, vol. 33, no. 1, pp. 5–41.

Wright, L. 2006, *The looming tower: Al-Qaeda and the road to 9/11*, Alfred A. Knopf Incorporated, New York.

Wright, R. 2019, 'The Caliphate's collapse', *New Yorker*, 23 April, viewed 29 December 2019, www.newyorker.com/news/our-columnists/isis-still-has-global-reach-despite-the-caliphates-collapse

Wright, T. 1986, *The religion of humanity: The impact of Comtean positivism on Victorian Britain*, Cambridge University Press, Cambridge.

Wright-Neville, D. 2010, *Dictionary of terrorism: Vol. 2*, Polity, London.

Yetiv, S. 2011, *The petroleum triangle: Oil, globalization, and terror*, Cornell University Press, New York.

Young, J. 2003, 'Merton with energy, Katz with structure: The sociology of vindictiveness and the criminology of transgression', *Theoretical Criminology*, vol. 7, no. 3, pp. 389–414.

Young, J. 2007, *The vertigo of late modernity*, Sage, London.

Young, J. 2011, *The criminological imagination*, Polity Press, Cambridge.

Younis, M. 2019, 'Four in 10 Americans embrace some form of socialism', Gallup, 20 May, viewed 29 December 2019, https://news.gallup.com/poll/257639/four-americans-embrace-form-socialism.aspx

Zawahiri, A. 2008, 'Al-Azhar: The lion's den: Interview with Shaykh Ayman al-Zawahiri', in *As Sahab* (eds), 21 November, viewed 10 January 2017, https://archive.org/details/The-all-Interviewes-with-Dr-Ayman-al-Zawahiri

Zelin, A. 2015, 'Picture or it didn't happen: A snapshot of the Islamic State's official media output', *Perspectives on Terrorism*, vol. 9, no. 4.

Zempi, I. and Awan, I. 2016, *Islamophobia: Lived experiences of online and offline victimisation*, Policy Press, Bristol.

Žižek, S. 2014, 'Isis is a disgrace to true fundamentalism', *New York Times*, 3 September.

Zoellick, R. 2001, 'Countering terror with trade', *Washington Post*, 20 September, viewed 10 May 2017, www.washingtonpost.com/archive/opinions/2001/09/20/countering-terror-with-trade/aa1e3f27-f069-4b66-b752-8d141876d0b7/

Zulaika, J. 2009, *Terrorism: The self-fulfilling prophecy*, University of Chicago Press.

Zulaika, J. 2012, 'Drones, witches and other flying objects: The force of fantasy in US counterterrorism', *Critical Studies on Terrorism*, vol. 5, no. 1, pp. 51–68.

Index

EU authorised representative for GPSR:
Easy Access System Europe, Mustamäe tee 50,
10621 Tallinn, Estonia
gpsr.requests@easproject.com

www.ingramcontent.com/pod-product-compliance
Lightning Source LLC
Chambersburg PA
CBHW051957270326
41929CB00015B/2694